The Delphian

A systematic plan of education, embracing the
world's progress and development of
The liberal arts
(Volume VII)

Delphian society

Alpha Editions

This edition published in 2019

ISBN : 9789389169447

Design and Setting By
Alpha Editions
email - alphaedis@gmail.com

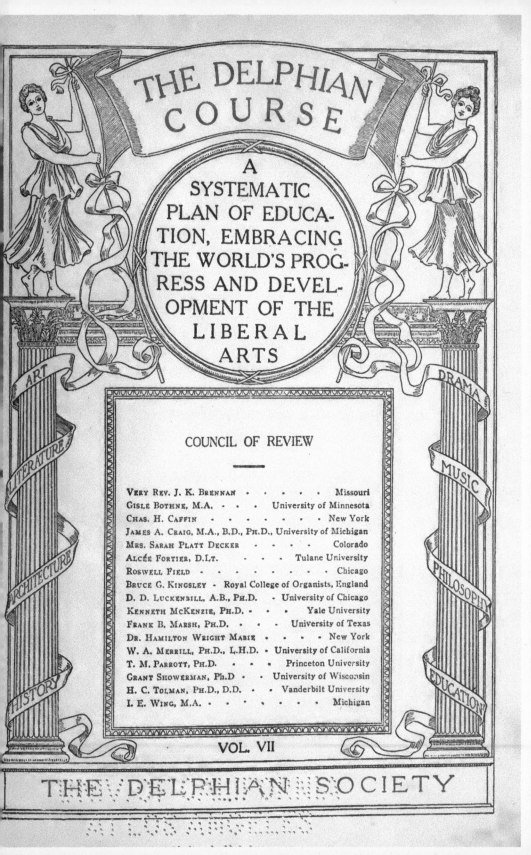

THE DELPHIAN COURSE

A SYSTEMATIC PLAN OF EDUCATION, EMBRACING THE WORLD'S PROGRESS AND DEVELOPMENT OF THE LIBERAL ARTS

ART · LITERATURE · ARCHITECTURE · HISTORY

DRAMA · MUSIC · PHILOSOPHY · EDUCATION

COUNCIL OF REVIEW

VERY REV. J. K. BRENNAN · · · · · · · · Missouri
GISLE BOTHNE, M.A. · · · · University of Minnesota
CHAS. H. CAFFIN · · · · · · · · New York
JAMES A. CRAIG, M.A., B.D., PH.D., University of Michigan
MRS. SARAH PLATT DECKER · · · · · Colorado
ALCÉE FORTIER, D.LT. · · · · Tulane University
ROSWELL FIELD · · · · · · · · Chicago
BRUCE G. KINGSLEY · Royal College of Organists, England
D. D. LUCKENBILL, A.B., PH.D. · University of Chicago
KENNETH MCKENZIE, PH.D. · · · Yale University
FRANK B. MARSH, PH.D. · · · University of Texas
DR. HAMILTON WRIGHT MABIE · · · New York
W. A. MERRILL, PH.D., L.H.D. · University of California
T. M. PARROTT, PH.D. · · · · Princeton University
GRANT SHOWERMAN, PH.D · · University of Wisconsin
H. C. TOLMAN, PH.D., D.D. · · Vanderbilt University
I. E. WING, M.A. · · · · · · · Michigan

VOL. VII

THE DELPHIAN SOCIETY

COMPOSITION, ELECTROTYPING, PRINTING
AND BINDING BY THE
W. B. CONKEY COMPANY
Hammond, Indiana

TABLE OF CONTENTS
PART VII

THE DRAMA.

FULL PAGE ILLUSTRATIONS

PART VII

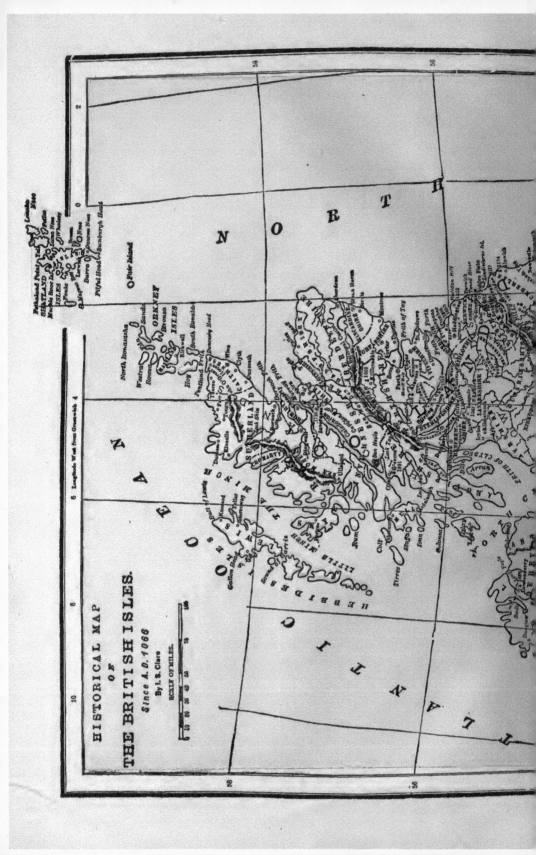

HISTORICAL MAP
OF
THE BRITISH ISLES.
Since A.D. 1066
By L. S. Clare
SCALE OF MILES.

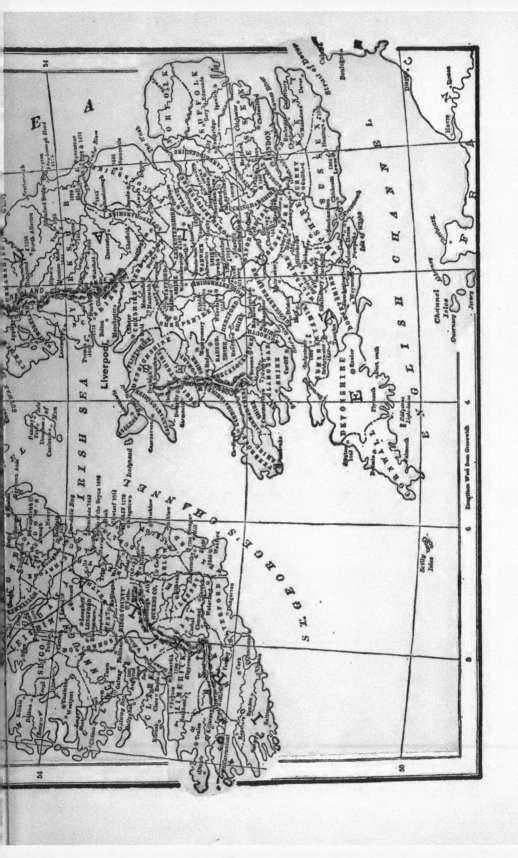

THE DRAMA

CHAPTER I.

GENERAL SURVEY.

POETRY and fiction are in a special sense the forms of writing through which the imagination finds expression. The essay happily lends itself to reason, sentiment and humor; the biography and history to the instinct for investigation, arrangement of facts and portraiture; the epic to narrative or to the easy flow of an imaginary or semi-historical stream of events; the ballad to the instinct for imaginative setting or recitation of incidents; the lyric to the singing impulse; the drama to the deep and compelling instinct to give action an expression suggestive of motion, energy, will, fate; to convey through it the tremendous struggles of contending wills; or to hold up to ridicule the weaknesses and foibles of men, their shallow conceits, their petty pride, their assumed dignity; to expose to merciless laughter the chasm between their conventional dignities and their pathetic weakness.

And these various forms of literature together make a free and full showing of human nature and the happenings of human experience. Goethe said that his works constituted one great confession; in like manner the books of the world show the very heart and soul of humanity and form a record of its experiences under historic conditions. This record is the more searching and complete because it has been, for the most part, unconsciously made. Homer was bent on telling the most interesting tradition of his race with such freshness and power of phrase that men would listen to it as men were listening at that time, in Oriental cities, to the earliest short stories; and, in the graphic telling of the ancient tale, he drew such pictures of manners and such portraits of persons, that he unconsciously made the most vital and varied disclosure of the genius and character of his race.

That race had a plastic imagination, which is the mother of artistic forms; a quick eye, an instinctive feeling for proportion and harmony of parts; and a genius for expression. Its mental

I

and moral traits, the sky and sea which framed its landscapes and created its atmosphere, made the Greeks not only colonizers, builders of cities, soldiers and traders, but painters and interpreters of life through writing, sculpture and architecture. They did not rest in the satisfactions of the senses and the pouring out of their energies in practical ways; their habits, activities, adventures early and readily rose out of the sphere of the material, incidental and necessary into the region of the poetic, universal and free. They gained such ease and power in the use of their materials and tools that they ceased to be drudges and became artists, and turned their work into play.

No literary form has greater majesty of thought, solidity of structure and beauty of phrase than the Greek tragedy; nor is any literary form more remote from our modern way of expression. The Greek play seems to us a highly artificial and conventional kind of drama; and yet it grew naturally out of the ways and habits of Greek country life. It grew out of doors, almost without intention, from a very simple form of worship of Dionysus; the god of the free, flowing, creative element in nature and life; the personification of those mysterious natural forces whose ebb and flow renew the freshness of the world every spring and give Nature endless variety and beauty; the personification of the highest inspirations in thought and of the most unrestrained outbreaks of passion. The story of the wonderings and adventures of Dionysus took hold of the imagination of the plain people and was recited, chanted and sung at the popular festivals of seedtime and harvest, the worshippers dressing themselves as satyrs in goat-skins; hence the word "tragedy."

The group about the rustic altar was first a kind of rude chorus; then the recitation of the dramatic parts of the story fell to one person, the chorus joining in at the end. Thus the different personages in the story were impersonated by different worshippers who had the gift of improvisation. Meanwhile the impulse for expression which made the Greeks artists was not satisfied with story and singing; the worshippers gave relief to their feelings by dancing. And so, by a natural evolution, the god and the men with whom he contended came to be personated by different worshippers, the story became dramatic, and what was at first a narrative gradually became a play.

As time went on, by an equally simple and natural process, the graver ideas for which the god stood were separated from the license and gayety which he also personified; the latter furnished the material for comedy, the former for tragedy. In both forms of drama the distinguishing characteristic is action; the will furnishes the motive power, and some kind of collision between the will and other wills or conditions supplies the materials. On the tragic stage the chief figure is always struggling, with other persons, with the laws of life, with the institutions of society, with the Gods, with Fate, with warring elements in his own nature. In Greek tragedy Œdipus wilfully ignored the warnings which ought to have put him on guard against the terrible offence he ignorantly committed; Agamemnon broke the sacred law of family life by sacrificing the life of his daughter; Prometheus defied the will of Zeus. In the Shakespearian drama Lear put himself into the power of his children, wilfully and violently asserting his will in the face of his knowledge of their characters; Othello abdicated his reason, made himself the victim of jealousy and blindly followed the lead of a treacherous servant; Macbeth surrendered himself to his ambition and set himself in conflict with the fundamental laws of society.

In French tragedy, as illustrated in fiction, the noble-hearted Jean Valjean struggles in vain to detach himself from his early offence; Pere Goriot is the victim of the greed and cruelty of his unnatural children; Madame Bovary seeks relief from the monotony of her life by sinning against her own nature and against society. Anna Karenina, the central figure in Tolstoi's great novel, follows her heart across the line of moral order and finds herself involved in a desperate struggle with organized society. Her tragedy is the collision of the individual will with the collective will of the world in which she lives.

This collision may be a lawless expression of individualism, a passionate assertion of the right of the individual will to have its way without regard to consequences, as in Richard III; it may be a daring outbreak of that supreme self-will which is the source of crime, as in Macbeth; or it may be a struggle for the free expression of the soul and for liberty to live one's life according to one's conscience, as in the case of Savonarola, Guido Bruno and John Huss. In a word, the collision which is the substance of tragedy, may be a crime against humanity as in the case of Tamburlane, or it may be a sublime sacrifice as in the case of Socrates; in every great social and political change, in all movements from the old order to the new, in the long struggle for freedom of mind and body, collision is involved; and tragedy is, therefore, an essential part of human history and experience.

This deep rootage in human experience gives tragedy its absorbing and, at times, almost overwhelming interest; while the greatness of its themes, evoking a kindred majesty of thought and of style, give it perhaps the foremost place among literary forms. It is true, neither Homer nor Dante nor Goethe were writers of tragedy; for "Faust," while it has tragic elements, is not, strictly speaking, a tragedy; and such plays as "Egmont" are not to be reckoned among the creative works of Goethe. But in all the foremost literature save the Roman, the German, the Russian, the tragedy holds a first place; and in Russian literature fiction is charged with tragic elements.

The Greek poets who gave life and form to the tragedy, had two great advantages over all their successors: the possession of a fund of legends and traditions which were the common property of their race, and a body of hearers inclusive of the entire citizenship and familiar from childhood with any incident or story put on the stage. The themes were majestic; the actors were gods, heroes, leaders of men; the manner was lofty and impressive; the theater was vast and open to the sky; and the whole city sat on the seats and hung breathless on the play. It dealt always with serious themes in a serious spirit, and was not only a high form of entertainment, but a religious function.

The Greek tragedy is summed up in three great names: Aeschylus, the central motive of whose plays was the implacable pursuit of the offender by Fate, a divine vengeance older than the gods themselves; Sophocles, the most perfect artist who has ever written in the tragic form, and in whose hands Fate takes on the aspect of a moral law; and Euripides, whom Mrs. Browning called "the human," who brought tragedy down from the region of gods and heroes to the level of human life, and in whose hands Fate became the source of pathos and sadness in human experience rather than iron-footed punishment tirelessly following the criminal.

The so-called dramatic unities, which have become the

special characteristics of the classical drama, involved the working out of the plot in one locality, the completion of the action within one day, and the direct bearing of all the incidents on the development of a single plot. The first two requirements were imposed by the conditions of the stage on which the plays were acted, and by the presence of the chorus throughout the play; unity of action was an expression of the Greek idea of the unity of a work of art.

From this highly developed drama the whole modern dramatic movement has been developed; for the influence of the Indian drama, of which Kalidasa's beautiful "Sakuntala" is most familiar to western readers, has been so slight that it may be disregarded. The Romans wrote real comedies, but their gifts were essentially rhetorical and the tragedies which survive are negligible. Italy was the first of the modern countries to recover classical art and the classical tradition, but its earliest plays were religious in motive and mediaeval in form; and, while writers of comedy like Goldoni caught the attention of other countries, the only writer of tragedy whose work has been widely read outside of Italy is Alfieri; a dramatist of passion and action, but a devout observer of the unities. The three greatest names in Spanish literature are Cervantes, Lope de Vega and Calderon. The genius of the author of "Don Quixote" was epic rather than dramatic, but one tragedy of lasting value stands to his credit. Lope de Vega was probably the most prolific writer of original quality in the history of literature: he is credited with the authorship of more than eighteen hundred plays! This means that he was a great improvisor rather than a great writer, and that his genius was prolific rather than creative in the higher sense of the word. That a man of such spontaneous and flowing invention should disregard the classic tradition and throw the unities to the winds seems almost inevitable. Calderon wrote in a more serious spirit and with far deeper regard for the rules of his art than Lope de Vega; but he, too, was a prolific writer and the magnitude of his production would have been impossible if his genius for improvisation had not found the Spanish drama easy in its demands on structural form and restraint of style. That drama was romantic in spirit, emotional in appeal and depended for its interest largely on incident. In style it was rhetorical and prolific of long speeches, often strikingly eloquent.

The early French drama, on the other hand, showed the French sense of proportion, order and symmetry; that inner logic of good taste which is of the essence of the French genius. Corneille, Racine and Boileau were the chief exemplars of the classical tradition in modern dramatic writing. Corneille was the greater genius, with natural elevation and dignity, finish of style and scrupulous care for good literary form as established by the French Academy; though, in the "Cid" he showed a tendency to break with the traditions. Racine had less force and vigor of imagination, but notable elegance, refinement and tenderness of feeling and perception. Boileau was a born conformist to the conventions of the classical drama, and one of the most notable expounders of its laws.

In England, from the very start, dramatic writers composed with a free hand; and, especially in tragedy, threw off at an early age the yoke of the unities and created a dramatic literature of great irregularity of form and richness of substance. Shakespeare wrote comedies of unsurpassed charm or of abounding wit, but his supreme work was in the field of tragedy. Since Aeschylus no writer of such genius for tragedy has appeared in any literature. He was indifferent to the unities, and the action in his plays often runs through a period of years, passes rapidly from place to place, weaves the tragic and the comic together with a free hand, and introduces two or three motives or carries on one or two subordinate plots contemporaneously with the main plot. The key of his plays is furnished by the phrase "character is destiny;" and to show the reaction of a man's deeds on his nature or the influence of a group of persons on one another Shakespeare takes whatever time is necessary. Love is one of the master motives in his plays; and love, while sometimes of sudden birth as in "Romeo and Juliet," does not flower and bear fruit in a day. The note of the Shakespearian tragedy is not the vengeance of the gods patiently pursuing a man until it overwhelms him; but the reaping of the harvest of a man's own sowing, the return of the deed to the doer.

Recent tragedy is far more subtle in its handling of motives than the older tragedy, depends less on objective action and more on the subjective impulses, tendencies and conditions created by temperament, and inheritance, and on conflicts born of economical and social circumstances; but its field is still the deeper experiences of humanity, its chief motive power is the will either in excess or in debility; and its note is still action.

The course of reading in dramatic literature presented in this volume, if intelligently followed, may be invaluable; for any plan or method which brings out the essential unity of books in the different fields doubles their value. To read a single play as if it were a thing complete in itself would be like seeing a field apart from the landscape of which it is part, or attempting to understand a man without taking into account his race, his country, and his age. Literature is an unfolding of the human spirit; an evolution of the mind of the race; every literary form has passed through a process of growth.

To understand the America of today one must know something of the Europe of the fifteenth and sixteenth centuries, when the mind of the old world was reaching out to the new world in many wonderful ways. To understand a poet of such beautiful simplicity as Longfellow, one must know a good deal of the history of the past, and of the origin of versification. A play cannot be thoroughly understood until one studies it in the light of earlier plays.

A knowledge of the drama is especially important to those who wish to understand literary movements in this country, because Americans are giving increasing attention to the writing of plays. From Colonial times plays have been written in this country, but they were experimental and, for the most part, of slight importance until a generation ago, when Bronson Howard put on the stage a group of dramas dealing with American subjects, fresh in feeling and effective in treatment. He was followed by playwrights who, like Augustus Thomas, had both the dramatic sense and the literary feeling; and these, in turn, have been the forerunners of a large group of younger men and women who have turned from the novel to the play as an effective form of dealing with ethical and social questions which appeal strongly to the emotions. Mr. Moody's "The Great Divide," Mr. Sheldon's "The Nigger," Mr. MacKaye's "The Scarecrow," Mrs. Marks' "The Piper," Mrs. Dargan's "The Shepherd" are a few titles taken almost at random from the rapidly-growing list of serious plays from American hands; plays of such importance that they register a genuine monument in dramatic literature, and prophesy a new chapter in the development of the American spirit.

LONDON BRIDGE IN THE DAYS OF ELIZABETH
Notice the Houses Built on the Bridge also the Heads Over the Gates.

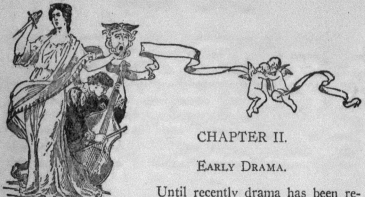

CHAPTER II.

Early Drama.

Until recently drama has been regarded as an expression of advanced civilization. However, modern investigation has shown that it is one of the oldest of the arts; movement and gesture doubtless antedating the spoken language. The old classification of poetry according to its supposed process of growth, drama following the epic and lyric, is somewhat misleading unless the perfected drama alone is signified. Extended study of primitive society shows that there was hardly a time so remote or a branch of the human family so undeveloped that need of diversion was not felt. This was found in war, in the hunt and, for quieter moments, in initiating these activities.

Lowest today in the social scale are tribes inhabiting Central Australia. For the purpose of investigation, scholars have gone to dwell temporarily among them, have been received into their clans and initiated into their tribal mysteries. Careful observation of their customs and manner of life, together with similar study of African tribes and others inhabiting some of the Malay islands, has aided materially in arriving at conclusions regarding the earliest peoples. Indications of a fondness for imitating animals and birds, as well as simple occupations and industries, are not lacking. In these we see the first obscure beginnings of dramatic expression.

Imitating the hunt is a favorite diversion of primitive tribes today, some representing the animals, others the hunters, while the rest find amusement in watching now the unconscious attitude of the dumb beasts, then the adroit craftiness of those pursuing. So intense may the excitement become that a slight accident might transform the whole assembly into blood-thirsty combatants.

In representing animals with which they were familiar, it is probable that early tribes, like those today, fixed upon certain marked peculiarities rather than upon the general appearance. An unusual gait, as in the case of the kangaroo, or some strange habit, caught the attention of a dawning intelligence. Later the idea of ornamenting themselves in the hides of the animals was conceived; also the notion of producing sounds similar to those emitted by bird and beast. Once awakened, human ingenuity suggested many variations and changes for this spirit of imitation.

It was customary for several American Indian tribes to dance both before setting out upon a warlike raid and after its conclusion. They first stimulated themselves to a high pitch of excitement, preparatory to battle; when victory was won, this was celebrated with feasting and joyful dances. When the dancers tarried for a brief rest, someone would recite thrilling incidents of the campaign, which would quickly throw the entire assembly into the ecstasies of the dance again.

In course of time it developed that dancing, gesture and recitation were frequently separated and no longer confused as before; but early peoples knew nothing of such differentiation. All three were co-mingled, as instinct prompted.

Dancing expresses the gladness of the heart. A little child dances away in glee when following some fresh impulse or fulfilling some desire. When the heart is heavy, the muscles are lifeless and the limbs droop; then as quickly as joy or passion seize hold of the mind, the muscles become tense and the limbs move instinctively. While we today are likely to express our thoughts by words alone, there are still many peoples who employ not only words but gesture and facial expression to convey the simplest impressions.

As a settled life supplanted a roving existence, industries developed. Men scratched the soil and sowed the seed; they wove nets to catch fish; gradually they forged rude implements. Imitation of these very occupations shortly manifested themselves. The movements of the dancers sometimes suggested the casting of a net, the rocking of a boat, the swaying of the reeds or standing grain tossed about or gently blown by fitful breezes. Some conception of these early dances may be obtained by watching the plays of little children who today find in similar movements a pleasure akin to that experienced by their remote ancestors.

Dances such as these were common among the Egyptians, but their placid life never stimulated them to any higher form of dramatic expression. Without the development of *will*, a perfected drama is impossible. The Egyptians were throughout the greater portion of their history a subservient people: subservient to kings, priests or foreigners, save on those few memorable occasions when conditions became too trying for even their endurance. Thus the *will* of the people as a whole never became a strong factor. In a large measure, the same was true of the Babylonians. We know that the Hebrews used the dance in connection with their worship, but here again we find no further development of dramatic expression. A wonderful drama survives in their literature—the Book of Job—but it is evident that this was never intended to be acted; the poet employed the form of dramatic poetry to set forth his lesson to mankind.

The Greeks were the first to produce a perfected drama; yet in the beginnings theirs had the same crude origin as the rest—song and dance and revelry made in honor of a deity who was believed to be pleased with such demonstrations.

Whatever the Greeks attempted they accomplished better than their contemporaries; such ideas as were theirs by inheritance or contact they passed on to others, but so beautified, so transfigured with their own touch, that it is often difficult to recognize their earlier forms. Worshipping beauty, inspired to make beautiful every art by the diversified land in which they dwelt, their drama astonishes and gratifies us today by its blended simplicity and masterly perfection.

It should not be imagined, however, that this transformation was quickly brought about. Centuries were involved in its process. From earliest times Dionysus, god of wine, was worshipped, particularly in the spring, when life started anew, and in the fall, when the harvest was gathered and wine made again from the luscious fruit. Since he was thought to be attended by a company of satyrs, half-men, half-goats, the goat was regarded as an acceptable offering. Indeed, there is rea-

son to believe that at first human sacrifices were made,
but early in the history of the Greeks this habit was abandoned,
animals being substituted at the altars.   Troops of merry-
makers dressed as satyrs formed in procession and circled
around the priest while the goat was sacrificed and rites observed in honor of the much loved god.   And here we have
the beginnings of the Greek chorus.   Our word tragedy is
directly derived from two Greek words: *tragos,* goat, and *ode,*
song—goat-song.

While little is definitely known of these remote celebrations, they continued year after year with marked regularity.
Communities were generally occupied similarly; they planted
the vine, tended it through the summer and in the fall gathered
the fruits of their toil.   In country districts of Greece today
one may see the jollity that accompanies the harvest and its
conclusion.   The new wine made, even now there is a temptation to enjoy to the utmost the felicitous occasion.   In early
times life apart from divinities was undreamed of; Dionysus
had taught men to cultivate the vine and all homage was due
to this friend and benefactor of mankind.   Offerings were
made at his altar and while his priest blessed the sacrifice,
troops of revelers sang his praises, going out through the
vicinity to shout and dance and improvise.   It is probable that
in time the chorus was much subdued, and that it received
considerable training.   We know that finally Thespis originated the plan of having the leader recite at times to rest the
chorus.   This leader became the first actor; Æschylus introduced a second, Sophocles a third.   More than three actors
were unknown on a Greek stage.   However, these might each
personify different characters and the use of boys for such
subordinate parts as messengers, slaves and the like was permitted.   Thus it is very evident that the Greek chorus was not
created to make possible the presentation of Greek plays but
that the drama was fitted into the chorus of long standing.

The origin of the Greek drama has already been considered
at length.   It is here reviewed only to show its place in the
long chain of dramatic development and particularly to touch
upon the presentation of the play itself.[1]

---

[1] Part III, p. 10 f.

Having their beginnings in religious celebrations then, we find these rude and boisterous dances crystallizing into plays. While we know that buffoonery and tragedy were once intermingled, by the time of Æschylus it had become the custom to separate the two and a satyr play was given at the close of a series of three tragedies to rest the audience. At the Greater Dionysia alone the leading poets presented their plays, while aspirants for fame and notice appeared at the Lenaea and Lesser Dionysia.

On the eve of the festival the statue of Dionysus was removed from his temple and carried to the theater, while processions of men, women and children passed through the streets. Sometimes these demonstrations lasted until the third day; before the statues of the twelve principal deities in the agora they would halt, while songs were sung and informal celebration made. The religious significance of these festivals was never lost sight of; throughout the independence of the ancient Greeks the best seat was reserved for the priest of Dionysus, while any disturbance occurring during the sacred celebration was severely punished as an affront to the deity himself.

There have occurred several periods of remarkable dramatic excellence—these as a rule following some unusual outburst of national spirit and patriotism. Such was the condition in Greece when the Great King had been repulsed and had fled with the remnant of his numerous but undisciplined army back to Persia. Then the Greeks came into a realization of their wonderful possibilities and they built those temples which, in ruins, delight us today; when they widened their boundaries and experimented in government; when they reached material prosperity and made a mighty stride forward in the fine arts. It is of this period of Greek drama that we know most—the period of Æschylus, Sophocles and Euripides. Of its condition previously we know only from references surviving in literature and in traditions handed down by later writers. But evidence is not wanting for this age of dramatic excellence—the most satisfying being copies of several of the plays themselves.

During the time of the Athenian Empire it was customary for the allies to send their contributions to Athens in the spring.

Visitors thronged the streets, coming at this season to enjoy the yearly presentation of plays. The tribute was brought into the theater and before the audience here gathered were presented the sons of soldiers fallen in battle, who had been educated at the expense of the state. They were declared free from its supervision and permitted to take their places as citizens. To be sure, incidents of this nature differed from time to time.

The three contesting poets whose group of three tragedies and a satyr play had been most acceptable to the judges now drew for their places in point of time. Each had one day in which to present his productions.

The very nature of the theater wherein these plays were given limited the dramatist greatly as to his theme. It should be remembered that the Greek theater was open to the sky, tier upon tier of seats rising above the orchestra or circular space in which the chorus and actors stood, and the fact that many thousand people might be accommodated here indicates at once that it must often have been difficult to hear all that was said. To magnify their appearance, the actors wore raised boots, or buskins and huge masks that towered high above their heads. Invariably the poets chose some story well known to all—some legend embedded in their history or some famous event. Thus if a portion of the words were lost, the general idea of the play could be easily followed. It required much skill and masterly genius to clothe old tales in new garments and make them agreeable to an audience that expressed its disapproval quite as frankly as its pleasure. Only comparatively few Greek plays remain to us, these doubtless being among the best produced. In spite of the fact that changed ideas make it impossible for us to even understand, sometimes, to say nothing of sympathizing with the plot of the tragedies, nevertheless the poets delineated their characters so well, told their story so graphically, that even in translation, wherein much of the beauty is lost, we find pleasure in reading these plays; and whenever they have been reproduced under circumstances similar to those for which they were written, they have been acceptable to modern audiences, although it need scarcely be noted that they are wholly unsuitable to our interior picture-frame stages of today.

There was no attempt at stage scenery; if a character arrived from afar, he explained whence he came; the chorus remained upon the stage throughout the play, making any attempt at change of locality unnatural. The mask was the most important part of the costume, and was made of linen. The actors wore the draped robe, so well known to us in Greek statuary, while menials wore the tunics of the workaday world. The mask enabled the audience to determine at a glance the general character of the actor; there were six masks for old men; eight for young; three for menials and eleven for women—they being represented always by youths.

Dire deeds were not shown upon the Greek stage, it being impracticable for men raised upon the high buskins and shut in by the towering masks to attempt them, even had the Greek temperament made this desirable. Tragedies were wrought elsewhere and merely reported to the audience. While we cannot imagine a present-day audience sitting patiently, not to say contentedly, from sunrise to sunset for several successive days witnessing such exhibitions as these, it must be remembered that the Greeks were fond of argument and oratory; there were no journals nor newspapers to bring tidings of a world beyond, and the presentations of some well known legend or tradition thus rendered filled them with gratification and roused their pride to greater undertakings. After the loss of Athenian independence and the succession of tyrants there was never again the same freedom allowed in satirizing the foibles of statesmen and ridicule of experiments in government as in the burlesques of earlier times. Instead, writers of comedy turned to domestic subjects. Beyond a question Menander was rarely gifted and a great favorite with his audiences, but, unfortunately, not one of his plays survives.

The Roman drama was largely an imitation of the Greek. Rome took over much of the civilization which the older country had developed; she could not supply nor acquire the delicate sense of proportion, of the fitness of things or appreciation of the beautiful so natural to the Greeks. In addition to the plays of Greek poets, which were at first shown among the Romans, Plautus and Terence wrote plays for the amusement of Roman audiences. However, they seemed to the Romans mere shadows of life, accustomed as they were to the scenes of circus and amphitheater. Those who were in the habit of witnessing the destruction of human as well as animal life for days together could not be expected to find plays sufficient. More popular than these were the mimes and pantomimes, which were, as one writer has noted, "always immoral and generally obscene."

Two changes were brought about when the Greek plays were transported to Rome; the chorus was dropped altogether and the stage was elevated. Contrary to earlier supposition, the Greeks never used an elevated stage. So widely did scholars differ on this point that in recent times the German government defrayed the cost of excavations on the sites of old Greek theaters. These proved beyond doubt that the orchestra of the Greeks contained no raised platform. Moreover, it has been shown that this very fact contributed to the comfort of the audience as the seats were then arranged. The Romans filled the orchestra with seats and raised the actors above them.

While the Roman theaters were modeled after the Greek, during the principate great extravagance was displayed in these buildings. Enormous awnings were spread over the open roof to ward off the rays of the sun; the air was refreshed by mixtures of wine, water and crocus juice which was piped to the highest tiers and sprinkled over the passages. Temporary theaters were erected by those who wished to win popular applause as a means of acquiring political preference. We read of one of these built to accommodate eighty thousand people, three stories in height. Each floor had its colonnade, the pillars of the first being of marble, the second of glass—at that time a costly commodity—and the third of gilded wood. Between the three hundred and sixty pillars were placed three thousand magnificent statues.

Another was raised in 53 to celebrate a funeral. We may judge of the princely sum which must have been required to build it by the comment which has come down to us from Pliny. "In the morning there were two wooden theaters each with its stage, on which plays were performed. The theaters turned their circular backs toward each other, so that the sounds from the one did not disturb the performance in the other. When the performance was ended, while all the spectators were still seated in their places, the two auditoriums were suddenly turned around so as to fit together and form a circus, an amphitheater, which was immediately made ready for warlike games."

In the dawning days of Christianity, the Roman stage had sunk to the lowest depths. All discriminating people, whether holding to the old religion or not, regarded the immorality as revolting and the debauchery shocking. To the Christians it was abhorrent. The Council of Arles in 314 A. D. decreed that "by mounting the stage the actors of comedy have given their support to worship of false gods and deserted their faith." If they persisted in so doing they were excommunicated. In 394 A. D. the Emperor Theodosius enacted that "images of actors should, out of respect for his person, be removed to a distance from his statues."

Acting was hereditary in families and the mere struggle for existence forced many to remain upon the boards. We know that during a plague in Rome when people generally were commanded to leave the city so far as possible, one thousand actors and actresses were bidden to remain.

Most of the early church fathers thundered their decrees against the stage and those who refrained from condemning it utterly were quite as vigorous in their protest against its abuse. However a few realized the fact that love of shows was too deeply rooted in the hearts of the populace to be easily crushed out, and rather than suffer the humiliation of many a preacher who found his audience more than once deserting for some particularly attractive spectacle, they spoke in greater moderation. When reading the following lines from Tertullian, who in his De Spectaculis exhorted Christians to forswear the plays, it should be remembered that the stage he condemned was so corrupt that it would not be tolerated today in any civilized country.

TERTULLIAN. DE SPECTACULIS.

Ye servants of God, about to draw near to God, that you may make solemn consecration of yourselves to Him, seek

well to understand the conditions of faith, the reasons of the
truth, the laws of Christian discipline, which forbid, among
other sins of the world, the pleasures of the public shows;
ye who have testified and confessed that you have already
done so, review the subject, that there may be no sinning,
whether through real or wilful ignorance.

Let us pass on now to theatrical exhibitions, which we
have already shown have a common origin with the circus,
and bear like idolatrous designations—even as from the first
they have borne the name of 'Ludi,' and equally minister to
idols. They resemble each other also in their pomp, having
the same procession to the scene of their display from temples
and altars and that mournful profusion of incense and blood,
with music of pipes and trumpets, all under the direction of
the soothsayer and the undertaker, those two foul masters of
funeral rites and sacrifices. . . . Venus and Bacchus
are close allies. These two evil spirts are in sworn confederacy with each other, as the patrons of drunkenness and
lust. . . . That immodesty of gesture and attire which
so specially and peculiarly characterizes the stage are conse-
crated to them. . . .

Having done enough, then, as we have said, in regard
to that principal argument, that there is in them all the taint
of idolatry, having sufficiently dealt with that, let us now
contrast the other characterization of the things of the show
with the things of God. God has enjoined us to deal calmly
and gently and quietly and peacefully with the Holy Spirit,
because these things are alone in keeping with the goodness
of His nature, with His tenderness and sensitiveness, not to
vex Him with rage, or ill-nature, or anger, or grief. Well,
how shall this be made to accord with the shows? For the
show always leads to spiritual agitation. For where there
is pleasure, there is keenness of feeling giving pleasure its
zest; and where there is keenness of feeling, there is rivalry
giving in turn its zest to that. Then, too, where you have
rivalry, you have rage, and bitterness, and wrath, and grief,
and all bad things which flow from them—the whole entirely
out of keeping with the religion of Christ.

. . . Are we not, in like manner, enjoined to put
away from us all immodesty? On this ground, again, we

are excluded from the theater, which is immodesty's own peculiar abode, where nothing is in repute but what elsewhere is disreputable. . . . Let the Senate, let all ranks, blush for very shame! . . . But if we ought to abominate all there is immodest, on what ground is it right to hear what we must not speak? For all licentiousness of speech, nay, every idle word, is condemned by God. Why, in the same way, is it right to look on what it is disgraceful to do? How is it that the things which defile a man in going out of his mouth, are not regarded as doing so when they go in at his eyes and ears?

Seated where there is nothing of God, will one be thinking of his Maker? Will there be peace in his soul when there is eager strife there for a charioteer? Wrought up into a frenzied excitement, will he learn to be modest? Nay, in the whole thing he will meet with no greater temptation than that gay attiring of the men and women. The very intermingling of emotions, the very agreements and disagreements with each other in the bestowment of their favors, where you have such close communion, blow up the sparks of passion. And then there is scarce any other object in going to the show but to see and be seen. When a tragic actor is declaiming, will one be giving thought to prophetic appeals? Amid the measures of the effeminate player, will he call up to himself a psalm? And when athletes are hard at struggle, will he be ready to proclaim that there be no striking again? And with his eye fixed upon the bites of bears and the sponge-nets of the net-fighters, can he be moved by compassion? May God avert from His people any such passionate eagerness after a cruel enjoyment! . . .

With such dainties as these let the devil's guests be feasted. The places and the times, the inviter too, are theirs. Our banquets, our nuptial joys, are yet to come. We cannot sit down in fellowship with them, as neither can they with us. Things go in this matter by their turns. Now they have gladness and we are troubled. For what is our wish but the apostle's, to leave the world, and be taken up into the fellowship of our Lord? You have your joys where you have your longings.

CHAPTER III.

DRAMATIC EXPRESSION IN THE MIDDLE AGES.

When Christianity attained power and influence the theater had fallen into such degradation that to reform it was impossible; to condemn it remained the only alternative. For generations it was wholly lost to view. When it rose again, it bore no relation to the drama of antiquity. Once more it sprang from the people and, as before, grew out of religious worship.

The ritual of the Church was full of dramatic possibilities, and a robed and disciplined clergy was also at hand. While Latin was unknown to people in general, it was, nevertheless, the language of the Church and its services. The masses were grossly ignorant, realizing little except what they witnessed with their own eyes. Consequently it followed that the priesthood had to devise a way to bring home to the worshippers the meaning of the Bible,—a book which they did not possess nor could have read. Thus the idea of acting out a portion of a Scriptural lesson was eagerly seized upon.

In England the terms miracle plays and mystery plays were often used interchangeably; strictly speaking, the term *mystery* was taken directly from the French *mystère,* the name of a scriptural play, while a miracle play, as the name implies, presented the life of some saint or some wonder wrought in behalf of religion. However, we find the words used occasionally without regard to this distinction.

Imagine the Christmas season to be at hand and the priests desirous of bringing home to every heart the beautiful Christmas story. They realized the need of reproducing each detail, for they could not depend upon the imaginative resources of the worshippers. The church itself was the scene of the little play and the priests were the actors. The presentation was not given as an additional feature but was substituted for part of the service itself. The skill with which the story might be portrayed depended wholly upon the capabilities of the priest in charge. In one corner of the church a real manger would be built and on Christmas Eve real cattle would feed near by. A mother and tiny babe would be shown, the baby's head pillowed on the mother's arm, light shining all around. A star of unwonted splendor would guide thither the wise men, who came from afar to worship and to bring offerings to the child. To this day in certain devout districts of Europe similar scenes are enacted at the Christmas season.

The Slaughter of the Innocents was celebrated on the twenty-eighth of December. On this occasion child-choristers, dressed in white and preceded by a lamb, would walk around the church in procession. Then they were supposed to be murdered by order of King Herod, after which an angel called them up to heaven, whither they pretended to ascend by rising and passing up into the choir. There a Te Deum was sung and the little play ended.

Easter time approaching, another lesson was to be impressed upon the dull minds of the worshippers. On Good Friday in many churches the crucifix was buried, accompanied by all the signs of mourning commonly attendant upon a burial. On Easter morn, amid glad songs, it was brought forth again. Music supplied any deficiency in the portrayal and additional characters were introduced and plays extended to meet the demands of changing conditions. The Resurrection of Lazarus, the Conversion of St. Paul, and the Passion were favorite subjects for such dramatization.

The oldest French drama surviving belongs to the twelfth century, and sets forth the story of Adam and Eve and their expulsion from the Garden of Eden. The directions written to guide its presentation still exist.

"Paradise shall be situated in a rather prominent place, and is to be hung all round with draperies and silk curtains to such a height that the persons who find themselves in Paradise are seen from their shoulders upwards. There shall be seen sweet smelling flowers and foliage; there shall be different trees covered with fruit, so that the place may appear very agreeable. The Salvator (Saviour) shall appear, robed in a chasuble; Adam and Eve place themselves in front of him. Adam dressed in a red tunic, Eve in a white garment and white silk veil; both rise, Adam nearest, bending his head,

Eve lower down. Adam shall be trained well to speak at the right moment, so that he may come neither too soon nor too late. Not only he, but all shall be well practiced in speaking calmly; they shall neither add nor omit any syllable of the metre; all shall express themselves in a distinct manner, and say in consecutive order all that is to be said."

The Lord explains to Adam his origin and duties; shows him the garden of Paradise; forbids him to touch the tree of knowledge. Adam answers in the submissive manner customary with the vassal swearing allegiance to his lord. Adam and Eve amuse themselves in the garden; devils appear and sneak about, showing Eve the forbidden fruit. She takes it and gives it to Adam. He is immediately aware of his sin and bursts forth in lamentations. God appears, expelling them from the garden. An angel with a fiery sword watches the gate of Paradise. Adam and Eve till the soil while devils plant thorns and thistles behind them. At last they are seized and dragged off to hell.

Presented within the church, there was little attempt at scenery. Often a series of three stories would be shown; for example, the Nativity, Slaughter of Innocents and Flight into Egypt. Each character had his own place or station in the cathedral; when he ceased to have longer a part in the action, his silence indicated his exit. In course of time the churches became too small for the throngs that gathered to witness the spectacles on feast days, and the priests utilized the more spacious quarters of the churchyard. When the churchyard or grounds around the cathedral became too cramped, public squares were used instead. In proportion as the distance between the church and the play increased, the hold of the priesthood upon the play decreased.

There had been from the beginning a possibility of the ludicrous, which increased as the laymen gained control of these plays. To be sure, the principal characters always retained their dignified and awe-inspiring bearing with a devout, mediæval audience. However, the devils who were ever on the watch for human souls whom they might snatch off to purgatory, Herod, Pilate, Noah and his shrewish wife and various lesser personalities of whom little was said in scriptural writing, gave opportunity for the spirit of levity to manifest itself. This the priests never encouraged and in those communities in which church authority was strongest, we find comparatively little of this tendency showing itself.

Understanding how thoroughly these plays given in the vernacular appealed to the masses, minstrels, story-tellers, jesters and the like eagerly seized upon them as a means of amusing the people. Knowing well that fun was welcome, they made the most of every opportunity. While public sentiment would have been outspoken regarding any infringement upon the purity and nobler bearing of many biblical characters, it appreciated the sport afforded by such minor ones as have been mentioned. The hell-mouth, into which sinful ones were triumphantly taken, supplied the greatest amusement and enjoyment. This spirit of buffoonery finally brought about an entire separation between the plays and the clergy. By 1300 we find that only certain scenes might longer be shown by the priests; in 1589 they were forbidden to longer act at all. After 1603 no plays were permitted within the churches.

In Italy and France a temporary stage was generally erected for the presentation of the plays. In England quite a different plan was followed. Here the guilds early undertook the presentation of the mystery plays, which soon grew to include the whole biblical story from the creation to the day of judgment. Four of these great cycles of plays have come down to us; those of York, Wakefield, Chester, and Coventry. Certain plays which were given in Cornwall still remain, but we have no other complete cycle, although we know that they were commonly given in various parts of England and Europe.

When a guild became sufficiently prosperous and strong, it aspired to do as the rest, and have a part in the great festival of its city. Application would be made to the authorities for permission to produce a play and for the assignment of a subject. It was not always easy to get this permission for, in order to supply a scene, sometimes the entire series would have to be again divided. Again, a new guild would take a scene previously played by some guild then declining. The third possibility was to take a play that had little or no connection with the general series.

Once allotted some share in the festival, a guild was required to acquit itself in a creditable manner. To meet the necessary expense, each member paid an annual tax. If a guild failed to do its part it was heavily fined. Two members of each organization were usually chosen as Pageant Masters. They collected the fees and paid out the money, fully accounting for it in the end.

If the play to be given was a new one, some one had to be found to write it; if an old one, it frequently had to be revised. Considerable care was exercised in apportioning the parts. Once decided upon, the rehearsals began. The men were too weary at night to rehearse, so they usually met from two to six in the early morning. Breakfast was then supplied them and they were paid a small fee. Eating and drinking were prominent features of the rehearsals.

In records accounting for money paid out we may read such items: "Paid to the players for rehearsals: To God, 2s, 8d; to Pilate his wife, 2s; to the Devil and Judas, 1s, 6d."

Each guild commonly owned the movable stage or pageant on which it gave its play. These pageants were scaffolds upon four or six wheels, and were divided into two compartments, an upper and a lower one. The upper one was open at the top and sides and was used as a stage. The lower one served as a dressing room. Trap doors through the floor led to the lower room, sometimes serving as hell; a small raised platform at the rear was heaven.

"At length the great day dawns. The narrow streets of the ancient city are crowded with holiday folks, who have come from far and near to see the plays. Lords and ladies from the castles and great houses of the country are here, with hosts of knights, esquires, men-at-arms, and grooms. Farmers have jogged into the city with wives or daughters; monks, palmers, pilgrims, mountebanks and peddlers, merchants, tradesmen and apprentices, all jostle and elbow each other in their anxiety to get a good place. The members of the crafts, who have assembled at the appointed spot almost before sunrise, are busy dressing for their parts, and putting the finishing touches to the finery of their pageants; all eagerly awaiting the signal to set out on their triumphant progress through the city."[1]

[1] Clarke: Miracle Play in England.

The heralds ride through the streets, reading the prologues to the performances. One by one the pageants start.
In order that all might witness the plays, several sites in the
city were decided upon for repeating the various scenes; thus
a play would start perhaps before some tavern door. After
the first guild had there given its allotted scene, that pageant
was drawn on to a second site, while pageant No. 2 came up
in front of the tavern and continued with the play. After
awhile pageants were playing simultaneously in several parts
of the city.

Archdeacon Rogers, who witnessed these pageants, wrote
this description of them: "The season of their performance
was Monday, Tuesday and Wednesday in Whitsun week.
The maner of these playes were every company had his
pagiant, or p'te, w'ch pagiants weare a high scafolde with
2 rowmes, a higher and a lower, upon 4 wheeles. In the
lower they apparelled themselves, and in the higher rowme
they played, being all open on the tope, that all behoulders
might heare and see at the Abay gates, and when the first
pagiante was played, it was wheeled to the highe crosse before
the Mayor, and so to every streete, and so every streete had
a pagiant playinge before them at one time, till all the pagiantes for the daye appoynted weare played, and when one
pagiant was neere ended, worde was broughte from streete
to streete, that so they mighte come in place thereof exceed-
inge orderlye, and all the streetes have their pagiants afore
them all at one time playinge togeather; to see w'ch playes
was greate resorte, and also scafoldes and stages made in the
streetes in those places where they determined to playe theire
pagiantes."

All parts, even those of women, were taken by men.
Until after Shakespeare's time no woman ever appeared upon
the stage. The devil afforded much amusement; Pilate and
Herod always had amusing rôles, while Noah's wife lent
plenty of humor to the ark scene.

"The English people were normally sound, but they were
coarse in habit and speech, after the manner of the time.
There was as much honest and sober living as today; the
grossness was not a matter of character, but of expression.
Men and women saw, without any consciousness of irrever-

ence or incongruity, the figure of Deity enthroned on a movable stage, with Cherubim gathered about Him, creating the world with the aid of images of birds and beasts, with branches plucked from trees, and with lanterns such as were carried about the streets at night."[2]

The wages paid to different actors varied. Noah is reported to have been paid 8d; his wife 1s. Sometimes one actor managed two or more parts: one named Fawston was paid 4d for hanging Judas, 4d for cock-crowing, and 5d for setting the world on fire in the last scene.

Scenery and accessories until the fifteenth century were limited and the imagination, now awakened from mediæval sleep, supplied much. A long cloth unrolled, half white, half black, showed the separation of light and darkness. More cloth with the stars sprinkled over it represented the skies and heavenly bodies. Gilt was much admired and all the spears, crosses, tools, etc., were coated over with it. God's wig, throne, even his face—until that proved injurious—was gilded. A huge barrel partly filled with stones produced an earthquake; globes represented the world and were burned at the day of judgment. Items in the records of expense are most enlightening to us. "Paid for the barrel for the earthquake 3d; paid for attending to the earthquake, 4d; paid for starch to make the storm, 6d; paid for making 3 worlds, 2s; paid for painting of the worlds, paid for setting the world on fire, 5d; paid for keeping the wind, 6d."

A fine hell mouth was an enviable possession. Smoke poured forth from a dragon's mouth, tin cans banged, and noise generally was kept up; the devil and his imps leaped in and out, snatching souls and carrying them to perdition. The devil wore horns and tail; lost souls wore robes of yellow and black to represent flames.

By the fifteenth century we find that the rivalry among the guilds led to much ostentation and display. The simplicity of earlier times disappeared, largely speaking. From two to five hundred people were often included in a festival. Each guild with its supporting friends tried to make the best possible showing. Robes became costly and the properties mul-

[2] H. W. Mabie: Life of Shakespeare.

tiplied. Finally the expense of defraying such a spectacle became such a burden that guilds petitioned the city to be released from the tax imposed upon them.

As the demand arose for something other than these religious plays, we find the moralities growing in favor. These form a connecting link between the scriptural and secular drama. Abstractions were used for the principal characters, and they impress us today as extremely monotonous. The vices and virtues were always in conflict; in the end the vices were punished and the virtues rewarded.

The old French morality, *Wise and Unwise*, well illustrates the general trend of morality plays. They meet from opposite sides of the stage. For a short time they walk together, but Wise is presently led by Reason to Faith, who gives him a lantern, saying: "Take care not to lose this torch —this light." Faith sends him to Contrition, who wants him to go to Confession. On the way Wise meets Humility, who asks him to discard his gorgeous attire. Yielding to Humility, Wise proceeds to Salvation, by guidance of Freewill.

Meantime Unwise has refused to accompany his early companion Wise. Rather, he elects to follow Idleness and Revolt. He visits a tavern where Folly and Debauchery rob him of his property. In grief he goes to Despair and to Bad End. Meanwhile Wise follows the path of virtue and has for companions: Chastity, Abstinence, Obedience, Diligence, Patience, and Wisdom, who lead him to Glory; but Unwise is killed finally by Bad End and his soul is taken by devils to hell.

The vices and virtues were known by the color of their costumes and by their general appearance. Faith was always robed in white; Hope in violet; Inspiration had the appearance of an angel; Hypocrisy, of a nun, while Good Work had the substantial aspect of an honest merchant.

ORDER OF THE PAGEANTS OF THE CORPUS CHRISTI PLAY IN THE CITY OF YORK, A. D. 1415.

Tanners.—God the Father Omnipotent creating and forming the heavens, the angels and archangels, Lucifer and the angels who fell with him into the pit.

Plasterers.—God the Father in his substance creating the earth and all things which are therein, in the space of five days.

Cardmakers.—God the Father forming Adam from the mud of the earth and making Eve from Adam's rib, and inspiring them with the breath of life.

Fullers.—God forbidding Adam and Eve to eat of the tree of life.

Coopers.—Adam and Eve and the tree between them, the serpent deceiving them with apples; God speaking to them and cursing the serpent, and an angel with a sword driving them out of Paradise.

Armorers.—Adam and Eve, an angel with a spade and distaff appointing them their labor.

Glovers.—Abel and Cain sacrificing victims.

Shipwrights.—God warning Noah to make an ark out of planed wood.

Fishmongers and Mariners.—Noah in the ark with his wife, three sons of Noah with their wives, with various animals.

Parchment-makers and Book-binders.—Abraham sacrificing his son Isaac on the altar.

Hisiers.—Moses lifting up the serpent in the wilderness, King Pharaoh, eight Jews looking on and wondering.

Spicers.—A doctor declaring the sayings of the prophets concerning the future birth of Christ. Mary, the angel saluting her; Mary saluting Elizabeth.

Pewterers and Founders.—Mary, Joseph wishing to send her away, the angels telling them to go over to Bethlehem.

STAGE AND CHORUS.—PASSION PLAY.

Tilers.—Mary, Joseph, a nurse, the child born and lying in a manger between an ox and an ass, and an angel speaking to the shepherds, and to the players in the next pageant.

Chandlers.—Shepherds speaking to one another, the star in the East, and angel announcing to the shepherds their great joy in the child which has been born.

Goldsmiths, Goldbeaters and Moneyers.—Three kings coming from the East, Herod questioning them about the child Jesus, and the son of Herod and two counsellors and a herald. Mary with the child, and the star above, and three kings offering gifts.

(Formerly) The House of St. Leonard, (now) Masons.—Mary, with the boy, Joseph, Anna, the nurse, with the young doves. Simeon receiving the boy into his arms, and the two sons of Simeon.

Marshalls.—Mary with the boy and Joseph fleeing into Egypt, at the bidding of the angel.

Girdlers, Nailers and Sawyers.—Herod, ordering the male children to be slain, four soldiers with lances, two counsellors of the king, and four women weeping for the death of their sons.

Spurriers and Lorimers.—Doctors, the boy Jesus sitting in the temple in the midst of them, asking them questions and replying to them, four Jews, Mary and Joseph seeking him, and finding him in the temple.

Barbers.—Jesus, John the Baptist baptizing him, and two angels attending.

Vinters.—Jesus on a pinnacle of the temple, and the devil tempting him with stones, and two angels attending, etc.

Curriers.—Peter, James and John; Jesus ascending into a mountain and transfiguring himself before them. Moses and Elias appearing and the voice of one speaking in a cloud.

Ironmongers.—Jesus, and Simon the leper asking Jesus to eat with him; two disciples, Mary Magdalene bathing Jesus' feet with her tears and drying them with her hair.

Plumbers and Patternmakers.—Jesus, two apostles, the woman taken in adultery, four Jews accusing her.

Pouchmakers, Bottlers and Capmakers.—Lazarus in the sepulchre, Mary Magdalene and Martha, and two Jews wondering.

Spinners and Vestmakers.—Jesus on an ass with its colt, twelve apostles following Jesus, six rich and six poor, eight boys with branches of palm, singing Blessed, etc., and Zaccheus climbing into a sycamore tree.

Cullers, Bladesmiths, Sheathers, Scalers, Bucklermakers and Horners.—Pilate, Caiaphas, two soldiers, three Jews, Judas selling Jesus.

Bakers.—The passover lamb, the Supper of the Lord, twelve apostles, Jesus girded with a towel, washing their feet, institution of the sacrament of the body of Christ in the new law, communion of the apostles.

Cordwainers.—Pilate, Caiaphas, Annas, fourteen armed soldiers, Malchus, Peter, James, John, Jesus and Judas kissing and betraying him.

Bowyers and Fletchers.—Jesus, Annas, Caiaphas and four Jews beating and scourging Jesus. Peter, the woman accusing Peter, and Malchus.

Tapestrymakers and Couchers.—Jesus, Pilate, Annas, Caiaphas, two counsellors and four Jews accusing Jesus.

Littesters.—Herod, two counsellors, four soldiers, Jesus and three Jews.

Cooks and Watercarriers.—Pilate, Annas, Caiaphas, two Jews, and Judas bringing back to them the thirty pieces of silver.

Pilemakers, Millers, Furriers, Hayesters, Bowlers.—Jesus, Pilate, Caiaphas, Annas, six soldiers holding spears with banners, and four others leading Jesus away from Herod, asking to have Barabbas released and Jesus crucified, and likewise binding and scourging him, and placing the crown of thorns upon his head; three soldiers casting lots for the clothing of Jesus.

Shearmen.—Jesus, stained with blood, bearing the cross to Calvary. Simon of Cyrene, the Jews compelling him to carry the cross; Mary the mother of Jesus; John the apostle then announcing the condemnation and passage of her son to Calvary. Veronica wiping the blood and sweat from the face of Jesus with a veil on which is imprinted the face of Jesus, and other women mourning for Jesus.

Pinmakers, Latenmakers, and Painters.—The cross, Jesus stretched upon it on the ground; four Jews scourging Him and binding Him with ropes, and afterwards lifting the cross, and the body of Jesus nailed to the cross on Mount Calvary.

Butchers and Poultry Dealers.—The cross, two thieves crucified, Jesus hanging on the cross between them, Mary the mother of Jesus, John, Mary, James, and Salome. A soldier with a lance, a servant with a sponge, Pilate, Annas, Caiaphas, the centurion, Joseph of Arimathea and Nicodemus, placing Him in the sepulchre.

Saddlers, Glaziers and Joiners.—Jesus conquering hell; twelve spirits, six good, and six evil.

Carpenters.—Jesus rising from the sepulchre, four armed soldiers, and the three Marys mourning. Pilate, Caiaphas, and Annas. A young man seated at the sepulchre clothed in white, speaking to the women.

Winedrawers.—Jesus, Mary Magdalene with aromatic spices.

Brokers and Woolpackers.—Jesus, Luke, and Cleophas in the guise of travelers.

Scriveners, Illuminators, Pardoners and Dubbers.—Jesus, Peter, John, James, Philip, and the other apostles with parts of a baked fish, and a honey-comb; and Thomas the apostle touching the wounds of Jesus.

Tailors.—Mary, John the evangelist, the eleven apostles, two angels, Jesus ascending before them, and four angels carrying a cloud.

Potters.—Mary, two angels, eleven apostles, and the Holy Spirit descending upon them, and four Jews wondering.

Drapers.—Jesus, Mary, Gabriel with two angels, two virgins and three Jews of Mary's acquaintance, eight apostles and two devils.

THE MYSTERY OF THE THREE MARIES.

CHARACTERS.

The Gardener—Jesus Christ.
The Three Maries: Mary Magdalene; Mary, Mother of
James, Mary Salome.
First Angel.
Second Angel.
(*Enter Mary Magdalene, and Mary, Mother of James.*)
Mary Magdalene.
What shall I do, alas!
My Lord went to the tomb,
   Today is the third day;
Go now see indeed
If he comes and rises,
   As he said to me truly.
Mary, Mother of James.
I will go and see
The body of him who redeemed me with pain,
   If it be risen again.
Great comfort he was to us;
That we should have seen his death!
      Alas! Alas!
                                    [*Enter Mary Salome.*

Mary Salome.
The third day is today;
If the body of Christ be risen,
   Go to see.
For the torment which he had
Is ever in my heart;
   This sorrow does not leave me.
                        [*Here she shall meet the other Maries.*
Mary Magdalene.
Women, joy to ye!
And Mary, mother of James,
   And Salome also.
Sorrow is in my heart, alas!
If the body of God himself is gone,
   Where may it be found?

Mary, Mother of James.
  So it is with me,—
  Much and great torment for him;
   If he will not, through his grace,
  Help me in a short time,
  My heart in me will break
   Very really through troubles.

Mary Salome.
  So with me is sorrow;
  May the Lord see my state
   After him.
  As he is head of sovereignty,
  I believe that out of the tomb
   Today he will rise.

Mary Magdalene.
  Oh! let us hasten at once,
  For the stone is raised
   From the tomb.
  Lord, how will it be this night,
  If I know not where goes
   The head of royalty?

Mary, Mother of James.
  And too long we have stayed,
  My Lord is gone his way
   Out of the tomb, surely.
  Alas! my heart is sick;
  I know not indeed if I shall see him,
   Who is very God.

Mary Salome.
  I know truly, and I believe it,
  That he is risen up
   In this day.
  How will it be to us now,
  That we find not our Lord?
   Alas! woe! woe!

      (The Dirge.)
   Alas! mourning I sing, mourning I call,
   Our Lord is dead that bought us all.

Mary Magdalene.
  Alas! it is through sorrows,
  My sweet Lord is dead
   Who was crucified.

      [*Mary Magdalene weeps at the tomb.*

  He bore, without complaining,

Much pain on his dear body,
    For the people of the world.
Mary, Mother of James.
    I cannot see the form
    Of him on any side;
        Alas! woe is me!
    I would like to speak with him,
    If it were his will,
        Very seriously.
Mary Salome.
    There is to me sharp longing
    In my heart always,
        And sorrow;
    Alas! my Lord Jesus,
    For thou art full of virtue,
        All mighty.

(*The Dirge.*)
    Alas, mourning I sing, mourning I call,
    Our Lord is dead that bought us all.

Mary Magdalene.
    Jesus Christ, Lord of Heaven,
    O hear now our voice;
    Who believes not in thee, miserable he!
        He will not be saved.
    When I think of his Passion,
    There is not any joy in my heart;
    Alas! that I cannot at once
        Speak to thee.
Mary, Mother of James.
    Gone he is to another land,
    And with him many angels;
    Alas! now for grief
    I am sorrowful.
    I pray thee, Lord of grace,
    To send a messenger to us,
    That something we may be knowing
        How it is to thee.
Mary Salome.
    O Jesus, full of mercy,
    Do think of us;
    To thy kingdom when we come,
        Hear our voice.
    For desire I become very sick,
    I cannot stand on my standing,

Alas! now what shall I do?
O Lord of Heaven!

(*The Dirge.*)

Alas, mourning I sing, mourning I call,
Our Lord is dead, that bought us all.

First Angel.

I know whom ye seek:
Jesus is not here,
For he is risen
To life in very earnest,
As I tell you,
Like as he is worthy.

Mary Magdalene.

O angel, now tell me,
The body (none, equal to him),
To what place is it gone),
Like as his grace is great,
Joy to me, with my eyes
To see him yet.

Second Angel.

O Mary, go forthwith,
Say to his disciples
And to Peter,
Like as he promised to them
He will go to Galilee
Very truly, without doubt.

Mary, Mother of James.

Now is he risen again indeed,
Jesus our Saviour,
Gone from the tomb,
Worship to him always;
He is Lord of heaven and earth,
Head of sovereignty.

Mary Salome.

Hence go we to the city,
And let us say in every place
As we have seen:
That Jesus is risen,
And from the tomb forth gone,
To heaven really.

Mary Magdalene.

Never to the city shall I go,
If I do not find my Lord,

Who was on the cross tree.
O Jesus, King of grace,
Joy to me once to see thee,
    Amen, amen.

Mary, Mother of James.
Mary, be with thee
All the blessings of women,
    And the blessing of Jesus Son of grace;
Of full heart I pray him,
Joy and grace always good to do
    To us now, from God the father.

Mary Magdalene.
My blessing on ye also,
From Christ, as he is gone to the tomb,
    Joy to ye to do well today.
Lord, give me the grace
Once to see thy face,
    If it be thy will with thee.

Mary Salome.
Amen, amen, let us seek
Christ, who redeemed us in pain,
    With his flesh and with his blood;
Much pain he suffered,
For love of the people of the world,
    And he is the King of power.

[*Here Mary, the mother of James, and Salome retire from the
    tomb, and sit down a little way from it.*
Mary Magdalene.
He who made heaven, as he is gone to the tomb,
After him great is my desire.
Christ, hear my voice, I pray also
That thou be with me at my end.

Lord Jesus, give me the grace,
As I may be worthy to find a meeting,
With thee today, in some sure place
That I may have a view and sight of thy face.

As thou art Creator of heaven and earth,
And a Redeemer to us always,
Christ my Saviour, hear, if it regards thee
Disclose to me, what I so much desire.

Through great longing I am quite weary,
And my body also, bones and back.
Where is there tonight any man who knows
Where I may yet find Christ full of sorrow?

[She goes to the garden.
[Enter the Gardener.

Gardener (*Jesus.*)

O woeful woman, where goest thou?
For grief thou prayest, cry out thou dost.
Weep not nor shriek, he whom thou seekest
Thou didst dry his feet with thy two plaits.

Mary Magdalene.

Good lord, if thou hast chanced to see
Christ my Saviour, where is he truly?
To see him I give thee my land;
Jesus, Son of grace, hear my desire.

Gardener.

O Mary, as I know thee to be
Within this world, one of his blood,
If thou shouldst see him before thee,
Couldst thou know him?

Mary Magdalene.

Well I do know the form
Of the son of Mary, named Jesus;
Since I see him not in any place,
I feel sorrow, else I would not sing "alas!"

(*And then Jesus shall shew his side to Mary Magdalene
and say:*)

Gardener.

Mary, see my five wounds,
Believe me truly to be risen;
To thee I give thanks for thy desire,
Joy in the land there shall be truly.

Mary Magdalene.

O dear Lord, who wast on the cross tree,
To me it becomes not to kiss thy head.
I would pray thee let me dare
Now to kiss once thy feet.

(Woman, touch me not!)

Gardener.

O woeful woman, touch me not near,
No, it will not serve, nor be for gain;
The time is not come;

462565

Until I go to heaven to my Father,
And I will return again to my country,—
To speak with thee.

Mary Magdalene.

Christ, hear my voice, say the hour
That thou comest from heaven again to earth
To speak with us.
Thy disciples are very sad,
And the Jews with violence always
Are round about them.

Gardener.

O Mary, tell them,
Truly I go to Galilee,
As I said;
And besides that, bear in memory to speak
Good comfort to Peter by me;
Much he is loved.

CHAPTER IV.

THE COMMEDIA DELL' ARTE.

The burden of producing a mystery play, or a cycle of them, fell upon a community as a whole. In England the various guilds embraced the greater portion of the citizen body; when each guild assumed the responsibility of one particular scene, the expense of the whole was in the end fairly well divided. Elsewhere, while spectacles might occur only occasionally, nevertheless when they were undertaken the reputation of the community was at stake, and no effort would be spared to make the celebration a success. Sometimes the visit of the sovereign or some special occasion as, for example, the celebration of a national holiday, might cause the citizens to prepare a cycle of plays. The rivalry in case of the guilds and the ambitions of a mediæval town would result in elaborate costumes, attractive settings and, in short, in gorgeous spectacles.

As time went on, however, acting came to be more and more confined to a class of people who made it a profession. As the production of plays fell to the share of individuals or small groups, there came to be a falling off of the splendid trappings and properties that had characterized the later miracle plays. Always poor, struggling for very existence, without a home, and often merely tolerated, the first professional actors had a sorry time. The first companies were formed in Italy and thence spread into other lands. Their equipment was slight; a draped platform served as a stage. However, one decided change occurred; since they played in all kinds of weather, they needed shelter from the elements, and so were obliged to provide a covered place in which to present their plays. This marks the beginning of the modern indoor theater.

The Commedia dell' Arte—Comedy of Art—had its birth in Italy of the Renaissance. It was improvised comedy —unwritten drama. The author, and manager in one, chose some subject, modified it to suit his needs, fixed the characters, devised certain situations, divided his material into acts and scenes, developed the plot and made the whole ready for his company. Then he decided to whom the various characters should be assigned, in which scenes they should appear, how long remain on the stage, what in general each should do and talk about. The rest was left to the actors themselves. Such skeletons of plays were known as scenarios. The French called them the canvas, the embroidery being done by the artists. Tables containing the plot of the play, the names of the characters represented, the entrances and exits and the cues for the music were posted up to assist the memories of the improvising actors. Beyond this, the success of the comedy rested wholly with the performers; their wit and repartee, their jokes and outbursts of feeling gave the whole success or failure. In time tradition furnished a common store of knowledge upon which the actor drew. Dialogues were to a great extent spontaneous; soliloquies were designed to give the audience such information as the action failed to supply.

We may infer from instructions for actors which survive from these years that many blunders must have occurred to mar the production when actors were unevenly matched or when they were all indifferently good. "The actors are enjoined to notice well where the scene is laid, so that one of them may not speak of Rome, where another has just mentioned Naples, or that he who comes from Spain may not say that he comes from Germany. They shall also pay close attention to the houses, and know where their own house is, so that they do not run into the wrong house, which always looks ridiculous. Nor is it well if a father cannot remember the name of his son or a lover of the beloved one."

To be a good actor a man needed not alone a rich store of knowledge, an elastic imagination and ready wit, but he must be quick to respond to the words and actions of his colleagues, thus to give the impression to those who witnessed the play that everything had been determined upon beforehand.

Riccoboni, a famous Italian actor, left a history of the Italian theater in which he dwelt at length upon the advantages of improvised comedy.

"Nobody can deny that it has a charm of its own, of which the written play can never boast. Improvisation gives opportunities for variety in playing, so that though we see the same canvas each time, it is nevertheless a different play. The actor who improvises, acts with more animation and in a more natural way than he who performs a part he has learned by heart. People feel better, and consequently say better, what they invent than what they borrow from others by means of the memory. But these advantages are purchased at the price of many difficulties; clever actors are required, moreover actors of even talent; for the drawback of improvisation is, that the art of even the best actors absolutely depends on his fellow-performer; if he has to act with a colleague who does not reply exactly at the right moment, or who interrupts him in the wrong place, his words miss part of their effect, or his spirit is gone. To an actor who depends on improvisation, it is not sufficient to have face, memory, voice, even senti-ment; if he is to distinguish himself, he must possess a lively and fertile imagination, a great faculty of expression, he must master all the subtleties of language, possess all the knowledge which is required for the different situations in which his part places him."

The inconstancy of husband and wife has ever appealed to Italian audiences. Today the well-worn plots are set forth in new dress continually. Especially during the Re-naissance they were popular. Sometimes it was the father who was deceived, more often the husband, and the fun of the play turned upon the completeness of his discomfiture. Intrigue and comic situation were the burden of these plays, which supply one link in the long chain of dramatic development. Their principal interest to us today lies in the effect they had upon later drama. Molière particularly owed much to the Commedia dell 'Arte, from which he borrowed many of his plots and situations.

Some there are who would find in the first companies of professional actors a survival of the professional actors of Rome, who during centuries of disturbance had in some mea-ger way ministered to the diversion of mankind. We know that acting was hereditary in families and that in Rome an actor's son was compelled to follow in his father's calling. While there were doubtless wandering minstrels, harpers and jesters who made their way from camp to camp, from court to court, and from town to town, nevertheless this theory is only a surmise and cannot be substantiated by existing evidence. Unquestionably in all ages there have been people more susceptible to emotion, more agile and more capable of entering into the spirit of dance, song and gesture than their fellows, but that there can be any direct connection between the professional actors of Rome and the first Italian companies of the Renaissance seems doubtful.

In these improvised comedies the same characters appeared again and again. The maids and valets correspond in a measure to the Greek slaves. The harlequins supplied much of the fun. In the earlier comedies they were stupid fools, always being imposed upon by everyone. Later they became clever jesters. Pantalone was a favorite and appeared in many places. He was the butt of all jokes; easily deceived, he would quickly fly into a passion which would pass away immediately. He was fond of the tavern and fond of women, generally occupying himself in courting them. He wore the long trousers known by his name, although they were changed after a time for long stockings and knickerbockers.

The Pedant was a well known character. Absent-minded, giving wise saws and sprinkling his sentences with Latin phrases, he would correspond to the recluse or scholar shown frequently upon the modern stage.

Pulcinella was the scoundrel who cheated on every hand, stole when he could and lied without conscience. In one comedy wherein he played his accustomed rôle, he is shown to belong to a band of gypsies. While one of his number is telling the fortune of a stupid peasant, Pulcinella decides to steal the farmer's donkey. Quietly slipping the halter from its head, the animal runs away, while he places the halter upon his own head. The peasant turning back to his load beholds in amazement the spectacle of a human being thus constrained, whereupon Pulcinella, always equal to the occasion, relates that in his boyhood he was disobedient to his mother, who laid the spell upon him to be a donkey for five years, five months, five days and five hours. This period has just elapsed and he is now himself again. He shakes hands with the peasant and thanks him for having been indulgent to him during his donkey days. The astonished peasant craves pardon for having seen in him only a donkey, and in response to Pulcinella's request that he be allowed to keep the halter as a remembrance, adds such coin as his slender purse permits.

It was in the presentation of these improvised plays that women were first employed on the stage in Italy. In 1636 a successful manager gave his reasons for preferring them. "I will never follow the custom of making boys play the parts of women or young girls, especially as I have seen the drawbacks of it in certain academies. In the first place, these young men do not know how to dress themselves in costumes which do not belong to their sex, so they are dressed at home by their women or flirting servant-girls, who frequently make fun with them. . . . Thus disguised in female attire, these children go out and present themselves in the town, chatting and joking with everybody, and they arrive at the theater in an untidy, disorderly state, so that their friends or teachers have to comb their hair again, paint them afresh, and arrange their collars and ornaments. . . .

"It is more natural that women should perform their own parts; they are able to dress themselves, and as they are respectable, they set a good example instead of creating scandal. . . .

"And besides, actresses are women like others. . . . They cannot err without its being known by all, and religion apart, they are bound to be more careful and discreet in their behavior than the women who can cover their fault with the cloak of hypocrisy."

From Italy the practice of having women impersonate feminine characters spread into France and England. Their grace and adaptability soon won for them a permanent place. However, women were still unknown upon the stage in Shakespeare's time, and audiences manifested their displeasure when they first appeared in England.

Another innovation was wrought by the managers of the Commedia dell 'Arte, this being the use of a curtain to separate the actors and the spectators. Since this required a platform enclosed on three sides, it brought into use what is known as the picture-frame stage,—"the fourth wall having been removed to allow us to watch what is happening within the room." The fact that this change was effected during the period of greatest excellence in the art of painting is significant.

CHAPTER V.
ENGLISH DRAMA.
INTERLUDES.

The term *interlude* was at first used of some of the moralities; however as time went on there came to be more and more a demand for plays other than religious. Frequently, too, the moralities were long and monotonous. A short witty play was desired for banquets and other special occasions, where guests did not wish to be reminded of death or the wages of sin. As a form of entertainment suitable to fill an intervening period which a host would make agreeable for his friends, the interlude became very popular.

There were two requisites demanded: first, the interlude must be brief; second, it must be humorous. For the most part interludes are read today only by students and the humor they possess seems to the present-day reader mild indeed. However, when compared with the older moralities they are the more acceptable.

We find the interlude used in contrast with the "stage-plays," the latter given out of doors in the summer time, and attended by large crowds of people. The interludes were generally given indoors before a limited circle of invited guests, and were suitable for inclement and winter weather. As might be expected, then, these were more aristocratic in spirit and were written to please more refined tastes than the so-called "stage plays."

Interludes required only four or five actors. They were made up of a series of dialogues. Sometimes they lack only a plot to make them comedy of a crude order. The following lines from the play *Sir Thomas Moore* give a very fair conception of their rendering in Early England.

SIR THOMAS MOORE.

Moore. Welcome, good friend; what is your will with me?
Player. My lord, my fellowes and myselfe
Are come to tender ye our willing service,
So please you to command us.

Moore. What, for a play, you meane?
Whom do you serve?
 Player. My Lord Cardinalles grace.
 Moore. My Lord Cardinalles players! now, trust me, welcome;
You happen hether in a luckie time,
To pleasure me, and benefit yourselves.
The Maior of London and some aldermen,
His lady and their wives, are my kinde guests
This night at supper: now, to have a play
Before the banquet, will be excellent.—
How think you, sonne Roper?
 Roper. 'Twill doo well, my lord,
And be right pleasing pastime to your guests.
 Moore. I prethee, tell me, what playes have ye?
 Player. Divers, my lord; *The Cradle of Securitie,*
Hit nayle o' th' head, Impacient Povertie,
The Play of Faure Pees, Diues and Lazarus,
Lustie Iuentus, and *The Marriage of Witt and Wisdome!*
 Moore. *The Marriage of Witt and Wisdome!* that, my lads;
Ile none but that; the theame is very good,
And may maintaine a liberall argument:
To marie witt to wisdome, asks some cunning;
Many have witt, that may come short of wisdome.
Weele see hoe Maister poet playes his part,
And whether witt or wisdome grace his arte.
Goe, make him drinke, and all his fellowes too.—
How manie are ye?
 Player. Foure men and a boy, sir.
 Moore. But one boy? then I see,
Ther's but fewe women in the play.
 Player. Three, my lord; Dame Science, Lady Vanitie,
And Wisdome she herselfe.
 Moore. And one boy play them all? bir lady, hees loden.
Well, my good fellowe, get ye straighte together,
And make ye readie with what haste ye may.—
Provide their supper gainste the play be doone,
Else shall we stay our guests here over long.—
Make haste, I pray ye.
 Player. We will, my lord.   [*Exit.*
 Moore. Where are the waytes? goe, bid them play,
To spend the time a while.   [*Enter lady.*
How now, madame?
 Lady. My lord, th' are coming hether.
 Moore. Th' are welcome. Wife, Ile tell ye one thing;

Our sport is somewhat mended; we shall have
A play tonight, *The Marriage of Witt and Wisdome,*
And acted by my good Lord Cardinalles players:
How like ye that, wife?

Lady. My lord, I like it well.
See, they are coming. . . .

Moore. What, are they readie?

Servant. My lord, one of the players craves to speak with you.

Moore. With me! where is he?

> [*Enter Inclination the Vice, readie.*

Incli. Heere, my lord.

Moore. How now, what's the matter?

Incli. We would desire your honor but to stay a little; one of
My fellows is but run to Oagles for a long beard for young
Witt, and heele be heere presently.

Moore. A long beard for young Witt! why, man, he may be
without a beard till he come to marriage, for witt goes not all by
the hayre. When comes Witt in?

Incli. In the second scene, next to the Prologue, my lord.

Moore. Why, play on till that sceane come, and by that time
Witt's beard will be growne, or else the fellowe returned with it.
And what part plaist thou?

Incli. Inclination the Vice, my lord.

Moore. Grammercies, now I may take the vice if I list; and
wherefore hast thou that bridle in thy hand?

Incli. I must be bridled anon, my lord.

Moore. And thou beest not sadled too, it makes no matter, for
then Witt's inclination may gallop so fast, that he will outstrip
Wisdome, and fall to follie.

Incli. Indeed, so he does to Lady Vanitie; but we have no
follie in our play.

Moore. Then ther's no witt in't, Ile be sworne; follie waites
on witt, as the shaddowe on the bodie, and where witt is ripest
there follie still is readiest.
But beginne, I prethee: weele rather allow a beardless
Witt than Witt all beard to have no braine.

Incli. Nay, he has his apparell on too, my lord, and therefore
he is the readier to enter.

Moore. Then, good Inclination, beginne at a venter.—

> [*Exit Inclination.*

My Lord Maior,
Witt lacks a beard, or else they would beginne:
Ide lend him mine, but that it is too thinne.
Silence, they come.

[*Trumpet sounds: enter Prologue.*
Pro. Now, for as much as in these latter dayes,
Throughout the whole world in every land,
Vice doth increase and vertue decays.
Iniquitie having the upper hand;
We therefore intend, good gentle audience,
A prettie short interlude to play at this present,
Desiring your leanne and quiet silence,
To shewe the same, as is meete and expedient.
It is called *The Marriage of Witt and Wisdome,*
A matter right pithie and pleasing to heare,
Whereof in breefe we will shewe the whole summe;
But I must be gon, for Witt doth appeare.

John Heywood was the most gifted of the interlude writers. Born probably in the year 1497, he died in 1580. Although but little is known of his private life, he was for some time a choir-boy of the Chapel Royal. When his voice changed he went to Oxford. Throughout his life he was a staunch Catholic, which brought him now the favor, now the disapproval, of the crown. During Queen Mary's reign he was attached to the Court and assisted at the presentation of plays and interludes. Ever devoted to his faith, he never-theless was unsparing in satirizing Church and ecclesiastical abuses.

In the *Play of Love*, Heywood still retained the general form of the old morality. Four characters are included: the Lover not Beloved; the Woman Beloved but not Loving; the Lover Beloved; Neither Loving nor Loved. *The Play of the Weather* is also of this earlier type.

Of the later plays, the *Four P's*, the *Merry Play between the Pardoner and the Friar*, and the *Merry Play between Johan the Husband, Tyb his Wife and Sir John the Priest* are best known. A conception of Heywood's style, as well as the nature of the interlude, may be gained from the following passages from the Four P's. In this series of dialogues, four travellers—the Pardoner, Pedlar, Palmer and 'Pothecary —meet and exchange experiences. Finally they accept the challenge to see which among them can tell the biggest lie. Even today a smile is provoked by the one which carried off the honors.

'Pothecary. By the mass, there is a great lie!
Pardoner. I never heard a greater, by our Lady!
Pedlar. A greater! Nay, know ye any so great?

THE FOUR P's.

Palmer. Now God be here; who keepeth this place?
Now by my faith I cry you mercy;
Of reason I must sue for grace,
My rudeness showeth me so homely.
Whereof your pardon axed and won,
I sue you, as courtesy doth me bind,
To tell this, which shall be begun,
In order as may come best in mind.
I am a Palmer, as ye see,
Which of my life much part have spent
In many a fair and far country.
As Pilgrims do of good intent.
At Jerusalem have I been
Before Christ's blessed sepulchre:
The mount of Calvary have I seen,
A holy place, you may be sure.
To Jehosaphat and Olivet
On foot, God wot, I went right bare;
Many a salt tear did I sweat,
Before thy carcase could come there.
Yet have I been at Rome also,
And gone the stations all a-row:
St. Peter's shrine and many mo,
Than, if I told all, ye do know.
Except that there be any such,
That hath been there, and diligently
Hath taken heed, and marked much,
Then can they speak as much as I.
Then at the Rhodes also I was;
And round about to Amias. . . .
To these, with many other one,
Devoutly have I prayed and gone,
Praying to them to pray for me
Unto the blessed Trinity,
By whose prayers and my daily pain
I trust the sooner to obtain
For my salvation, grace, and mercy.
For be ye sure I think surely,

Who seeketh saints for Christ's sake,
And namely such as pain do take
On foot, to punish their frail body,
Shall thereby merit more highly
Than by anything done by man.
 Pardoner. And when ye have gone as far as ye can,
For all your labor and ghostly intent,
Ye will come home as wise as ye went.
 Pardoner. Nay, 'fore God, sir, then did I rage;
I think ye right well occupied,
To seek these saints on every side.
Also your pain I not dispraise it;
But yet I discommend your wit:
And ere we go, even shall ye,
If you in this will answer me.
I pray you show what the cause is,
Ye went all these pilgrimages?
 Palmer. Forsooth, this life I did begin
To rid the bondage of my sin:
For which these saints rehearsed ere this
I have both sought and seen, I wis;
Beseeching them to bear record
Of all my pain unto the Lord,
That giveth all remission,
Upon each man's contrition;
And by their good mediation,
Upon mine humble submission,
I trust to have in very deed
For my sould health the better speed.
 Pardoner. Now is your own confession likely
To make yourself a fool quickly.
For I perceive ye would obtain
No other thing for all your pain,
But only grace your soul to save:
Now mark in this what wit ye have!
To seek so far, and help so nigh;
Even here at home is remedy;
For at your door myself doth dwell,
Who could have saved your soul as well
As all your wide wandering shall do,
Though ye went thrice to Jericho.
Now since ye might have sped at home,
What have ye won by running to Rome?
 Palmer. If this be true that ye have moved,

Then is my wit indeed reproved.
But let us hear first what ye are?
 Pardoner. Truly I am a pardoner.
 Palmer. Truly a pardoner! that may be true;
But a true pardoner doth not ensue.
Right seldom is it seen, or never,
That truth and pardoners dwell together,
For be your pardons never so great,
Yet them to enlarge ye will not let
With such lies that ofttimes, Christ wot,
Ye seem to have that ye have not.
Wherefore, I went myself to the self thing
In every place and without saying:
Had as much pardon there assuredly,
As ye can promise me here doubtfully.
Howbeit, I think ye do speak of,
And no whit of pardon granted
In any place where I have haunted:
Yet of my labor I nothing repent;
God hath respected how each time is spent;
And as in his knowledge all is regarded,
So by his goodness all is rewarded.
 Pardoner. By the first part of this last tale,
It seemeth ye came of late from the ale.
For reason on your side so far doth fail,
That ye leave reasoning, and begin to rail.
Wherein you forget your own part clearly,
For you be as untrue as I:
And in one point ye are beyond me.
For you may lie by authority,
And all that have wandered so far,
That no man can be their controller.
And where you esteem your labor so much,
I say again my pardons are such,
That if there were a thousand souls on a heap,
I would bring them to heaven as good cheap.
As ye have brought yourself on pilgrimage,
In the least quarter of your voyage,
Which is far a side heaven, by God:
There your labor and pardon is odd.
With small cost and without any pain,
These pardons bring them to heaven plain;
Give me but a penny or two pence,
And as soon as the soul departeth hence,

In half-an-hour, or three-quarters at the most,
The soul is in heaven with the Holy Ghost.
   'Pothecary. Send ye any souls to heaven by water?
   Pardoner. If we do, sir, what is the matter?
   'Pothecary. By God, I have a dry soul should thither;
I pray you let our souls go to heaven together,
So busy you twain be in soul's health;
May not a 'pothecary come in by stealth?
Yes, that I will, by St. Anthony,
And, by the leave of this company,
Prove ye false knaves both, ere we go,
In part of your sayings, as this, lo!
Thou by thy travail thinkest heaven to get;
And thou by pardons and relics countest no let,
To send thine own soul to heaven sure;
And all other whom thou list to procure.
If I took an action, then were they blank;
For like thieves the knaves rob away my thank.
All souls in heaven having relief,
Shall they send your crafts? nay, thank mine chief.
No soul, ye know, entereth heaven-gate,
Till from the body he be separate;
And whom have ye known die honestly,
Without help of the 'pothecary? . . .
   Pardoner. If ye had killed a thousand in an hour's
     space,
When come they to heaven dying out of grace?
   'Pothecary. If a thousand pardons about your necks
     were tied,
When come they to heaven, if they never died?
   Palmer. Long life after good works indeed
Doth hinder man's receipt of mead;
And death before one duty done,
May make us think we die too soon.
Yet better tarry a thing than have it;
Than go too soon, and vainly crave it.
   Pardoner. The longer ye dwell in communication,
The less shall ye like this imagination.
For ye may perceive, even at the first chop,
Your tale is trapped in such a stop.
That at the least ye seem worse than we.
   'Pothecary. By the mass, I hold us nought all three.

[*Enter Pedlar.*

Pedlar. By our lady, then have I gone wrong;
And yet to be here I thought it long.
  'Pothecary. Ye have gone wrong no whit,
I praise your fortune and your wit,
That can direct you so discreetly
To plant you in this company.
Thou a Palmer, and thou a Pardoner,
I a 'Pothecary.
  Pedlar. And I a Pedlar.
  'Pothecary. Now, on my faith, well watched;
Where the devil were we four hatched?
  Pedlar. That maketh no matter, since we be matched,
I could be merry if that I had catched
Some money for part of the ware in my pack.
  'Pothecary. What the devil hast thou there at thy back?
  Pedlar. What! dost thou not know that every pedlar
In all kinds of trifles must be a meddler?
Specially in women's triflings;
Those use we chiefly above all things,
Which things to see, if ye be disposed,
Behold what ware is here disclosed;
This gear showeth itself in such beauty,
That each man thinketh it saith, *Come, buy me!*
Look where yourself can like to be chooser,
Yourself shall make price, though I be loser.
Is here nothing for my father Palmer?
Have ye not a wanton in a corner,
For all your walking to holy places?
By Christ, I have heard of as strange cases,
Who liveth in love, and love would win,
Even at this pack he must begin.
Wherein is right many a proper token,
Of which by name part shall be spoken:
Gloves, pins, combs, glasses unspotted,
Pomades, hooks, and laces knotted;
Brooches, rings, and all manner of beads;
Laces, round and flat, for women's heads;
Needles, thread, thimble, shears, and all such knacks,
Where lovers be, no such things lack;
Slipers, swathbands, ribbons, and sleeve laces,
Girdles, knives, purses, and pincases.
  'Pothecary. Do women buy their pincases of you?
  Pedlar. Yea, that they do. I make God a vow.

'Pothecary. So mot I thrive them for my part,
I beshrew thy knave's naked heart,
For making my wife's pincase so wide,
The pins fall out, they cannot abide;
Great pins she must have, one or other;
If she lose one, she will find another.
Wherein I find cause to complain:
New pins to her pleasure and to my pain!
    Pardoner. Sir, ye seem well-seen in women's causes,
I pray you to tell me what causeth this:
That women, after their arising,
Be so long in their apparelling?
    Pedlar. Forsooth, women have many lets,
And they be masked in many nets;
As frontlets, fillets, partlets, and bracelets;
And then their bonnets and their poignets:
By these lets and nets the let is such,
That speed is small when haste is much. . . .
And now have I found one mastery,
That ye can do differently;
And is nother selling and buying,
But even on very lying.
And all ye three can lie as well,
As can the falsest devil in hell.
And though afore ye heard me grudge
In greater matters to be your judge,
Yet in lying I can some skill,
And if I shall be judge, I will.
And be you sure, without flattery,
Where my conscience findeth the mastery,
There shall my judgment straight be found,
Though I might win a thousand pound.
    Palmer. Sir, for lying, though I can do it;
Yet am I loth to go for it.
    Pedlar. Ye have no cause for fear, be bold,
For ye may here lie uncontrolled.
And ye in this have good advantage,
For lying is your common usage.
And you in lying be well sped,
For all your crapt doth stand in falsehood.
Ye need not care who shall begin;
For each of you may hope to win.
Now speak all three even as ye find;
Be ye agreed to follow my mind?

Palmer. Though nother of us yet had lied,
Yet what we can do is untried;
For as yet we have devised nothing,
But answered you and given you hearing. . . .
   'Pothecary. I did a cure no longer ago,
But in *anno domini millesimo,*
On a young woman so young and fair,
That never have I seen a gayer. . . .
   Pardoner. Well, sir, then mark what I can say.
I have been a pardoner many a day,
And done greater cures ghostly
Than ever did he bodily. . . .
   Palmer. His tale is all much perilous;
But part is much more marvellous:
As where he said the devils would complain,
That women put them to such pain.
Be their conditions so crooked and crabbed,
Frowardly fashioned, so wayward and wrabbed.
So far in division, and stirring such strife,
That all the devils be weary of their life.
This in effect he told for truth.
Whereby much marvel to me ensueth,
That women in hell such shrews can be,
And here so gentle, as far as I see.
Yet have I seen many a mile,
And many a woman in the while.
Not one good city, town, or borough
In Christendom, but I have been thorough,
And this I would ye should understand,
I have seen women five hundred thousand;
And oft with them have long time tarried.
Yet in all places where I have been,
Of all the women I have seen,
I never saw nor knew in my conscience
Any one woman out of patience.
   'Pothecary. By the mass, there is a great lie.
   Pardoner. I never heard a greater, by our Lady.
   Pedlar. A greater! Nay, know ye any so great?

CHAPTER VI.

MASQUES.

The masque came into England from the south. In favored Italy, under its blue skies, in its splendor-loving cities, the masque was a spectacle of wondrous beauty. It charmed by its costumes, properties and unexpected effects; the poetry was lost in the maze of spectacular glory. Dancing, music, declamation and lyric poetry were all intermingled. The demands made upon the actors were that they should be fine looking, dignified, and gorgeously apparelled. Naturally, then, this form of entertainment appealed to the wealthy.

Florence and Venice were cities wherein the masque, viewed as a spectacle, reached its height. The Florentines were always fond of festivals and sumptuous entertainment. Venice had the advantage of its unparalleled waterways. For the celebration of weddings and festivals masques were in great favor.

Castiglione tells us of a performance given in Urbine in 1513. In the first act the legend of Jason was portrayed. After the sowing of the dragon's teeth, warriors came forth through trap doors and slew one another. In another act Neptune rode in a chariot, drawn by monsters of the seas; in still another, Juno drawn by her peacocks, rode in majestic calm. The citizens of Florence in more elaborate display combined sculpture, painting, music and tableaux. In 1515 the *Music-Masque of Dreams* (Il Canto de 'Sogni) was produced. All human life was conceived to be under the domination of Morpheus. As in a dream Wealth, Glory, Fame, Ambition, Hope and Love passed while one slumbered, each attended by followers and genii, the latter wearing bats' wings upon their shoulders. Madness was attended by Bacchantes and Satyrs, adorned with ivy and the vine. "Classical mythology was racked to furnish forth the several emblems of elephants and dolphins, tortoises and tigers, unicorns and falcons. Blooming youth and wrinkled age, the grisly ugliness of witches and the lucid beauty of Olympian gods, human forms and bestial monsters, were blent together, interchanged and combined in the slow-moving panorama."

In Venice the visit of a distinguished prince was sometimes celebrated by a regatta, where guild vied with guild for dazzling and artistic effects. Such repetition was tendered Henry of Anjou in 1574. Senators, aristocracy and gentry made lavish display. For days the city bore the aspect of one continued masque. Each guild had its brigatine, emblematic of its calling. Silk-weavers spread costly silken banners to the breezes; goldsmiths were resplendent with priceless gems; mirror-makers covered masts with glasses, to throw bright reflections around about; swordsmiths used their arms effectively in the peaceful cause of decoration.

Brought from sunny Italy to sombre England, the masque failed to retain its splendour and extravagance. Music and dancing, together with lyric poetry, were employed and costumes were as fine as circumstances permitted. One change we may note: the poetry became more important and no longer was relegated to a subordinate place. Consequently the English masques may be read with pleasure, while the Italian masques were less capable of expression in writing.

Here was a mode of entertainment worthy of royalty itself, and kings and princes, queens and princesses, made up the courtly actors in these spectacles. Favored indeed were those invited to witness festivals like these. While always the amusement of the rich, masques were by no means confined to the nobility; no wedding, no reception to foreign prince was complete without one masque. In Scott's story of *Kenilworth* we may read of one given in honor of Elizabeth's visit to the Earl of Leicester's castle, which there is some reason to think Shakespeare saw as a boy.

The titles of Ben Jonson's masques give indication of their variety: *Masque of Blankness; Masque of Beauty; Masque of Owls; of Queens; of Time; of Pan; of Oberon.*

The last imposing masque given in England as a court function was provided by Charles I. and Henrietta Marie in 1640, not long before the outburst of the civil war.

PAN'S ANNIVERSARY; OR, THE SHEPHERD'S HOLYDAY.

(As it was presented at court before King James.)

(The Scene-Arcadia.)

First Nymph. Thus, thus begin the yearly rites
Are due to Pan on these bright nights;
His morn now riseth and invites
To sports, to dances and delights:
　All envious and profane, away,
　This is the shepherd's holyday.
Second Nymph. Strew, strew the glad and smiling
　ground
With every flower, yet not confound:
The primrose drop, the spring's own spouse,
Bright day's-eyes, and the lips of cows,
　The garden-star, the queen of May,
　The rose, to crown the holyday.
Third Nymph. Drop, drop, you violets; change your
　hues,
Now red, now pale, as lovers' use;
And in your death go out as well
As when you lived unto the smell:
　That from your odour all may say,
　This is the shepherd's holyday.
Shepherd. Well done, my pretty ones, rain roses still,
Until the last be dropt: then hence, and fill
Your fragrant prickles for a second shower.
Bring corn-flag, tulips, and Adonis' flower,
Fair ox-eye, goldy-locks, and columbine,
Pinks, goulands, king-cups, and sweet sops-in-wine,
Blue harebells, pagles, pansies, calaminth,
Flower-gentle, and the fair-haired hyacinth;
Bring rich carnations, flower-de-luces, lilies,
The checqued, and purple-ringed daffodillies,
Bright crown-imperial, kingspear, holyhocks,
Sweet Venus-navel, and soft lady-smocks;
Bring too some branches forth of Daphne's hair,
And gladdest myrtle for these posts to wear,
With spikenard weaved, and marjoram between,
And starred with yellow-golds, and meadow-queen,

That when the altar, as it ought, is drest,
More odour come not from the phoenix' nest;
The breath thereof Panchaia may envy,
The colours China and the light the sky.

(The Scene opens, and in it are the Masquers discovered sitting about the Fountain of Light, the *Musicians* attired like the *Priests of Pan*, standing in the work beneath them, when entereth to the old Shepherd)

(*A Fencer, flourishing.*)

Fencer. Room for an old trophy of time; a son of the sword, a servant of Mars, the minion of the Muses, and a master of fence! One that hath shown his quarters, and played his prizes at all the games of Greece in his time; as fencing, wrestling, leaping, dancing, what not? and hath now ushered hither by the light of my long sword, certain bold boys of Bœotia, who are come to challenge the Arcadians at their own sports, call them forth on their own holyday, and dance them down on their own green-swarth.

Shepherd. 'Tis boldly attempted, and must be a Bœotian enterprise, by the face of it, from all the parts of Greece else, especially at this time, when the best and bravest spirits of Arcadia, called together by the excellent Arcas, are yonder sitting about the Fountain of Light, in consultation of what honours they may do the great Pan, by increase of anniversary rites fitted to the music of his peace.

Fencer. Peace to thy Pan, and mum to thy music, swain; there is a tinker of Thebes a coming, called Epam, with his kettle, will make all Arcadia ring of him. What are your sports for the purpose—say? If singing, you shall be sung down; if dancing, danced down. There is no more to be done with you, but know what;—which is it; and you are in smoke, gone, vapoured, vanished, blown, and, as a man would say in a word of two syllables, nothing.

Shepherd. This is short, though not so sweet. Surely the better part of the solemnity here will be dancing.

Fencer. Enough; they shall be met with instantly in their own sphere, the sphere of their own activity, a dance. But by whom, expect: no, Cynætheian, nor Satyrs; but, as I have said, boys of Bœotia, things of Thebes, (the town is ours, shepherd), mad merry Greeks, lads of life, that have no gall in us, but all air and sweetness. A tooth-drawer is our foreman, that if there be but a bitter tooth in the company, it may be called out at a twitch: he doth command any man's teeth out of his head upon

the point of his poniard; or tickles them forth with his riding
rod: he draws teeth a horseback at full speed, yet he will dance
a foot, he hath given his word: he is a yoeman of the mouth to
the whole brotherhood, and is charged to see their gums be clean
and their breath sweet, at a minute's warning. Then comes my
learned Theban, the tinker I told you of, with his kettledrum
before and after, a master of music and a man of metal, he beats
the march to the tune of Ticklefoot, Pam, Pam, Pam, brave Epam
with a nondas. That's the strain.

Shepherd. A high one!

Fencer. Which is followed by the trace and tract of an excellent juggler, that can juggle with every joint about him, from
head to heel. He can do tricks with his toes, wind silk and thread
pearl with them, as nimble a fine fellow of his feet as his hands:
for there is a noble corn-cutter, his companion, hath so pared
and finified them—I need he hath taken it into his care to reform
the feet of all, and fit all their footing to a form! only one splay
foot in the company, and he is a bellows-mender allowed, who
hath the looking to of all their lungs by patent, and by his
place is to set that leg afore still, and with his puffs keeps them
in breath during pleasure; a tinderbox-man, to strike new fire
into them at every turn, and where he spies any brave spark
that is in danger to go out, ply him with a match presently.

Shepherd. A most politic provision!

Fencer. Nay, we have made our provisions beyond example,
I hope. For to these there is annexed a clock-keeper, a grave
person as Time himself, who is to see that they all keep time
to a nick, and move every elbow in order, every knee in compass. He is to wind them up and draw them down, as he sees
cause: then there is a subtle, shrewd-bearded sir, that hath been
a politician, but is now a maker of mouse-traps, a great inginer
yet: and he is to catch the ladies' favours in the dance with
certain cringes he is to make; and to bait their benevolence.
Nor can we doubt of the success, for we have a prophet amongst
us of that peremptory pate, a tailor or master fashioner, that
hath found it out in a painted cloth, or some old hanging, (for
those are his library), that we must conquer in such a time, and
such a half time; therefore bids us go on cross-legged, or however thread the needles of our happiness, go through-stitch with
all, unwind the clew of our cares; he hath taken measure of our
minds, and will fit our fortune to our footing. And to better
assure us, at his own charge brings his philosopher with him,
a great clerk, who, they say, can write, and it is shrewdly suspected but he can read too. And he is to take the whole dances

from the foot by brachygraphy, and so make a memorial, if not a map of the business. Come forth, lads, and do your own turns. How like you this, shepherd? was not this gear gotten on a holyday?

Shepherd. Faith, your folly may deserve pardon because it hath delighted: but beware of presuming, or how you offer comparison with persons so near deities. Behold where they are that have not forgiven you, whom should you provoke again with the like, they will justly punish that with anger which they now dismiss with contempt. Away!

To the Masquers.

And come, you prime Arcadians, forth, that taught
   By Pan the rites of true society,
From his loud music all your manners wrought,
   And made your commonwealth a harmony;
Commending so to all posterity
   Your innocence from that fair fount of light,
As you still sit without the injury
   Of any rudeness folly can, or spite:
Dance from the top of Lycæan mountain
   Down to this valley, and with nearer eye
Enjoy what long in that illumined fountain
   You did far off, but yet with wonder, spy.

Hymn I.

First Nymph. Of Pan we sing, the best of singers, Pan,
That taught us swains how first to tune our lays;
And on the pipe more airs than Phœbus can.
   Chorus. Hear, O you groves, and hills resound his
   praise.
   Second Nymph. Of Pan we sing, the best of leaders,
   Pan,
That leads the Naiads and the Dryads forth;
And to their dances more than Hermes can.
   Chorus. Hear, O you groves, and hills resound his
   worth.
   Third Nymph. Of Pan we sing, the best of hunters,
   Pan,
That drives the hart to seek unused ways;
And in the chase more than Sylvanus can.

Chorus. Hear, O you groves, and hills resound his praise.

Second Nymph. Of Pan we sing, the best of shepherds, Pan,

That keeps our flocks and us, and both leads forth
To better pastures than great Pales can.

Chorus. Hear, O you groves, and hills resound his worth.

And while his powers and praises thus we sing,
The valleys let rebound, and all the rivers ring.

HYMN II.

Pan is our All, by him we breathe, we live,
  We move, we are; 'tis he our lambs doth rear,
Our flocks doth bless, and from the store doth give
  The warm and finer fleeces that we wear.
  He keeps away all heats and colds,
  Drives all diseases from our folds;
  Makes everywhere the spring to dwell,
  The ewes to feed, their udders swell;
  But if he frown, the sheep, alas!
  The shepherds wither, and the grass.
Chorus. Strive, strive to please him then, by still increasing thus
The rites are due to him, who doth all right for us.

HYMN III.

    If yet, if yet,
Pan's orgies you will further fit,
See where the silver-footed fays do sit,
  The nymphs of wood and water;
  Each tree's and fountain's daughter!
  Go take them forth, it will be good
To see some wave it like a wood,
And others wind it like a flood;
    In springs,
    And rings,
Till the applause it brings,
  Wakes Echo from her seat,
  The closes to repeat.
(Echo. *The closes to repeat.*)
Echo the truest oracle on ground,
  Though nothing but a sound.

(Echo. *Though nothing but a sound.*)
Beloved of Pan, the valleys' queen.
(Echo. *The valleys' queen.*)
And often heard, though never seen.
(Echo. *Though never seen.*)

Fencer. Room, room there; where are you, shepherd? I am come again, with my second part of my bold bloods, the brave gamesters; who assure you by me, that they perceive no such wonder in all is done here but that they dare adventure another trial. They look for some sheepish devices here in Arcadia, not these, and therefore a hall! a hall! they demand.

Shepherd. Nay, then they are past pity, let them come, and not expect the anger of a deity to pursue them, but meet them. They have their punishment with their fact: they shall be sheep.

Fencer. O spare me, by the law of nations, I am but their ambassador.

Shepherd. You speak in time, sir. Now let them return with their solid heads, and carry their stupidity into Bœotia, whence they brought it, with an emblem of themselves and their country. This is too pure an air for so gross brains.

To the Nymphs.

End you the rites, and so be eased
Of these, and then great Pan is pleased.

Hymn IV.

Great Pan, the father of our peace and pleasure,
  Who gives us all this leisure,
Hear what thy hallowed troop of herdsmen pray
  For this their holyday.
And how their vows to thee they in Lycæus pay.
  Chorus. So may our ewes receive the mounting rams,
And we bring thee the earliest of our lambs:
So may the first of all our fells be thine,
And both the beestning of our goats and kine;
  As thou our folds dost still secure,
  And keep'st our fountains sweet and pure;
Drivest hence the wolf, the tod, the brock,
Or other vermin from the flock.
That we, preserved by thee, and thou observed by us,
May both live safe in shade of thy loved Maenalus.
  Shepherd. Now each return unto his charge,
And though today you've lived at large,

And well your flocks have fed their fill,
Yet do not trust your hirelings still.
See yond' they go, and timely do
The office you have put them to;
But if you often give this leave,
Your sheep and you they will deceive.
    And thus it endeth.

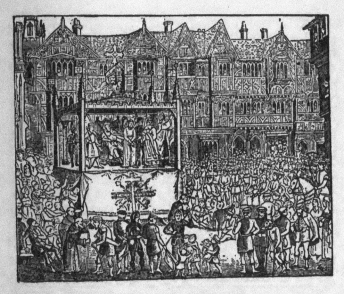

A MIRACLE PLAY AT COVENTRY.
From an Old Print.

CHAPTER VII.

ELIZABETHAN AUDIENCES AND THEATERS.

Under the Tudors England outgrew mediævalism and became a modern nation. A spirit of nationality boldly asserted itself, resulting in part from the ecclesiastical break with Rome, and still more from the uniting of all factions to withstand the attack of Spain, together with the consequent elation occasioned by the splendid victory over the Armada. These feelings were further stimulated by news of unexpected discoveries beyond the seas, bringing whole continents into the view of Europe.

It is difficult for us today to fully understand the England of those years. Feudalism, with its disintegrating tendencies, was gone; in place of many centers, men were coming to the realization of one united country. Yet, while feudalism was extinct, its showy trappings remained and the spirit of chivalry which it had engendered was still potent.

Rumor and surmise were abroad through the land. Stories of the new found countries were everywhere rife and no report was too extravagant to gain credence. Imaginations were thrilled with tales which met the ear, and no fancy was deemed incapable of realization. A play written of the lately found lands contained this sentence: "Why, man, in that country the very frying-pans are made of pure gold!" Men dreamed of personal riches; the nation hoped for extended territory, trade and profit. All hearts were roused to fresh desire.

Nevertheless, England was still in the making. Few towns had paved streets; none were lighted save by the dim flicker of lanterns carried by belated pedestrians. Garbage was thrown into the streets; passersby must needs exercise caution to evade the bucketful of water likely at any moment to be thrown from some window. So unsanitary were conditions that pestilence wiped out a goodly part of the population every few years. The homes of the simplest laborers today contain many comforts unknown at that time in the dwellings of the most prosperous. Chimneys were but recently devised, and in the majority of houses smoke was still allowed to find its way along

MIDSUMMER NIGHT'S DREAM.—FUSELI.

the walls to a hole left for its escape in the roof. Nobles tossed bones to the dogs from the banquet tables. Although large sums were expended for apparel,—the queen taking pride in her three thousand gowns,—yet few had beds which would be today thought tolerable, and pillows were regarded as the portion of the sick. No delicacy of speech hampered the expression of people in whom passions were powerful. War and strife had accustomed men to bloodshed; pillage upon the high seas was countenanced by the queen herself. Men glorified in their strength and in their freedom. Subjects debarred from polite society today were then freely discussed; coarse language was the rule rather than the exception.

One misses much in the plays of Shakespeare if ignorant of men as he knew them and life as his contemporaries lived it. Drama, more closely than other forms of literature, reflects the life of the people. It is true to its own age while, at the same time, if it be enduring, it reflects that which is permanent in man, beneath all the exteriors that social customs may create. Particularly does the Elizabethan drama mirror life peculiar to the years which produced it.

People travelled extensively in the sixteenth century. It was customary for young men to finish their education by travel in France, Spain and, more particularly, in Italy—the country which had given birth to the Renaissance and under its spell had produced wonderful buildings and masterpieces of art. Jonson and Shakespeare satirized the habit of these youths who returned to their native land with foreign accent, language, habits and dress. Contact and culture had not yet brought about the uniformity we find among men amid old civilizations. "Every one lived in his own humor and openly avowed his tastes."

In spite of the crudities, coarse speech, dirt and vices of the times, the English people were sound to the core. They admired strength, courage, truth, fair dealing and justice. Their worst qualities were apparent on the surface; no incipient moral decay was working at the roots of their society. The race was young and its faults were those common to men who are not far remote from the elemental things. They loved beauty and appreciated the sublime. In short, the English nation was still in the rough but had already a vision of its future possibilities and greatness.

The Renaissance which found its highest expression in painting among the Italians, in England expressed itself most completely in the drama. People could not wait to hear a story told—they must see it acted. The revival of the classics had spread over all England and many English women, as well as men, were acquainted with Latin and Greek. Queen Elizabeth found time amid her pressing cares to read Greek daily; Lady Jane Grey preferred study to the pleasures of the chase. Reverence for authority, so binding in the middle ages, had given way to the spirit of investigation. Men wished to find out facts for themselves; they wished also to know what the past had to offer them. The invention of printing made possible the distribution of reading material, previously the luxury of the rich alone; the Bible, sole property of the Church, had been rendered into the vernacular and given to the people. Education and learning had received a mighty impulse, while the masses were fast becoming more enlightened.

We should not fail to note the contradictions which this age presents. Superstitions still held men enthralled; they believed in the potency of a charm, the maliciousness of witches, the existence of fairies and "the evidence of things not seen" was very real to them. For years after they tried to make gold by the mixture of chemicals and even entertained the possibility of creating life itself, if they could but discover the proper combinations. Audiences composed of people holding these beliefs found such monsters as Caliban, witches, ghosts and fairies acceptable to a degree which we can scarcely understand.

During the middle ages all were walled to insure protection. The wall of London was standing in the days of Queen Elizabeth, although the town was no longer confined within it. From the river by the Tower, it followed a semicircular course around the city, terminating again at the Thames. Seven gates gave access to the newer region which had grown up beyond it to the north. South of the river another district was growing. The London bridge connected the city with Southwark but the river itself was the convenient highway for travel and traffic. Short flights of stairs led to the water's edge where boatmen plied their passage back and forth, up and down, to satisfy the needs of the passengers, who paid fares varying according to the distance covered. As the boatsman set out upon his trip he cried: "Eastward Ho!" "Southward Ho!" "Westward Ho!" to warn others of his intended direction. We find that when the first theaters sprang up in London they were located beyond the wall to the north, and across the river to the south. Not until after the Restoration were they allowed within the limits of the city proper.

When the first strolling companies came into England from other lands, they exhibited in such places as they found convenient. Most favorable in point of general plan were the English inns. Pictures of old Tabard and other inns of this period have made the general form of the inn-court familiar to us. Galleries usually extended around the entire three sides, supplying places where the more careful and comfort-loving might witness the plays in safety from the pressing throng which filled the court-yard. This particular arrangement should be noted for, strange to say, when it later came to the question of providing play-houses and having no earlier models to which they could turn, the very plan of the inn-court was copied and such in general was the aspect of the Shakespearean theaters.

Prior to 1564 there were no permanent theaters in England. Moreover, players were merely tolerated at public places; noise and disturbances interrupted the play, and those who suffered the actors to give their productions were insolent and overbearing in many cases. More serious still was the problem of collecting a stipulated fee. Companies were obliged to accept such contributions as their audiences saw fit to make and many took advantage of the opportunity to witness the spectacles free. Nevertheless, there were advantages in playing at the inns, for these were the centers around which people gathered, there being considerable travel throughout the country.

The Puritan spirit was growing in England. It will be remembered that the Puritans condemned much that we regard as essential to our very happiness and comfort now,—art, painting, gay music, all luxuries and most reading, except that of a religious nature or in the form of hymns. From the rise of Puritanism in England these tendencies were manifest, but as they became more apparent by the increase of adherents to this mode of worship, the struggle became more pronounced. Fortunate it was for the drama that the Tudor and Stuart rulers were fond of plays and gave them unceasing encouragement.

In 1576 James Burbage, father of Richard Burbage, the famous actor, leased a lot outside the city wall near Bishop's Gate, and built a house which he called The Theatre. The word was not in common use at the time, *playhouse* being the term generally applied. The next year The Curtain was erected in the same neighborhood. At that time a curtain used as today for the purpose of shutting the stage from the view of the audience was unknown; no such barrier existed until some time afterward. This playhouse took its name from the locality which had long been known as Curtayne Close.

The entertainment supplied at these places was rough and crude. The first English playwrights had not yet begun to produce those plays which made Shakespeare's greater efforts possible.

The terms of the lease governing Burbage's tenure allowed him the privilege of removing the building when his term expired, but the landlord appears to have been a quarrelsome fellow who refused to recognize this privilege. Whereupon Burbage and other actors pulled down the structure by force and used the material in the construction of The Globe.

Before his death, James Burbage also started the Blackfriars Theater, on the south bank of the river. This took its name from the fact that it was built on land formerly belonging to the monastery of the Blackfriars. It is very probable that Burbage secured it for the reason that, having been monastic property, it was free from many of the petty restrictions that might be used to annoy a manager at a time when Puritan sentiment was growing in England and disabilities were placed as often as possible upon actors and their place of action. These two playhouses are most interesting to us because of Shakespeare's close association with them. Other early public theaters were the Rose, the Fortune, Red Bull and the Swan. Each had its sign—the Globe being known by the figure of Atlas supporting the world, the Fortune by the Goddess of Fortune, and so on.

While the public theaters were open only in summer, private theaters were open for a longer season. There appear to have been but three private playhouses in early London: the Cockpit, Salisbury Court and, most important, the Blackfriars. These were entirely roofed over and were provided with artificial lights, so that plays might be given at five o'clock instead of in the afternoon—which time alone the public theaters were used. Patronized by the nobility, boxes or small rooms composing the balconies around the room, were rented by regular patrons who kept the keys for these boxes in their own possession. Seats were provided for spectators in these private theaters, and the audiences were quiet and well behaved.

The public theaters were less comfortable. Only the stage and boxes were roofed, the central portion of the building being open to the sky. Those who wished to pay for the privilege could secure seats around the room, or, in the case of favored patrons, on the stage itself. Others found places in the pit and either stood throughout the performance or sat upon the earth. They drank, played cards, ate apples and nuts, quarreled and noisily deported themselves. Women who coveted favorable opinion did not frequent the public theaters, and on the stage feminine parts were played by youths until after the Restoration. An Englishman who visited Italy in 1608, after the Fortune had been built, made this comment in a letter: "I was at one of their playhouses, where I saw a comedy acted. The house is very beggarly and bare in comparison with our stately playhouses in England, neither can their acting compare with ours for apparell, shews, and musick. Here I observed certain things that I never saw before, for I saw women act, a thing I never saw before; and they performed with as good grace, action, gesture and whatsoever convenient for a play as I ever saw a masculine actor."

Each theater had playwrights who wrote for it exclusively. The Blackfriars was celebrated for its excellent orchestra. However, this was no expense to the management since it appears that the musicians paid an annual stipend for the privilege of thus coming before the notice of wealthy patrons.

The following description of London theaters was written
by a Dutch visitor to that city in 1596: "There are in London four theaters of noteworthy beauty, which bear different
names according to their signs. In each of them a different
play is daily performed before the people. The two most
magnificent of these are situated across the Thames on the
south side, and are called from the signs suspended over them:
'The Rose' and 'The Swan.' Two others, 'The Theater' and
'The Curtain,' are situated outside the town to the north,
on the road which is entered through 'the episcopal gate,' generally called Bishopgate. There is also a fifth, but of a different construction, meant for the baiting of wild beasts, in
which many bears, bulls and dogs of an extraordinary size are
fed in separate dens and cages, which are baited to fight, and
thus afford a most delightful spectacle to the people. Of
all the theaters the largest and most magnificent is the one
whose sign is a Swan, as it holds three thousand persons, and
is built of flint, of which there is a large abundance in England, supported by wooden pillars. The paint that covers
these pillars produces such an excellent imitation of marble
that it baffles even the sharpest eye."

Could we be set back into that year and visit those playhouses as did this foreign guest, our description would be
very different. He compared the English stage with others
of his day; we should find it crude indeed in comparison with
the simplest theater of today. Whether we witnessed the
afternoon performance in a public theater, beginning at three
o'clock, or one later in the day at the Blackfriars, by the dim
lamps then available, it would seem to us as if the actors were
moving about in semi-darkness. In the Globe we would find
the noise of the groundlings—as those occupying the pit were
called—deafening. If, as frequently happened, the prologue
in a black robe should come forward to repeat his lines, and
an insolent young noble stalked in upon the stage, shouting:
"Boy, a stool," without regard to the speaker, we should again
find existing conditions intolerable. The groundlings hissed
those spectators upon the stage who carried on their conversation regardless of the play and often threw nuts and apples
at them. The young dandies, however, were there to see and
be seen and they cared little for the approval or disapproval
of the commoners.

The ceiling of the stage was usually covered with blue, to represent the sky; but when tragedy was to be enacted, it was hung with black. The handbills were usually printed in black, but for tragedy in gory red. When the hour for the play drew near, the flag was hoisted above the playhouse to announce that entertainment was therein provided; trumpeters gave signal of the opening play. Scenery was cheap and scarce. A board hung out in front indicated to those who could read the locality in which the scene was laid. Being hampered by no change of scenery, playwrights constantly changed the situation. They had many elements to satisfy: the more discerning who would follow the main story and plot; the less attentive who were diverted by the variety set in the play, and the most ignorant who would appreciate only the broadest jokes and jests. It is for this reason that Shakespeare's plays have to be adapted for present-day use. It would be a practical impossibility, with modern demand for change of scene, to give a Shakespearean play in such time as the audience would be willing to remain as spectators.

After a time the more discriminating awoke to the bare, inartistic appearance of the stage. Sir Philip Sidney's ridicule of it is often quoted: "Where you shall have Asis of the one side and Afric of the other, and so many other under-kingdoms, that the player, when he cometh in, must ever begin with telling where he is (or else the tale will not be conceived). Now ye shall have three ladies walk to gather flowers, and then we must believe the stage to be a garden. By and by we hear news of a shipwreck in the same place, and then we are to blame if we accept it not for a rock. Upon the back of that comes out a hideous monster, with fire and smoke, and then the miserable beholders are bound to take it for a cave. While in the meantime, two armies fly in, represented with four swords and bucklers, and then what hard heart will not receive it for a pitched field?"

At first sight we are impressed with the unexpected number of theaters in early times, but upon closer examination it develops that the same theater was known by different names at different periods. Thus the Cockpit and Phœnix were identical; the Whitefriars and Salisbury Court, and others. The picture we know today of the Globe theater un-

fortunately is not of the building used in Shakespeare's time.
That burned in 1613, during a presentation of Henry VIII.
The roof was thatched, and a shot from a cannon in use on
the stage set the whole in flames in a moment. Later it was
rebuilt in a more substantial manner.

In spite of efforts on the part of Puritans to suppress the
theaters, or at least to limit their number to two, the seven
playhouses mentioned continued to entertain the people until
the outbreak of the civil war. The act which caused their
suppression was thus worded:

"Whereas the distressed Estate of Ireland, steeped in her
own Bloode, and the distracted Estate of England, threatened
with a cloud of Bloode, by a Civill Warre, call for all possible
meanes to appease and avert the Wrath of God appearing in
these judgments; amongst which Fastinif and Prayer have
often been tried to be very effectual, have been lately and are
still enjoyned, and whereas publick Sports do not well agree
with publick Calamities, nor publick playes with the Seasons
of Humiliation, this being an Exercise of sad and pious solemnity, and the other being Spectacles of, too commonly expressing lacivious Mirth and Levitie. It is therefore thought fit,
and Ordained by the Lords and Commons in this Parliament
Assembled, that while these sad Causes and set times of Humiliation do continue, publick Stage-players shall cease and
be foreborne. Instead of which are recommended to the people of this Land, the profitable and seasonable Consideration
of Repentance, Reconciliation, and Peace with God, which
probably may produce outward peace and prosperity, and bring
again Times of Joy and Gladness to these Nations."

THE BANKSIDE, SOUTHWARK, SHOWING THE GLOBE THEATER

CHAPTER VIII.

FORERUNNERS OF SHAKESPEARE.

Admirers of Shakespeare's plays once wrote as though he had found the drama undeveloped, and by his own transcendent genius had raised it to a height before unknown and since unequalled. This is true only in part. Even if Shakespeare had not belonged to the Elizabethan age, a period which produced a Marlowe and a Jonson would have been remarkable. No writer comes suddenly into view, creates a form of literature and disappears to leave generations to marvel at his achievements. Geniuses are made possible by the efforts of countless men who have gone before and prepared the way. Shakespeare was indebted to miracle and morality plays; to masques and interludes; to earlier dramatists whose plays were well known to him and, even to a greater extent, to Marlowe. These contributed ideas and conceptions which the master turned to use by his consummate skill. A knowledge of the conditions of the stage as he found it helps us to estimate the more clearly his own accomplishment and to intelligently follow his own growing strength and power.

Although miracle plays ceased to be acted in the cities, nevertheless, they continued for many years in country places. It is not unlikely that Shakespeare witnessed the well meant efforts of mechanics to provide entertainment; his humorous portrayal of Bottom the Weaver in *Midsummer Night's Dream* gives indication that similar attempts had been known to him.

Each theater had in its possession many plays which had been written for its use in years bygone; these it was customary for new playwrights to work over and put upon the stage in new attire. In those days there were no copyrights and to have had a play printed would have meant its loss as exclusive property. London of those times could not supply endless audiences to witness a play repeated for months, as it can today. It contained about one hundred thousand people, and the same ones filled the theaters each week. To run a play a few times and then preserve it for occasional use was as much a manager could hope to do.

Thus we may understand how it came about that no edition of Shakespeare's plays appeared before his death; we can also understand how it was that his first work as a playwright was the recasting of such plays as he found available. Critics are agreed that Titus Andronicus, his first effort, was his only in part.

The revival of the classics brought an acquaintance with the Latin dramatists—Plautus, Terence and Seneca—into England and from their study of these plays writers learned something of dramatic technique. They adopted the division of plays into five acts and in other respects improved the structure of the plays. However, English productions were original in spirit and at no time has the English drama been blind imitation of that of other nationalities.

Subjects for plays abounded everywhere. They were located in France, Spain, Italy; in ancient Rome and Greece. Comic situations were supplied by street and tavern and by the home as well. Historical subjects suddenly grew in favor after the defeat of the Armada, for Englishmen were proud of their victory and were filled with a desire to know more of the steps by which their country had risen to power. Audiences were far from critical. Such inconsistencies as having a scene placed in Italy and enacted by men who were indisputably English in every particular, did not disconcert them in the least. They merely required that a play should merge from one scene to another without interruption, and that it should hold their attention from beginning to end. And there were many classes to satisfy: the more discriminating who would enjoy the portrayal of character and the possibilities of the play; others who would find the variety of scenes sufficiently diverting; and finally the more ignorant whose attention could be held only by means of coarse tavern scenes and broad humor. Since a large portion of the audience remained standing throughout the performance, they must be amused if they were to be kept quiet.

Of the early group of playwrights, whose plays were holding London audiences when Shakespeare came as a young man to seek his fortune in the capital city, Lyly, Peele, Greene, Kyd and Marlowe were best known. Marlowe was greatest among them. The others are interesting to us today chiefly for their part in the gradual development of the English drama and for their influence upon the style of the future poet. Otherwise, it is doubtful whether present day readers would give them more than passing attention.

John Lyly was born in 1552. He was graduated at Oxford and at the age of twenty-seven published a book which brought him fame. It was called *Eupheus, the Anatomy of Wit.* Somewhat later a second part, entitled *Eupheus, his England,* followed. The popularity of this story, largely composed of views on love, philosophy, social conduct and travel, was due to what was shortly recognized as a defect: namely, a bombastic style where the language greatly outweighs the matter. The title has given rise to the derivative *euphuism,* which is used to indicate that particular style of writing.

Of Lyle's plays, the best is *Campaspe,* based upon an incident in Alexander's triumphant progress into Greece. Having conquered Thebes and fallen in love with the beautiful captive, Campaspe, he orders Appelles to paint her picture. Discovering that the artist has been completely won over by the charming maid, the conqueror generously withdraws to take up the burden of conquest again, realizing that his personal pleasure must be set aside for the duties which his position force upon him. Lyly tried for many years to gain appointment as Master of Revels at the court of Elizabeth. Undoubtedly he deemed this story one suited to win the favor of the Virgin Queen.

"Lyly was emphatically a discoverer. He discovered euphuism, and created fashionable affectation, which ran its course of more than twenty years. He discovered the dialogue of repartee in witty prose. He discovered the ambiguity of sexes, as a motive of dramatic curiosity. He discovered what effective use might be made of the occasional lyric as an adjunct to dramatic action. He discovered the suggestion of dramatic dreaming. He discovered the combination of Masque and Drama, which gave rise to the Courtly or Romantic Comedy."

A Most Excellent Comedie of Alexander, Campaspe, and Diogenes.

(Played before the Queens Majestie on twelfe day at night, by her Majestie's Children and the Children of Paules.)

(*The Prologue at the Black-Friers.*)

They that fear the stinging of waspes make fannes of peacocks tailes, whose spots are like eyes; and Lepidus, which could not sleepe for the chattering of birds, set up a beast whose head was like a dragon: and we, which stand in awe of report, are compelled to set before our owle Pallas shield, thinking by her vertue to cover the others deformity. It was a sign of famine to Egypt when the Nyle flowed lesse than twelve cubites or more than eighteene; and it may threaten despaire unto us if we be lesse courteous than you looke for or more cumbersome. But, as Thesus, being promised to be broughte to an eagles nest, and traveling all the day, found but a wren in a hedge, yet said, "This is a bird:" so, we hope, if the shower of our swelling mountaine seeme to bring forth some elephant, performe but a mouse, you will gently say, "This is a beast." Basill softly touched yieldeth a sweete sent, but chafed in the hand, a ranke savour: we feare, even so, that our labors slightly glanced on will breed some content, but examined in the proofe, small commendation. The haste in performing shall be our excuse. There went two nights to the begetting of Hercules; feathers appeare not on the phœnix under seven months; and the mulberie is twelve in budding; but our travailes are like the hares, who at one time bringeth forth, nourisheth, and engendreth againe, or like the brood of trochilus, whose eggs in the same moment that they are laid become birds. But, howsoever we finish our worke, we crave pardon if we offend in matter, and patience if we transgresse in manners. We have mixed mirth with councell, and discipline with delight, thinking it not amisse in the same garden to sow pot-hearbes that we set flowers. But we hope, as harts that cast their hornes, snakes their skins, eagles their bills, become more fresh for any other labour; so, our charge being shaken off, we shall be fit for greater matters. But, least, like the Myndians, we make our gates greater than our towne, and that our play runs out at the preface, we here conclude,—wishing that, although there be in your precise judgments an universall mislike, yet we may enjoy by your wonted courtesies a generall silence.

ACTUS PRIMUS. SCAENA SECUNDA.

(*The market-place.*)

Manes. I serve instead of a master a mouse, whose house is a tub, whose dinner is a crust, and whose bed is a board.

Psyllus. Then thou art in a state of life which philosophers commend; a crum for thy supper, an hand for thy cup, and thy clothes for thy sheets; for *Natura paucis contenta.*

Grani. Manes, it is pitie so proper a man should be cast away upon a philosopher; but that Diogenes, that dogge, should have Manes, that dogbolt, it grieveth nature and spiteth art; the one having found thee so dissolute—absolute, I would say—in bodie, the other so single—singular—in minde.

Manes. Are you merry? It is a signe by the trip of your tongue and the toyes of your head that you have done that today which I have not done these three dayes.

Psyllus. What's that?

Manes. Dined.

Grani. I thinke Diogenes keepes but cold cheare.

Manes. I would it were so; but he keepeth neither hot nor cold.

Grani. What then? luke-warm? That made Manes runne from his master the last day.

Psyllus. Manes had reason, for his name foretold as much.

Manes. My name? how so, sir boy?

Psyllus. You know that it is called *mons, a mouendo,* because it stands still.

Manes. Good.

Psyllus. And thou art named Manes, a *manendo,* because thou runnest away.

Manes. Passing reasons! I did not run away, but retire.

Psyllus. To a prison, because thou wouldst have leisure to contemplate.

Manes. I will prove that my body was immortal, because it was in prison.

Grani. As how?

Manes. Did your masters never teach you that the soule is immortal?

Grani. Yes.

Manes. And the bodie is the prison of the soule?

Grani. True.

Manes. Why then, this:—to make my body immortal, I put it in prison.

Grani. Oh, bad!

Psyllus. Excellent ill!

Manes. You may see how dull a fasting wit is. Therefore, Psyllus, let us go to supper with Granichus. Plato is the best fellow of all philosophers. Give me him that reades in the morning in the schoole and at noone in the kitchin. . . .

ACTUS PRIMUS. SCAENA TERTIA.

(Alexander's palace.)

Melippus. I had never such ado to warne schollers to come before a king! First. I came to Crisippus, a tall, leane, old madman, willing him presently to appeare before Alexander. He stood staring on my face, neither moving his eyes nor his body. I urging him to give some answer, he tooke up a booke, sate downe, and saide nothing. Mekissa, his maide, told me it was his manner, and that oftentimes she was fain to thrust meat into his mouth, for that he would rather starve than cease study. Well, thought I, seeing bookish men are so blockish and great clearkes such simple courtiers, I will neither be partaker of their commons nor their commendations. From thence I came to Plato and to Aristotle and to divers others, none refusing to come saving an olde, obscure fellow, who, sitting in a tub turned towards the sunne, read Greeke to a young boy. Him when I willed to appeare before Alexander, he answered, "If Alexander would fain see me, let him come to me." "Why," said I, "he is a king." He answered, "Why, I am a philosopher." "Why, but he is Alexander!" "I; but I am Diogenes." I was half angry to see one so crooked in his shape to be so crabbed in his sayings; so going my way, I said, "Thou shall repent it, if thou comest not to Alexander." "Nay," smiling answered he, "Alexander may repent it, if he come not to Diogenes; vertue must be sought, not offered." And, so, turning himselfe to his cell, he grunted I know not what, like a pig under a tub. But I must be gone, the philosophers are coming.

(*Enter philosophers.*)

Plato. It is difficult controversie, Aristotle, and rather to be wondered at than beleeved, how natural causes should worke supernatural effects.

Arist. I do not so much stand upon the apparition that is seene in the moon, neither the Demonium of Socrates, as that I cannot by natural reason give any reason of the ebbing and flowing of the sea; which makes me in the depth of my studies to cry out, *O ens entium, miserere mei!*

Plato. Cleanthes and you attribute so much to nature by searching for things which are not to be found, that, whilest you study a cause of your owne, you omit the occasion itselfe. There is no man so savage in whom resteth not this divine particle; that there is an omnipotent, eternal and divine mover, which may be called God.

Cleant. I am of this minde, that the first mover, which you terme God, is the instrument of all the movings which we attribute to nature. The earth, which is mass, swimmeth on the sea, seasons divide themselves, fruits growing in themselves, and the majestie of the sky, the whole firmament of the world, *and* whatsoever else appeareth miraculous,—what man almost of meane capacity but can prove it natural?

Anaxar. These causes shall be debated at our philosophers' feast, in which controversie I will take part, Aristotle, that there is a *Natura naturans,* and yet not God.

Crates. And I with Plato that there is *Deus optimus maximus,* and not Nature.

Arist. Here cometh Alexander.

Alex. I see, Hephestion, that these philosophers are here attending for us.

Hephest. They are not philosophers if they know not their duties.

Alex. But I much marvel Diogenes should be so dogged.

Hep. I do not thinke but his excuse will be better than Melippus' message.

Alex. I will go see him, Hephestion, because I long to see him that would Alexander to come.—Aristotle and the rest, since my coming from Thebes to Athens, from a place of conquest to a palace of quiet, I have resolved with myselfe in my court to have as many philosophers as I had in my camp souldiers. My court shall be a schoole, wherein I will have used as great doctrine in peace as I did in warre discipline.

Arist. We are all here ready to be commanded, and glad we are that we are commanded, for that nothing better becommeth kings than literature, which maketh them come as neare to the gods in wisdome as they do in dignity.

Alex. It is so, Aristotle, but there is yet among you, yea, and of your bringing up, that sought to destroy Alexander,— Calistenes, Aristotle, whose treasons against his prince shall not be borne out with the reasons of his philosophy.

Arist. If ever mischief entered into the heart of Calistenes, let Calistenes suffer for it; but that Aristotle ever imagined any such thing of Calistenes, Aristotle doth deny.

Alex. Well, Aristotle. kindred may blinde thee, and affection me; but in kings causes I will not stand to schollers arguments. This meeting shall be for a commandment that you frequent my court. Instruct the young with rules, confirme the olde with reasons; let your lines be answerable to your learnings, lest my proceedings be contrary to my promises.

Hephest. You said you would aske every one of them a question which yesternight none of us could answere.

Alex. I will. Plato, of all beasts which is the subtilest?

Plato. That which a man hitherto never knew.

Alex. Aristotle, how should a man be thought a god?

Arist. In doing a thing impossible for a man.

Alex. Crisippus, which was first, the day or the night?

Crisp. The day, by a day.

Alex. Indeede strange questions must have strange answers. Cleanthes, what say you, is life or death the stronger?

Clea. Life, that suffereth so many troubles.

Alex. Crates, how long should a man live?

Crates. Till he thinke it better to die than to live.

Alex. Anaxarchus, whether doth the sea or the earth bring forth most creatures?

Anax. The earth, for the sea is but a part of the earth.

Alex. Hephestion, me thinkes they have answered all well, and in such questions I meane often to try them.

Hephest. It is better to have in your court a wise man than in your ground a golden mine. Therefore would I leave war, to study wisdome, were I Alexander.

Alex. So would I, were I Hephestion. But come, let us go and give release, as I promised, to our Theban thralls.   [*Exit.*

Plato. Thou art fortunate, Aristotle, that Alexander is thy scholler.

Arist. And all you happy that he is your sovereigne.

Crisp. I could like the man well, if he could be contented to be but a man.

Arist. He seeketh to draw nere to the gods in knowledge, not to be a god.

[*Enter Diogenes.*

Plato. Let us question a little with Diogenes why he went not with us to Alexander. Diogenes, thou didst forget thy duty, that thou wentest not with us to the king.

Diog. And you your profession, that went to the king.

Plato. Thou takest as great pride to be peevish as others do glory to be virtuous.

Diog. And thou as great honour, being a philosopher, to be thought courtlike as others shame, that be courtiers, to be accounted philosophers.

Arist. These austere manners set aside, it is well knowne that thou didst counterfeite money.

Diog. And thou thy manners, in that thou didst not counterfeite money.

Arist. Thou hast reason to contemne the court, being both in body and minde too crooked for a courtier.

Diog. As good to be crooked and indeavor to make myselfe straight, from the court, as be straight and learne to be crooked at the court.

Cr. Thou thinkest it a grace to be opposite against Alexander.

Diog. And thou to be iump with Alexander.

Anax. Let us go, for in contemning him we shall better please him than in wondering at him.

Arist. Plato, what doest thou thinke of Diogenes?

Plato. To be Socrates furious. Let us go. . . .

Alex. My case were light, Hephestion, and not worthy to be called love, if reason were a remedie, or sentences could salve that sense cannot conceive. Little do you know and therefore slightly do you regard the dead embers in a private person or live coals in a great prince, whose passions and thoughts do as far exceed others in extremetie as their callings do in majesty. An eclipse in the sunne is more than the falling of a starre; none can conceive the torments of a king unlesse he be a king, whose desires are not inferiour to their dignities. And then judge, Hephestion, if the agonies of love be dangerous in a subject, whether they be not more than deadly unto Alexander, whose deepe and not-to-be conceived sighes cleave the heart in

shivers, whose wounded thoughts can neither be expressed nor
endured. Cease then, Hephestion, with arguments to seeke to
refell that which with their deitie the gods cannot resist; and
let this suffice to answere thee, that it is a king that loveth, and
Alexander, whose affections are not to be measured by reason,
being immortal, nor, I feare me, to be borne, being intolerable.

Hephest. I must needs yield, when neither reason nor counsell can be heard.

Alex. Yield, Hephestion, for Alexander doth love, and therefore must obtaine.

Hephest. Supposes she loves you not? Affection cometh not
by appointment or birth, and then as good hated as enforced.

Alex. I am a king, and will command.

Hephest. You may, to yield to lust by force, but to consent
to love by feare you cannot.

Alex. Why? What is that which Alexander may not conquer as he list?

Hephest. Why, that which you say the gods cannot resist,—
love.

Alex. I am a conqueror, she a captive; I as fortunate as she
faire; my greatness may answere her wants and the gifts of my
mind the modestie of hers; is it not likely then that she should
love? Is it not reasonable?

Hephest. You say that in love there is no reason; and therefore there can be no likelihood.

Alex. No more, Hephestion! In this case I will use mine
owne counsell, and in all other thine advice; thou mayest be a
good souldier, but never good lover. Call my page. (*Enter
page.*) Sirrah, go presently to Apelles and will him to come to
me without either delay or excuse.

Page. I go.

Alex. In the meane season, to recreate my spirits, being so
neere, we will go see Diogenes. And see where his tub is!
Diogenes!

Diog. Who calleth?

Alex. Alexander. How happened it that you would not
come out of your tub to my palace?

Diog. Because it was as far from my tub to your palace as
from your palace to my tub.

Alex. Why then, doest thou owe no reverence to kings?

Diog. No.

Alex. Why so?

Diog. Because they be no gods.

Alex. They be gods of the earth.

Diog. Yea, gods of earth.

Alex. Plato is not of thy minde.

Diog. I am glad of it.

Alex. Why?

Diog. Because I would have none of Diogenes minde but Diogenes.

Alex. If Alexander have anything that may pleasure Diogenes, let me know, and take it.

Diog. Then take not from me that you cannot give me,— the light of the world.

Alex. What doest thou want?

Diog. Nothing that you have.

Alex. I have the world at command.

Diog. And I in contempt.

Alex. Thou shalt live no longer than I.

Diog. But I shall die, whether you will or no.

Alex. How should one learn to be content?

Diog. Unlearne to covet.

Alex. Hephestion, were I not Alexander, I would wish to be Diogenes!

Hephest. He is dogged, but discreet; I cannot tell how sharpe, with a kind of sweetness; full of wit, yet too-too wayward.

Alex. Diogenes, when I come this way againe, I will both see thee and confer with thee.

Diog. Do.

ROBERT GREENE.

Nothing definite is known of the life of Thomas Kyd. Few of his plays have survived. These are of a type in favor among early Elizabethan audiences, but wholly unsuited to present-day ideas or ideals. *The Spanish Tragedy* is the best known among them. Characterizing this and others of its type a modern critic has said: "The action of these tragedies was a prolonged tempest. Blows fell like hailstones; swords flashed like lightning; threats roared like thunder; poison was poured out like rain." And again: "There are, at least, five murders, two suicides, two judicial executions, and one death in duel. . . . Few of the characters survive to bury the dead, and these few are of secondary importance."

Robert Greene was born about 1550, in Norwich. He received his degree from Cambridge in 1578. Like Peele and Marlowe, his life was one of continued debauchery and dissipation. Following the custom of the English youth of his time, he acquired all the social vices of the Italians during his sojourn in their country; drink and self indulgence of every variety followed his return home. However, he found time to write several plays and lyrics which give evidence of his gifts. Such jovial and convivial society as later grew up among men of unconventional but irreprehensible habits did not exist at that time and for one who did not easily find his way among the so-called respectable element, there was nothing left but the dregs of society; and this social stratum Greene, Peele and Marlowe explored to the depths. Times of repentance came to Greene, as his autobiography attests; but he was too weak to conquer his habits, which in the end conquered him.

Greene's plays lack plot but he knew how to tell a story so as to hold an audience to the end. *The Looking-Glass for London, James the Fourth* and *Friar Bacon and Friar Bungay* are among his best productions.

FRIAR BACON AND FRIAR BUNGAY.

Post. Fair lovely damsell, which way leads this path?
How might I post me unto *Fresingfield?*
Which footpath leadeth to the keeper's lodge?
Margaret. Your way is ready, and this path is right;
My selfe do dwell hereby in *Fresingfield:*
And if the keeper be the man you seeke,
I am his daughter; may I know the cause?
Post. Lovely, and once beloved of my lord,
No marvaile if his eye was lodged so low,
When brighter beauty is not in the heavens.
The *Lincolne* earle hath sent you letters here,
And, with them, just an hundred pounds in gold.
Sweete, boony wench, read them and make reply.
Margaret. The scrolles that *Ione* sent *Danäé,*
Wrapt in rich closures of fine burnished gold,.
Were not more welcome than these lines to me.
Tell me, whilst that I do unrip the seales,
.Lives *Lacie* well, how fares my lovely Lord?
Post. Well, if that wealth may make men to live well.

(Margaret reads the letter.)

The bloomes of the Almond tree grow in a night, and vanish in a morne; the flies Hæmeræ take life with the Sun, and die with the dew; fancie that slippeth in with a gase, goeth out with a winke; and too timely loves have ever the shortest length. I write this as thy grefe, and my folly, who at *Fresingfield* loved that which time hath taught me to be but meane dainties; eyes are dissemblers, and fancie is but queasie; therefore know, Margaret, I have chosen a Spanish Ladie to be my wife, cheefe waiting woman to the Princess *Ellinour;* a Lady faire, and no lesse faire than thy selfe, honorable and wealthy. In that I forsake thee I leave thee to thine owne liking; and for thy dowrie I have sent thee an hundred pounds; and even assure thee of my favour, which shall availe thee and thine much. Farewell.

Not thine, nor his owne,

Edward Lacie.

Fond Atae, doomer of bad boding fates,
That wrappes proud Fortune in thy snaky locks,
Didst thou inchant my byrth-day with such stars
As lightened mischiefe from their infancie?
If heavens had vowed, if stars had made decree,
To shew on me their froward influence,
If *Lacie* had but loved, heavens, hell, and all
Could not have wronged the patience of my minde.
  Post. It grieves me, damsell; but the Earle is forst
To love the Lady by the Kings command.
  Margaret. The wealth combinde within the English
    shelves,
Europes commander, nor the English King,
Should not have moved the love of *Peggie* from her Lord.
  Post. What answere shall I return to my Lord?
  Margaret. First, for thou camst from *Lacie* whom I
    loved—
Ah, give me leave to sigh at every thought!
Take thou, my friend, the hundred pound he sent,
For *Margaret's* resolution craves no dower.
The world shall be to her as vanitie,
Wealth, trash; love, hate; pleasure, dispair:
For I will straight to stately *Fremingham,*
And in the abbey there be shorne a Nun,
And yield my love and liberty to God.
Fellow, I give thee this, not for the newes,
For those be hatefull unto Margaret,

But for that *Lacies* man, once *Margarets* love.

    Post. What I have heard, what passions I have seene,
Ile make report of them unto the Earle.

    Margaret. Say that she joyes his fancies be at rest,
And prays that his misfortune may be hers. . . .

ACT. V.

[*Enter Margaret in Nuns apparell, Keeper, her father and
   friend.*

    Keep. Margaret, be not so headstrong in these vows:
Oh, burie not such beautie in a cell,
That *England* hath held famous for the hue!
Thy father's haire, like to the silver bloomes
That beautify the shrubs of *Affrica,*
Shall fall before the dated time of death,
Thus to forgo his lovely *Margaret.*

    Mar. Ah, father, when the harmonie of heaven
Soundeth the measures of a lively faith,
The vaine illusions of this flattering world
Seems odious to the thoughts of *Margaret.*
I loved once, Lord *Lacie* was my love;
And now I hate my selfe for that I loved,
And doted more on him than on my God.
For this I scourge my selfe with sharpe repents.
But now the touch of such aspiring sinnes
Tells me all love is lust but love of heavens;
That beautie used for love is vanitie;
The world contains nought but alluring baits,
Pride, flatterie, and inconstant thoughts.
To shun the pricks of death, I leave the world,
And vow to meditate on heavenly blisse,
To live in *Framingham* a holy Nunne,
Holy and pure in conscience and in deed;
And for to wish all maides to learne of me,
To seeke heaven's joy before earth's vanitie.

    Friend. And will you then, *Margaret*, be shorn a
      Nunne, and so leave us all? .

    Margaret. Now farewell, world, the engin of all woe!
Farewell to friends and father! welcome Christ!
Adew to daintie robes! this base attire
Better befits an humble minde to God
Than all the shewe of rich abilliments.
Farewell, oh Love, and with fond Love farewell,

Sweet *Lacie*, whom I loved once so deere!
Ever be well, but never in my thoughts,
Least I offend to thinke on *Lacie's* love:
But even to that, as to the rest, farewell!
    [*Enter Lacie, Warrain, Ermsbie, booted and spurd.*
   Lacie. Come on, my wags, weere neere the Keeper's
    lodge,
Here have I oft walked in the watrie Meades,
And chatted with my lovely *Margaret.*
   Warraine. Sirha, *Ned*, is not this the Keeper?
   Lacie. 'Tis the same.
   Ermsbie. The old lecher hath gotten holy mutton to
    him: a Nunne, my lord.
   Lacie. Keeper, how farest thou? holla man, what
    cheere?
How doth *Peggie* thy daughter and my love?
   Keeper. Ah, good my lord! oh, wo is me for *Pegge!*
See where she stands clad in her Nunnes attire,
Readie to be shorne in *Framingham*s
She leaves the world because she left your love.
Oh, good my lord, persuade her if you can.
   Lacie. Why, how now, *Margaret?* what, a malecontent?
A Nunne? what holy father taught you this,
To taske your selfe to such a tedious life
As die a maid? twere injurie to me
To smother up such beautie in a cell.
   Margaret. Lord *Lacie*, thinking of my former misse,
How fond the prime of wanton yeares were spent
In Love, (Oh fie upon that fond conceite,
Whose hap and essence hangeth in the eye!),
I leave both love and loves content at once,
Betaking me to him that is true love,
And leaving all the world for love of him.
   Lacie. Whence, *Peggie*, comes this Metamorphosis?
What, shorne a Nunne, and I have from the Court
Posted with coursers to convey thee hence
To *Windsore*, where our Marriage shall be kept!
Thy wedding robes are in the tailor's hands,
Come, *Peggy*, leave these peremptorie vows.
   Margaret. Did not my lord resign his interest,
And make divorce twixt *Margaret* and him?
   Lacie. 'Twas but to try sweete *Peggie's* constancie.
But will faire *Margaret* leave her love and Lord?

Margaret. Is not heaven's joy before earth's fading
  blisse,
And life above sweeter than life in love?
  Lacie. Why, then, *Margaret* will be shorne a Nunne?
  Margaret. *Margaret* hath made a vow which may not
  be revokt.
  Warraine. We cannot stay, my Lord; and if she be so
  strict,
Our leisure graunts us not to woo a fresh.
  Ermsbie. Choose you, faire damsell, yet the choice is
  yours,
Either a solemn Nunnerie, or the Court,
God, or Lord *Lacie;* which contents you best,
To be a Nun, or else Lord *Lacie's* wife?
  Lacie. A good notion. *Peggie,* your answere must be
  short.
  Margaret. The flesh is fraile; my Lord doth know it
  well,
That when he comes with his enchanting face,
What so ere betide I cannot say him nay.
Off goes the habite of a maiden's heart,
And, seeing Fortune will, faire *Fremingham,*
And all the shew of holy Nuns, farewell.
Lacie for me, if he will be my lord.
  Lacie. *Peggie,* thy Lord, thy love, thy husband.
Trust me, by truth of knighthood, that the King
Stayes for to marry matchless *Ellinour,*
Until I bring thee richly to the Court,
That one day may both marry her and thee.
How sayest thou, Keeper? art thou glad of this?
  Keeper. As if the English King had given
The parke and deere of *Fresingfield* to me.
  Erms. I pray thee, my Lord of Sussex, why art thou
  in a browne studie?
  Warraine. To see the nature of women, that be they
  never so neare God, yet they love to die in a man's
  armes.
  Lacie. What have you fit for breakfast? we have hied
  and posted all this night to *Fresingfield.*
  Margaret. Butter and cheese, and humbls of a deere,
Such as poor Keepers have within their lodge.
  Lacie. And not a bottle of wine?
  Margaret. Weele find one for my Lord.

Lacie. Come, *Sussex*, lets in; we shall have more, for she speaks least, to hold her promise sure.

(*Friar Bacon's Cell.*)

[*Enter a devill to seeke Miles.*

Devill. How restless are the ghosts of hellish spirites, When every charmer with his Magick spells Calls us from nine-fold trenched Phlegiton, To scud and over-scoure the earth in post, Upon the speedie wings of swiftest winds! Now *Bacon* hath raised me from the darkest deepe, To search about the world for *Miles* his man, For *Miles,* and to torment his lazy bones, For careless watching of his Brasen head. See where he comes: Oh, he is mine!

Miles. A scholler, quoth you! marry, sir, I would I had bene made a botlemaker when I was made a scholler; for I can get neither to be a Deacon, Reader, nor Schoolmaister; another saith my head is as full of Latine as an egg is full of oatmeale; thus I am tormented that the devil and Frier *Bacon* haunts me. Good Lord, heers one of my maisters devils. Ille go speake to him. What, maister Plutus, how chere you?

Devill. Doost thou know me?

Miles. Know you, sir! why, are not you one of my maisters devils, that were wont to come to my maister Doctor *Bacon*, at Brazen-nose?

Devill. Yes, marry, am I.

Miles. Good Lord, M. Plutus, I have seene you a thousand times at my maisters, and yet I had never the manners to make you drinke. But sir, I am glad to see how conformable you are to the statute. I warrant you, hees as yeomanly a man as you shall see: marke you, Maisters, heers a plaine, honest man, without welt or garde, but I pray you, sir, do you come lately from hell?

Devill. I marry: how then?

Miles. Faith, 'tis a place I have desired long to see: have you not good tipling houses there? may not a man have a lustie fire there, a pot of good ale, a paire of cardes, a swinging peece of chalk, and a browne toast that will clap a white wastcoat on a cup of good drinke?

Devill. All this you may have there.

Miles. You are for me, friende, and I am for you. But I pray you, may I not have an office there?

Devill. Yes, a thousand; what wouldst thou be?

Miles. By my troth, sir, in a place where I may profit my selfe. I know hell is a hot place, and men are marvailous drie, and much drinke is spent there; I would be a tapster.

Devill. Thou shalt.

Miles. Theres nothing lets me from going with you, but that 'tis a long journey, and I have never a horse.

Devill. Thou shalt ride on my backe.

Miles. Now surely here's a courteous devill, that for to pleasure his friend, will not stick to make a Jade of himselfe. But say you, goodman friend, let me move a question to you.

Devill. What's that?

Miles. I pray you, whether is your pace a trot or an amble?

Devill. An amble.

Miles. 'Tis well; but take heed it be not a trot. But 'tis no matter, Ile prevent it.

Devill. What doest?

Miles. Marry, friend, I put on my spurs; for if I find your pace either a trot, or else uneasie, Ile put you to a false gallop, Ile make you feele the benefit of my spurs.

Devill. Get up on my backe.

Miles. O Lord, here's even a goodly marvell, when a man rides to hell on the Devill's back.

THE BEAR-BAITING GARDEN.

CHAPTER IX.

Forerunners of Shakespeare: Peele and Marlowe.

George Peele was born about 1558 in Devonshire, graduating at Oxford. His life was singularly like that of his friend Greene, so that any consideration of it would be but comparing one form of dissoluteness with another—if indeed either left any untried. Probably he influenced Shakespeare and the future drama least of any of the group. His *Arraignment of Paris,* a masque or court comedy, and *David and Bethsabe* are best known.

The Arraignment of Paris.

Venus. But pray you, tell me, Juno, was it so,
As Pallas told me here the tale of Echo.
   Juno. She was a nymph indeed, as Pallas tells,
A walker, such as in these thickets dwells;
And as she told what subtle juggling pranks
She play'd with Juno, so she told her thanks:
A tattling trull to come at every call,
And now, forsooth, nor tongue nor life at all.
And though perhaps she was a help to Jove,
And held me chat he might court his love,
Believe me, dames, I am of this opinion,
He took but little pleasure in the minion;
And whatsoe'er his scapes have been beside,
Dare say for him, 'a never strayed so wide:
A lovely nut-brown lass or lusty trull
Have power perhaps to make a god a bull.
   Venus. Gramercy, gentle Juno, for that jest;
I' faith, that item was worth all the rest.
   Pal. No matter, Venus, howsoe'er you scorn,
My father Jove at that time ware the horn.
   Juno. Had every wanton god above, Venus, not better
     luck,
Then heaven would be a pleasant park, and Mars a lusty
     buck.
   Venus. Tut, Mars hath horns to butt withal, although
     no bull 'a shows,

'A never needs to mask in nets, 'a fears no jealous froes.

   Juno.   Forsooth, the better is his turn, for, if 'a speak too loud,

Must find some shift to shadow him, a net or else a cloud.

   Pal.   No more of this, fair goddesses; unrip not so your shames,

To stand all naked to the world, that bene such heavenly dames.

   Juno.   Nay, Pallas, that's a common trick with Venus well we know.

And all the gods in heaven have seen her naked long ago.

   Venus.   And then she was so fair and bright, and lovely and so trim,

As Mars is but for Venus' tooth, and she will sport with him;

And, but me list not here to make comparison with Jove,

Mars is no ranger, Juno, he, in evry open grove.

   Pal.   Too much of this: we wander far, the skies begin to scowl;

Retire we to Diana's bower, the weather will be foul.   . .

   Juno.   Pallas, the storm is past and gone, and Phœbus clears the skies,

And, lo, behold a ball of gold, a fair and worthy prize!

   Venus.   This posy wills the apple to the fairest given be;

Then is it mine, for Venus hight the fairest of the three.

   Pal.   The fairest here, as fair is meant, am I, ye do me wrong;

And if the fairest have it must, to me it doth belong.

   Juno.   Then Juno may it not enjoy, so every one says no,

But I will prove myself the fairest, ere I lose it so.

                        [Reads the posy.

The brief is this, *Detur pulcherrimae,*

Let this unto the fairest given be,

. The fairest of the three,—and I am she.

   Pal.   *Detur pulcherrimae,*

Let this unto the fairest given be,

The fairest of the three,—and I am she.

   Venus.   *Detur pulcherrimae,*

Let this unto the fairest given be,

The fairest of the three,—and I am she.

   Juno.   My face is fair; but yet the majesty,

That all the gods in heaven have seen in me,
Have made them choose me, of the planets seven,
To be the wife of Jove and queen of heaven.
If, then, this prize be but bequeathed to beauty,
The only she that wins this prize am I.
    Venus. That Venus is the fairest, this doth prove,
That Venus is the lovely Queen of Love:
The name of Venus is indeed but beauty,
And men me fairest call per excellency.
If, then, this prize be but bequeathed to beauty,
The only she that wins this prize am I.
    Pal. To stand on terms of beauty as you take it,
Believe me, ladies, is but to mistake it.
The beauty that this subtle prize must win,
No outward beauty hight, but dwells within;
And sift it as you please, and you shall find,
This beauty is the beauty of the mind:
This fairness, virtue hight in general,
That many branches hath in special;
This beauty wisdom hight, whereof am I,
By heaven appointed, goddess worthily.
And look how much the mind, the better part,
Doth overpass the body in desert,
So much the mistress of those gifts divine
Excels thy beauty, and that state of thine.
Then, if this prize be thus bequeathed to beauty,
The only she that wins this prize am I.
    Venus. Nay, Pallas, by your leave you wander clean:
We must not construe hereof as you mean,
But take the sense as it is plainly meant;
And let the fairest ha't, I am content.
    Pal. Our reasons will be infinite, I trow,
Unless unto some other point we grow:
But first here's none, methinks, disposed to yield,
And none but will with words maintain the field.
    Juno. Then, if you will, t' avoid a tedious grudge,
Refer it to the sentence of a judge;
Whoe'er he be that cometh next in place,
Let him bestow the ball and end the case.
    Venus. So can it not go wrong with me at all.
    Pal. I am agreed, however it befall:
And yet by common doom, so may it be,
I may be said the fairest of the three.

Juno. Then yonder, lo, that shepherd swain is he,
That must be umpire in this controversy!

                              [*Enter Paris.*
Venus. Juno, in happy time, I do accept the man;
It seemeth by his looks some skill of love he can.
Paris. The nymph is gone, and I, all solitary,
Must wend to tend my charge, oppressed with melancholy
This day (or else me fails my shepherd's skill)
Will tide me passing good or passing ill.
Juno. Shepherd, abash not, though at sudden thus
Thou be arrived by ignorance among us,
Not earthly but divine, and goddesses all three;
Juno, Pallas, Venus, these our titles be.
Nor fear to speak for reverence of the place,
Chosen to end a hard and doubtful case.
This apple, lo (nor ask thou whence it came),
Is to be given unto the fairest dame!
And fairest is, nor she, nor she, but she,
Whom, shepherd, thou shalt fairest name to be.
This is thy charge; fulfil without offence,
And she that wins shall give thee recompense.
Pal. Dread not to speak, for we have chosen thee,
Sith in this case we can no judges be.
Venus. And, shepherd, say that I the fairest am,
And thou shalt win good guerdon for the same.
Juno. Nay, shepherd, look upon my stately grace,
Because the pomp that 'longs to Juno's mace
Thou mayst not see; and think Queen Juno's name,
To whom old shepherds title works of fame,
Is mighty, and may easily suffice,
At Phœbus' hand, to gain a golden prize.
And for thy meed, sith I am queen of riches,
Shepherd, I will reward thee with great monarchies,
Empires, and kingdoms, heaps of massy gold,
Sceptres and diadems curious to behold,
Rich robes, of sumptuous workmanship and cost,
And thousand things whereof I make no boast:
The mould whereon thou treadest shall be of Tagus'
    sands,
And Xanthus shall run liquid gold for thee to wash they
    hands;
And if thou like to tend thy flock, and not from them to
    fly,

Their fleeces shall be curled gold to please their master's
    eye;
And last, to set thy heart on fire, give this one fruit to
    me,
And, shepherd, lo, this tree of gold will I bestow on thee!

Juno's Show.

(Hereupon did rise a Tree of Gold with diadems and crowns of gold.)

The ground whereon it grows, the grass, the root of gold,
The body and the bark of gold, all glistering to behold,
The leaves of burnished gold, the fruits that thereon grow
Are diadems set with pearl in gold, in gorgeous glistering show;
And if this tree of gold in Lieu may not suffice,
Require a grove of golden trees, so Juno bears the prize.

    Pal. Me list not tempt thee with decaying wealth,
Which is embassed by want of lusty health;
But if thou have a mind to fly above,
Y-crowned with fame, near to the seat of Jove,
If thou aspire to wisdom's worthiness,
Whereof thou mayst not see the brightness,
If thou desire honour of chivalry,
To be renown'd for happy victory,
To fight it out, and in the champion field
To shroud thee under Pallas' warlike shield,
To prance on barbed steeds, this honour, lo,
My self for guerdon shall on thee bestow!
And for encouragement, that thou mayst see
What famous knights Dame Pallas' warriors be,
Behold in Pallas' honour here they come,
Marching along with sound of thundering drum.

Pallas' Show.

        [*Enter Nine Knights.*
    Venus. Come, shepherd, come, sweet shepherd, look on
    me,
These bene too hot alarums these for thee:
But if thou wilt give me the golden ball,
Cupid, my boy, shall ha't to play withal,
That, whensoever this apple he shall see,

The God of Love himself shall think on thee,
And bid thee look and choose, and he will wound
Whereso thy fancy's object shall be found;
And lightly, when he shoots, he doth not miss:
And I will give thee many a lovely kiss,
And come and play with thee on Ida here;
And if thou wilt a face that hath no peer,
A gallant girl, a lusty minion trull,
That can give sport to thee thy bellyfull,
To ravish all thy beating veins with joy,
Here is a lass of Venus' court, my boy,
Here, gentle shepherd, here's for thee a piece,
The fairest face, the flower of gallant Greece.

VENUS' SHOW.

[Enter Helen, attended by Cupids.
Paris. Most heavenly dames, was never man as I,
Poor shepherd swain so happy and unhappy;
The least of these delights that you devise,
Able to rape and dazzle human eyes.
But since my silence may not pardon'd be,
And I appoint which is the fairest she,
Pardon, most sacred dames, sith one, not all,
By Paris' doom must have this golden ball;
Thy beauty, stately Juno, dame divine,
That like to Phœbus' golden beams doth shine,
Approves itself to be most excellent;
But that fair face that doth me most content,
Sith fair, fair dames, is neither she nor she,
But she whom I shall fairest deem to be,
That face is hers that hight the Queen of Love,
Whose sweetness doth both gods and creatures move;
                        [Gives the ball to Venus.
And if the fairest face deserve the ball
Fair Venus, ladies, bears it from ye all.
   Venus. And in this ball doth Venus more delight
Than in her lovely boy fair Cupid's sight.
Come, shepherd, come; sweet Venus is thy friend;
No matter how thou other gods offend.
                        [Exit with Paris.
   Juno. But he shall rue and ban the dismal day

Wherein his Venus bare the ball away;
And heaven and earth just witnesses shall be,
I will revenge it on his progeny.   .
   Pal. Well, Juno, whether we be lief or loth,
Venus hath got the apple from us both.

Marlowe far surpassed his friends and co-playwrights.
Son of a shoemaker, he was born in 1564, the year of Shakespeare's birth, at Canterbury. He, too, was trained in one of
the universities of England, his college being Cambridge. He
quickly formed those associations with the libertines and riot-
ers who were his companions throughout his short life. Dying
in a tavern brawl in his thirtieth year, he had accomplished
much in the intervening years, in spite of his irregularities.
Tamburlaine was his first production and it made him the talk
of the hour. *Dr. Faustus*, the plot of which Goethe later
developed so marvelously, and the *Jew of Malta* rapidly followed.

To Marlowe Shakespeare owed much. It would be difficult to surmise what that great master might have been without him. With unerring judgment, he saw at a glance and
never lost sight of the superiority of his predecessor, for while
these men were born the same year, Marlowe had met his
death before Shakespeare had scarcely become known.

This in short was Marlowe's service to the English drama:
he found it something vague and indefinite; he left it stamped
with a form that it still bears. It would have been a difficult
thing to have explained wherein the charm of the stage lay
when Marlowe first became associated with it. The devil of
the old miracle play still made fun for the groundlings; not
infrequently plays which at first gave promise of comedy fell
into the progress of a morality. Interludes and masques were
intermingled; many plays were thrown into rhyme; plots were
often lacking entirely and always poorly developed; characters
were faintly drawn or, again, strong characters lost their importance in the story. In brief, drama was a maze and its
very future hung in the balance.

Marlowe mastered the idea of a plot and gave it logical
development, unified action and interest and created bold
characters. He simplified details and relegated jesters and

clowns to the background. Quite as important, he made blank
verse the medium of dramatic expression and in his own
plays showed its flexibility and hitherto unknown possibilities. For these services Marlowe merits the name he has received, father of the English drama.

THE JEW OF MALTA.

ACT THE FIRST—SCENE I.

(Enter Barabas in his counting house, with heaps of gold before him.)

> *Bar.* So that of thus much that return was made:
> And of the third part of the Persian ships,
> There was the venture summed and satisfied.
> As for those Samnites, and the men of Uz,
> That bought my Spanish oils, and wines of Greece,
> Here have I purst their paltry silverlings.
> Fie! what a trouble 'tis to count this trash.
> Well fare the Arabians, who so richly pay
> The things they traffic for with wedge of gold,
> Whereof a man may easily in a day
> Tell that which may maintain him all his life.
> The needy groom that never fingered groat,
> Would make a miracle of this much coin;
> But he whose steel-barred coffers are crammed full,
> And all his lifetime hath been tired,
> Wearying his fingers' ends with telling it,
> Would in his age be loth to labour so,
> And for a pound to sweat himself to death.
> Give me the merchants of the Indian mines,
> That trade in metal of the purest mould;
> The wealthy Moor, that in the eastern rocks
> Without control can pick his riches up,
> And in his house keep pearl like pebble stones,
> Receive them free, and sell them by the weight;
> Bags of fiery opals, sapphires, amethysts,
> Jacinths, hard topaz, grass-green emeralds,
> Beauteous rubies, sparkling diamonds,
> And seld-seen costly stones of so great price,
> As one of them indifferently rated,
> And of a carat of this quantity,
> May serve in peril of calamity

To ransom great kings from captivity.
This is the ware wherein consists my wealth;
And thus methinks should men of judgment frame
Their means of traffic from the vulgar trade,
And as their wealth increaseth, so inclose
Infinite riches in a little room.
But now how stands the wind?
Into what corner peers my halycon's bill?
Ha! to the east? yes; see how stands the vanes?
East and by south; why then I hope my ships
I sent for Egypt and the bordering isles
Are gotten up by Nilus winding banks;
Mine argosy from Alexandria,
Loaden with spice and silks, now under sail,
Are smoothly gliding down by Candy shore
To Malta, through our Mediterranean Sea.
But who comes here? How now?

                          [Enter a Merchant.

  Merch. Barabas, thy ships are safe,
Riding in Malta Road; and all the merchants
With other merchandise are safe arrived,
And have sent me to know whether yourself
Will come and custom them.

  Bar. The ships are safe, thou say'st, and richly fraught.

  Merch. They are.

  Bar. Why then go bid them come ashore,
And bring with them their bills of entry:
I hope our credit in the custom-house
Will serve as well as I were present there.
Go send 'em threescore camels, thirty mules,
And twenty wagons to bring up the ware.
But art thou master in a ship of mine,
And is thy credit not enough for that?

  Merch. The very custom barely comes to more
Than many merchants of the town are worth,
And therefore far exceeds my credit, sir.

  Bar. Go tell 'em the Jew of Malta sent thee, man;
Tush! who amongst them knows not Barabas?

  Merch. I go.

  Bar. So then, there's somewhat come.
Sirrah, which of my ships art thou master of?

  Merch. Of the Speranza, sir

  Bar. And saw'st thou not
Mine argosy at Alexandria?

Thou could'st not come from Egypt, or by Caire
But at the entry there into the sea,
Where Nilus pays his tribute to the main:
Thou needs must sail by Alexandria.
 Merch. I neither saw them nor inquired of them;
But this we heard some of our seamen say,
They wondered how you durst with so much wealth
Trust such a crazed vessel, and so far.
 Bar. Tush! they are wise! I know her and her strength.
But go, go thou thy ways, discharge thy ship,
And bid my factor bring his loading in.
[Exit Merchant.
And yet I wonder at this argosy.
[Enter a second Merchant.
 Second Merch. Thine argosy from Alexandria,
Know, Barabas, doth ride in Malta Road,
Laden with riches, and exceeding store
Of Persian silks, of gold, and orient pearl.
 Bar. How chance you came not with those other ships
That sailed by Egypt?
 Second Merch. We saw them not.
 Bar. Belike they coasted round by Candy shore
About their oils, or other businesses.
But 'twas ill done of you to come so far
Without the aid or conduct of their ships.
 Second Merch. Sir, we were wafted by a Spanish fleet,
That never left us till within a league,
That had the galleys of the Turk in chase.
 Bar. Oh!—they were going up to Sicily:—
Well, go.
And bid the merchants and my men despatch
And come ashore, and see the fraught discharged.
 Second Merch. I go.   [*Exit.*
 Bar. Thus trowls our fortune in by land and sea,
And thus are we on every side enriched:
These are the blessings promised to the Jews,
And herein was old Abram's happiness:
What more may heaven do for earthly man
Than thus to pour out plenty in their laps,
Ripping the bowels of the earth for them,
Making the seas their servants, and the winds
To drive their substance with successful blasts?
Who hateth me but for my happiness?
Or who is honoured now but for his wealth?

Rather had I a Jew he hated thus,
Then pitied in a Christian poverty:
For I can see no fruits in all their faith,
But malice, falsehood and excessive pride,
Which methinks fits not their profession.
Haply some hapless man hath conscience,
And for his conscience lives in beggary.
They say we are a scattered nation;
I cannot tell, but we have scrambled up
More wealth by far than those that brag of faith.
There's Kirriah Jarim, the great Jew of Greece,
Obed in Bairseth, Nones in Portugal,
Myself in Malta, some in Italy,
Many in France, and wealthy every one;
Aye, wealthier far than any Christian.
I must confess we come not to be kings,
That's not our fault; Alas, our number's few,
And crowns come either by succession,
Or urged by force; and nothing violent,
Oft have I heard, can be permanent.
Give us a peaceful rule, make Christians kings,
That thirst so much for principality.
I have no charge, nor many children,
But one sole daughter, whom I hold as dear
As Agamemnon did his Iphigene:
And all I have is hers. But who comes here?

                                    [Enter three Jews.

   First Jew. Tush, tell me not 'twas done of policy.
   Second Jew. Come, therefore let us go to Barabas,
For he can counsel best in these affairs;
And here he comes.
   Bar. Why how now, countrymen!
Why flock you thus to me in multitudes?
What accident's betided to the Jews?
   First Jew. A fleet of warlike galleys, Barabas,
Are come from Turkey, and lie in our road:
And they this day sit in the council-house
To entertain them and their embassy.
   Bar. Why let 'em come, so they come not to war;
Or let 'em war, so we be conquerors;
Nay, let 'em combat, conquer, and kill all!
So they spare me, my daughter and my wealth.
   First Jew. Were it for confirmation of a league,
They would not come in warlike manner thus.

Second Jew. I fear their coming will affect us all.

Bar. Fond men, what dream you of their multitudes,
What need they treat of peace that are in league?
The Turks and those of Malta are in league.
Tut, tut, there's some other matter in't.

First Jew. Why, Barabas, they come for peace or war.

Bar. Haply for neither, but to pass along
Towards Venice by the Adriatic Sea;
With whom they have attempted many times,
But never could effect their stratagem.

Third Jew. And very wisely said. It may be so.

Second Jew. But there's a meeting in the senate-house,
And all the Jews in Malta must be there.

Bar. Hum; all the Jews in Malta must be there?
Aye, like enough, why then let every man
Provide him, and be there for fashion-sake,
If anything shall there concern our state
Assure yourselves I'll look unto—myself.

First Jew. I know you will; well, brethren, let us go.

Second Jew. Let's take our leaves; farewell, good
     Barabas.

Bar. Farewell, Zaareth, farewell Temainte.
                                        [*Exit Jews.*

And Barabas now search this secret out,
Summon thy sense, call thy wits together;
These silly men mistake the matter clean.
Long to the Turk did Malta contribute;
Which tribute, all in policy I fear,
The Turk has let increase to such a sum,
As all the wealth in Malta cannot pay;
And now by that advantage thinks belike
To seize upon the town; Aye, that he seeks,
Howe'er the world go, I'll make sure for one,
And seek in time to intercept the worst,
Warily guarding that which I have got.
Ego mihimet sum semper proximus.
Why let 'em enter, let 'em take the town. . . .
[*Enter Governor of Malta, Knights, met by Bassoes of
     the Turk.*

Gov. Now, officers, have you done?

Off. Aye, my lord, we have seized upon the goods
And wares of Barabas, which being valued
Amount to more than all the wealth in Malta.
And of the other we have seized half.

Gov. Then we'll take order for the residue.

Bar. Well, then, my lord, say are you satisfied?
You have my goods, my money, and my wealth,
My ships, my store, and all that I enjoyed;
And, having all, you can request no more;
Unless your unrelenting flinty hearts
Suppress all pity in your stony breasts,
And now shall move you to bereave my life.

Gov. No, Barabas, to stain our hands with blood
Is far from us and our profession.

Bar. Why, I esteem the injury far less
To take the lives of miserable men
Than be the causes of their misery.
You have my wealth, the labour of my life,
The comfort of mine age, my children's hope,
And therefore ne'er distinguish of the wrong.

Gov. Content thee, Barabas, thou hast naught but
right.

Bar. Your extreme right does me exceeding wrong;
But take it to you, i' the devil's name.

Gov. Come, let us in, and gather of these goods
The money for this tribute of the Turk.

First Knight. 'Tis necessary that be looked unto:
For if we break our day, we break our league,
And that will prove but simple policy.

[*Exit, except Jews.*

Bar. Aye, policy! that's their profession,
And not simplicity, as they suggest.
The plagues of Egypt, and the curse of heaven
Earth's barrenness, and all men's hatred
Inflict upon them, thou great *Primus Motor!*
And here upon my knees, striking the earth,
I ban their souls to everlasting pains
And extreme tortures of the fiery deep,
That thus have dealt with me in my distress.

First Jew. Oh yet be patient, gentle Barabas.

Bar. Oh silly brethren, born to see this day:
Why stand you thus unmoved with my laments?
Why weep you not to think upon my wrongs?
Why pine not I, and die in this distress?

First Jew. Why, Barabas, as hardly can we brook
The cruel handling of ourselves in this;
Thou seest they have taken half our goods.

Bar. Why did you yield to their extortion?
You were a multitude, and I but one;
And of me only have they taken all.
  First Jew. Yet, brother Barabas, remember Job.
  Bar. What tell you me of Job? . . .
  First Jew. Come, let us leave him in this ireful mood,
Our words will but increase his ecstasy.
  Second Jew. On, then; but trust me 'tis a misery
To see a man in such affliction;
Farewell, Barabas!   [*Exit.*
  Bar. Aye, fare you well.
See the simplicity of these base slaves,
Who, for the villians have no wit themselves,
Think me to be a senseless lump of clay
That will with every water wash to dirt:
No, Barabas is born to better chance,
And framed of finer mould than common men,
That measure naught but by the present time.
A reaching thought will search his deepest wits,
And cast with cunning for the time to come:
For evils are apt to happen every day—
But whither wends my beauteous Abigail?
                          [*Enter Abigail, his daughter.*
Oh, what has made my lovely daughter sad?
What, woman, moan not for a little loss;
Thy father hath enough in store for thee.
  Abg. Not for myself, but aged Barabas:
Father, for thee lamenteth Abigail:
But I will learn to leave these fruitless tears,
And, urged thereto with my afflictions,
With fierce exclaims run to the senate-house,
And in the senate reprehend them all,
And rend theirs hearts with tearing of my hair,
Till they reduce the wrongs done to my father.
  Bar. No, Abigail, things past recovery
Are hardly cured with exclamations.
Be silent, daughter, sufferance breeds ease,
And time may yield us an occasion
Which on the sudden cannot serve the turn.
Besides, my girl, think me not all so fond
As negligently to forego so much
Without provision for thyself and me.
Ten thousand portagues, besides great pearls,
Rich costly jewels, and stones infinite,

Fearing the worst of this before it fell,
I closely hid.

    Abig. Where, father?

    Bar. In the house, my girl.

    Abig. Then shall they ne'er be seen of Barabas:
For they have seized upon thy house and wares.

    Bar. But they will give me leave once more, I trow,
To go into my house.

    Abig. That they may not:
For there I left the Governor placing nuns,
Displacing me; and of thy house they mean
To make a nunnery, where none but their own sect
Must enter in; men generally barred.

    Bar. My gold! my gold! and all my wealth is gone.
You partial heavens, have I deserved this plague?
What will you oppose me thus, luckless stars,
To make me desperate in my poverty?
I'll rouse my senses and awake myself.
Daughter, I have it! thou perceiv'st the plight
Wherein these Christians have oppressed me;
Be ruled by me, for in extremity
We ought to make no bar of policy.

    Abig. Father, whate'er it be to injure them
That have so manifestly wronged us,
What will not Abigail attempt?

    Bar. Why, so;
Then thus, thou told'st me they have turned my house
Into a nunnery, and some nuns are there.

    Abig. I did.

    Bar. Then, Abigail, there must my girl
Intreat the abbess to be entertained.

    Abig. How, as a nun?

    Bar. Aye, daughter, for religion
Hides many mischiefs from suspicion.

    Abig. Aye, but father they will suspect me there.

    Bar. Let 'em suspect, but be thou so precise
As they may think it done of holiness.
Intreat 'em fair, and give them friendly speech,
And seem to them as if thy sins were great,
Till thou hast gotten to be entertained.

    Abig. Thus father shall I much dissemble.

    Bar. Tush! as good dissemble that thou never meant'st,
As first mean truth and then dissemble it,—
A counterfeit profession is better

Than unforseen hypocrisy.

Abig. Well father, say I be entertained,
What then shall follow?

Bar. This shall follow then;
There have I hid, close underneath the plank
That runs along the upper chamber floor,
The gold and jewels which I kept for thee.
But here they come; be cunning, Abigail.

Abig. Then father, go with me.

Bar. No, Abigail, in this
It is not necessary I be seen;
For I will seem offended with thee for't:
Be close, my girl, for this must fetch my gold.

CHAPTER X.

SHAKESPEARE.

"Pride of his own, and wonder of this age,
Who first created, and yet rules, the Stage,
Bold to design, all powerful to express,
Shakespeare each passion drew in every dress:
Great above rule, and imitating none;
Rich without borrowing, nature was his own.
Yet in his sense debas'd by gross alloy:
As gold in mines lies mix'd with dirt and clay.
Now, eagle-wing'd, his heavenward flight he takes;
The big stage thunders, and the soul awakes:
Now, low on earth, a kindred reptile creeps;
Sad Hamlet quibbles, and the hearer sleeps."

DAVID MALLET.—1759.

Who knows whether Shakespeare might not have thought less, if he had read more? Who knows if he might not have laboured under the load of Johnson's learning, as Enceldaus under Ætna? His mighty genius, indeed, though the most mountainous oppression, would have breathed out some of his inextinguishable fire; yet possibly he might not have risen up into that giant, that much more than common man, at which we now gaze with amazement and delight. Perhaps he was as learned as his dramatic province required; for whatever other learning he wanted, he was master of two books unknown to many of the profoundly read: the book of Nature, and that of Man.—EDWARD YOUNG.

The work of a correct and regular writer is a garden accurately formed and diligently planted, varied with shades, and scented with flowers; the composition of Shakespeare is a forest, in which oaks extend their branches, and pines tower in the air, interspersed sometimes with weeds and brambles, and sometimes giving shelter to myrtles and to roses; filling the eye with awful pomp, and gratifying the mind with endless diversity. Other poets display cabinets of precious rarities, minutely finished, wrought into shape, and polished into brightness. Shakespeare opens a mine which contains gold and diamonds in inexhaustible plenty, though clouded by incrustations, debased by impurities, and mingled with a mass of meaner minerals.—*Samuel Johnson's preface to Shakespeare's Works.*

William Shakespeare was born in Stratford-on-Avon in 1564. The twenty-third of April is celebrated as his birthday, but the exact date has been a matter of controversy. His father was John Shakespeare, a dealer in wool and general produce in the little town of Stratford. His mother, Mary Arden, was the daughter of a prosperous farmer belonging to the gentry.

Only a few facts are definitely known regarding the life of Shakespeare previous to his removal to London in his twenty-first year. Time alone determines who shall prove immortal and it has frequently been the case that the ones who have left most minute personal history have been soonest relegated to oblivion. Shakespeare's contemporaries deemed him gifted but they did not realize his greatness; he himself never dreamed that posterity could find information regarding his personal life of interest. Instead of considering it remarkable that little is established today regarding Shakespeare's boyhood and youth, it should be recalled that even now, in an age of personal and family history, few are recording data concerning the youth of this generation. Although dispute has arisen over incidents pertaining to the years passed in Stratford, nevertheless the following is in the main accepted.

As a boy Shakespeare attended the grammar school of Stratford. Latin and Greek were taught in the grammar schools of this period. Ben Jonson is responsible for the statement that Shakespeare "knew little Latin and less Greek." It should, however, be remembered in this connection that Jonson was a classical student, and many a college professor might today make the same comment of students, who, notwithstanding, possess after all a fair comprehension of classical literature. At the early age of thirteen we find the boy taken from school to help his father, and whatever education he afterwards received, he gained for himself.

It is known that John Shakespeare was very fond of plays. Doubtless the son often accompanied his father to nearby places where strolling companies were presenting such entertainment as they could supply. He was probably familiar with the various forms of plays then current.

In his nineteenth year Shakespeare married Ann Hathaway, several years his senior. To them, three children were born: Susanna, Hamnet, and Judith. To the lasting grief of his father, Hamnet died in boyhood; Susanna married one Dr. Hall, and Judith, a farmer by the name of Quinby. Various indications would lead to the conclusion that Shakespeare was not happy in his married relations; his long sojourn in London is sometimes cited in this connection. However, he returned frequently to visit his family and when he retired from active life, went back to Stratford and made his home there.

Many religions have found in the Bible substantiation for their creeds and beliefs, and similarly, various theories may be borne out by passages from Shakespeare's plays. While many an author has left his personality so stamped upon his work that from it his entire life might be reconstructed, it is, nevertheless, dangerous to try to prove either domestic happiness or dearth of it from these plays. His life appears to have been a mingling of light and shadow, joy and grief, common to men, while he enjoyed the gratification of acknowledged success which is the portion of the few. Shakespeare was a writer of plays, then demanded by popular voice. At first, like other playwrights of his time, he merely worked over old plays; as he developed in his art, he grew to realize that only what he made his own satisfied; that while subjects for the stage abounded on every hand, the plays which were wholly his own creation, the creatures of his brain, gave keenest pleasure to others and most satisfaction to himself. He quickly learned all the others had to teach and by his inborn power soared far above them. His more mature plays must of necessity contain the kernel of his philosophy of life, the conclusions of his experience and observation. However, it is very certain that could he read today the countless volumes that have been written on his views of religion, morality, folk-lore, flower-lore and the many other topics which are developed from extracts culled from his plays, he would be filled with amazement.

Those who would enjoy to the utmost these dramatic masterpieces would find it wisest to avoid for a time all critical

treatises of the plays, and, having first become familiar with
the England of Shakespeare's time, together with some knowledge of the trend of dramatic development to the Elizabethan
period, confine themselves to the plays themselves. Better still
is it to see them played—for they were produced for the stage
rather than the library. Having read and reread them, and
watched them progress with gifted as well as amateur artists,
one grows at last to understand their superiority to most that
the theater supplies. Shakespeare was a genius and belongs
to no time or place. As certain painters and sculptors have
caught a vision of life universal, so did he know it in all its
phases and was able to express it in any key.

Titus Andronicus is believed to be Shakespeare's only in
part, being evidently some old play which he remade for the
Globe. It partakes of the style of Kyd's *Spanish Tragedy*
and abounds with horrors and cruelty. We may feel sure
that its redeeming characteristics are the results of its contact with Shakespeare: its plot is well defined and frequent
touches suggestive of the future dramatist abound. "A breeze
from the Warwickshire glades blows fresh at times through
the reeking atmosphere, and amidst the festering corruption of
a decadent society we have glimpses of nature that make us
less forlorn."

A series of comedies bearing both promise and stamp of
immaturity followed: *Love's Labor Lost, The Comedy of
Errors,* and *Two Gentlemen of Verona.* The chronicle plays
succeeded rapidly, giving examples of kingly strength and
kingly weakness. King John, Richard II., and Henry VI.
portrayed failure through weakness; Henry IV., Henry V.,
and Richard III. success in strength. A patriotic public gave
these plays hearty welcome and by them were taught, as Scott's
contemporaries two hundred years later by the Waverley novels, their past history. While Shakespeare never limited himself to records in the matter of detail, he nevertheless caught
the spirit of the growing nation and in characters that were
keenly alive, he set the successive steps of their progress before the people in glowing colors.

A Midsummer Night's Dream belongs to Shakespeare's
early period. It is in reality a masque and offers a rare portrayal of fairies and fairyland. Titania, Oberon and Puck

are not lifeless echoes of a wonderbook, but they deport themselves as we feel sure fairies would do should they suddenly materialize.

A tradition survives that Merry Wives of Windsor was composed in a fortnight to please the queen, who had asked to see Falstaff in love. It forms a connecting link between the chronicle plays and the more mature comedies, which include As You Like It, Twelfth Night and Much Ado about Nothing.

After these brilliant productions, the poet turned again to tragedy. Meantime he had suffered much and had come into the fullness of life's struggle, wherein so often the minor chords prevail. Grief for his son and suffering, of which only his sonnets give hint, held their spell over him. Then it was that he wrote his wonderful tragedies: Hamlet, King Lear, Othello, Julius Cæsar and Macbeth which alone would have left him supreme in English drama. They bear evidence of the master hand that is unafraid and feels the confidence of battles fought and won. They show profoundly the depth of Shakespeare's power.

The Tempest was a product of the times, reports of newly found lands having stirred men's imaginations beyond any thing previously known. The island which he created for the amusement of his audiences, together with the creatures inhabiting it, were not more remarkable than the reports which sailors brought back from distant shores.

No Shakespearean plays are more generally read and acted than Merchant of Venice and Romeo and Juliet; while the Taming of the Shrew and the The Winter's Tale are not infrequently shown upon the modern stage. The two Roman plays, Anthony and Cleopatra and Coriolanus are occasionally given.

Whole libraries of critical and analytic literature concerning Shakespeare and his inimitable plays have been forthcoming. No comprehensive course of literary study in any modern country is complete without some consideration of his works. His marvelous understanding of human nature, which a recent critic styled as "almost uncanny," his broad sympathy with every living creature, his unfailing wit and humor which takes the sting from the bitterest wrong, and his ability to unveil to others what was so evident to his rare vision, place him above all modern dramatists.

THE TRAGEDY OF KING LEAR.

ACT FIRST.—SCENE ONE. *King Lear's palace.*

[*Enter Kent, Gloucester, and Edmund.*

Kent. I thought the king had more affected the Duke of Albany than Cornwall.

Glou. It did always seem so to us: but now, in the division of the kingdom, it appears not which of the dukes he values most; for equalities are so weighed that curiosity in neither can make choice of either's moiety.

Kent. Is not this your son, my lord?

Glou. His breeding, sir, hath been at my charge: I have so often blushed to acknowledge him that now I am brazed to it. Do you smell a fault?

Kent. I cannot wish the fault undone, the issue of it being so proper.

Glou. But I have, sir, a son by order of law, some year elder than this, who yet is no dearer in my account: though this knave came something saucily into the world, yet was his mother fair, and he must be acknowledged. Do you know this noble gentleman, Edmund?

Edm. No, my lord.

Glou. My lord of Kent: remember him hereafter as my honourable friend.

Edm. My services to your lordship.

Kent. I must love you, and sue to know you better.

Edm. Sir, I shall study deserving.

Glou. He hath been out nine years, and away he shall again. The king is coming.

[*Sennet. Enter one bearing a coronet, King Lear, Cornwall, Albany, Goneril, Regan, Cordelia, and Attendants.*

Lear. Attend the lords of France and Burgundy, Gloucester.

Glou. I shall, my liege.

[*Exeunt Gloucester and Edmund.*

Lear. Meantime we shall express our darker purpose.
Give me the map there. Know we have divided
In three our kingdom: and 'tis our fast intent
To shake all cares and business from our age,
Conferring them on younger strengths, while we
Unburthen'd crawl toward death. Our son of Cornwall,
And you, our no less loving son of Albany,

SUNSET SPLENDOR IN SOUTHERN SEAS.

We have this hour a constant will to publish
Our daughters' several dowers, that future strife
May be prevented now. The princes, France and Bur-
    gundy,
Great rivals in our youngest daughter's love,
Long in our court have made their amorous sojourn,
And here are to be answer'd. Tell me, my daughters,
Since now we will divest us both of rule,
Interest of territory, cares of state,
Which of you shall we say doth love us most?
That we our largest bounty may extend
Where nature doth with merit challenge. Goneril,
Our eldest-born, speak first.
    Gon. Sir, I love you more than words can wield the
    matter,
Dearer than eye-sight, space and liberty,
Beyond what can be valued, rich or rare,
No less than life, with grace, health, beauty, honour,
As much as child e'er loved or father found;
A love that makes breath poor and speech unable;
Beyond all manner of so much I love you.
    Cor. [*Aside*] What shall Cordelia do? Love, and be
    silent.
    Lear. Of all these bounds, even from this line to this,
With shadowy forests and with champains rich'd,
With plenteous rivers and wide-skirted meads,
We make thee lady. To thine and Albany's issue
Be this perpetual. What says our second daughter,
Our dearest Regan, wife of Cornwall? Speak.
    Reg. I am made of that self metal as my sister,
And prize me at her worth. In my true heart
I find she names my very deed of love;
Only she comes too short; that I profess
Myself an enemy to all other joys
Which the most precious square of sense possesses,
And find I am alone felicitate
In your dear highness' love.
    Cor. [*Aside*]   Then poor Cordelia!
And yet not so, since I am sure my love's
More ponderous than my tongue.
    Lear. To thee and thine hereditary ever
Remain this ample third of our fair kingdom,
No less in space, validity and pleasure,
Than that conferr'd on Goneril. Now, our joy,

Although the last, not least, to whose young love
The vines of France and milk of Burgundy
Strive to be interess'd, what can you say to draw
A third more opulent than your sisters? Speak.
  Cor. Nothing, my lord.
  Lear. Nothing!
  Cor. Nothing.
  Lear. Nothing will come of nothing: speak again.
  Cor. Unhappy that I am, I cannot heave
My heart into my mouth: I love your majesty
According to my bond; nor more nor less.
  Lear. How, how, Cordelia! mend your speech a little,
Lest it may mar your fortunes.
  Cor.   Good my lord,
You have begot me, bred me, loved me: I
Return those duties back as are right fit,
Obey you, love you, and most honour you.
Why have my sisters husbands, if they say
They love you all? Haply, when shall I wed,
That lord whose hand must take my plight shall carry
Half my love with him, half my care and duty:
Sure, I shall never marry like my sisters,
To love my father all.
  Lear. But goes thy heart with this?
  Cor.   Ay, good my lord.
  Lear. So young, and so untender?
  Cor. So young, my lord, and true.
  Lear. Let it be so; thy truth then be thy dower:
For, by the sacred radiance of the sun,
The mysteries of Hecate, and the night;
By all the operation of the orbs
From whom we do exist and cease to be;
Here I disclaim all my paternal care,
Propinquity and property of blood,
And as a stranger to my heart and me
Hold thee from this for ever. The barbarous Scythian,
Or he that makes his generation messes
To gorge his appetite, shall to my bosom
Be as well neighbour'd, pitied and relieved,
As thou my sometime daughter.
  Kent.   Good my liege,—
  Lear. Peace, Kent!
Come not between the dragon and his wrath.
I loved her most, and thought to set my rest

On her kind nursery. Hence, and avoid my sight!
So be my grave my peace, as here I give
Her father's heart from her! Call France. Who stirs?
Call Burgundy. Cornwall and Albany,
With my two daughters' dowers digest this third:
Let pride, which she calls plainness, marry her.
I do invest you jointly with my power,
Pre-eminence and all the large effects
That troop with majesty. Ourself, by monthly course,
With reservation of an hundred knights
By you to be sustain'd, shall our abode
Make with you by due turns. Only we still retain
The name and all the additions to a king;
The sway, revenue, execution of the rest,
Beloved sons, be yours: which to confirm,
This coronet part betwixt you.

    Kent.   Royal Lear,
Whom I have ever honour'd as my king,
Loved as my father, as my master follow'd,
As my great patron thought on in my prayers,—
    Lear. The bow is bent and drawn; make from the shaft.
    Kent. Let it fall rather, though the fork invade
The region of my heart: be Kent unmannerly,
When Lear is mad. What wouldst thou do, old man?
Think'st thou that duty shall have dread to speak,
When power to flattery bows? To plainness honour's
    bound,
When majesty stoops to folly. Reverse thy doom,
And in thy best consideration check
This hideous rashness: answer my life my judgment,
Thy youngest daughter does not love thee least;
Nor are those empty-hearted whose low sound
Reverbs no hollowness.

    Lear.   Kent, on thy life, no more.
    Kent. My life I never held but as a pawn
To wage against thy enemies, nor fear to lose it,
Thy safety being the motive.
    Lear.   Out of my sight!
    Kent. See better, Lear, and let me still remain
The true blank of thine eye.
    Lear. Now, by Apollo,—
    Kent.   Now, by Apollo, king,

Thou swear'st thy gods in vain.

    Lear.   O, vassal! miscreant!
                          [Laying his hand on his sword.

    Alb. }
    Corn. }   Dear sir, forbear.

    Kent. Do;
Kill thy physician, and the fee bestow
Upon the foul disease. Revoke thy doom;
Or, whilst I can vent clamour from my throat,
I'll tell thee thou dost evil.

    Lear.   Hear me, recreant!
On thy allegiance, hear me!
Since thou hast sought to make us break our vow,
Which we durst never yet, and with strain'd pride
To come between our sentence and our power,
Which nor our nature nor our place can bear,
Our potency make good, take thy reward.
Five days we do allot thee, for provision
To shield thee from diseases of the world,
And on the sixth to turn thy hated back
Upon our kingdom: if on the tenth day following
Thy banish'd trunk be found in our dominions,
The moment is thy death. Away! By Jupiter,
This shall not be revoked.

    Kent. Fare thee well, king: sith thus thou wilt appear,
Freedom lives hence, and banishment is here.
[*To Cordelia*] The gods to their dear shelter take thee,
    maid,
That justly think'st and hast more rightly said!
[*To Regan and Goneril*] And your large speeches may
    your deeds approve,
That good effects may spring from words of love.
Thus Kent, O princes, bids you all adieu;
He'll shape his old course in a country new.   [*Exit.*
Flourish. Re-enter Gloucester, with France, Burgundy,
    and Attendants.

    Glou. Here's France and Burgundy, my noble lord.

    Lear. My lord of Burgundy,
We first address towards you, who with this king
Hath rivall'd for our daughter: what, in the least,
Will you require in present dower with her,
Or cease your quest of love?

    Bur.   Most royal majesty,
I crave no more than what your highness offer'd,

Nor will you tender less.

   Lear.   Right noble Burgundy,
When she was dear to us, we did hold her so;
But now her price is fall'n. Sir, there she stands:
If aught within that little seeming distance,
Or all of it, with our displeasure pieced.
And nothing more, may fitly like your grace,
She's there, and she is yours.

   Bur.   I know no answer.

   Lear. Will you, with those infirmities she owes,
Unfriended, new adopted to our hate,
Dower'd with our curse and stranger'd with our oath,
Take her, or leave her?

   Bur.   Pardon me, royal sir;
Election makes not up on such conditions.

   Lear. Then leave her, sir; for, by the power that made me,
I tell you all her wealth. [*To France*] For you, great king,
I would not from your love make such a stray,
To match you where I hate; therefore beseech you
To avert your liking a more worthier way
Than on a wretch whom nature is ashamed
Almost to acknowledge hers.

   France.   This is most strange,
That she, that even but now was your best object,
The argument of your praise, balm of your age,
Most best, most dearest, should in this trice of time
Commit a thing so monstrous, to dismantle
So many folds of favour. Sure, her offence
Must be of such unnatural degree
That monsters it, or your fore-vouch'd affection
Fall'n into taint: which to believe of her,
Must be a faith that reason without miracle
Could never plant in me.

   Cor.   I yet beseech your majesty,—
If for I want that glib and oily art,
To speak and purpose not, since what I well intend,
I'll do't before I speak,—that you make known
It is no vicious blot murder, or foulness,
No unchaste action, or dishonour'd step,
That hath deprived me of your grace and favour;
But even for want of that for which I am richer,
A still-soliciting eye, and such a tongue

As I am glad I have not, though not to have it
Hath lost me in your liking.
    Lear.   Better thou
Hadst not been born than not to have pleased me better.
    France. Is it but this? a tardiness in nature
Which often leaves the history unspoke
That it intends to do? My lord of Burgundy,
What say you to the lady? Love's not love
When it is mingled with regards that stand
Aloof from the entire point. Will you have her?
She is herself a dowry.
    Bur.   Royal Lear,
Give but that portion which yourself proposed,
And here I take Cordelia by the hand,
Duchess of Burgundy.
    Lear. Nothing: I have sworn; I am firm.
    Bur. I am sorry then you have so lost a father
That you must lose a husband.
    Cor.   Peace be with Burgundy!
Since that respects of fortune are his love,
I shall not be his wife.
    France. Fairest Cordelia, that art most rich being poor,
Most choice forsaken, and most loved despised,
Thee and thy virtues here I seize upon:
Be it lawful I take up what's cast away.
Gods, gods! 'tis strange that from their cold'st neglect
My love should kindle to inflamed respect.
Thy dowerless daughter, king, thrown to my chance,
Is queen of us, of ours, and our fair France:
Not all the dukes of waterish Burgundy
Can buy this unprized precious maid of me.
Bid them farewell, Cordelia, though unkind:
Thou losest here, a better where to find.
    Lear. Thou hast her, France: let her be thine, for we
Have no such daughter, nor shall ever see
That face of hers again. Therefore be gone
Without our grace, our love, our benison.
Come, noble Burgundy.
                    [*Flourish. Exeunt all but France,*
                         Goneril, Regan, and Cordelia.
    France. Bid farewell to your sisters.
    Cor. The jewels of our father, with wash'd eyes
Cordelia leaves you: I know you what you are;
And, like a sister, am most loath to call

Your faults as they are named. Use well our father:
To your professed bosoms I commit him:
But yet, alas, stood I within his grace,
I would prefer him to a better place.
So farewell to you both.
   Reg. Prescribe not us our duties.
   Gon.   Let your study
Be to content your lord, who hath received you
At fortune's alms. You have obedience scanted,
And well are worth the want that you have wanted.
   Cor. Time shall unfold what plaited cunning hides:
Who cover faults, at last shame them derides.
Well may you prosper!
   France.   Come, my fair Cordelia.
                 [Exeunt France and Cordelia.

   Gon. Sister, it is not a little I have to say of what most
nearly appertains to us both. I think our father will hence to-
night.

   Reg. That's most certain, and with you; next month with us.

   Gon. You see how full of changes his age is; the observation
we have made of it hath not been little: he always loved our
sister most; and with what poor judgment he hath now cast
her off appears too grossly.

   Reg. 'Tis the infirmity of his age: yet he hath ever but slen-
derly known himself.

   Gon. The best and soundest of his time hath been but rash;
then must we look to receive from his age, not alone the imperfections of long ingrafted condition, but therewithal the unruly
waywardness that infirm and choleric years bring with them.

   Reg. Such unconstant starts are we like to have from him
as this of Kent's banishment.

   Gon. There is further compliment of leave-taking between
France and him. Pray you, let's hit together: if our father carry
authority with such dispositions as he bears, this last surrender
of his will but offend us.

   Reg. We shall further think on't.

   Gon. We must do something, and i' the heat.   *[Exeunt.*

SCENE 2. *Another part of the heath. Storm still.*

                          [Enter Lear and Fool.
   Lear. Blow, winds, and crack your cheeks! rage! blow!
You cataracts and hurricanes, spout

Till you have drench'd our steeples, drown'd the cocks!
You sulphurous and thought-executing fires,
Vaunt-couriers to oak-cleaving thunderbolts,
Singe my white head! And thou, all-shaking thunder,
Smite flat the thick rotundity o' the world!
Crack nature's moulds, all germins spill at once
That make ingrateful man!

Fool. O nuncle, court holy-water in a dry house is better
than this rain-water out o' door. Good nuncle, in, and ask thy
daughters' blessing: here's a night unites neither wise man nor
fool.

    Lear. Rumble thy bellyful! Spit, fire! spout, rain!
Nor rain, wind, thunder, fire, are my daughters:
I tax not you, you elements, with unkindness;
I never gave you kingdom, call'd you children,
You owe me no subscription: then let fall
Your horrible pleasure; here I stand, your slave,
A poor, infirm, weak and despised old man:
But yet I call you servile ministers,
That have with two pernicious daughters join'd
Your high-engender'd battles 'gainst a head
So old and white as this. O! O! 'tis foul!

Fool. He that has a house to put's head in has a good head-
piece.

           The man that makes his toe
             What he his heart should make
          Shall of a corn cry woe,
             And turn his sleep to wake.

For there was never yet fair woman but she made mouths
in a glass.

    Lear. No, I will be the pattern of all patience; I will say
nothing.

                                 [Enter Kent.

    Kent. Who's there?

    Fool. Marry, here's a wise man and a fool.

    Kent. Alas, sir, are you here? things that love night
Love not such nights as these; the wrathful skies
Gallow the very wanderers of the dark,
And make them peep their caves: since I was man,
Such sheets of fire, such bursts of horrid thunder,
Such groans of roaring wind and rain, I never
Remember to have heard: man's nature cannot carry

The affliction nor the fear.

Lear.   Let the great gods,
That keep this dreadful pother o'er our heads,
Find out their enemies now. Tremble, thou wretch,
That has within thee undivulged crimes,
Unwhipp'd of justice: hide thee, thou bloody hand;
Thou perjured, and thou simular man of virtue
That art incestuous: caitiff, to pieces shake,
That under covert and convenient seeming
Hast practised on man's life: close pent-up guilts,
Rive your concealing continents and cry
These dreadful summoners grace. I am a man
More sinn'd against than sinning.

Kent.   Alack, bare-headed!
Gracious my lord, hard by here is a hovel;
Some friendship will it lend you 'gainst the tempest:
Repose you there; while I to this hard house—
More harder than the stones whereof 'tis raised;
Which even but now, demanding after you,
Denied me to come in—return, and force
Their scanted courtesy.

Lear.   My wits begin to turn.
Come on, my boy: how dost, my boy? art cold?
I am cold myself. Where is this straw, my fellow?
The art of our necessities is strange,
That can make vile things precious. Come, your hovel.
Poor fool and knave, I have one part in my heart
That's sorry yet for thee.

Fool. [*Singing*]
 He that has and a little tiny wit,—
 With hey, ho, the wind and the rain,—
 Must make content with his fortunes fit,
 For the rain it raineth every day.

Lear. True, my good boy. Come bring us to this hovel.
         [*Exeunt.*

THE MERCHANT OF VENICE.

ACT I. SCENE I. *Venice. A street.*

[*Enter Antonio, Salarino, and Salanio.*

Ant. In sooth, I know not why I am so sad:
It wearies me; you say it wearies you;
But how I caught it, found it, or come by it,
What stuff 't is made of, whereof it is born,
I am to learn;
And such a want-wit sadness makes of me,
That I have much ado to know myself.
  Salar. Your mind is tossing on the ocean;
There, where your argosies with portly sail,
Like signiors and rich burghers on the flood,
Or, as it were, the pageants of the sea,
Do overpeer the petty traffickers,
That curtsy to them, do them reverence,
As they fly by them with their woven wings.
  Salan. Believe me, sir, had I such venture forth,
The better part of my affections would
Be with my hopes abroad. I should be still
Plucking the grass, to know where sits the wind,
Peering in maps for ports and piers and roads;
And every object that might make me fear
Misfortune to my ventures, out of doubt
Would make me sad.
  Salar.   My wind cooling my broth
Would blow me to an ague, when I thought
What harm a wind too great at sea might do.
I should not see the sandy hour-glass run,
But I should think of shallows and of flats,
And see my wealthy Andrew docked in sand,
Vailing her high-top lower than her ribs
To kiss her burial. Should I go to church
And see the holy edifice of stone,
And not bethink me straight of dangerous rocks,
Which touching but my gentle vessel's side,
Would scatter all her spices on the stream,
Enrobe the roaring waters with my silks,
And, in a word, but even now worth this,

And now worth nothing? Shall I have the thought
To think on this, and shall I lack the thought
That such a thing bechanced would make me sad?
But tell not me; I know, Antonio
Is sad to think upon his merchandise.

Ant. Believe me, no: I thank my fortune for it,
My ventures are not in one bottom trusted,
Nor to one place; nor is my whole estate
Upon the fortune of this present year:
Therefore my merchandise makes me not sad.

Salar. Why, then you are in love.

Ant.   Fie, fie!

Salar. Not in love neither? Then let us say you are
     sad,
Because you are not merry: and 'twere as easy
For you to laugh and leap and say you are merry,
Because you are not sad. Now, by two-headed Janus,
Nature hath framed strange fellows in her time:
Some that will evermore peep through their eyes
And laugh like parrots at a bag-piper,
And other of such vinegar aspect
That they'll not show their teeth in way of smile,
Though Nestor swear the jest be laughable.

               [*Enter Bassanio, Lorenzo, and Gratiano.*

Salan. Here comes Bassanio, your most noble kinsman,
Gratiano and Lorenzo. Fare ye well:
We leave you now with better company.

Salar. I would have stayed till I had made you merry,
If worthier friends had not prevented me.

Ant. Your worth is very dear in my regard.
I take it, your own business calls on you
And you embrace the occasion to depart.

Salar. Good morrow, my good lords.

Bass. Good signiors both, when shall we laugh? say,
     when?
You grow exceeding strange: must it be so?

Salar. We'll make our leisures to attend on yours.

               [*Exeunt Salarino and Salanio.*

Lor. My Lord Bassanio, since you have found Antonio,
We two will leave you: but at dinner-time,
I pray you, have in mind where we must meet.

Bass. I will not fail you.

Gra. You look not well, Signior Antonio;

You have too much respect upon the world: ·
They lose it that do buy it with much care:
Believe me, you are marvellously changed.
   Ant. I hold the world but as the world, Gratiano;
A stage where every man must play a part,
And mine a sad one.
   Gra.   Let me play the fool:
With mirth and laughter let old wrinkles come,
And let my liver rather heat with wine
Than my heart cool with mortifying groans.
Why should a man, whose blood is warm within,
Sit like his grandsire cut in alabaster?
Sleep when he wakes and creep into the jaundice
By being peevish? I tell thee what, Antonio—
I love thee, and it is my love that speaks—
There are a sort of men whose visages
Do cream and mantle like a standing pond,
And do a wilful stillness entertain,
With purpose to be dressed in an opinion
Of wisdom, gravity, profound conceit,
As who should say "I am Sir Oracle,
And when I ope my lips let no dog bark!"
O my Antonio, I do know of these
That therefore only are reputed wise
For saying nothing, when, I am very sure,
If they should speak, would almost damn those ears
Which, hearing them, would call their brothers fools.
I'll tell thee more of this another time:
But fish not, with this melancholy bait,
For this fool gudgeon, this opinion.
Come, good Lorenzo. Fare ye well awhile:
I'll end my exhortation after dinner.
   Lor. Well, we will leave you then till dinner-time:
I must be one of these same dumb wise men,
For Gratiano never lets me speak.
   Gra. Well, keep me company but two years more.
Thou shalt not know the sound of thine own tongue.
   Ant. Farewell: I'll grow a talker for this gear.
   Gra. Thanks, i' faith, for silence is only commendable
In a neat's tongue dried.
                  [*Exeunt Gratiano and Lorenzo.*
   Ant. Is that any thing now?
   Bass. Gratiano speaks an infinite deal of nothing, more

than any man in all Venice. His reasons are as two grains
of wheat hid in two bushels of chaff: you shall seek all day
ere you find them, and when you have them, they are not
worth the search.

Ant. Well, tell me now what lady is the same.
To whom you swore a secret pilgrimage,
That you to-day promised to tell me of?

Bass. 'T is not unknown to you, Antonio,
How much I have disabled mine estate,
By something showing a more swelling port
Than my faint means would grant continuance:
Nor do I now make moan to be abridged
From such a noble rate; but my chief care
Is to come fairly off from the great debts
Wherein my time something too prodigal
Hath left me gaged. To you, Antonio,
I owe the most, in money and in love,
And from your love I have a warranty
To unburden all my plots and purposes
How to get clear of all the debts I owe.

Ant. I pray you, good Bassanio, let me know it;
And if it stand, as you yourself still do,
Within the eye of honour, be assured,
My purse, my person, my extremest means,
Lie all unlocked to your occasions.

Bass. In my school-days, when I had lost one shaft,
I shot his fellow of the self-same flight
The self-same way with more advised watch,
To find the other forth, and by adventuring both
I oft found both: I urge this childhood proof,
Because what follows is pure innocence.
I owe you much, and, like a wilful youth,
That which I owe is lost; but if you please
To shoot another arrow that self way
Which you did shoot the first, I do not doubt,
As I will watch the aim, or to find both
Or bring your latter hazard back again
And thankfully rest debtor for the first.

Ant. You know me well, and herein spent but time
To wind about my love with circumstance;
And out of doubt you do me now more wrong
In making question of my uttermost
Than if you had made waste of all I have:

Then do but say to me what I should do
That in your knowledge may by me be done,
And I am prest unto it: therefore, speak.

 Bass. In Belmont is a lady richly left;
And she is fair and, fairer than that word,
Of wondrous virtues: sometimes from her eyes
I did receive fair speechless messages:
Her name is Portia, nothing undervalued
To Cato's daughter, Brutus' Portia:
Nor is the wide world ignorant of her worth,
For the four winds blow in from every coast
Renowned suitors; and her sunny locks
Hang on her temples like a golden fleece;
Which makes her seat of Belmont Colchos' strand,
And many Jasons come in quest of her.
O my Antonio, had I but the means
To hold a rival place with one of them,
I have a mind presages me such thrift,
That I should questionless be fortunate!

 Ant. Thou know'st that all my fortunes are at sea:
Neither have I money nor commodity
To raise a present sum: therefore go forth;
Try what my credit can in Venice do:
That shall be racked, even to the uttermost,
To furnish thee to Belmont, to fair Portia.
Go, presently inquire, and so will I,
Where money is; and I no question make
To have it of my trust or for my sake. [*Exeunt.*

SCENE II. *Belmont. A room in Portia's house.*
       [*Enter Portia and Nerissa.*

 Por. By my troth, Nerissa, my little body is aweary of this great world.

 Ner. You would be, sweet madam, if your miseries were in the same abundance as your good fortunes are: and yet, for aught I see, they are as sick that surfeit with too much as they that starve with nothing. It is no mean happiness, therefore, to be seated in the mean: superfluity comes sooner by white hairs, but competency lives longer.

 Por. Good sentences and well pronounced.

 Ner. They would be better, if well followed.

 Por. If to do were as easy as to know what were good to do,

chapels had been churches and poor men's cottages princes' palaces. It is a good divine that follows his own instructions: I
can easier teach twenty what were good to be done, than be one
of the twenty to follow mine own teaching. The brain may devise laws for the blood, but a hot temper leaps o'er a cold decree:
such a hare is madness the youth, to skip o'er the meshes of good
counsel the cripple. But this reasoning is not in the fashion to
choose me a husband. O me, the word choose! I may neither
choose whom I would nor refuse whom I dislike; so is the will
of a living daughter curbed by the will of a dead father. Is it
not hard, Nerissa, that I cannot choose one nor refuse none?

Ner. Your father was ever virtuous; and holy men at their
death have good inspirations: therefore the lottery, that he hath
devised in these three chests of gold, silver and lead, whereof
who chooses his meaning chooses you, will, no doubt, never be
chosen by any rightly but one who you shall rightly love. But
what warmth is there in your affection towards any of these
princely suitors that are already come?

Por. I pray thee, over-name them; and as thou namest them,
I will describe them; and, according to my description, level at
my affection.

Ner. First, there is the Neapolitan prince.

Por. Ay, that's a colt indeed, for he doth nothing but talk of
his horse; and he makes it a great appropriation to his own good
parts, that he can shoe him himself.

Ner. Then there is the County Palatine.

Por. He doth nothing but frown, as who should say "If
you will not have me, choose:" he hears merry tales and smiles
not: I fear he will prove the weeping philosopher when he grows
old, being so full of unmannerly sadness in his youth. I had
rather be married to a death's-head with a bone in his mouth
than to either of these. God defend me from these two!

Ner. How say you by the French lord, Monsieur Le Bon?

Por. God made him, and therefore let him pass for a man.
In truth, I know it is a sin to be a mocker: but, he! why, he hath
a horse better than the Neapolitan's, a better bad habit of frown-
ing than the Count Palatine; he is every man in no man; if a
throstle sing, he falls straight a capering: he will fence with his
own shadow: if I should marry him, I should marry twenty hus-

bands. If he would despise me, I would forgive him, for if he love me to madness, I shall never requite him.

Ner. What say you, then, to Falconbridge, the young baron of England?

Por. You know I say nothing to him, for he understands not me, nor I him: he hath neither Latin, French, nor Italian, and you will come into the court and swear that I have a poor penny-worth in the English. He is a proper man's picture, but, alas, who can converse with a dumb-show? How oddly he is suited! I think he bought his doublet in Italy, his round hose in France, his bonnet in Germany and his behaviour every where.

Ner. What think you of the Scottish lord, his neighbour?

Por. That he hath a neighbourly charity in him, for he borrowed a box of the ear of the Englishman and swore he would pay him again when he was able; I think the Frenchman became his surety and sealed under for another.

Ner. How like you the young German, the Duke of Saxony's nephew?

Por. Very vilely in the morning, when he is sober, and most vilely in the afternoon, when he is drunk: when he is best, he is little worse than a man, and when he is worst, he is little better than a beast: an the worst fall that ever fell, I hope I shall make shift to go without him.

Ner. If he should offer to choose, and choose the right casket, you should refuse to perform your father's will, if you should refuse to accept him.

Por. Therefore, for fear of the worst, I pray thee, set a deep glass of rhenish wine on the contrary casket, for if the Devil be within and that temptation without, I know he will choose it. I will do anything, Nerissa, ere I'll be married to a sponge.

Ner. You need not fear, lady, the having any of these lords: they have acquainted me with their determinations; which is, indeed, to return to their home and to trouble you with no more suit, unless you may be won by some other sort than your father's imposition depending on the caskets.

Por. If I live to be as old as Sibylla, I will die as chaste as Diana, unless I be obtained by the manner of my father's will. I am glad this parcel of wooers are so reasonable, for there is not one among them but I dote on his very absence, and I pray God grant them a fair departure.

TROPICAL FAIRYLAND.—LUZON.

Ner. Do you not remember, lady, in your father's time, a Venetian, a scholar and a soldier, that came hither in company of the Marquis Montferrat?

Por. Yes, yes, it was Bassanio,—as I think, so was he called.

Ner. True, madam: he, of all the men that ever my foolish eyes looked upon, was the best deserving a fair lady.

Por. I remember him well, and I remember him worthy of thy praise.

[*Enter a Serving-Man.*

How now! What news?

Serv. The four strangers seek for you, madam, to take their leave: and there is a forerunner come from a fifth, the Prince of Morocco, who brings word the Prince his master will be here tonight.

Por. If I could bid the fifth welcome with so good a heart as I can bid the other four farewell, I should be glad of his approach: if he had the condition of a saint and the complexion of a devil, I had rather he should shrive me than wive me. Come, Nerissa. Sirrah, go before.

While we shut the gates upon one wooer, another knocks at the
  door.   [*Exeunt.*

Scene.—*A Court of Justice in Venice.*

Duke. Go one, and call the Jew into court.

Salanio. He is ready at the door: he comes, my lord.
            [*Enter Shylock.*

Duke. Make room, and let him stand before our face.
Shylock, the world thinks, and I think so too,
That thou but lead'st this fashion of thy malice
To the last hour of act; and then 'tis thought
Thou'lt show thy mercy and remorse, more strange,
Than is thy strange apparent cruelty;
And where thou now exact'st the penalty,
Which is a pound of this poor merchant's flesh,
Thou wilt not only lose the forfeiture,
But, touched with human gentleness and love,
Forgive a moiety of the principal;
Glancing an eye of pity on his losses,

VII—9

That have of late so huddled on his back,
Enow to press a royal merchant down.
We all expect a gentle answer, Jew.
     Shylock. I have possessed your grace of what I purpose;
And by our holy Sabbath have I sworn
To have the due and forfeit of my bond.
If you deny it, let the danger light
Upon your charter and your city's freedom.
You'll ask me, why I rather choose to have
A weight of carrion flesh than to receive
Three thousand ducats: I'll not answer that:
But, say, it is my humor: is it answered?
What if my house be troubled with a rat,
And I be pleased to give ten thousand ducats·
To have it baned? What, are you answered yet?
     Bassanio. This is no answer, thou unfeeling man,
To excuse the current of thy cruelty.
     Shylock. I am not bound to please thee with my answer.
     Bassanio. For thy three thousand ducats here is six.
     Shylock. If every ducat in six thousand ducats
Were in six parts, and every part a ducat,
I would not draw them;—I would have my bond.
     Duke. How shalt thou hope for mercy, rendering none?
     Shylock. What judgment shall I dread, doing no wrong?
You have among you many a purchased slave,
Which, like your asses, and your dogs and mules
You use in abject and in slavish parts,
Because you bought them: shall I say to you,
Let them be free, marry them to your heirs?
Why sweat they under burthens? let their beds
Be made as soft as yours, and let their palates
Be seasoned with such viands? You will answer
"The slaves are ours:" so do I answer you:
The pound of flesh, which I demand of him,
Is dearly bought; 'tis mine, and I will have it.
If you deny me, fie upon your law!
There is no force in the decrees of Venice.
I stand for judgment: answer: shall I have · ·
     Duke. Upon my power I may dismiss this court,
Unless Bellario, a learned doctor,
Whom I have sent for to determine this.
Come here to-day.

A messenger appears with a letter from Bellario, stating that he cannot come, but sends a young doctor Balthasar in his stead.

Duke. You hear the learned Bellario, what he writes:
And here, I take it, is the doctor come.
                       [*Enter Portia, dressed like a doctor of laws*
Give me your hand. Came you from old Bellario?
   Portia. I did, my lord.
   Duke. You are welcome: take your place.
Are you acquainted with the difference
That holds this present question in the court?
   Portia. I am informéd throughly of the cause.
Which is the merchant here, and which the Jew?
   Duke. Antonio and old Shylock, both stand forth.
   Portia. Is your name Shylock?
   Shylock. Shylock is my name.
   Portia. Of a strange nature is the suit you follow;
Yet in such rule that the Venetian law
Cannot impugn you as you do proceed.
[*To Antonio*] You stand within his danger, do you not?
   Antonio. Aye, so he says.
   Portia. Do you confess the bond?
   Antonio. I do.
   Portia. Then must the Jew be merciful.
   Shylock. On what compulsion must I? tell me that.
   Portia. The quality of mercy is not strained,
It droppeth as the gentle rain from heaven
Upon the place beneath; it is twice blest;
It blesseth him that gives and him that takes:
'Tis mightiest in the mightiest: it becomes
The thronéd monarch better than his crown;
His sceptre shows the force of temporal power,
The attribute to awe and majesty,
Wherein doth sit the dread and fear of kings;
But mercy is above this sceptred sway;
It is enthroned in the hearts of kings,
It is an attribute to God himself;
And earthly power doth then show likest God's
When mercy seasons justice. Therefore, Jew,
Though justice be thy plea, consider this,
That, in the course of justice, none of us
Should see salvation: we do pray for mercy;

And that same prayer doth teach us all to render
The deeds of mercy.   I have spoke thus much
To mitigate the justice of thy plea,
Which if thou follow, this strict court of Venice
Must needs give sentence 'gainst the merchant there.
 Shylock. My deeds upon my head!   I crave the law,
The penalty and forfeit of my bond.
 Portia. Is he not able to discharge the money?
 Bassanio. Yes, here I tender it for him in the court;
Yea, twice the sum: if that will not suffice,
I will be bound to pay it ten times o'er,
On forfeit of my hands, my head, my heart:
If this will not suffice, it must appear
That malice bears down truth.   And I beseech you,
Wrest once the law to your authority:
To do a great right, do a little wrong,
And curb this cruel devil of his will.
 Portia. It must not be; there is no power in Venice
Can alter a decree established:
'Twill be recorded for a precedent,
And many an error by the same example
Will rush into the state: it cannot be.
 Shylock. A Daniel come to judgment! yea, a Daniel:
O wise young judge, how I do honor thee!
 Portia. I pray you, let me look upon the bond.
 Shylock. Here 'tis, most reverend doctor, here it is.
 Portia. Shylock, there's thrice thy money offered
  thee.
 Shylock. An oath, an oath, I have an oath in heaven:
Shall I lay perjury upon my soul?
No, not for Venice.
 Portia. Why, this bond is forfeit;
And lawfully by this the Jew may claim
A pound of flesh, to be by him cut off
Nearest the merchant's heart.   Be merciful:
Take thrice thy money; bid me tear the bond.
 Shylock. When it is paid according to the tenor.
It doth appear you are a worthy judge;
You know the law, your exposition
Hath been most sound: I charge you by the law,
Whereof you are a well-deserving pillar,
Proceed to judgment: by my soul I swear

There is no power in the tongue of man
To alter me: I stay here on my bond.

Antonio. Most heartily I do beseech the court
To give the judgment.

Portia. Why then, thus it is:
You must prepare your bosom for his knife.

Shylock. O noble judge! O excellent young man!

Portia. For the intent and purpose of the law,
Hath full relation to the penalty
Which here appeareth due upon the bond.

Shylock. 'Tis very true: O wise and upright judge!
How much more elder art thou than thy looks!

Portia. Have by some surgeon, Shylock, on your charge,
To stop his wounds, lest he do bleed to death.

Shylock. Is it so nominated in the bond?

Portia. It is not so expressed: but what of that?
'Twere good you do so much for charity.

Shylock. I cannot find it: 'tis not in the bond.

Portia. Come, merchant, have you anything to say?

Antonio. But little: I am armed and well prepared.
Give me your hand, Bassanio: fare you well!
Grieve not that I am fallen to this for you;
Repent not you that you shall lose your friend,
And he repents not that he pays your debt;
For if the Jew do cut but deep enough,
I'll pay it instantly with all my heart.

Bassanio. Antonio, I am married to a wife [Portia],
Which is as dear to me as life itself;
But life itself, my wife, and all the world,
Are not with me esteemed above thy life:
I would lose all, ay, sacrifice them all
Here to this devil, to deliver you.

Portia. Your wife would give you little thanks for that,
If she were by, to hear you make the offer.

Shylock. We trifle time: I pray thee, pursue sentence.

Portia. A pound of that same merchant's flesh is thine:
The court awards it, and the law doth give it.

Shylock. Most rightful judge!

Portia. And you must cut this flesh from off his breast:
The law allows it, and the court awards it.

Shylock. Most learned judge! A sentence! Come, prepare!

Portia. Tarry a little; there is something else.
This bond doth give thee here no jot of blood;
The words expressly are, "a pound of flesh."
Take then thy bond, take thou thy pound of flesh;
But, in the cutting it, if thou dost shed
One drop of Christian blood, thy lands and goods
Are, by the laws of Venice, confiscate
Unto the state of Venice.

Gratiano. O upright judge! Mark, Jew: O learned judge!

Shylock. Is that the law?

Portia. Thyself shall see the act:
For, as thou urgest justice, be assured
Thou shalt have justice, more than thou desirest.

Gratiano. O learned judge! Mark, Jew: a learned judge!

Shylock. I take this offer, then; pay the bond thrice
And let the Christian go.

Bassanio. Here is the money.

Portia. Soft!
The Jew shall have all justice; soft! no haste:
He shall have nothing but the penalty.

Gratiano. O Jew! an upright judge, a learned judge!

Portia. Therefore prepare thee to cut off the flesh.
Shed thou no blood, nor cut thou less, nor more,—
But just a pound of flesh: if thou tak'st more
Or less than a just pound, be it but so much
As makes it light or heavy in the substance,
Or the division of the twentieth part
Of one poor scruple,—nay, if the scale do turn
But in the estimation of a hair,—
Thou diest, and all thy goods are confiscate.

Gratiano. A second Daniel,—a Daniel, Jew!
Now infidel, I have thee on the hip.

Portia. Why doth the Jew pause? take thy forfeiture.

Shylock. Give me my principal, and let me go.

Bassanio. I have it ready for thee; here it is.

Portia. He hath refused it in the open court:
He shall have merely justice and his bond.

Gratiano. A Daniel, still say I, a second Daniel!
I thank thee, Jew, for teaching me that word.

Shylock. Shall I not have barely my principal?

Portia. Thou shalt have nothing but the forfeiture,
To be so taken at thy peril, Jew,

Shylock. Why, then the devil give him good of it!
I'll stay no longer question.

Portia. Tarry, Jew:
The law hath yet another hold on you.
It is enacted in the laws of Venice,
If it be proved against an alien,
That by direct or indirect attempts
He seek the life of any citizen,
The party 'gainst the which he doth contrive
Shall seize one-half his goods; the other half
Comes to the privy coffer of the state;
And the offender's life lies in the mercy
Of the duke only, 'gainst all other voice.
In which predicament, I say, thou stand'st:
For it appears by manifest proceeding,
That, indirectly, and directly too,
Thou hast contrived against the very life
Of the defendant; and thou hast incurred
The danger formerly by me rehearsed.
Down, therefore, and beg mercy of the duke.

Duke. That thou shalt see the difference of our spirit,
I pardon thee thy life before thou ask it:
For half thy wealth, it is Antonio's:
The other half comes to the general state,
Which humbleness may drive unto a fine.

Portia. Ay, for the state, not for Antonio.

Shylock. Nay, take my life and all; pardon not that:
You take my house when you do take the prop
That doth sustain my house; you take my life
When you do take the means whereby I live.

Portia. What mercy can you render him, Antonio?

Antonio. So please my lord the duke and all the court
To quit the fine for one-half of his goods;

I am content, so he will let me have
The other half in use, to render it,
Upon his death, unto the gentleman
That lately stole his daughter.
Two things provided more,—that, for this favor,
He presently become a Christian;
The other that he do record a gift,
Here in the court, of all he dies possessed,
Unto his son Lorenzo and his daughter.

    Duke. He shall do this, or else I do recant
The pardon that I late pronouncéd here.

    Portia. Art thou contented, Jew? what dost thou say?

    Shylock. I am content.

    Portia. Clerk, draw a deed of gift.

    Shylock. I pray you give me leave to go from hence;
I am not well; send the deed after me,
And I will sign it.   [*Exit Shylock.*

THE TEMPEST

ACT I.

SCENE I. *On a ship at sea: a tempestuous noise of thunder and lightning heard.*

Enter a Ship-Master *and* a Boatswain.

Mast. Boatswain!

Boats. Here, Master: what cheer?

Mast. Good, speak to th' mariners: fall to 't, yarely, or we run ourselves aground: bestir, bestir.   [*Exit.*

Enter Mariners.

Boats. Heigh, my hearts! cheerly, cheerly, my hearts! yare, yare! Take in the topsail. Tend to th' master's whistle. Blow, till thou burst thy wind, if room enough!

Enter ALONSO, SEBASTIAN, ANTONIO, FERDINAND, GONZALO, *and others.*

Alon. Good boatswain, have care. Where's the master? Play the men.

Boats. I pray now, keep below.

Ant. Where is the master, boson?

Boats. Do you not hear him? You mar our labour: keep your cabins: you do assist the storm.

Gon. Nay, good, be patient.

Boats. When the sea is. Hence! What cares these roarers for the name of king? To cabin: silence! trouble us not.

Gon. Good, yet remember whom thou hast aboard.

Boats. None that I more love than myself. You are a counsellor; if you can command these elements to silence, and work the peace of the present, we will not hand a rope more; use your authority: if you cannot, give thanks you have liv'd so long, and make yourself ready in your cabin for the mischance of the hour, if it so hap. Cheerly, good hearts! Out of our way, I say.   [*Exit.*

Gon. I have great comfort from this fellow: methinks he hath no drowning mark upon him; his complexion is perfect gallows. Stand fast, good Fate, to his hanging: make the rope

137

of his destiny our cable, for our own doth little advantage.   If
he be not born to be hang'd, our case is miserable.   .   .   .

[*Exeunt.*

SCENE II.   *The island.   Before* PROSPERO'S *cell.*
Enter PROSPERO *and* MIRANDA.

Mir.   If by your art, my dearest father, you have
Put the wild waters in this roar, allay them.
The sky, it seems, would pour down stinking pitch,
But that the sea, mounting to the welkin's cheek,   •
Dashes the fire out.   O, I have suffered
With those that I saw suffer: a brave vessel,
Who had, no doubt, some noble creature in her,
Dash'd all to pieces.   O, the cry did knock
Against my very heart.   Poor souls, they perish'd.
Had I been any god of power, I would
Have sunk the sea within the earth or ere
It should the good ship so have swallow'd and
The fraughting souls within her.
  Pros.   Be collected:
No more amazement.   Tell your piteous heart
There's no harm done.
  Mir.   O, woe the day!
  Pros.   No harm.
I have done nothing but in care of thee,
Of thee, my dear one, thee, my daughter, who
Art ignorant of what thou art, nought knowing
Of whence I am, nor that I am more better
Than Prospero, master of a full poor cell,
And thy no greater father.
  Mir.   More to know
Did never meddle with my thoughts.
  Pros.   'T is time
I should inform thee farther.   Lend thy hand,
And pluck my magic garment from me.   So:

[*Lays down his mantle.*

Lie there, my art.   Wipe thou thine eyes; have comfort.
The direful spectacle of the wrack, which touch'd
The very virtue of compassion in thee,
I have with such provision in mine art
So safely order'd that there is no soul—

No, not so much perdition as an hair
Betid to any creature in the vessel
Which thou heard'st cry, which thou saw'st sink. Sit down;
For thou must now know farther.

 Mir.   You have often
Begun to tell me what I am, but stopp'd
And left me to a bootless inquisition,
Concluding, "Stay: not yet."

 Pros.   The hour's now come;
The very minute bids thee ope thine ear;
Obey and be attentive. Canst thou remember
A time before we came unto this cell?
I do not think thou canst, for then thou wast not
Out three years old.

 Mir.   Certainly, sir, I can.

 Pros. By what? by any other house or person?
Of any thing the image tell me that
Hath kept with thy remembrance.

 Mir.   'T is far off
And rather like a dream than an assurance
That my remembrance warrants. Had I not
Four or five women once that tended me?

 Pros. Thou hadst, and more, Miranda. But how is it
That this lives in thy mind? What seest thou else
In the dark backward and abysm of time?
If thou remember'st aught ere thou cam'st here,
How thou cam'st here thou may'st.

 Mir.   But that I do not.

 Pros. Twelve year since, Miranda, twelve year since,
Thy father was the Duke of Milan and
A prince of power.

 Mir.   Sir, are not you my father?

 Pros. Thy mother was a piece of virtue, and
She said thou wast my daughter; and thy father
Was Duke of Milan; and thou his only heir
And princess no worse issued.

 Mir.   O the heavens!
What foul play had we, that we came from thence?
Or blessed was't we did?

Pros.   Both, both, my girl:
By foul play, as thou say'st, were we heaved thence,
But blessedly holp thither.
   Mir.   O, my heart bleeds
To think o' th' teen that I have turned you to,
Which is from my remembrance! Please you, farther.
   Pros.   My brother and thy uncle, call'd Antonio—
I pray thee, mark me—that a brother should
Be so perfidious!—he whom next thyself
Of all the world I lov'd, and to him put
The manage of my state; as at that time
Through all the signories it was the first,
And Prospero the prime duke, being so reputed
In dignity, and for the liberal arts
Without a parallel; those being all my study,
The government I cast upon my brother
And to my state grew stranger, being transported
And rapt in secret studies. Thy false uncle—
Dost thou attend me?
   Mir.   Sir, most heedfully.
   Pros.   Being once perfected how to grant suits,
How to deny them, who t' advance and who
To trash for overtopping, new created
The creatures that were mine, I say, or chang'd 'em,
Or else new form'd 'em; having both the key
Of officer and office, set all hearts i' th' state
To what tune pleas'd his ear; that now he was
The ivy which had hid my princely trunk,
And suck'd my verdure out on 't. Thou attend'st not.
   Mir.   O, good sir, I do.
   Pros.   I pray thee, mark me.
I, thus neglecting worldly ends, all dedicated
To closeness and the bettering of my mind
With that which, but by being so retir'd,
O'er-priz'd all popular rate, in my false brother
Awak'd an evil nature; and my trust,
Like a good parent, did beget of him
A falsehood, in its contrary as great
As my trust was; which had indeed no limit.
A confidence sans bound. He being thus lorded,

Not only with what my revenue yielded,
But what my power might else exact, like one
Who having unto truth, by telling of it,
Made such a sinner of his memory,
To credit his own lie, he did believe
He was indeed the duke; out o' th' substitution,
And executing th' outward face of royalty,
With all prerogative: hence his ambition growing—
Dost thou hear?
    Mir.   Your tale, sir, would cure deafness.
    Pros. To have no screen between this part he play'd
And him he play'd it for, he needs will be
Absolute Milan. Me, poor man!—my library
Was dukedom large enough: of temporal royalties
He thinks me now incapable; confederates—
So dry he was for sway—wi' th' King of Naples
To give him annual tribute, do him homage,
Subject his coronet to his crown, and bend
The dukedom yet unbow'd—alas, poor Milan!—
To most ignoble stooping.
    Mir.   O the heavens!
    Pros. Mark his condition and th' event; then tell me
If this might be a brother.
    Mir.   I should sin
To think but nobly of my grandmother;
Good wombs have borne bad sons.
    Pros.   Now the condition.
This King of Naples, being an enemy
To me inveterate, hearkens my brother's suit;
Which was, that he, in lieu o' th' premises,
Of homage and I know not how much tribute,
Should presently extirpate me and mine
Out of the dukedom, and confer fair Milan
With all the honours on my brother: whereon,
A treacherous army levied, one midnight
Fated to th' purpose did Antonio open
The gates of Milan, and, i' th' dead of darkness,
The ministers for the purpose hurri'd thence
Me and thy crying self.
    Mir.   Alack, for pity!

I, not remembering how I cri'd out then,
Will cry it o'er again: it is a hint
That wrings mine eyes to 't.
    Pros.   Hear a little further,
And then I'll bring thee to the present business
Which now's upon 's; without the which this story
Were most impertinent.
    Mir.   Wherefore did they not
That hour destroy us?
    Pros.   Well demanded, wench:
My tale provokes that question. Dear, they durst not,
So dear the love my people bore me, nor set
A mark so bloody on the business, but
With colours fairer painted their foul ends.
In few, they hurried us aboard a bark,
Bore us some leagues to sea; where they prepar'd
A rotten carcass of a boat, not rigg'd,
Nor tackle, sail, nor mast; the very rats
Instinctively had quit it: there they hoist us,
To cry to th' sea that roar'd to us, to sigh
To th' winds whose pity, sighing back again,
Did us but loving wrong.
    Mir.   Alack, what trouble
Was I then to you!
    Pros.   O, a cherubin
Thou wast that did preserve me. Thou didst smile.
Infused with a fortitude from heaven,
When I have deck'd the sea with drops full salt,
Under my burthen groan'd; which rais'd in me
An undergoing stomach, to bear up
Against what should ensue.
    Mir.   How came we ashore?
    Pros. By Providence divine.
Some food we had and some fresh water that
A noble Neapolitan, Gonzalo,
Out of his charity being then appointed
Master of this design, did give us, with
Rich garments, linens, stuffs and necessaries,
Which since have steadied much; so, of his gentleness,
Knowing I lov'd my books, he furnish'd me

From mine own library with volumes that
I prize above my dukedom.
    Mir.   Would I might
But ever see that man!
    Pros.   Now I arise: [*Puts on his robe.*
Sit still, and hear the last of our sea-sorrow.
Here in this island we arriv'd; and here
Have I, thy schoolmaster, made thee more profit
Than other princess can that have more time
For vainer hours and tutors not so careful.
    Mir. Heavens thank you for 't! And now, I pray
        you, sir,
For still 't is beating in my mind, your reason
For raising this sea-storm?
    Pros.   Know thus far forth.
By accident most strange, bountiful Fortune,
Now my dear lady, hath mine enemies
Brought to this shore; and by my prescience
I find my zenith doth depend upon
A most auspicious star, whose influence
If now I court not but omit, my fortunes
Will ever after droop. Here cease more questions:
Thou art inclin'd to sleep; 't is a good dulness,
And give it way: I know thou canst not choose.
                            [*Miranda sleeps.*
Come away, servant, come. I am ready now.
Approach, my Ariel, come.

Enter ARIEL.

    Ari. All hail, great master! grave sir, hail! I come
To answer thy best pleasure; be 't to fly,
To swim, to dive into the fire, to ride
On the curl'd clouds, to thy strong bidding task
Ariel and all his quality.
    Pros.   Hast thou, spirit,
Perform'd to point the tempest that I bade thee?
    Ari. To every article.
I boarded the king's ship; now on the beak,
Now in the waist, the deck, in every cabin,
I flam'd amazement: sometime I 'ld divide,

And burn in many places; on the topmast,
The yards and bowsprit, would I flame distinctly,
Then meet and join.   Jove's lightnings, the precursors
O' th' dreadful thunder-claps, more momentary
And sight-outrunning were not; the fire and cracks
Of sulphurous roaring the most mighty Neptune
Seem'd to besiege, and make his bold waves tremble,
Yea, his dread trident shake.

  Pros.   My brave spirit!
Who was so firm, so constant, that this coil
Would not infect his reason?

  Ari.   Not a soul
But felt a fever of the mad and play'd
Some tricks of desperation.   All but mariners
Plung'd in the foaming brine and quit the vessel,
Then all afire with me: the king's son, Ferdinand,
With hair up-staring,—then like reeds, not hair,—
Was the first man that leap'd; cried, "Hell is empty,
And all the devils are here."

  Pros.   Why, that's my spirit!
But was not this nigh shore?

  Ari.   Close by, my master.
  Pros.   But are they, Ariel, safe?
  Ari.   Not a hair perish'd;
On their sustaining garments not a blemish,
But fresher than before: and, as thou bad'st me,
In troops I have dispers'd them 'bout the isle.
The king's son have I landed by himself;
Whom I left cooling of the air with sighs
In an odd angle of the isle and sitting,
His arms in this sad knot.

  Pros.   Of the king's ship
The mariners say how thou hast dispos'd
And all the rest o' th' fleet.

  Ari.   Safely in harbour
Is the king's ship: in the deep nook, where once
Thou call'dst me up at midnight to fetch dew
From the still-vex'd Bermoothes, there she 's hid:
The mariners all under hatches stow'd;
Who. with a charm join'd to their suffer'd labour,

I have left asleep: and for the rest o' th' fleet
Which I dispers'd, they all have met again
And are upon the Mediterranean flote,
Bound sadly home for Naples,
Supposing that they say the king's ship wrack'd
And his great person perish.
    Pros.   Ariel, thy charge
Exactly is perform'd: but there's more work.
What is the time o' th' day?
    Ari.   Past the mid season.
    Pros. At least two glasses. The time 'twixt six and now
Must by us both be spent most preciously.
    Ari. Is there more toil? Since thou dost give me pains,
Let me remember thee what thou hast promis'd,
Which is not yet perform'd me.
    Pros.   How now? moody?
What is 't thou canst demand?
    Ari.   My liberty.
    Pros. Before the time be out? no more? . . .

ACT IV.

Scene I. *Before* Prospero's *cell.*

Enter Prospero, Ferdinand, *and* Miranda.

    Pros. If I have too austerely punish'd you,
Your compensation makes amends, for I
Have given you here a third of mine own life,
Or that for which I live; who once again
I tender to thy hand: all thy vexations
Were but my trials of thy love, and thou
Hast strangely stood the test: here, afore Heaven,
I ratify this my rich gift. O Ferdinand,
Do not smile at me that I boast her off,
For thou shalt find she will outstrip all praise
And make it halt behind her.
    Fer.   I do believe it
Against an oracle.
    Pros. Then, as my gift and thine own acquisition
Worthily purchas'd, take my daughter: but
If thou dost break her virgin-knot before
VII—10

All sanctimonious ceremonies may
With full and holy rite be minister'd,
No sweet aspersion shall the heavens let fall
To make this contract grow; but barren hate,
Sour-eyed disdain and discord shall bestrew
The union of your bed with weeds so loathly
That you shall hate it both: therefore take heed,
As Hymen's lamps shall light you.

Fer.   As I hope
For quiet days, fair issue and long life,
With such love as 't is now, the murkiest den, ·
The most opportune place, the strong'st suggestion
Our worser genius can, shall never melt
Mine honour into lust, to take away
The edge of that day's celebration
When I shall think, or Phœbus' steeds are founder'd,
Or Night kept chain'd below.

Pros.   Fairly spoke.
Sit then and talk with her; she is thine own.
What, Ariel! my industrious servant, Ariel!

Enter ARIEL.

Ari. What would my potent master? here I am.

Pros. Thou and thy meaner fellows your last service
Did worthily perform; and I must use you
In such another trick. Go bring the rabble,
O'er whom I give thee power, here to this place:
Incite them to quick motion; for I must
Bestow upon the eyes of this young couple
Some vanity of mine art; it is my promise,
And they expect it from me.

Ari.   Presently?

Pros. Ay, with a twink.

Ari. Before you can say "come" and "go,"
        And breathe twice and cry "so, so,"
        Each one, tripping on his toe,
        Will be here with mop and mow.
        Do you love me, master? no?

Pros. Dearly, my delicate Ariel. Do not approach
Till thou dost hear me call.

Ari.   Well, I conceive.   [*Exit.*

  Pros. Look thou be true; do not give dalliance
Too much the rein: the strongest oaths are straw
To the fire i' th' blood: be more abstemious,
Or else, good night your vow!

  Fer.   I warrant you, sir;
The white cold virgin snow upon my heart
Abates the ardour of my liver.

  Pros.   Well.
Now come, my Ariel! bring a corollary,
Rather than want a spirit: appear, and pertly!
No tongue! all eyes! be silent.   [*Soft music.*

ACT V.

SCENE I. *Before* PROSPERO's *cell.*

Enter PROSPERO *in his magic robes, and* ARIEL.

  Pros. Now does my project gather to a head:
My charms crack not; my spirits obey; and time
Goes upright with his carriage. How's the day?

  Ari. On the sixth hour; at which time, my lord,
You said our work should cease.

  Pros.   I did say so,
When first I rais'd the tempest. Say, my spirit,
How fares the king and 's followers?

  Ari.   Confin'd together
In the same fashion as you gave in charge,
Just as you left them; all prisoners, sir,
In the line-grove which weather-fends your cell;
They cannot budge till your release. The king,
His brother and yours, abide all three distracted,
And the remainder mourning over them,
Brimful of sorrow and dismay; but chiefly
Him that you term'd, sir, "The good old lord, Gonzalo;"
His tears run down his beard, like winter's drops
From eaves of reeds. Your charm so strongly works 'em
That if you now beheld them, your affections
Would become tender.

  Pros.   Dost thou think so, spirit?

  Ari. Mine would, sir, were I human.

Pros.   And mine shall.
Hast thou, which art but air, a touch, a feeling
Of their afflictions, and shall not myself,
One of their kind, that relish all as sharply
Passion as they, be kindlier mov'd than thou art?
Though with their high wrongs I am struck to the quick,
Yet with my nobler reason 'gainst my fury
Do I take part: the rarer action is
In virtue than in vengeance: they being penitent,
The sole drift of my purpose doth extend
Not a frown further. Go release them, Ariel:
My charms I'll break, their senses I'll restore,
And they shall be themselves.
    Ari.   I'll fetch them, sir.   [*Exit.*
    Pros.   Ye elves of hills, brooks, standing lakes and groves,
And ye that on the sands with printless foot
Do chase the ebbing Neptune and do fly him
When he comes back; you demi-puppets that
By moonshine do the green sour ringlets make,
Whereof the ewe not bites, and you whose pastime
Is to make midnight mushrooms, that rejoice
To hear the solemn curfew; by whose aid,
Weak masters though ye be, I have bedimm'd
The noontide sun, call'd forth the mutinous winds,
And 'twixt the green sea and the azur'd vault
Set roaring war: to the dread rattling thunder
Have I given fire and rifted Jove's stout oak
With his own bolt; the strong-bas'd promontory
Have I made shake and by the spurs pluck'd up
The pine and cedar: graves at my command
Have waked their sleepers, op'd, and let 'em forth
By my so potent art. But this rough magic
I here abjure, and, when I have requir'd
Some heavenly music, which even now I do,
To work mine end upon their senses that
This airy charm is for, I'll break my staff,
Bury it certain fathoms in the earth,
And deeper than did ever plummet sound
I'll drown my book.   [*Solemn music.*

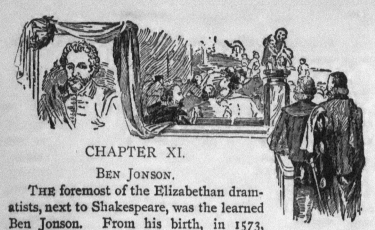

CHAPTER XI.

BEN JONSON.

THE foremost of the Elizabethan dramatists, next to Shakespeare, was the learned Ben Jonson. From his birth, in 1573, to his 'first success as a play-writer, in 1598, not much is definitely known, except that he was of Scotch descent, got his schooling at Westminster and Cambridge, and did 'prentice work for his stepfather—a bricklayer. This he left for service as a volunteer with the army in the Low Countries. When back in London the stage was Ben's clear destiny, first as one of the actors, but soon as actor-author, in which double capacity Shakespeare had already earned fame and fortune. The young playwright had a few months' experience of jail-life for having killed a brother-actor in a duel,—and here he became a Catholic. His earliest comedy, or the earliest performed, was played by the Lord Chamberlain's company, and one of the characters was acted by Shakespeare. This was "Every Man in his Humor." From this sprang the friendship, none the less cordial if tinctured with envy on Jonson's side, between the genial rivals at the Mermaid Tavern. To this play succeeded sundry patchwork contributions to other men's plays; and then "Every Man Out of his Humor," which was performed in the presence of Queen Elizabeth. In 1600 Jonson sought to win her favor by a skillful piece of flattery, entitled "Cynthia's Revels," in which certain satirical passages wounded the dignity of Dekker and Marston, two of his associate playwrights, and provoked a retort from the former. Hearing that this was coming, Jonson hurried the production of "The Poetaster," ridiculing the pettiness of the versemakers. Within a year or two the jibing satirists were friends again, collaborating in other plays. The classical tragedy entitled "Sejanus, his Fall," was performed in 1603, with Shakespeare in one of the parts.

The general run of Jonson's dramas is in the opposite direction to that of popularity: the narrative is involved, the wit bright and pungent, but hammered out too finely, and the dialogue overlaid with pedantic veneering. The intellectual strength underneath is unmistakable. His more serious plays may be described as Dekker describes their author: "Large of frame, bony, meagre of flesh (in his earlier years), pockmarked, and with eager eyes for piercing glances and for soaring up to the heights of poetry." His comedies, including "Volpone, or, The Fox;" "Epicœne, or, The Silent Woman;" "The Alchemist;" "Bartholemew Fair," and "The Devil is an Ass," were written prior to 1616, when for ten years he ceased to write for the stage.

The death of Queen Elizabeth found Jonson turning to the concocting of masques and similar entertainments, which won the patronage of the king and nobility, in whose houses they were performed. He succeeded better as poet than as dramatist. Here and there in his plays—especially in the tragedy, "Catiline, his Conspiracy"—are lyrics of the true ring; and in his collections—"The Forest" and "Under-woods"—are many examples of pure poetry in various measures, on varied themes. His "Epigrams," too, of which he was tenderly proud, displayed his versatility of handiwork. In 1618 Jonson tramped from London to Scotland, where he sojourned with congenial Drummond of Hawthornden, whose recorded "Conversations" give a vivid picture of the English-man. Despite his laureate pension Jonson was impecunious. He says his plays had not brought him two hundred pounds in all. So in 1625 he took to play-making again, without great results. On the failure of the latest comedy, called "The New Inn," Jonson published an epilogue protest against the neglect on the part of the King and Queen. To this Charles I. replied with the annual grant of £100, and a tierce of Canary wine, which long continued to be the laureate's perquisite. His latter days were gladdened by the homage of all lovers of literature. Jonson died on August 6, 1637, in his sixty-fourth year.

SIR EPICURE MAMMON.

SCENE.—*Subtle the Alchemist's House.*

Mammon. Come on, sir. Now you set your foot on shore
In *novo orbe.* Here's the rich Peru:
And then within, sir, are the golden mines,
Great Solomon's Ophir! He was sailing to 't
Three years, but we have reached it in ten months.
This is the day wherein to all my friends
I will pronounce the happy word, Be rich.
This day you shall be *spectatissimi.*
You shall no more deal with the hollow die,
Or the frail card. No more be at charge of keeping
The livery punk for the young heir, that must
Seal at all hours in his shirt. No more,
If he deny, ha' him beaten to 't, as he is
That brings him the commodity. No more
Shall thirst of satin, or the covetous hunger
Of velvet entrails for a rude-spun cloak
To be displayed at Madam Augusta's, make
The sons of Sword and Hazard fall before
The golden calf, and on their knees whole nights
Commit idolatry with wine and trumpets;
Or go a-feasting after drum and ensign;
No more of this. You shall start up young viceroys,
And have your punques and punquetees, my Surly:
And unto thee I speak it first, Be rich.
Where is my Subtle there? within ho—
    Face (within). Sir, he'll come to you by and by.
    Mam. That's his fire-drake,
His Lungs, his Zephyrus, he that puffs his coals
Till he firk nature up in her own centre.
You are not faithful, sir. This night I'll change
All that is metal in thy house to gold:
And early in the morning will I send
To all the plumbers and the pewterers,
And buy their tin and lead up; and to Lothbury
For all the copper.
    Surly. What, and turn that too?

Mam. Yes, and I'll purchase Devonshire and Cornwall,
And make them perfect Indies! You admire now?

Sur. No, faith.

Mam. But when you see the effects of the great medicine!
Of which one part projected on a hundred
Of Mercury, or Venus, or the Moon,
Shall turn it to as many of the Sun;
Nay, to a thousand, so *ad infinitum:*
You will believe me.

Sur. Yes, when I see 't, I will.

Mam. Ha! why,
Do you think I fable with you? I assure you,
He that has once the flower of the Sun,
The perfect Ruby, which we call Elixir,
Not only can do that, but by its virtue
Can confer honor, love, respect, long life,
Give safety, valor, yea and victory,
To whom he will. In eight and twenty days
I'll make an old man of fourscore a child.

Sur. No doubt; he's that already.

Mam. Nay, I mean,
Restore his years, renew him like an eagle,
To the fifth age; make him get sons and daughters,
Young giants, as our philosophers have done
(The ancient patriarchs afore the flood,)
By taking, once a week, on a knife's point,
The quantity of a grain of mustard of it,
Become stout Marses and beget young Cupids.

Sur. The decayed vestals of Pickt-hatch would thank you,
That keep the fire alive there.

Mam. 'Tis the secret
Of nature naturized 'gainst all infections,
Cures all diseases, coming of all causes;
A month's grief in a day; a year's in twelve;
And of what age soever, in a month:
Past all the doses of your drugging doctors;
I'll undertake withal to fright the plague
Out o' the kingdom in three months.

Sur. And I'll
Be bound the players shall sing your praises, then,
Without their poets.

Mam. Sir, I'll do 't. Meantime,

I'll give away so much unto my man,
Shall serve the whole city with preservative
Weekly; each house his dose, and at the rate—
  Sur. As he that built the water-work does with water!
  Mam. You are incredulous.
  Sur. Faith, I have humor.
I would not willingly be gulled. Your Stone
Cannot transmute me.
  Mam. Pertinax Surly,
Will you believe antiquity? Records?
I'll show you a book, where Moses and his sister,
And Solomon, have written of the art!
Aye, and a treatise penned by Adam.
  Sur. How?
  Mam. Of the Philosopher's Stone and in High Dutch.
  Sur. Did Adam write, sir, in High Dutch?
  Mam. He did;
Which proves it was the primitive tongue.
  Sur. What paper?
  Mam. Cedar-board.
  Sur. O that, indeed, they say,
Will last 'gainst worms.
  Mam. 'Tis like your Irish wood
'Gainst cobwebs. I have a piece of Jason's fleece too.
Which was no other than a book of Alchemy,
Writ in large sheep-skin, a good fat ram-vellum.
Such was Pythagoras' Thigh, Pandora's Tub,
And all that fable of Medea's charms,
The manner of our work; the bulls, our furnace,
Still breathing fire: our *Argent-vive*, the Dragon:
The Dragon's teeth, Mercury sublimate,
That keeps the whiteness, hardness and the biting:
And they are gathered into Jason's helm,
(Th' Alembick,) and then sowed in Mars his field,
And thence sublimed so often, till they are fixed.
Both this, the Hesperian Garden, Cadmus' Story,
Jove's Shower, the Boon of Midas, Argus' Eyes,
Boccace his Demogorgon, thousands more,
All abstract riddles of our Stone.

BEAUMONT AND FLETCHER.

Two young men of the Elizabethan dramatic group found themselves united by a rare sympathy of ideal friendship and a like genius, which endured till death. The twinship of Beaumont and Fletcher was that of soul as well as intellect. Their work is a perfect harmony of diverse powers, and it is as unnecessary as it is difficult to apportion its beauties to one or the other of its gifted creators.

John Fletcher was born in 1579, and Francis Beaumont in 1584, or 1585. Fletcher's father ultimately became Bishop of London, but the youth had a hard struggle to live, being orphaned at seventeen. He had been through Cambridge, and thence to London, with the usual experience of a hack writer for the stage. Beaumont's father was on the bench of the common pleas, with the honors of knighthood. He left Oxford without graduating, entered the Inner Temple bar, and took to paraphrasing tales from Ovid. Very soon this pair of literary adventurers embarked upon their communistic career, sharing bed and board and clothes, as they shared in their toil and ambition. They were playwrights from necessity and poets by choice. Whether they had produced an earlier play than "Philaster; or, Love Lies a-Bleeding," is not known. It was their first success, and was performed in 1609, if not the year before; but they had both enjoyed the distinction of prefixing poems of their own to the published version of Jonson's comedy "Volpone," in 1607, when Fletcher was twenty-eight and Beaumont only twenty-two. Within eight years Beaumont died, only a few weeks before the death of Shakespeare. Their principal joint works were written between 1607 and 1612, as Beaumont wrote no more for the stage after his marriage in 1613. The best collected edition of the plays "by Beaumont and Fletcher" did not appear until thirty-one years after Beaumont's death and twenty-two years after Fletcher's, and the latter was sole author of many which bore their joint names.

Of their best plays, accepted as of their authorship, these five rank highest: "Philaster," "A King no King," "The

Maid's Tragedy," "The Scornful Lady," and "Four Plays in One." It is possible that others had some share in the "Cupid's Revenge," the "Coxcomb," and the "Captain." There are no fewer than fifty-six dramas in all in which traces, at least, of both writers are found, but chiefly of Fletcher. The "Woman Hater," and the "Masque of the Inner Temple," and "The Honest Man's Fortune," are regarded as Beaumont's work. Fletcher collaborated with Shakespeare in "The Two Noble Kinsmen." In loftiness of imagination, purity of style and strength, Beaumont surpassed the more exuberant and lighter touch of his co-worker. Their masterpieces are "Philaster" and ' The Maid's Tragedy," splendid examples of poetical romance at its highest. Where Beaumont excelled in pathos, the elder sparkled in wit and drollery; yet the former produced the brilliant burlesque on the romance of chivalry (ridiculed a few years earlier by Cervantes in his "Don Quixote"), entitled the "Knight of the Burning Pestle." Fletcher's greatest comedy, perhaps his chief work, is "Rule a Wife and Have a Wife;" and not much inferior in merit, though belonging to another order of mixed comedy and romance, are "The Little French Lawyer," "The Custom of the Country," "The Wild-goose Chase," and "The Noble Gentleman,"—the last being pure extravaganza. The poetical element which informs the whole range of Beaumont and Fletcher's dramatic pieces has already been remarked upon; but, outside the plays proper, both are entitled to rank with the foremost poets of even their golden age. Though cast in dramatic form, Fletcher's famous "Faithful Shepherdess" is a lyrical gem of purest ray. His touch here is matched with the sweetest notes of Milton, whose "Comus" owes much to this first model.

Fletcher's death occurred in 1625. Where both had the gift it is ungracious to seek to draw comparisons of merit. Great as each was in the literary art, together they compounded a body of dramatic and lyric poetry which Shakespeare need not have hesitated to own. The exquisite charm of their lighter verse is not surpassed, in all that gives immortality to human work, by the more impressive volume of their writings for the theatre.

PHILASTER'S JEALOUSY.

IN the tragi-comedy "Philaster, or Love Lies a-Bleeding," Philaster finds the boy Bellario in the forest, and takes him into his service. Afterwards he gives the boy as servant to the princess Arethusa, with whom he is in love. Bellario serves both faithfully, but the prince becomes jealous. Eventually it turns out that the boy is a girl who had disguised herself to be near Philaster, whom she had loved hopelessly.

Bellario. Health to you, my lord;
The princess doth commend her love, her life,
And this unto you.
    Philaster. O Bellario,
Now I perceive she loves me, she does show it
In loving thee, my boy; she has made thee brave.
    Bell. My lord, she has attired me past my wish,
Past my desert, more fit for her attendant,
Though far unfit for me who do attend.
    Phi. Thou art grown courtly, boy. O let all women
That love black deeds learn to dissemble here.
Here by this paper she does write to me
As if her heart were mines of adamant
To all the world besides, but unto me
A maiden snow that melted with my looks.
Tell me, my boy, how doth the princess use thee?
For I shall guess her love to me by that.
    Bell. Scarce like her servant, but as if I were
Something allied to her, or had preserved
Her life three times by my fidelity;
As mothers fond do use their only sons;
As I'd use one that's left unto my trust,
For whom my life should pay if he met harm,
So does she use me.
    Phi. Why this is wondrous well:
But what kind language does she feed thee with?
    Bell. Why, she does tell me, she will trust my youth
With all her loving secrets, and does call me
Her pretty servant, bids me weep no more
For leaving you; she'll see my services
Regarded: and such words of that soft strain,

That I am nearer weeping when she ends
Than ere she spake.

   Phi. This is much better still.

   Bell. Are you ill, my lord?

   Phi. Ill? No, Bellario.

   Bell. Methinks your words
Fall not from off your tongue so evenly,
Nor is there in your looks that quietness,
That I was wont to see.

   Phi. Thou art deceived, boy.—And she strokes thy head?

   Bell. Yes.

   Phi. And she does clap thy cheeks?

   Bell. She does, my lord.

   Phi. And she does kiss thee, boy, ha?

   Bell. How, my lord?

   Phi. She kisses thee?

   Bell. Not so, my lord.

   Phi. Come, come, I know she does.

   Bell. No, by my life.
Ay, now I see why my disturbed thoughts
Were so perplexed when first I went to her;
My heart held augury. You are abused,
Some villain has abused you; I do see
Whereto you tend; fall rocks upon his head,
That put this to you; 'tis some subtle train
To bring that noble frame of yours to naught.

   Phi. Thou think'st I will be angry with thee. Come,
Thou shall know all my drift. I hate her more
Than I love happiness, and placed thee there
To pry with narrow eyes into her deeds.
Hast thou discovered? is she fallen to lust,
As I would wish her? Speak some comfort to me.

   Bell. My lord, you did mistake the boy you sent,
Had she a sin that way, hid from the world,
I would not aid
Her base desires; but what I came to know
As servant to her, I would not reveal,
To make my life last ages.

   Phi. O my heart!
This is a salve worse than the main disease.
Tell me thy thoughts; for I will know the least
That dwells within thee, or will rip thy heart

To know it; I will see thy thoughts as plain
As I do know thy face.

    Bell. Why, so you do.
She is (for aught I know), by all the gods,
As chaste as ice; but were she foul as hell,
And I did know it, thus; the breath of kings,
The points of swords, tortures, nor bulls of brass,
Should draw it from me.

    Phi. Then it is no time
To dally with thee; I will take thy life,
For I do hate thee; I could curse thee now.

    Bell. If you do hate, you
   could not curse me
   worse;
The gods have not a pun-
   ishment in store
Greater for me than is your
   hate.

    Phi. Fie, fie,
So young and so dissemb-
   ling! fearest thou not
   death?
Can boys contemn that?

    Bell. Oh, what boy is he
Can be content to live to be
   a man,
That sees the best of men
   thus passionate,
Thus without reason?

    Phi. Oh, but thou dost not
   know what 'tis to die.

    Bell. Yes, I do know, my lord!
'Tis less than to be born; a lasting sleep;
A quiet resting from all jealousy;
A thing we all pursue; I know besides
It is but giving over of a game
That must be lost.

    Phi. But there are pains, false boy,
For perjured souls; think but on these, and then
Thy heart will melt, and thou wilt utter all.

    Bell. May they fall all upon me whilst I live,
If I be perjured, or have ever thought

Of that you charge me with; if I be false,
Send me to suffer in those punishments
You speak of; kill me.
   Phi. Oh, what should I do?
Why, who can but believe him? He does swear
So earnestly, that if it were not true,
The gods would not endure him. Rise, Bellario;
Thy protestations are so deep, and thou
Dost look so truly when thou utter'st them,
That though I know them false, as were my hopes,
I cannot urge thee further; but thou wert
To blame to injure me, for I must love
Thy honest looks, and take no revenge upon
Thy tender youth: a love from me to thee
Is firm whate'er thou dost: it troubles me
That I have called the blood out of thy cheeks,
That did so well become thee: but, good boy,
Let me not see thee more; something is done
That will distract me, that will make me mad,
If I behold thee; if thou tender'st me,
Let me not see thee.
   Bell. I will fly as far
As there is morning, ere I give distaste
To that most honored mind. But through these tears
Shed at my hopeless parting, I can see
A world of treason practised upon you,
And her, and me. Farewell for evermore;
If you shall hear that sorrow struck me dead,
And after find me loyal, let there be
A tear shed from you in my memory,
And I shall rest at peace.

THE HOME-MADE DUKE.

IN Beaumont and Fletcher's play, "The Noble Gentleman," an intriguing wife and her companions persuade Monsieur Mount-Marine that the king has conferred many favors on him and made him a duke. Their purpose is to keep him in the city that they may spend his money. Afterwards, in further prosecution of the same design, they pretend to have been ordered to unmake the poor dupe.

SCENE—*A room in the house of Marine.*

Longueville. Where's Monsieur Mount-Marine?
Gentleman. Why, there he stands; will ye aught with him?

Long. Yes.

Good-day, Monsieur Marine!

    Marine. Good-day to you.

    Long. His majesty doth recommend himself

Most kindly to you, sir, and hath, by me,

Sent you this favor: kneel down; rise a knight!

    Mar. I thank his majesty!

    Long. And he doth further

Request you not to leave the court so soon;

For though your former merits have been slighted,

After this time there shall no office fall

Worthy your spirit (as he doth confess

There's none so great) but you shall surely have it.

    Gent. (*aside to Marine*). Do you hear? If you yield yet,

       you are an ass.

    Mar. I'll show my service to his majesty

In greater things than these; but for this small one

I must entreat his highness to excuse me.

    Long. I'll bear your knightly words unto the king,

And bring his princely answer back again.   [*Exit.*

    Gent. Well said! Be resolute a while; I know

There is a tide of honors coming on;

I warrant you!   [*Enter Beaufort.*

    Beaufort. Where is this new-made knight?

    Mar. Here, sir.

    Beau. Let me enfold you in my arms,

Then call you lord! the king will have it so:

Who doth entreat your lordship to remember

His message sent to you by Longueville.

    Gent. If you be dirty, and dare not mount aloft,

You may yield now; I know what I would do.

    Mar. Peace! I will fit him.—Tell his majesty

I am a subject, and I do confess

I serve a gracious prince, that thus hath heaped

Honors on me without desert; but yet

As for the message, business urgeth me,

I must begone, and he must pardon me,

Were he ten thousand kings and emperors.

    Beau. I'll tell him so.

    Gent. (*aside*). Why, this was like yourself!

    Beau. As he hath wrought him, 'tis the finest fellow

That e'er was Christmas-lord! he carries it

So truly to the life, as though he were
One of the plot to gull himself.   [*Exit.*

  Gent. Why, so!
You sent the wisest and the shrewdest answer
Unto the king, I swear, my honored friend,
That ever any subject sent his liege.

  Mar. Nay, now I know I have him on the hip,
I'll follow it.   [*Enter Longueville.*

  Long. My honorable lord!
Give me your noble hand, right courteous peer,
And from henceforward be a courtly earl;
The king so wills, and subjects must obey:
Only he doth desire you to consider
Of his request.

  Gent. Why, faith, you are well, my lord;
Yield to him.

  Mar. Yield? Why, 'twas my plot—

  Gent. Nay,
'Twas your wife's plot.

  Mar. To get preferment by it.
And thinks he now to pop me in the mouth
But with an earldom? I'll be one step higher.

  Gent. (*aside*). It is the finest lord! I am afraid anon
He will stand upon't to share the kingdom with him.
     [*Enter Beaufort.*

  Beau. Where's this courtly earl?
His majesty commends his love unto you,
And will you but now grant to his request,
He bids you be a duke, and choose of whence.

  Gent. Why, if you yield not now, you are undone;
What can you wish to have more, but the kingdom?

  Mar. So please his majesty, I would be duke
Of Burgundy, because I like the place.

  Beau. I know the king is pleased.

  Mar. Then will I stay,
And kiss his highness' hand.

  Beau. His majesty
Will be a glad man when he hears it.

  Long. (*aside to the Gent.*). But how shall we keep this from
     the world's ear,
That some one tell him not, he is no duke?

  Gent. We'll think of that anon.—Why, gentlemen,

VII- -*1*

Is this a gracious habit for a duke?
Each gentle body set a finger to,
To pluck the clouds of these his riding weeds
From off the orient sun, off his best clothes;
I'll pluck one boot and spur off.   [*They pluck him.*

   Long. I another.

   Beau. I'll pluck his jerkin off.

   Gent. Sit down, my lord.—

Both his spurs off at once, good Longueville!
And, Beaufort, take that scarf off, and that hat.
Now set your gracious foot to this of mine;
One pluck will do it; so! Off with the other!

   Long. Lo, thus your servant Longueville doth pluck
The trophy of your former gentry off.
Off with his jerkin, Beaufort!

   Gent. Didst thou never see
A nimble tailor stand so in his stockings,
Whilst some friend helped to pluck his jerkin off,
To dance a jig?   [*Enter Jaques*

   Long. Here's his man Jaques come,
Booted and ready still.

   Jaques. My mistress stays.
Why, how now, sir? What does your worship mean,
To pluck your grave and thrifty habit off?

   Mar. My slippers, Jaques!

   Long. O thou mighty duke!
Pardon this man, that thus hath trespassed,
In ignorance.

   Mar. I pardon him.

   Long. Jaques!
His grace's slippers!

   Jaques. Why, what's the matter?

   Long. Footman, he's a duke:
The king hath raised him above all his land.   [*Enter Lady.*

   Gent. See, see my mistress!

   Long. (*aside*). Let's observe their greeting

   Lady. Unto your will, as every good wife ought,
I have turned all my thoughts, and now am ready.

   Mar. O wife, I am not worthy to kiss
The least of all thy toes, much less thy thumb,
Which yet I would be bold with! All thy counsel
Hath been to me angelical; but mine

To thee hath been most dirty, like my mind.
Dear duchess, I must stay.

   Lady. What! are you mad,
To make me dress and undress, turn and wind me,
Because you find me pliant? Said I not
The whole world should not alter me, if once
I were resolved? and now you call me duchess·
Why, what's the matter?

   Mar. Lo! a knight doth kneel.

   Lady. A knight?

   Mar. A lord.

   Lady. A fool.

   Mar. I say doth kneel
An earl, a duke.

   Long. In drawers.

   Beau. Without shoes.

   Lady. Sure you are lunatic!

   Gent. No, honored duchess
If you dare but believe your servant's truth,
I know he is a duke.

   Lady. Your grace's pardon. . . . .

   Long. The choicest fortunes wait upon our duke!

   Gent. And give him all content and happiness!

   Beau. Let his great name live to the end of time!

   Mar. We thank you, and are pleased to give you notice
We shall at fitter times wait on your loves;
Till when, be near us.

   Long. May it please your grace
To see the city? 't will be to the minds
And much contentment of the doubtful people.

   Mar. I am determined so. Till my return,
I leave my honored duchess to her chamber.
Be careful of your health! I pray you be so.

   Gent. Your grace shall suffer us, your humble servants,
To give attendance, fit so great a person,
Upon your body?

   Mar. I am pleased so.

   Long. (*aside*). Away, good Beaufort; raise a guard sufficient
To keep him from the reach of tongues; be quick!
And, do you hear? remember how the streets
Must be disposed for cries and salutations—
Your grace determines not to see the king?

Mar. Not yet; I shall be ready ten days hence
To kiss his highness' hand, and give him thanks,
As it is fit I should, for his great bounty.
Set forward, gentlemen!

Groom. Room for the duke there!   [*They issue forth.*
Room there afore; sound! Room, and keep your places.
And you may see enough; keep your places!

Long. These people are too far unmannered, thus
To stop your grace's way with multitudes.

Mar. Rebuke them not, good monsieur. 'Tis their loves,
Which I will answer, if it please my stars
To spare me life and health.

2 Gent. God bless your grace!

Mar. And you, with all my heart.

1 Gent. Now Heaven preserve you!

Mar. I thank you too.

2 Gent. Now Heaven save your grace!

Mar. I thank you all.

Beau. On there before!

Mar. Stand, gentlemen!
Stay yet a while; I'm minded to impart
My love to these good people, and my friends,
Whose love and prayers for my greatness
Are equal in abundance. Note me well,
And with my words my heart; for as the tree——

Long. Your grace had best beware; 't will be informed
Your greatness with the people.

Mar. I had more,
My honest and ingenuous people: but
The weight of business hath prevented me;
I am called from you; but this tree I speak of
Shall bring forth fruit, I hope, to your content;
And so, I share my bowels amongst you all.

All. A noble duke! a very noble duke!

.   .   .   .   .

1 Gent. Afore there, gentlemen!

2 Gent. You are fairly met, good monsieur
            Mount-Marine!

1 Gent. Be advised! the time is altered.

2 Gent. Is he not the same man he was afore?

Mar. Still the same man to you, sir.

Long. You have received mighty grace; be thankful.

Gent. Let me not die in ignorance.

Long. You shall not:

Then know, the king out of his love, hath pleased
To style him duke of Burgundy.
  Gent. Oh, great duke,
Thus low I plead for pardon, and desire
To be enroll'd amongst your poorest slaves.
  Mar. Sir, you have mercy, and withal my hand;
From henceforth let me call you one of mine.
  Gent. Make room afore there, and dismiss the people!
  Mar. Every man to his house in peace and quiet!
  People. Now Heaven preserve the duke! Heaven
            bless the duke!
Your grace is well return'd.
  Mar. As well as may be;
Never in younger health, never more able:
I mean to be your bed-fellow this night;
Let me have good encounter.
  Beau. Bless me, Heaven,
What a hot meat this greatness is!
  Long. It may be so;
For I'll be sworn he hath not got a snap
This two months on my knowledge, or her woman
Is damn'd for swearing it.
  Mar. I thank you, gentlemen, for your attendance,
And also your great pains! Pray know my lodgings
Better and oftner; do so, gentlemen!
Now, by my honour, as I am a prince,
I speak sincerely, know my lodgings better,
And be not strangers! I shall see your service
Under your deservings, when you least expect—
  All. We humbly thank your grace for this great favour.

CHAPTER XII.

THE DRAMA OF THE RESTORATION.

The closing of the theaters by Parliament at the outbreak
of the civil war threw a large number of professional actors
out of employment.   Some found places in the royal army;
others drifted about, doing whatever they could to make
a living.   However, the Puritan element, which had worked
so incessantly for the undoing of the theaters, was not everywhere equally strong, and sometimes players banded together
and strolled about through the country, presenting plays as
they were able. The offense being partly in the name, they prepared *drolls*—humorous and farcical sketches taken generally
from plays.   The *drolls* were welcomed at fairs and elsewhere
when people congregated for some relaxation other than religious service. One of the most popular appears to have been
the *droll* entitled: *Bottom the Weaver,* from *Midsummer
Night's Dream.* Actors who were too daring in violating the
law came sometimes to grief; we read of an entire company
being "hauled off to jail in their stage clothes."

With the return of the Stuarts a reaction set in.   Only
part of England was Puritan and even many Puritans had
grown weary of the rule under the Commonwealth.   Particularly did the royalists welcome a return of the old régime.
They plunged into pleasures so long forbidden with great
zest.   The king brought back to his native land the worst of
that life he had known at the French Court.   At no other time
has morality witnessed such an ebb.   Yet the corruption of
society was not general; it affected the Court and those in
any way attached to it, while the people as a whole retained
the wholesome moral tone so characteristic of the English
nation.

Charles II. shared the love of plays peculiar to his house
and the Tudors. He encouraged players and made immediate
plans for the building of new theaters. However, the plays
in favor were not those which had delighted Elizabethan
audiences. Nor was this to have been expected. Many years
had passed since that mighty outburst of dramatic literature

which caught the ear of the people and stimulated them to renewed energy. The conditions which had produced it were gone forever. Fresh interests filled the minds of all; a break had come in the chain of dramatic development and it could not be resumed where it had been broken. The beginning of a dramatic decline had begun soon after the death of Shakespeare. The plays of Beaumont and Fletcher held popular appreciation but they lacked the strength and originality of the Elizabethan dramas.

It is important to note that the Restoration drama ceased to be national. Instead, it became the expression of that life which was peculiar to the Court and its admirers. Corrupt and sensual, it demanded these elements in its plays.

As has been repeatedly stated, the drama far more than any other form of literature mirrors the life of the people. While it may be local and pertain especially to the age and country which produces it, nevertheless if it be destined to survive, it will reach beneath the surface and treat of themes which are potent in all ages and with which people generally can sympathize. As quickly as it comes to reflect the life of an exclusive body of people, living under circumstances which at once place them in a class by themselves with experiences that the average person cannot adequately grasp, the drama is no longer national, to be sure, but furthermore it lacks vitality to long endure.

Sensuality pervaded the Court and its followers. A profligate ruler set an example which many of his subjects were not slow to follow. Those whose days and nights were filled to the brim with intrigue and all kinds of self-indulgence, would not be attracted to plays bearing a strong moral tone. The coarser the jest, the more abandoned the character, the more dissipated the rake, the better did it please. The king encouraged the writing of plays and favored comedy. Those who wrote it did so particularly to win royal favor. The result was inevitable. Women attended the theaters masked, allowing a license which could hardly have been otherwise tolerated. Small wonder was it that the pious Puritan stood aghast at the spectacles which the theater often presented.

In addition to the immoral tendencies just noted, the Restoration drama became a political medium. Party feeling ran high. Prologues and epilogues gave opportunity for political harangues. Plays were written to satirize individuals and parties. One finds in these plays indications of popular feeling in political matters.

Dryden remains the most imposing figure of the seventeenth century. It is safe to say that the best that was done in the interest of the drama was done by him. Belonging to an age known today as artificial, he labored for style rather than content. At first he tried to bring back rhyme as the language of the play, but at length was obliged to abandon it.

One of the wittiest of Restoration playwrights was Congreve, who wrote but four comedies. Few men have enjoyed more praise and commendation during their life than he. Being genial and clever, social leaders and scholars welcomed him alike. His style is clear and vivid; he never used a word too much. But for the criticism common to plays of this period, that the lack of reputations, honor and character grows monotonous when it becomes the general rule, his plays are today entertaining to read. *The Double Dealer, The Old Bachelor* and *The Way of the World* were played for many years. Today they are seldom read except by those who wish to profit by Congreve's unusual mastery of diction.

It would afford the general reader but scant pleasure and small profit to follow the productions that filled the Restoration period. They are known merely as names for the most part, and those which survive are interesting only to the student of this century.

Only three enduring plays were forthcoming during the eighteenth century—all comedies: Goldsmith's *She Stoops to Conquer*, and Sheridan's *Rivals* and *School for Scandal*. These are occasionally presented on the stage today and always carry the favorable appreciation of their audiences.

The drama fell into a decline. The novel took its place. People ceased to gather so frequently at the playhouse for diversion and found it more frequently by their own firesides with stories that thrilled them as their forefathers had been thrilled by Marlowe, Peele and Greene, by Shakespeare and Ben Jonson. Theaters did not cease to be; on the contrary, they multiplied as the population increased. However they no longer held the same place in the lives of people generally.

THE DOUBLE DEALER.

(*A Gallery in Lord Touchwood's House.*)

Mellefont. Ned, Ned, whither so fast? what, turned flincher? why, you won't leave us?

Careless. Where are the women? I'm weary of guzzling, and begin to think them the better company.

Mel. Then thy reason staggers, and thou'rt almost drunk.

Care. No, faith, but your fools grow noisy; and if a man must endure the noise of words without sense, I think the women have more musical voices, and become nonsense better.

Mel. Why, they are at the end of the gallery, retired to their tea and scandal, according to their ancient custom, after dinner; but I made a pretense to follow you, because I had something to say to you in private, and I am not like to have many opportunities this evening.

Care. And here's this coxcomb most critically come to interrupt you. [*Enter Brisk.*

Brisk. Boys, boys, lads, where are you? What, do you give ground! mortgage for a bottle, ha? Careless, this is your trick; you're always spoiling company by leaving it.

Care. And thou art always spoiling company by coming into it.

Brisk. Pooh! ha! ha! ha! I know you envy me; spite, proud spite, by the gods! and burning envy. I'll be judged by Mellefont here, who gives and takes raillery better than you or I. Pshaw, man! when I say you spoil company by leaving it, I mean you leave nobody for the company to laugh at. I think there I was with you, ha, Mellefont?

Mel. On my word, Brisk, that was a home-thrust; you have silenced him.

Brisk. Oh, my dear Mellefont, let me perish if thou art not the soul of conversation, the very essence of wit, and spirit of wine!—The deuce take me, if there were three good things said, or one understood, since thy amputation from the body of our society.—He! I think that's pretty and metaphorical enough: egad I could not have said it out of thy company, Careless, ha?

Care. Hum, ay, what is't?

Brisk. O, *mon cœur!* what is't? Nay gad I'll punish you for want of apprehension: the deuce take me if I tell you.

Mel. No, no, hang him, he has no taste.—But, dear Brisk, excuse me, I have a little business.

Care. Prithee get thee gone; thou seest we are serious.

Mel. We'll come immediately, if you'll but go in, and keep up good-humour and sense in the company; prithee do, they'll fall asleep else.

Brisk. Egad, so they will. Well, I will, I will, egad, you shall command me from the zenith to the nadir.—But the deuce take me if I say a good thing till you come. But prithee, dear rogue, make haste, prithee make haste, I shall burst else.—And yonder's your uncle, my Lord Touchwood, swears he'll disinherit you, and Sir Paul Plyant threatens to disclaim you for a son-in-law, and my Lord Froth won't dance at your wedding tomorrow, nor, the deuce take me, I won't write your epithalamium—and see what a condition you're like to be brought to.

Mel. Well, I'll speak but three words, and follow you.

Brisk. Enough, enough.—Careless, bring your apprehension along with you.

Care. Pert coxcomb!

Mel. Faith, 'tis a good-natured coxcomb, and has very entertaining follies; you must be more humane to him; at this juncture, it will do me service. I'll tell you though, I would have mirth continued this day at any rate; though patience purchase folly, and attention be paid with noise; there are times when sense may be unseasonable, as well as truth. Prithee, do thou wear none today; but allow Brisk to have wit, that thou may seem a fool.

Care. Why, how now? why this extravagant proposition?

Mel. Oh, I would have no room for serious design, for I am jealous of a plot. I would have noise and impertinence keep my Lady Touchwood's head from working; for hell is not more busy than her brain, nor contains more devils than her imaginations.

Care. I thought your fear of her had been over. Is not tomorrow appointed for your marriage with Cynthia; and her father, Sir Paul Plyant, come to settle the writings this day, on purpose?

Mel. True; but you shall judge whether I have not reason to be alarmed. None besides you and Maskwell are acquainted with the secret of my Aunt Touchwood's violent passion for me. Since my first refusal of her addresses, she has endeavored to do me all ill offices with my uncle; yet has managed 'em with that subtlety that to him they have borne the face of kindness; while her malice, like a dark lantern, only shone upon me where it was directed. . . .

(Gallery in Lord Touchwood's House.)

[*Enter Lady Froth and Cynthia.*

Cyn. Indeed, madam! Is it possible your ladyship could have been so much in love?

Lady Froth. I could not sleep; I did not sleep one wink for three weeks together.

Cyn. Prodigious! I wonder want of sleep, and so much love, and so much wit as your ladyship has, did not turn your brain.

Lady Froth. O my dear Cynthia, you must not rally your friend.—But really, as you say, I wonder, too;—but then I had a way: for between you and me, I had whimsies and vapours, but I gave them vent.

Cyn. How pray, madam?

Lady Froth. Oh, I writ, writ abundantly;—do you never write?

Cyn. Write what?

Lady Froth. Songs, elegies, satires, encomiums, panegyrics, lampoons, plays, and heroic poems.

Cyn. O Lord, not I, madam; I'm content to be a courteous reader.

Lady Froth. O inconsistent! in love, and not write! if my lord and I had been both of your temper, we had never come together.—O bless me! what a sad thing would that have been, if my lord and I should never have met!

Cyn. Then neither my lord nor you would ever have met with your match, on my conscience.

Lady Froth. O' my conscience, no more we should; thou sayest right; for sure my Lord Froth is as fine a gentleman and as much a man of quality! Ah, nothing at all of the common air!—I think I may say he wants nothing but a blue ribbon and a star to make him shine, the very phosphorus of our hemisphere. Do you understand those two hard words? if you don't, I'll explain 'em to you.

Cyn. Yes, yes, madam, I'm not so ignorant. (*Aside.*) At least I won't own it, to be troubled with your instructions.

Lady Froth. Nay, I beg your pardon; but being derived from the Greek, I thought you might have escaped the etymology.—But I'm the more amazed to find you a woman of letters, and not write! bless me! how can Mellefont believe you love him?

Cyn. Why faith, madam, he that won't take my word, shall never have it under my hand.

Lady Froth. I vow Mellefont's a pretty gentleman, but me-thinks he wants a manner.

Cyn. A manner? what's that, madam?

Lady Froth. Some distinguishing quality, as for example, the *bel air* or *brilliant* of Mr. Brisk; the solemnity, yet complaisance of my lord, or something of his own that should look a little *je ne sais quoi;* he is too much a mediocrity, in my mind.

Cyn. He does not indeed affect either pertness or formality, for which I like him. Here he comes.

[*Enter Lord Froth, Mellefont, and Brisk.*

Cyn. (aside). Impertinent creature! I could almost be angry with her now.

Lady Froth. My lord, I have been telling Cynthia how much I have been in love with you, I swear I have; I'm not ashamed to own it now. Ah, it makes my heart leap! I vow, I sigh when I think on't; my dear lord, ha! ha! ha! do you remember, my lord?

Lord Froth. Pleasant creature! perfectly well—Ah, that look! ay, there it is! who could resist? 'was so my heart was made a captive first, and ever since 't has been in love with happy slavery.

Lady Froth. O that tongue! that dear deceitful tongue! that charming softness in your mien, and then your bow! Good my lord, bow as you did when I gave you my picture; here, suppose this my picture.—(*Gives him a pocket mirror.*) Pray mind, my lord; ah, he bows charmingly!—Nay, my lord, you shan't kiss it so much, I shall grow jealous, I vow now.

Lord Froth. I saw myself there and kissed it for your sake.

Lady Froth. Ah, gallantry to the last degree!—Mr. Brisk, you're a judge; was ever anything so well bred as my lord?

Brisk. Never anything but your ladyship, let me perish!

Lady Froth. Oh, prettily turned again! let me die, but you have a great deal of wit!—Mr. Mellefont, don't you think Mr. Brisk has a world of wit?

Mel. Oh yes, madam!

Brisk. O dear, madam—

Lady Froth. An infinite deal?

Brisk. O Heavens, madam—

Lady Froth. More wit than anybody?

Brisk. I'm everlastingly your humble servant, deuce take me, madam.

Lord Froth. Don't you think us a happy couple?

Cyn. I vow my lord, I think you are the happiest couple in the world; for you are not only happy in one another and when you are together, but happy in yourselves, and by yourselves.

Lord Froth. I hope Mellefont will make a good husband, too.

Cyn. 'Tis my interest to believe he will, my lord.

Lord Froth. D'ye think he'll love you as well as I do my wife? I'm afraid not.

Cyn. I believe he'll love me better.

Lord Froth. Heavens! that can never be; but why do you think so?

Cyn. Because he has not so much reason to be fond of himself.

Lord Froth. Oh, your humble servant for that, dear madam. —Well, Mellefont, you'll be a happy creature.

Mel. Ay, my lord, I shall have the same reason for my happiness that your lordship has, I shall think myself happy.

Lord Froth. Ah, that's all.

Brisk (to Lady Froth). Your ladyship's in the right; but, egad, I'm wholly turned to satire. I confess I write but seldom, but when I do—keen iambics, egad! But my lord was telling me, your ladyship has made an essay toward an heroic poem.

Lady Froth. Did my lord tell you? yes, I vow and the subject is my lord's love to me. And what do you think I call it? I dare swear you won't guess—"The Syllabub;" ha! ha! ha!

Brisk. Because my lord's title is Froth, egad; deuce take me, very *à propos* and surprising, ha! ha! ha!

Lady Froth. He! ay, is not it?—And then I call my lord Spumoso, and myself—what do you think I call myself?

Brisk. Lactilla, maybe; 'gad I cannot tell.

Lady Froth. Biddy, that's all; just my own name.

Brisk. Biddy! egad, very pretty!—Deuce take me if your ladyship has not the art of surprising the most naturally in the world!—I hope you'll make me happy in communicating the poem.

Lady Froth. O you must be my confidant, I must ask your advice.

Brisk. I'm your humble servant, let me perish!—I presume your ladyship has read Rossu?

Lady Froth. O yes, and Rapin, and Dacier upon Aristotle and Horace.—My lord, you must not be jealous, I'm communicating all to Mr. Brisk.

Lord Froth. No, no, I'll allow Mr. Brisk; have you nothing about you to show him, my dear?

Lady Froth. Yes, I believe I have.—Mr. Brisk, come, will you go into the next room, and there I'll show you what I have.

Lord Froth. I'll walk a turn in the garden, and come to you.

[*Exit Lord and Lady Froth and Brisk.*

Mel. You're thoughtful, Cynthia?

Cyn. I'm thinking, though marriage makes man and wife one flesh, it leaves them still two fools; and they become more conspicuous by setting off one another.

Mel. That's only when two fools meet, and their follies are opposed.

Cyn. Nay, I have known two wits to meet, and by the opposition of their wit render themselves as ridiculous as fools. 'Tis an odd game we're going to play at; what think you of drawing stakes, and giving over in time?

Mel. No, hang't, that's not endeavoring to win, because it's possible we may lose; since we have shuffled and cut, let's e'en turn up trump now.

Cyn. Then I find it's like cards: if either of us have a good hand, it is an accident of fortune.

Mel. No, marriage is rather like a game at bowls; Fortune indeed makes the match, and the two nearest, and sometimes the two farthest, are together; but the game depends entirely upon judgment.

Cyn. Still it is a game, and consequently one of us must be a loser.

Mel. Not at all; only a friendly trial of skill, and the winnings to be laid out in an entertainment;—What's here, the music? (*Musicians cross the stage.*) Oh, my lord has promised the company a new song; we'll get 'em to give it to us by the way. Pray let us have the favour of you, to practice the song before the company hear it.

SONG.

Cynthia frowns whene'er I woo her,
Yet she's vexed if I give over;
Much she fears I should undo her,
But much more to lose her lover;
Thus in doubting she refuses:
And not winning, thus she loses.
Prithee, Cynthia, look behind you,
Age and wrinkles will o'ertake you;

Then, too late, desire will find you,
When the power must forsake you:
Think, O think, o' the sad condition,
To be past, yet wish fruition!

Mel. You shall have my thanks below.

S. S.
SHAKESPEARE'S COAT OF ARMS

R. B. SHERIDAN.

WIT and high spirits ran in the family from the Thomas Sheridan, D. D., who was Dean Swift's boon companion in Ireland. This clergyman's son combined the profession of acting with ambitious efforts to reform the prevailing system of education, and with such success that Oxford and Cambridge conferred on him their honorary degrees after listening to his lectures. He played *Hamlet* and similar prominent parts, being regarded as second only to Garrick. His romantic marriage resulted in the birth of the dramatist at Dublin in 1751. The father's means, with expectations from his educational scheme, permitted Richard to lead the idle life of a beau of the period, though he produced a few dramatic sketches. As the lover of Miss Linley, the young daughter of a popular composer, and singer at his concerts, Sheridan outrivalled a Captain Matthews, a married suitor, and fought two duels with him. A secret marriage had taken place between the young pair, as the girl's father objected to Sheridan. Not until 1773 were they openly married. On her slender fortune they lived in high style in London, a shrewd scheme for winning friends worth having. When he produced his first comedy, "The Rivals," in 1775, these influential friends made it the talk of the town, which ensured Sheridan good returns. In association with Linley as composer, he produced his opera, "The Duenna," in the same year, the success of which enabled him to buy, first, one half of Garrick's share in Drury Lane theatre, and, two years afterwards, the other half. In 1777 was produced "The School for Scandal," which stands at the head of all comedies by reason of the unbroken level of its wit, its crisp action and keen satire. Though in fact inferior as a work of art to "The Rivals," it has remained till the present day the most popular comedy that holds the stage. The amusing farcical piece, "The Critic," appeared in 1779, and twenty years later the tragedy of "Pizarro," but the dramatist's talents now found new occupation in politics. As their Parliamentary candidate, Sheridan paid the voters of the borough of Stafford five guineas each for electing him their member. His mastery of subjects and skill in oratory at once won him the favor of statesmen. Fox gave him office, leading to his becoming Secretary of the Treasury while yet a young man. When the impeachment of Warren Hastings was under discussion Sheridan spoke for three hours, with so powerful an effect that the House adjourned until it could recover its calmness. His four days' speech on the same topic has been described by Macaulay. His great speeches rank among the worthiest traditions of oratory. The break-up of the Whig party and the death of Fox left Sheridan isolated, and he used his influence as a social companion of the Prince Regent to keep it in the cold. The latter years of Sheridan tell a melancholy story. They were wild days at best; drink and gambling were the rule in fashionable society, and the bloated faces of statesmen and orators, and the shattering of great fortunes on the card table, were common spectacles. Sheridan's gay temperament made him the easiest prey to all the popular vices. The theatre, his only support for thirty years, suffered from his reckless ways, his health was ruined, his parliamentary influence waned under the scandals he courted rather than stopped. Twice his theatre was burnt out. Debts of every kind piled upon his head a load too heavy for a much stronger man than ever he was, and so, hunted by and hiding from the sheriff's officers, at last he found release in death, which came in 1816. Nevertheless, Richard Brinsley Sheridan was buried with all the outward honors among his betters in genius and character in Westminster Abbey.

BOB ACRES' DUEL.

(From "The Rivals.")

Sir Lucius O' Trigger. Mr. Acres, I am delighted to embrace you.

Acres. My dear Sir Lucius, I kiss your hands.

Sir L. Pray, my friend, what has brought you so suddenly to Bath?

Acres. 'Faith, I have followed Cupid's Jack-a-lantern, and find myself in a quagmire at last. In short, I have been very ill-used, Sir Lucius. I don't choose to mention names, but look on me as a very ill-used gentleman.

Sir L. Pray, what is the case? I ask no names.

Acres. Mark me, Sir Lucius:—I fall as deep as need be in love with a young lady—her friends take my part—I follow her to Bath—send word of my arrival—and receive answer that the lady is to be otherwise disposed of. This, Sir Lucius, I call being ill-used.

Sir L. Very ill, upon my conscience! Pray, can you divine the cause of it?

Acres. Why, there's the matter! She has another lover, one Beverley, who, I am told, is now in Bath. Odds slanders and lies! he must be at the bottom of it.

Sir L. A rival in the case, is there?—and you think he has supplanted you unfairly?

Acres. Unfairly! to be sure he has. He never could have done it fairly.

Sir L. Then sure you know what is to be done?

Acres. Not I, upon my soul.

Sir. L. We wear no swords here—but you understand me.

Acres. What! fight him?

Sir L. Ay, to be sure; what can I mean else?

Acres. But he has given me no provocation.

Sir L. Now I think he has given you the greatest provocation in the world. Can a man commit a more heinous offence against another than to fall in love with the same woman? Oh, by my soul, it is the most unpardonable breach of friendship.

Acres. Breach of friendship! Ay, ay; but I have no acquaintance with this man. I never saw him in my life.

Sir L. That's no argument at all—he has the less right, then, to take such a liberty.

Acres. 'Gad, that's true—I grow full of anger, Sir Lucius— I fire apace! Odds hilts and blades! I find a man may have a deal of valor in him and not know it. But couldn't I contrive to have a little right on my side?

Sir L. What the devil signifies *right* when your *honor* is concerned? Do you think Achilles or my little Alexander the Great ever inquired where the right lay? No, by my soul, they drew their broadswords, and left the lazy sons of peace to settle the justice of it.

Acres. Your words are a grenadier's march to my heart. I believe courage must be catching. I certainly do feel a kind of valor rising, as it were—a kind of courage, as I may say—Odds flints, pans, and triggers! I'll challenge him directly.

Sir L. Ah! my little friend, if I had Blunderbuss Hall here I could show you a range of ancestry, in the O'Trigger line, that would furnish the New Room, every one of whom had killed his man. For though the mansion-house and dirty acres have slipped through my fingers, I thank Heaven our honor and the family pictures are as fresh as ever.

Acres. Oh, Sir Lucius, I háve had ancestors too!—every man of them colonel or captain in the militia! Odds balls and barrels! say no more—I'm braced for it. The thunder of your words has soured the milk of human kindness in my breast! Zounds! as the man in the play says, "I could do such deeds"——

Sir L. Come, come, there must be no passion at all in the case; these things should always be done civilly.

Acres. I must be in a passion, Sir Lucius—I must be in a rage! —Dear Sir Lucius, let me be in a rage, if you love me. Come, here's pen and paper. (*Sits down to write.*) I would the ink were red! Indite, I say, indite. How shall I begin? Odds bullets and blades! I'll write a good bold hand, however.

Sir L. Pray compose yourself. [*Sits down.*

Acres. Come, now, shall I begin with an oath? Do, Sir Lucius, let me begin with a dam'me!

Sir L. Pho, pho! do the thing decently, and like a Christian. Begin now—"Sir"—

Acres. That's too civil by half.

Sir L. "To prevent the confusion that might arise"—

Acres. (*Writing and repeating.*) "To prevent the confusion which might arise"—Well?—

Sir L. "From our both addressing the same lady"—

Acres. Ay—there's the reason—"same lady"—Well?—

Sir L. "I shall expect the honor of your company"—

Acres. Zounds, I'm not asking him to dinner!

Sir L. Pray, be easy.

Acres. Well, then, "honor of your company"—

Sir L. "To settle our pretensions"—

Acres. Well?

Sir L. Let me see—aye, King's Mead-fields will do—"in King's Mead-fields."

Acres. So, that's down. Well, I'll fold it up presently; my own crest—a hand and dagger—shall be the seal.

Sir L. You see, now, this little explanation will put a stop at once to all confusion or misunderstanding that might arise between you.

Acres. Ay, we fight to prevent any misunderstanding.

Sir L. Now, I'll leave you to fix your own time. Take my advice and you'll decide it this evening, if you can; then, let the worse come of it, 'twill be off your mind to-morrow.

Acres. Very true.

Sir L. So I shall see nothing more of you unless it be by letter, till the evening. I would do myself the honor to carry your message, but, to tell you a secret, I believe I shall have just such another affair on my own hands. There is a gay captain here who put a jest on me lately at the expense of my country, and I only want to fall in with the gentleman to call him out.

Acres. By my valor, I should like to see you fight first. Odds life! I should like to see you kill him, if it was only to get a little lesson.

Sir L. I shall be very proud of instructing you. Well, for the present—but remember now, when you meet your antagonist, do everything in a mild and agreeable manner. Let your courage be as keen, but at the same time as polished, as your sword.

[*Exit Sir Lucius.*

[*While Acres seals the letter, David his servant enters.*

David. Then, by the mass, sir, I would do no such thing! Ne'er a Sir Lucifer in the kingdom should make me fight when I wa'n't so minded. Oons! what will the old lady say when she hears o't!

Acres. But my honor, David, my honor! I must be very careful of my honor.

David. Ay, by the mass, and I would be very careful of it; and I think, in return, my honor couldn't do less than be very careful of me.

Acres. Odds blades! David, no gentleman will ever risk the loss of his honor!

David. I say, then, it would be but civil in *honor* never to risk the loss of a *gentleman*. Look ye, master, this *honor* seems to me a marvellous false friend; ay, truly, a very courtier-like servant. Put the case, I was a gentleman (which, thank Heaven, no one can say of me), well—my honor makes me quarrel with another gentleman of my acquaintance. So—we fight. (Pleasant enough that!) Boh! I kill him (the more's my luck.) Now, pray, who gets the profit of it? Why, my *honor*. But put the case that he kills me! By the mass! I go to the worms, and my honor whips over to my enemy.

Acres. No, David, in that case—odds crowns and laurels! your honor follows you to the grave.

David. Now that's just the place where I could make a shift to do without it.

Acres. Zounds! David, you are a coward!—It doesn't become my valor to listen to you. What, shall I disgrace my ancestors? Think of that, David—think what it would be to disgrace my ancestors!

David. Under favor, the surest way of not disgracing them is to keep as long as you can out of their company. Look'ee now, master, to go to them in such haste—with an ounce of lead in your brains—I should think might as well be let alone. Our ancestors are very good kind of folks; but they are the last people I should choose to have a visiting acquaintance with.

Acres. But, David, now, you don't think there is such very, very, *very* great danger, hey?—Odds life!—people often fight without any mischief done!

David. By the mass, I think 'tis ten to one against you!—Oons! here to meet some lion-headed fellow, I warrant, with his d——d double-barrelled swords and cut-and-thrust pistols! Lord bless us! it makes me tremble to think o't—those be such desperate bloody-minded weapons! Well, I never could abide 'em!—from a child I never could fancy 'em!—I suppose there a'n't been so merciless a beast in the world as your loaded pistol.

Acres. Zounds! I *won't* be afraid—odds fire and fury! you sha'n't make me afraid—Here is the challenge, and I have sent for my dear friend, Jack Absolute, to carry it for me.

David. Ay, i' the name of mischief, let *him* be the messenger. —For my part, I wouldn't lend a hand to it for the best horse in your stable. By the mass, it don't look like another letter!—It is, as I may say, a designing and malicious-looking letter!—and I warrant smells of gunpowder, like a soldier's pouch!—Oons! I wouldn't swear it mayn't go off.   [*Drops it in alarm.*

Acres. (*Starting.*) Out, you poltroon!—you ha'n't the valor of a grasshopper.

David. Well, I say no more—'twill be sad news, to be sure, at Clod Hall—but I ha' done. How Phillis will howl when she hears of it!—ay, poor bitch, she little thinks what shooting her master's going after!—and I warrant old Crop, who has carried your honor, field and road, these ten years, will curse the hour he was born!   [*Whimpering.*

Acres. It won't do, David—so get along, you coward—I am determined to fight while I'm in the mind.   [*Enter servant.*

Serv. Captain Absolute, sir.

Acres. Oh! show him up.   [*Exit servant.*

David. (*On his knees.*) Well, Heaven send we be all alive this time to-morrow.

Acres. What's that?—Don't provoke me, David!

David. Good-bye, master.   [*Exit David, whimpering.*

Acres. Get along, you cowardly, dastardly, croaking raven.
          [*Enter Captain Absolute.*

Capt. A. What's the matter, Bob?

Acres. A vile, sheep-hearted blockhead; if I hadn't the valor of St. George, and the dragon to boot—

Capt. A. But what do you want with me, Bob?

Acres. Oh! there—(*Gives him the challenge.*)

Capt. A. "To Ensign Beverley." (*Aside.*) So, what's going on now? Well, what's this?.

Acres. A challenge!

Capt. A. Indeed! Why, you won't fight him, will you, Bob?

Acres. 'Egad, but I will, Jack. Sir Lucius has brought me to it. He has left me full of rage—and I'll fight this evening, that so much good passion mayn't be wasted.

Capt. A. But what have I to do with this?

Acres. Why, as I think you know something of this fellow, I want you to find him out for me, and give him this mortal defiance.

Capt. A. Well, give it me, and, trust me, he gets it.

Acres. Thank you, my dear friend, my dear Jack; but it is giving you a great deal of trouble.

Capt. A. Not in the least I beg you won't mention it. No trouble in the world, I assure you.

Mrs. Siddons.—Gainsborough.

Acres. You are very kind. What it is to have a friend!—you couldn't be my second, could you, Jack?

Capt. A. Why no, Bob, not in *this* affair—it would not be quite so proper.

Acres. Well, then, I must get my friend Sir Lucius. I shall have your good wishes, however, Jack?

Capt. A. Whenever he meets you, believe me. [*Enter servant.*

Serv. Sir Anthony Absolute is below, inquiring for the Captain.

Capt. A. I'll come instantly.—Well, my little hero, success attend you. [*Going.*

Acres. Stay, stay, Jack. If Beverley should ask you what kind of a man your friend Acres is, do tell him I am a devil of a fellow—will you, Jack?

Capt. A. To be sure I shall. I'll say you're a determined dog —hey, Bob?

Acres. Ay, do, do—and if that frightens him, 'egad, perhaps he mayn't come. So tell him I generally kill a man a week; will you, Jack?

Capt. A. I will, I will; I'll say you are called in the country "Fighting Bob."

Acres. Right, right—'tis all to prevent mischief; for I don't want to take his life, if I clear my honor.

Capt. A. No! That's very kind of you.

Acres. Why, you don't wish me to kill him; do you, Jack?

Capt. A. No, upon my soul, I do not. But a devil of a fellow, hey? [*Going.*

Acres. True, true. But stay—stay, Jack; you may add that you never saw me in such a rage before—a most devouring rage.

Capt. A. I will, I will.

Acres. Remember, Jack—a determined dog!

Capt. A. Ay, ay—"Fighting Bob." [*Exeunt severally.*

King's Mead-fields.—Enter Sir Lucius and Acres, with pistols.

Acres. By my valor! then, Sir Lucius, forty yards is a good distance. Odds levels and aims! I say it is a good distance.

Sir L. It is for muskets or small fieldpieces; upon my conscience, Mr. Acres, you must leave these things to me. Stay, now; I'll show you. (*Measures six paces.*) There, now, that is a very pretty distance—a pretty gentleman's distance.

Acres. Zounds! we might as well fight in a sentry-box! I tell you, Sir Lucius, the further he is off, the cooler I shall take my aim.

Sir L. 'Faith, then, I suppose you would aim at him best of all if he was out of sight!

Acres. No, Sir Lucius; but I should think forty, or eight-and-thirty yards—

Sir L. Pho, pho! Nonsense! Three or four feet between the mouths of your pistols is as good as a mile.

Acres. Odds bullets, no!—by my valor! there is no merit in killing him so near. Do, my dear Sir Lucius, let me bring him down at a long shot—a long shot, Sir Lucius, if you love me!

Sir L. Well, the gentleman's friend and I must settle that. But tell me now, Mr. Acres, in case of an accident, is there any little will or commission I conld execute for you?

Acres. I am much obliged to you, Sir Lucius; but I don't understand—

Sir L. Why, you may think there's no being shot at without a little risk—and if an unlucky bullet should carry a quietus with it—I say, it will be no time then to be bothering you about family matters.

Acres. A quietus!

Sir L. For instance, now—if that should be the case—would you choose to be pickled and sent home?—Or would it be the same to you to lie here in the Abbey?—I'm told there is very snug lying in the Abbey.

Acres. Pickled!—Snug lying in the Abbey!—Odds tremors! Sir Lucius, don't talk so!

Sir L. I suppose, Mr. Acres, you never were engaged in an affair of this kind before?

Acres. No, Sir Lucius, never before, (*aside*) and never will again, if I get out of this.

Sir L. Ah, that's a pity!—there's nothing like being used to a thing.—Pray, now, how would you receive the gentleman's shot?

Acres. Odds files! I've practised that. There, Sir Lucius, there—(*puts himself in an attitude*)—a side-front, hey!—Odd! I'll make myself small enough—I'll stand edgeways.

Sir L. Now, you're quite out—for if you stand so when I take my aim——(*leveling at him.*)

Acres. Zounds, Sir Lucius! are you sure it is not cocked?

Sir L. Never fear.

Acres. But—but—you don't know; it may go off of its own head.

Sir L. Pho! be easy. Well, now if I hit you in the body, my bullet has a double chance; for if it misses a vital part on your right side, 'twill be very hard if it don't succeed on the left.

Acres. A vital part!

Sir L. But, there—fix yourself so (*placing him,*) let him see the broadside of your full front. (*Sir Lucius places him face to face, then turns and goes to the left. Acres has in the interim turned his back in great perturbation.*) Oh, bother! do you call that the broadside of your front? (*Acres turns reluctantly.*) There —now a ball or two may pass clean through your body, and never do you any harm at all.

Acres. Clean through me! A ball or two clean through me!

Sir. L. Ay, may they—and it is much the genteelest attitude into the bargain.

Acres. Look ye! Sir Lucius—I'd just as lieve be shot in an awkward posture as a genteel one.—So, by my valor! I will stand edgeways.

Sir L. (*Looking at his watch.*) Sure they don't mean to disappoint us!

Acres. (*Aside.*) I hope they do.

Sir L. Hah! no, 'faith—I think I see them coming.

Acres. Hey?—what?—coming!

Sir L. Ay, who are those yonder, getting over the stile?

Acres. There are two of them, indeed! well, let them come— hey, Sir Lucius?—We—we—we—we—won't run (*takes his arm*).

Sir L. Run?

Acres. No, I say—we *won't* run, by my valor!

Sir L. What the devil's the matter with you?

Acres. Nothing—nothing—my dear friend—my dear Sir Lucius—but I—I—I don't feel quite so bold, somehow, as I did.

Sir L. O fie! consider your honor.

Acres. Ay, true—my honor—do, Sir Lucius, edge in a word or two, every now and then, about my honor.

Sir L. (*Looking.*) Well, here they're coming.

Acres. Sir Lucius, if I wa'n't with you I should almost think I was afraid—if my valor should leave me!—valor will come and go.

Sir L. Then pray keep it fast, while you have it.

Acres. Sir Lucius—I doubt it is going—yes, my valor is certainly going! it is sneaking off!—I feel it oozing out, as it were, at the palms of my hands!

Sir L. Your honor, your honor! Here they are.

Acres. O mercy!—now—that I was safe at Clod Hall! or could be shot before I was aware! [*Enter Faulkland and Captain Absolute.*

Sir L. Gentlemen, your most obedient—hah! what? Captain Absolute!—So, I suppose, sir, you are come here, just like my-self—to do a kind office, first for your friend—then to proceed to business on your own account.

Acres. What, Jack! my dear Jack! my dear friend!

[*Shakes his hand.*

Capt. A. Harkye, Bob, Beverley's at hand. [*Acres retreats to left.*

Sir L. Well, Mr. Acres—I don't blame your saluting the gen-tleman civilly. (*To Faulkland*) So Mr. Beverley, if you'll choose your weapons, the Captain and I will measure the ground.

Faulk. My weapons, sir!

Acres. Odds life! Sir Lucius, I'm not going to fight Mr. Faulkland; these are my particular friends!

[*Shakes hands with Faulkland—goes back.*

Sir. L. What, sir, did you not come here to fight Mr. Acres?

Faulk. Not I, upon my word, sir.

Sir L. Well, now, that's mighty provoking! But I hope, Mr. Faulkland, as there are three of us come on purpose for the game—you won't be so cantankerous as to spoil the party by standing out.

Capt. A. Oh pray, Faulkland, fight to oblige Sir Lucius.

Faulk. Nay, if Mr. Acres is so bent on the matter.

Acres. No, no, Mr. Faulkland—I'll bear my disappointment like a Christian. Look ye, Sir Lucius, there's no occasion at all for me to fight; and if it is the same to you, I'd as lieve let it alone.

Sir L. Observe me, Mr. Acres—I must not be trifled with. You have certainly challenged somebody, and you came here to fight him—now, if that gentleman is willing to represent him—I can't see, for my soul, why it isn't just the same thing.

Acres. Why no, Sir Lucius, I tell you 'tis one Beverley I've challenged—a fellow, you see, that dare not show his face. If he were here I'd make him give up his pretensions directly.

Capt. A. Hold, Bob—let me set you right—there is no such man as Beverley in the case. The person who assumed that name is before you; and as his pretensions are the same in both characters, he is ready to support them in whatever way you may please.

Sir L. Well, this is lucky. (*Slaps him on the back.*) Now you have an opportunity.

Acres. What, quarrel with my dear friend Jack Absolute!— not if he were fifty Beverleys! (*Shakes his hand warmly.*) Zounds! Sir Lucius, you would not have me be so unnatural!

Sir L. Upon my conscience, Mr. Acres, your valor has oozed away with a vengeance!

Acres Not in the least! odds backs and abettors! I'll be your second with all my heart—and if you should get a quietus, you may command me entirely. I'll get you snug lying in the Abbey here; or pickle you, and send you over to Blunderbuss Hall, or anything of the kind, with the greatest pleasure.

Sir L. Pho, pho! you are little better than a coward.

Acres. Mind, gentlemen, he calls me a coward; coward was the word, by my valor!

Sir L. Well, sir?

Acres. Very well, sir. (*Gently.*) Look ye, Sir Lucius, 'tisn't that I mind the word coward. Coward may be said in joke; but if you had called me a poltroon, odds daggers and balls!—

Sir L. (*Sternly.*) Well, sir?

Acres. I should have thought you a very ill-bred man.

Sir L. Pho! you are beneath my notice.

Acres. I'm very glad of it.

Capt. A. Nay, Sir Lucius, you can't have a better second than my friend Acres. He is a most determined dog—called in the country Fighting Bob. He generally kills a man a week—don't you, Bob?

Acres. Ay—at home!

CHAPTER XIII.

EARLY ENGLISH ACTORS.

In 1603 King James granted a license to the company
playing at the Globe and Blackfriars, and henceforth they
called themselves "His Majesty's Servants." From that time
forward the fortunes of the professional actors continued to
improve. Acting was held in higher esteem as players ceased
to be people of little or no means and became possessed of
property and substance. In their wills prominent actors styled
themselves "gentlemen," and they were welcomed as genial
companions by the talented of the age.

Most brilliant among the clever group that made up the
company for which Shakespeare wrote and with which he
himself sometimes acted was Richard Burbage son of James
Burbage—who erected the first theater in England. Tragedy
was his rôle and to him fell the honor of first impersonating
Brutus, Hamlet, Lear, Macbeth and other of Shakespeare's
immortal heroes. When he died, in 1618, it was felt that
these mighty parts were lost forever.

"He's gone, and with him what a world are dead,
  Friends every one, and what a blank instead!
  Take him for all in all, he was a man
  Not to be match'd, and no age can.
  No more young Hamlet, though but scant of breath,
  Shall cry 'Revenge' for his dear father's death;
  Poor Romeo never more shall tears beget
  For Juliet's love and cruel Capulet:
  Harry shall not be seen as king or prince,
  They died with thee, dear Dick."

William Kempe, another of this celebrated band, is reputed to have been an actor as well as a clown. The parts of Launcelot Gobbo, Shallow, Touchstone, and the first Gravedigger were originally played by him.

When the civil war broke out, the theaters were closed by act of Parliament. Having prospered by royal patronage, players took up arms in defense of the king. Those too advanced in years to serve in the army often suffered for the mere necessities of life, save in those rare cases where thy were able to find other employment. As quickly as peace and the Stuarts were restored, actors began immediately to gather once more in London.

The reverses of war and the diligence of the Puritans brought about the destruction of the old theaters; few remained at the time of the Restoration. King Charles II. gave permission for the construction of two new ones—the first in Drury Lane, its company to be known as the King's Company; the other in Salisbury Court, the company known as the Duke of York's. Several of the actors who made up these companies returned from service in the royal army; Burt, the tragedian in the King's Company, had been a cornet of cavalry; Mohun, a major—by which title he continued to be known on the theater bills. Hart, Shakespeare's grandnephew, played with the King's Company. Previous to the war he had played women's parts. Youths continued to act feminine parts for some years, but Pepys mentions the third of January, 1661, as the time he first saw women playing on the stage. Nell Gwynne appeared first at Drury Lane in 1665, being then fifteen years of age. Ill fitted for tragedy, she was admirably suited to lighter parts and was an adept at mimicry.

The rivalry between the two theaters became very keen and at length the king commanded the two companies to consolidate. This gratified some and offended other of the actors but it temporarily adjusted those rivalries which were threatening to undermine the whole theatrical business. Of those who composed the "amalgamated company"—as it was called —best remembered is Thomas Betterton. He was a great favorite with Pope and Dryden, with Addison and Steele and we find him frequently mentioned by them. His style of delivery would seem ponderous and heavy today, but a contemporary critic testified to the gratification he afforded his listeners. "I never heard a line in tragedy come from Betterton, wherein my judgment, my ear and my imagination were not fully satisfied." He acted Hamlet when seventy years of age and died only three days after his last appearance in "The Maid's Tragedy."

The dim lights afforded by the eighteenth century made it imperative that actors should be brought as near the spectators as possible. For this reason the stage projected far into the audience room. The Elizabethan custom of permitting spectators to sit upon the stage still continued, although it impeded the performers and interfered seriously with the play. "Juliet frequently lay in her tomb surrounded by some scores of people, and Macbeth, returning from the murder of Duncan, had to force his way through a crowd of beaux." Having heard Hamlet complain that the air was very cold, shortly before he threw off his hat upon the appearance of the ghost, one considerate woman carefully placed it back upon his head—to the overwhelming amusement of royalty present. Efforts were made for almost a century to free the stage from auditors and Garrick succeeded in doing so only when in 1762 he contracted the stage and thus supplied greater seating capacity.

With insufficient light, scenic effects were not practical and throughout the eighteenth century costumes were frequently shabby and inappropriate. It was the habit of the nobility to send discarded clothing to the theaters, so, while the hero might appear in old and tattered apparel, serving maids might be decked out in elaborate robes similar to those of the dames whom they were serving. The result was not so disconcerting as it would seem, since only those seated near could observe details carefully in the dim light.

David Garrick inaugurated a new era in the profession of acting. Having taken minor parts under an assumed name, he appeared first under his own in December, 1741. No actor has ever carried the support of the theater-going world more constantly than he.

"Nature had done so much for him that he could not help being an actor. His eye was so penetrating, so speaking, his brow so movable, and all his features so plastic and so accommodating, that wherever his mind impelled them they would go, and before his tongue could give the text his countenance would express the spirit and passion of the part he was charged with." In the matter of delivery Garrick abandoned the ponderous, sonorous style of his predecessors and was always natural. His presentation of Lear was magnificent and perhaps no subsequent actor has ever given the mad Lear so marvellously.

The custom which London actors follow today of going to Stratford the week of the birthday each year and presenting some of Shakespeare's plays, originated with Garrick, who undertook to do so in 1768. However, this little town had not yet awakened to its good fortune of having given birth to a genius so widely loved that men from the ends of the earth would come to do him homage. The people gave scant welcome to their distinguished guests and a storm of unusual fury rendered many of the plans impractical.

Garrick was generous to a fault, and through his influence various worthy movements were facilitated. The proceeds of his last night, June 10, 1776, were turned to swell a fund for superannuated actors, established ten years before.

Macklin, Barry and Foote were all prominent on the London stage during this period. However, it may be doubted whether any of them contributed greatly to the future interpretations of their favorite roles, or whether they exercised lasting influence on the development of acting. Macklin lacked the power to concentrate; his disposition made it difficult for others to work with him and he was to be found now with one, now with another company. In an exhaustive study of theatrical art all three would have a place.

Elizabeth Barry, Mrs. Bracegirdle and Mrs. Mountfort were among the first women to win fame in dramatic rôles. Mrs. Bowman was another of their company and when these four unusually handsome women appeared together on the stage, the audience gave them immoderate applause. Mrs. Barry's interpretation of Lady Macbeth was much appreciated; her mantle descended to Mrs. Porter—long her understudy.

Of all the eighteenth century comedy queens, Peg Woffington, as she was generally called, enjoyed great popularity.

Possessing the failings common to many of the actresses of
her generation, these seem to have been quickly forgiven her
in view of her humor, quick wit and pleasing appearance.
Her fine figure and dashing manner held her audiences attentive.

The greatest tragedy queen was unquestionably Sarah
Siddons, daughter of Roger Kemble, the manager of an itin-
erant company.   She came of a family all of whom were
actors; when but a tiny child she was brought upon the stage.
Growing into a beautiful woman, possessed of queenly bearing
and noble manner, she commanded at once the respect and
admiration of those with whom she came in contact.

She never held the warm affection which many another
distinguished actress has done, for although an incomparable
artist in her best years, she was regarded as a disagreeable,
disobliging woman of strong mercenary instincts.   Yet who-
ever witnessed her acting was deeply affected by it.   Those
supporting her in the play would sometimes be rendered
unfit for their parts by the intense tragedy and pathos of her
playing.   Washington Irving writes that he was strangely
moved by her.   Hazlitt, who was not likely to be unduly agitated, spoke often of her splendid interpretations.

"The homage she has received is greater than that which
is paid to queens.   The enthusiasm she excited had something
idolatrous about it; she was regarded less with admiration
than with wonder, as if a being of a superior order had
dropped from another sphere to awe the world with the
majesty of her appearance.   She raised tragedy to the skies,
or brought it down from thence.   It was something above
nature.   We can conceive of no other grander.   She embodied
to our imagination the fables of mythology, of the heroic and
deified mortals of elder time.   She was not less than a goddess, or than a prophetess inspired by the gods.   Power
was seated on her brow; passion emanated from her breast
as from a shrine.   She was tragedy personified. . . . She
not only hushed the tumultuous shouts of the pit in breathless expectation, and quenched the blaze of surrounding beauty
in silent tears, but to the retired and lonely student, through
long years of solitude, her face shone as if an angel appeared
from heaven; her name has been as if a voice had opened the

chambers of the human heart, or as if a trumpet had awakened the sleeping and the dead. To have seen Mrs. Siddons was an event in every one's life."

Yet she who elicited this praise was a complete failure when she first appeared in London to play Portia. Never successful in comedy, after she had gone back to the country towns and had perfected her art, she took London by storm and held her audiences for many years.

We are made familiar with her queenly form by Gainsborough's portrait, while Reynolds painted her in her tragedy rôle.

Mrs. Siddons' brother, John Philip Kemble was an actor of considerable note. All the family found a place in the profession but the rest did not win particular distinction.

In this survey of early players, Edmund Kean has a place. At the age of three he was brought upon the stage to take the part of Cupid. During his boyhood and youth he struggled against dire poverty and fortune turned her face for many a year. Finally given a place at Drury Lane, his popularity came by storm. Like Garrick and unlike Kemble, he thrust aside the artificial and recalled the natural in his acting. Shylock, Hamlet, Othello, Richard—he made them all live again and endowed them with new power.

Kean's later life was full of irregularities and confusion. His wonderful talents were squandered and the public, always fickle and vacillating, gave him signals of its disapproval quite as often as of its appreciation. It is doubtful if today audiences would allow prevailing opinions concerning an artist's private life to influence its recognition of his wonderful powers of transforming himself into beings of an imaginary world.

As conditions under which plays are given have improved and facilities for excellent lighting have made all descriptions of scenic effects possible, actors have been able to depend more upon pleasing settings and less upon their own acting. Sometimes it seems as though these very improvements have been gained at the expense of acting. Modern times have produced a few gifted actors—for example, Irving in England and Mansfield in the United States. Yet even these men have lacked the tremendous and overpowering fire of the earlier players. It is possible that the near future, which is generally regarded as holding much in store along dramatic lines, may bring forth one who shall be greater than Garrick or Kean.

"What the acting of the pre-rebellion age was like we can only surmise; but that the greatest era of dramatic literature, written, be it remembered, *solely for the stage,* must have been rich in dramatic exponents, is past doubt, and analogy would lead us to believe that the style of Burbage, Alleyn, and their contemporaries, like that of Marlowe and Shakespeare, was vivid, full of fire, broad, rather than subtle, prone to bombast and exaggeration, doubtless, but grand and impressive. With the Restoration was introduced the cold, turgid, artificial manner of the French theater, which, however, in the person of a Betterton, as in that of a Baron, was rendered grand and sublime, and full of intellectual power. Garrick brought us back to nature; Kemble restored the artificial, until the dazzling genius of Edmund Kean, the last of the great Shakespearean actors, once more gave us warmth and energy for classical correctness; Macready effected a compromise, and united the salient points of the two schools with something of his own."*

* Baker: English Actors, Vol. 2, 285.

CHAPTER XIV.

RECENT ENGLISH DRAMATISTS.

After generations of makeshift upon the stage, drama at last comes into a renaissance. Constant demand for amusement and diversion has long been met by such substitutes for plays as staged novels and combinations of comic opera and farce. The advent of Ibsen marks the beginning of the revival. Since he sounded a new note, other gifted dramatists have appeared: Hauptmann, Sudermann, Maeterlinck, Pinero and others. While we are too near these writers to correctly estimate them, and although it is not possible at the present time to make predictions for the drama of the future, many will agree with those critics who have said, while frankly acknowledging their powerlessness to forecast the future, that it is possible even now to point out certain qualities that the coming drama will not possess. It will not be a story thrown into the form of a play on the supposition that a successful book means an acceptable drama; novels and plays are written with different purposes, are subjected to different treatment and intended for entirely different needs—one to be enjoyed at leisure, frequently alone; the other, to be witnessed with others at some definite time and place.

The future drama will not be brilliant conversation, devoid of plot and action—as has been true of several recent plays. It will not be a production contrived to supply a reason for ambitious managers to present startling and unexpected scenery before a bewildered public. The scenery will be the frame in which the picture is set and will be subservient to the play—the play will not be lost in the setting. Moreover, leading theaters will provide plays that will be worthy of intelligent beings—not variety shows or extravaganzas.

The stage is one of the most potent factors in civilization. It mirrors life and can wield power granted to neither pulpit nor platform, if only it be worthily served. Primarily, the theater is to supply diversion and entertainment. However, this can be done in ways which shall strengthen, build up, inspire and ennoble as well as in ways that are trifling, superficial and whimsical. Vaudevilles fill a necessary place in our present civilization and the ends they serve have been met in some form for hundreds of years; picture shows are pleasing and instructive and have their part to fill; musical extravaganzas are always popular and fit into our social structure; but the drama is to be compared with painting, sculpture, poetry and music. It is one of the fine arts and should be exalted—not dragged into the mire. Upholding ideals, it demands respect; supplying pleasure and recreation, it merits regard; as a means of placing before us pictures of life, wherein we may see in miniature the struggle which characterizes all phases of existence, it becomes the great teacher of humanity, teaching not by precept but example.

Every problem which humanity has to meet may become a suitable subject for a play; but to be enduring, it must be treated earnestly and delicately. Nothing is more quickly offensive than flippancy in the treatment of matters which are vital to the welfare and happiness of mankind. Nothing is more harmful than the ruthless tearing away of that which people revere. It is idle to hold that some topics are suited to the stage and others are not. All subjects that interest people as a whole are capable of dramatic treatment, whether they touch upon religious, industrial, political or social relations. Whether they become living plays will depend upon the consummate skill of the playwright, upon his understanding of men and upon his power to see what may be local and temporary and what is universal and abiding.

Ibsen viewed the marriage relation resulting from treatment of women as though they were little children or playthings, and created a drama that will live, which caught the ear of the people, and which even now has had an effect upon the thought of our age. Pinero presented the time-worn problem: how can those whose past lives have been irregular leave the past wholly behind them and live for the present and future alone? And the answer was the inevitable one that they can't. Kennedy watched a Christian world repeat creeds and profess its subscription to the tenets of a religion whose cornerstone is *the brotherhood of men,* and then, in every human relationship act in contradiction of that principle, and wrote a play which forced people to view the striking inconsistency.

The time is ripe for dramatic literature. The old idols are crumbling. People are wearied of the hypocrisy and shams of life. The way has been prepared and there is reason to think that the present century may produce the masterhand.

Of the many aspiring English playwrights of the present time, three alone are here considered. Pinero, who is probably justly regarded as England's foremost dramatist; Bernard Shaw, the dramatic satirist; and Kennedy, who while English by birth and training, has achieved his success largely in America.

Arthur Wing Pinero was born in London in 1854, the son of a barrister. For several years he was connected with the stage as an actor, being associated for a portion of that time with the Henry Irving company. This training served him in good stead and doubtless to it he owes his great skill in the mastery of stage craft.

His first efforts were farces, which met with excellent success; The Magistrate, The School-mistress, Dandy Dick and The Amazons were best of these writings. They indicated dramatic possibilities for their young author.

Pinero's first domestic drama was Sweet Lavender—a play of no special plot, but wholesome in its portrayal of good women, honest men, genial humor and refined wit. In recent years Pinero has confined himself generally to so-called problem plays. The Profligate, Iris, The Second Mrs. Tanqueray, are all well known.

If Pinero's message as conveyed through his plays was to be briefly summarized, perhaps it might be expressed in this way: that weakness is as bad as crime, self-indulgence brings results as inevitably as vice, that disregard for social laws will bring its own reward. The plays are expressed in clear, concise language and no modern dramatist has more complete understanding of dramatic technique.

PINERO.

THE SECOND MRS. TANQUERAY.

(Aubrey Tanqueray, entertaining three old friends at dinner, has just announced his approaching marriage, suggesting that their future relations may be affected by it. During his temporary absence, his friends discuss with dismay his foreboding sentence: "My marriage isn't even the conventional sort of marriage likely to satisfy society.")

Drummle (anxiously). Deuce take it, the man's second marriage mustn't be another mistake.

Jayne. You knew him in his short married life, Cayley. Terribly unsatisfactory, wasn't it?

Drummle. Well (*looking at the door*) I quite closed that door?

Misquith. Yes. (*Settles himself on the sofa; Jayne is seated in an arm-chair.*)

Drummle (smoking with his back to the fire). He married a Miss Herriott; that was in the year eighteen—confound dates—twenty years ago. She was a lovely creature—by Jove, she was! By religion a Roman Catholic. She was one of your cold sort, you know—all marble arms and black velvet. I remember her with painful distinctness as the only woman who ever made me nervous.

Misquith. Ha, ha!

Drummle. He loved her—to distraction, as they say. Jupiter, how fervently that poor devil courted her! But I don't believe she allowed him even to squeeze her fingers. She *was* an iceberg! As for kissing, the mere contact would have given him chapped lips. However, he married her and took her away, the latter greatly to my relief.

Jayne. Abroad, you mean?

Drummle. Eh? Yes. I imagine he gratified her by renting a villa in Lapland, but I don't know. After a while they returned, and then I saw how wofully Aubrey had miscalculated results.

Jayne. Miscalculated—?

Drummle. He had reckoned, poor wretch, that in the early days of marriage she would thaw; but she didn't. I used to picture him closing his doors and making up the fire in the hope of seeing her features relax. Bless her, the thaw never set in! I believe she kept a thermometer in her stays and always regis-

tered ten degrees below zero. However, in time a child came—
a daughter.

Jayne. Didn't that—?

Drummle. Not a bit of it; it made matters worse. Frightened at her failure to stir up in him some sympathetic religious
belief, she determined upon strong measures with regard to the
child. He opposed her for a miserable year or so, but she wore
him down, and the insensible little brat was placed in a convent,
first in France, then in Ireland. Not long afterwards the mother
died, strangely enough, of a fever, the only warmth, I believe,
that ever came to that woman's body.

Misquith. Don't, Cayley.

Jayne. The child is living, we know.

Drummle. Yes, if you choose to call it living. Miss Tanqueray—a young woman of nineteen now—is in the Loretto convent at Armagh. She professes to have found her true vocation
in a religious life, and within a month or two will take final
vows.

Misquith. He ought to have removed his daughter from the
convent when the mother died.

Drummle. Yes, yes, but absolutely at the end there was reconciliation between husband and wife, and she won his promise
that the child should complete her conventual education. He
reaped his reward. When he attempted to gain his girl's confidence and affection he was too late; he found he was dealing
with the spirit of the mother.

SECOND ACT.

Aubrey. Sunshine! Spring!

Paula (glancing at the clock). Exactly six minutes.

Aubrey. Six minutes?

Paula. Six minutes, Aubrey dear, since you made your last
remark.

Aubrey. I beg your pardon: I was reading my letters. Have
you seen Ellean this morning?

Paula (coldly). Your last observation but one was about
Ellean.

Aubrey. Dearest, what shall I talk about?

Paula. Ellean breakfasted two hours ago, Morgan tells me,
and then went out walking with her dog.

Aubrey She wraps up warmly, I hope; this sunshine is
deceptive.

Paula. I ran about the lawn last night, after dinner, in satin shoes. Were you anxious about me?

Aubrey. Certainly.

Paula (*melting*). Really?

Aubrey. You make me wretchedly anxious; you delight in doing incautious things. You are incurable.

Paula. Ah, what a beast I am! (*Going to him and kissing him, then glancing at the letters by his side.*) A letter from Cayley?

Aubrey. He is waiting very near here, with Mrs. ————. Very near here.

Paula. With the lady whose chimneys we have the honour of contemplating from our windows?

Aubrey. With Mrs. Cortelyon—yes.

Paula. Mrs. Cortelyon! The woman who might have set the example of calling upon me when we first threw out roots in this deadly-lively soil! Deuce take Mrs. Cortelyon!

Aubrey. Hush! my dear girl!

Paula (*returning to her seat*). Oh, I know she's an old acquaintance of yours—and of the first Mrs. Tanqueray. And she joins the rest of 'em in slapping the second Mrs. Tanqueray in the face. However, I have my revenge—she's six-and-forty, and I wish nothing worse to happen to any woman.

Aubrey. Well, she's going to town, Cayley says here, and his visit's at an end. He's coming over this morning to call on you. Shall we ask him to transfer himself to us? Do say yes.

Paula. Yes.

Aubrey (*gladly*). Ah, ha! old Cayley.

Paula (*coldly*). He'll amuse *you*.

Aubrey. And you, too.

Paula. Because you find a companion, shall I be boisterously hilarious?

Aubrey. Come, come. He talks London, and you know you like that.

Paula. London! London or Heaven! which is farther from me! Oh! I've no patience with you! You'll kill me with this life! (*She selects some flowers from a vase on the table, cuts and arranges them, and fastens them in her bodice.*) What is my existence, Sunday to Saturday? In the morning, a drive down to the village, with the groom, to give my orders to the tradespeople. At lunch, you and Ellean. In the afternoon, a novel, the newspapers; if fine, another drive—if fine! Tea—you and Ellean. Then two hours of dusk; then dinner—you and Ellean. Then a game of Besique, you and I, while Ellean reads a religious book in a dull corner. Then a yawn from me, another from you, a sigh from Ellean; three figures suddenly rise— Good-night, good-night, good-night! (*imitating a kiss*) God bless you! Ah!

Aubrey. Yes, yes, Paula—yes, dearest—that's what it is *now.* But by and bye, if people begin to come round us—

Paula. Hah! That's where we've made the mistake, my friend Aubrey. (*Pointing to the window.*) Do you believe these people will *ever* come round us? Your former crony, Mrs. Cortelyon? Or the grim old vicar, or that wife of his whose huge nose is positively indecent? Or the Ullathornes, or the Gollons, or Lady William Petres? I know better! And when the young ones gradually take the place of the old, there will still remain the sacred tradition that the dreadful person who lives at the top of the hill is never, under any circumstances, to be called upon! And so we shall go on here, year in and year out, until the sap is run out of our lives, and we're stale and dry and withered from sheer, solitary respectability. Upon my word, I wonder we didn't see that we should have been far happier if we'd gone in for the devil-may-care, café-living sort of life in town! After all, *I* have a set, and you might have joined it.

FOURTH ACT.

Aubrey. Perhaps now she'll propose to return to the convent —well, she must.

Paula. Would you like to keep her with you and—and leave me?

Aubrey. Paula—!

Paula. You needn't be afraid I'd go back to—what I was. I couldn't.

Aubrey. S-sh, for God's sake! We—you and I—we'll get out of this place. . . . What a fool I was to come here again!

Paula. You lived here with your first wife!

Aubrey. We'll get out of this place and go abroad again, and begin afresh.

Paula. Begin afresh?

Aubrey. There's no reason why the future shouldn't be happy for us—no reason that I can see—

Paula. Aubrey!

Aubrey. Yes?

Paula. You'll never forget this, you know.

Aubrey. This?

Paula. Tonight, and everything that's led up to it. Our coming here, Ellean, our quarrels—cat and dog!—Mrs. Cortelyon, the Orreyeds, this man! What an everlasting nightmare for you!

Aubrey. Oh, we can forget it, if we choose.

Paula. That was always your cry. How *can* one do it?

Aubrey. We'll make our calculations solely for the future, talk about the future, think about the future.

Paula. I believe the future is only the past again, entered through another gate.

Aubrey. That's an awful belief.

Paula. Tonight proves it. You must see now that, do what we will, go where we will, you'll be continually reminded of—what I was. I see it.

Aubrey. You're frightened tonight; meeting this man has frightened you. But that sort of thing isn't likely to recur. The world isn't quite so small as all that.

Paula. Isn't it? The only great distances it contains are those we carry within our selves—the distances, that separate husbands and wives, for instance. And so it'll be with us. You'll do your best—oh, I know that—you're a good fellow. But circumstances will be too strong for you in the end, mark my words.

Aubrey. Paula—!

Paula. Of course I'm pretty now—I'm pretty still—and a pretty woman, whatever else she may be, is always—well, endurable. But even now I notice that the lines of my face are getting deeper; so are the hollows about my eyes. Yes, my face is covered with little shadows that usen't to be there. Oh, I know I'm going off! I hate paint and dye and those messes, but by and bye, I shall drift the way of the others; I sha'n't be able to help myself. And then, some day,—perhaps very suddenly, under a queer, fantastic light at night or in the glare of the morning,—that horrid, irresistible truth that physical repulsion forces on men and women will come to you, and you'll sicken at me.

Aubrey. I—!

Paula. You'll see me then, at last, with other people's eyes; you'll see me just as your daughter does now, as all wholesome folks see women like me. And I shall have no weapon to fight with—not one serviceable little bit of prettiness left me to defend myself with! A worn-out creature—broken up, very likely, some time before I ought to be—my hair bright, my eyes dull, my body too thin, or too stout, my cheeks raddled and ruddled—a ghost, a wreck, a caricature, a candle that gutters, call such an end what you like! Oh, Aubrey, what shall I be able to say to you then? And this is the future you talk about! I know it!— I know it!

BERNARD SHAW.

George Bernard Shaw was born in Dublin July 26, 1856. Like his countryman Dean Swift, Shaw is a satirist. Due to prevailing tendencies of the times he has thrown his writings into dramatic form; however, they are likely to endure as literature rather than as plays. Characterized by little or no action, they are brilliant dialogues and conversations rather than productions adapted to the stage.

The circumstances under which Shaw grew up caused him to ascribe small value to the traditions and conventionalities of society. The shams of life were early apparent to him and aroused his contempt. This he made no attempt to conceal. Again, he has never been afraid of being egotistical, but frankly confesses the trait, claiming it as a virtue. He says: "I am ashamed neither of my work nor the way it is done. . . . I like explaining its merits to the huge majority who don't know good work from bad. It does them good; and it does me good, curing me of nervousness, laziness and snobbishness."

Probably no writer of any age has evoked more varied criticism than that which has greeted Shaw. To some he has seemed merely a wit, whose every remark was signal for a laugh; to others, a conceited person whose one object was to shock society and ridicule existing customs; to others still, his has been the voice of one crying in the wilderness. Generally some intermediary view is safest. Shaw was born in an age of changing ideas and ideals. The old gods have been passing away; many new ones have been contending for their places. He sees so much cant in religion, so much pretense in society, so much crushing out of individuality by established customs that he cries out against it all. No moderate statements would win him an ear. The satirist and social reformer must always be extremists.

To one who looks beneath the surface, the use and abuse of names and phrases must ever be an exasperation, fit only for ridicule. "The sanctity of the family and of the home, for instance, has become a protecting cloud about the sentimental tyrannies of husbands, wives and children, each striving to obtain and control the other, and resulting in a nebulous and shallow indifference to everything but externals and names. Education, another favoured god, becomes the systematic curriculum—cramming of the young—the intellectual slaughter of the innocents—with what result? A rising generation and a generation just risen with no further intelligence than an infinite capacity for being deceived. And to name but one more—democracy—the people's will: expressing itself forever in the faded and tawdry pomp and circumstance of an outworn feudalism; lauding its free and popular institutions to the skies, and using what privileges its possesses, grudgingly or not at all, at the dictation of the stale rhetoric of politicians."

Who today does the things he wishes to do, in the way he would like to do them? Who if he were honest would not have to confess that his life is hedged about by rulings of social custom, which however they may hamper or impede, yet appear to be paramount? Shaw's message is to assert one's freedom; work out your individuality; stand out against conventionalities; freedom and desire are not synonymous with vice—they work for progress and attainment.

In his youth Shaw gave himself over to novel writing; for his stories, however, he was successful in finding a publisher only when he had won fame from his plays. Even these brought quite as violent censure as gratifying praise—this phrase itself being misleading in so much as Shaw holds himself indifferent to either. He has explained his lack of popular appreciation by the following incident:

"He (an oculist) tested my eyesight one evening, and informed me that it was quite uninteresting to him because it was 'normal.' I naturally took this to mean that it was like everybody else's; but he rejected this construction as paradoxical, and hastened to explain to me that I was an exceptional and highly fortunate person optically, 'normal' sight conferring the power of seeing things accurately, and being enjoyed by only about ten per cent of the population, the remaining ninety per cent being abnormal. I immediately perceived the explanation of my want of success in fiction. My mind's eye, like my body's, was 'normal'; it saw things differently from other people's eyes, and saw them better."

Man and Superman, Plays Pleasant and Unpleasant, Getting Married, Plays for Puritans, The Doctor's Dilemma and *John Bull's Other Island* are his best known plays. He has also written essays and social treatises.

GETTING MARRIED.

Collins (putting the cake on the table). Well, look at that, ma'am! Ain't it odd that after all the weddings he's given away at, the General can't stand the sight of a wedding cake yet. It always seems to give him the same shock.

Mrs. Bridgenorth. Well, it's his last shock. You have married the whole family now, Collins.

Collins. Except your sister, ma'am. A fine character of a lady, ma'am, is Miss Grantham. I have an ambition to arrange her wedding breakfast.

Mrs. Bridgenorth. She won't marry, Collins.

Collins. Bless you, ma'am, they all say that. You and me said it, I'll lay. I did, anyhow.

Mrs. Bridgenorth. No; marriage came natural to me. I should have thought it did to you, too.

Collins. No, ma'am; it didn't come natural. My wife had to break me into it. It came natural to her; she's what you might call a regular old hen. Always wants to have her family within sight of her. Wouldn't go to bed unless she knew they was all safe at home and the door locked, and the lights out. Always wants her luggage in the carriage with her. Always goes and makes the engine driver promise her to be careful. She's a born wife and mother, ma'am. That's why my children all ran away from home.

Mrs. Bridgenorth. Did you ever feel inclined to run away, Collins?

Collins. Oh yes, ma'am, yes; very often. But when it came to the point I couldn't bear to hurt her feelings. She's a sensitive, affectionate, anxious soul; and she was never brought up to know what freedom is to some people. You see, family life is all the life she knows, she's like a bird born in a cage, that would die if you let it loose in the woods. When I thought how little it was to a man of my easy temper to put up with her, and how deep it would hurt her to think it was because I didn't care for her, I always put off running away till next time; and so in the end I never ran away at all. I daresay it was good for me to be took such care of; but it cut me away from all my old friends something dreadful, ma'am; especially the women, ma'am. She never gave them a chance; she didn't indeed. She never understood that married people should take holidays from one another if they are to keep at all fresh. Not that I ever got tired of her, ma'am; but my! how I used to get tired of home life sometimes. I used to catch myself envying my brother George: I positively did, ma'am. . . .

The General. Listen to me, Lesbia. For the tenth and last time—

Lesbia. On Florence's wedding morning, two years ago, you said "For the ninth and last time."

The General. We are two years older, Lesbia. I'm fifty: you are—

Lesbia. Yes, I know. It's no use, Boxer. When will you be old enough to take no for an answer?

The General. Never, Lesbia, never. You have never given me a real reason for refusing me yet. I once thought it was somebody else. There were lots of fellows after you; but now they've all given it up and married. Lesbia, tell me your secret. Why—

Lesbia. Oh! you've been smoking. Keep away, you wretch.

The General. But for that pipe I could not have faced you without breaking down. It has soothed me and nerved me.

Lesbia. Well, it has nerved me to tell you why I'm going to be an old maid.

The General. Don't say that, Lesbia. It's not natural; it's not right: it's—

Lesbia. It may not be natural; but it happens all the same. You'll find plenty of women like me, if you care to look for them; women with lots of character and good looks and money and offers, who won't and don't get married. Can't you guess why?

The General. I can understand when there is another.

Lesbia. Yes, but there isn't another. Besides, do you suppose I think, at my time of life, that the difference between one decent sort of man and another is worth bothering about?

The General. The heart has its preferences, Lesbia. One image, and one only, gets indelibly—

Lesbia. Yes. Excuse my interrupting you so often; but your sentiments are so correct that I always know what you are going to say before you finish. You see, Boxer, everybody is not like you. You are a sentimental noodle; you don't see women as they really are. You don't see me as I really am. Now I do see men as they really are. I see you as you really are.

The General. No: don't say that, Lesbia.

Lesbia. I'm a regular old maid. I'm very particular about my belongings. I like to have my own house, and to have it to myself. I have a very keen sense of beauty and fitness and cleanliness and order. I am proud of my independence and jealous for it. I have a sufficiently well-stocked mind to be very good company for myself if I have plenty of books and music. The one thing I never could stand is a great lout of a man smoking all over my house and going to sleep in his chair after dinner, and untidying everything. Ugh!

The General. But love—

Lesbia. Oh, love! Have you no imagination? Do you think I have never been in love with wonderful men? heroes! archangels! princes! sages! even fascinating rascals! and had the strangest adventures with them? Do you know what it is to look at a mere man after that? a man with his boots in every corner, and the smell of his tobacco in every curtain? . . .

Mrs. Bridgenorth. Lesbia, Boxer, here's a pretty mess!

The Genera.. What's the matter?

Mrs. Bridgenorth. Reginald's in London, and wants to come to the wedding.

The General. Well, dash my buttons!

Lesbia. Oh, all right, let him come.

The General. Let him come! Why, the decree has not been made absolute yet. Is he to walk in here to Edith's wedding, reeking from the Divorce Court?

Mrs. Bridgenorth. It's too bad. No; I can't forgive him, Lesbia, really. A man of Reginald's age, with a young wife— the best of girls, and as pretty as she can be—to go off with a common woman from the streets! Ugh!

Lesbia. You must make allowances. What can you expect? Reginald was always weak. He was brought up to be weak. The family property was all mortgaged when he inherited it. He had to struggle along in constant money difficulties, hustled by his solicitors, morally bullied by the Barmecide, and physically bullied by Boxer, while they two were fighting their own way and getting well trained. You know very well he couldn't afford to marry until the mortgages were cleared, and he was over fifty. And then of course he made a fool of himself marrying a child like Leo.

The General. But to hit her! Absolutely to hit her! He knocked her down—knocked her flat on a flower bed in the presence of his gardener. He! the head of the family. . . . I'd cut Reginald dead if I met him in the street.

Mrs. Bridgenorth. Besides, Leo's coming. They'd meet. It's impossible, Lesbia.

Lesbia. Oh, I forgot that. That settles it. He mustn't come.

The General. Of course he mustn't. You tell him that if he enters this house I'll leave it; and so will every decent man and woman in it.

Collins. Mr. *Reginald,* ma'am.

The General. Well, dash my buttons!!

Reginald. Alice, it's no use. I can't stay away from Edith's wedding. Good morning, Lesbia. How are you, Boxer?

The General. I was just telling Alice, sir, that if you entered this house I should leave it.

Reginald. Well, don't let me detain you, old chap. When you start calling people Sir, you're not particularly good company.

Lesbia. Don't you begin to quarrel. That won't improve the situation.

Mrs. Bridgenorth. I think you might have waited until you got my answer, Rejjy.

Reginald. It's so jolly easy to say No in a letter. Won't you let me stay?

Mrs. Bridgenorth. How can I? Leo's coming.

Reginald. Well, she won't mind.

The General. Won't mind! ! ! ! . .

Collins (*again appearing*). Mrs. Reginald, ma'am.

Lesbia. No, no. Ask her to—

Mrs. Bridgenorth. Oh, how unfortunate!

The General. Well, dash my buttons!

Leo. Good morning. How do, Alice? Why so gloomy, General? Oh, Rejjy! What will the king's proctor say?

Reginald. Damn the King's Proctor!

Leo. Naughty. Well, I suppose I must kiss you; but don't any of you tell. Have you kept all your promises?

Reginald. Oh, don't begin bothering about those—

Leo. Have? You? Kept? Your? Premises? Have you rubbed your head with the lotion every night?

The General. Leo: forgiveness is one of the most beautiful traits in a woman's nature; but there are things that should not be forgiven to a man. When a man knocks a woman down—

VII—14

Reginald. The man that would raise his hand to a woman, save in the way of a kindness, is unworthy of the name of Bridgenorth.

The General. Oh, well, if Leo does not mind, of course I have no more to say. But I think you might, out of consideration for the family, beat your wife in private and not in the presence of the gardener.

Reginald. What's the good of beating your wife unless there's a witness to prove it afterwards? You don't suppose a man beats his wife for the fun of it, do you? How could she have got her divorce if I hadn't beaten her? Nice state of things that!

The General. Do you mean to tell me that you did it in cold blood, simply to get rid of your wife?

Reginald. No, I didn't: I did it to get her rid of me. What would you do if you were fool enough to marry a woman thirty years younger than yourself, and then found that she didn't care for you, and was in love with a young fellow with a face like a mushroom.

Leo. He has not. And you are most unkind to say I didn't care for you. Nobody could have been fonder of you.

Reginald. A nice way of showing your fondness! I had to go out and dig that flower bed all over with my hands to soften it. I had to pick all the stones out of it. And then she complained that I hadn't done it properly, because she got a worm down her neck. . . . And then I'm held up in the public court for cruelty and adultery, and turned away from Edith's wedding by Alice, and lectured by you, a bachelor, and a precious green one at that! What do you know about it?

The General. Am I to understand that the whole case was one of collusion?

Reginald. Of course it was. Half the cases are collusions; what are people to do? And what do you take me for, that you should have the cheek to pretend to believe all that rot about my knocking Leo about and leaving her for—for a—Ugh! you should have seen her.

The General. This is perfectly astonishing to me. Why did you do it? Why did Leo allow it?

Reginald. You'd better ask her.

Leo. I'm sure I never thought it would be so horrid for Rejjy. I offered honorably to do it myself, and let him divorce me, but he wouldn't. And he said himself that it was the only way to do it that way. I never saw the hateful creature until that day in Court. If he had only shown her to me before, I should never have allowed it.

Mrs. Bridgenorth. You did all this for Leo's sake, Rejjy?

Reginald. I shouldn't mind it a bit if it were for Leo's sake. But to have to do it to make room for that mushroom-faced serpent—!

The General. What right had he to be made room for? Are you in your senses? What right?

Reginald. The right of being a young man, suitable to a young woman. I had no right at my age to marry Leo; she knew no more about life than a child.

Leo. I knew a great deal more about it than a great baby like you. I'm sure I don't know how you'll get on with no one to take care of you; I often lie awake at night thinking about it. And now you've made me thoroughly miserable.

Reginald. Serve you right! (*She weeps*). There: don't get into a tantrum, Leo.

Lesbia. May one ask who is the mushroom-faced serpent?

Leo. He isn't.

Reginald. Sinjon Hotchkiss, of course.

Mrs. Bridgenorth. Sinjon Hotchkiss! Why, he's coming to the wedding!

Reginald. What! In that case I'm off.

Leo. No you shan't. You promised to be nice to him.

The General. No, don't go, old chap. Not from Edith's wedding.

Mrs. Bridgenorth. Oh, do stay, Rejjy. I shall really be hurt if you desert us.

Lesbia. Better stay, Reginald. You must meet him sooner or later.

Reginald. A moment ago when I wanted to stay you were all shoving me out of the house. Now that I want to go, you won't let me.

Mrs. Bridgenorth. I shall send a note to Mr. Hotchkiss not to come.

Leo. (*weeping*). Oh, Alice!

Reginald. Oh well, let her have her way. Let her have her mushroom. Let him come. Let them all come.

CHARLES RANN KENNEDY.

The Terrible Meek.

First act stage play, for three voices; to be played in darkness.

A Peasant Woman, an Army Officer, a Soldier.
Time: Time of Darkness.
Place: A Wind-Swept Hill.
Woman is weeping. Captain tries to depart.
Captain. Listen. I will tell you. . . . I am a soldier. I have been helping to build kingdoms for over twenty years. I have never known any other trade. Soldiery, bloodshed, murder; that's my business. My hands are crimson with it. That's what empire means.

In the city I come from, it is the chief concern of the people. Building kingdoms, rule, empire. They're proud of it. The little children in the schools are drilled in obedience to it; they are taught hymns in praise of it: they are brought up to reverence its symbols. When they wave its standard above them, they shout, they leap, they make wild and joyful noises; like animals, like wolves, like little brute beasts. Children! Young children! Their parents encourage them in it; it never occurs to them to feel ashamed; they would be treated like lepers if they felt ashamed. That's what empire does to human beings in the city I come from. It springs from fear—a peculiar kind of fear they call courage.

And so we go on building our kingdoms—the kingdoms of this world. We stretch out our hands, greedy, grasping, tyrannical, to possess the earth. Domination, power, glory, money, merchandise, luxury, these are the things we aim at; but what we really gain is pest and famine, grudge labour, the enslaved hate of men and women, ghosts, dead and death-breathing ghosts that haunt our lives forever. It can't last; it never has lasted, this building in blood and fear. Already our kingdoms begin to totter. Possess the earth! We have lost it. We never did possess it. We have lost both earth and ourselves in trying to possess it; for the soul of the earth is man and the love of him; and we have made of both, a desolation.

Soldier. Well, I 'ope I know my duty, sir. I on'y obeyed orders. Come to that, sir, arskin' your pawdon, it was you as give them orders. I s'pose *you* knew orl right wot it was 'e done?

Captain. No, I don't know exactly, either. I am only just beginning to find out. We both did our duty, as you call it, in blindness.

Soldier. That's strange langwidge to be comin' from *your* lips, Captain.

Captain. Strange thoughts have been coming to me during the last six hours. ·

. . . .

Captain. You yourself, of course, had nothing at all against him? Nothing personal, nothing political, I mean. No more than I had.

Soldier. Lor' bless you, no, sir. Rather liked 'im the bit I saw of 'im.

Captain. Only they—the long-faced gentlemen—found him guilty. Oh, of course, they had to hand him over to the magistrate.

Soldier. Yes, blarst them. What did they want ter go an' do that for?

Captain. It was perhaps their—duty, don't you see?

Soldier (*taken aback on the sacred word*). Oh, was it? Well, since you put it in that way, o' course. . . .

Captain. Then, again, came the magistrate's duty. I suppose he found he had some duty in the matter? Did *he* very much object to this horrible thing that had been said?

Soldier. Not much! 'E ain't that sort, not this fellow! . . .

Captain. Was that charge proved against the prisoner?

Soldier. They 'ad witnesses, I suppose. On'y you know wot witnesses are, in a case like this, sir. Got their orders, you understand.

Captain. And, of course, they all did their duty. That sacred obligation was attended to. They obeyed.

Soldier. I don't know. Don't arsk me. I know nuthin' abaht it.

. . . .

Captain. Whereupon, though we were practically ignorant as to the charges upon which this man was convicted: though we had grave doubts as to whether he were guilty at all; and while it is perfectly certain that we had nothing against him personally, that we even liked him, sympathized with him, pitied him; it became *our* duty, our sworn, our sacred duty, to do to him—the terrible thing we did just now.

Soldier. I can't see wot you're drivin' at, sir. You wouldn't 'ave a man go agen 'is duty, would you?

Captain. I'm trying to make up my mind. I don't know. I'm blind. I don't think I know what duty is.

Soldier. It's perfectly plain, sir. Arter all, duty *is* duty, ain't it?

Captain. Yes, it doesn't seem to be very much else.

Soldier. 'Ow do you mean, sir.

Captain. Well, for instance, it doesn't seem to be love or neighborliness or pity or understanding or anything that comes out hot and fierce from the heart of a man. Duty! Duty! We talk of duty! What sort of a devil's duties are there in the world, do you think, when they lead blindly, wantonly, wickedly, to the murder of such a man as this?

Soldier. We, far as I'm concerned, I on'y obeyed my orders.

Captain. Orders! Obeyed orders!

Soldier. Well, sir, it was you as give them to me.

Captain. Good God, man, why didn't you strike me in the blasphemous teeth, the hour I gave them?

Soldier. Me, sir? Strike my superior officer!

Captain. You struck this defenseless man. You had no scruples about his superiority. You struck him to the death.

Soldier (*hotly*). I on'y did my duty!

Captain. We have murdered our brother. We have destroyed a woman's child.

Soldier. I on'y obeyed my orders. When my superior officer says, *Kill a man,* why, I just kill 'im, that's orl. O' course I kill 'im. Wot's a soldier for? That's duty! (*With sudden lust.*) Blood and 'ell! I'd kill 'im soon as look at 'im, yes, I would, if 'e was Gawd aht of 'Eaven, 'Imself! . . . Not as I 'ave anythin' personal agen this pore devil. On'y I *do* know my duty.

CHAPTER XV.

FRENCH DRAMA.

France has experienced no such national outburst of dramatic power as manifested itself in ancient Greece or Elizabethan England. Nevertheless, the drama has during two distinct periods been the most important form of literature; during the age of Molière or, generally speaking, during the seventeenth century, and in the earlier portion of the nineteenth century; while today it is surmised that France, together with other leading European countries, is approaching a dramatic Renaissance.

Corneille, Molière, and Racine are the great names of the seventeenth century, that of Molière towering above the others as Shakespeare's soars above his contemporaries. Yet the work of all three was important and any extended study of dramatic development must take each largely into account. Molière is unquestionably the greatest name in French literature and his service to the drama is comparable to that rendered by the poet of Avon.

A classical revival characterized the eighteenth century, manifesting itself in all forms of art—whether sculpture, painting, music, poetry or the drama. Not alone because they loved the ancient models, but because they realized that whatever art had withstood the test of time must of necessity exemplify true and abiding laws, did men devote themselves to the ancient masters and become their disciples. While there is profound justice in the view, yet imitation soon becomes servile and the close of the century brought stagnation—further progress being impossible while artists were thus confined to established forms. Particularly had the drama been stifled by rigid adherence to the "three unities" and other rules which, had they ever been vital, were far from essential in modern France.

From the sway of the classicists, the pendulum swung to the other extreme and the Romantic school arose in youthful enthusiasm. No longer should men revert to the past; in their eagerness to cut loose from the fetters that had held art bound, the best products of the classic school were swept away with the worst.

Scribe was the first to apply these new ideas to the writing of plays. Although conspicuous for his intuitive knowledge of stagecraft he was not a deep thinker. Beyond any playwright the world has produced, he knew the stage and its possibilities—what it could create and how desired results could be obtained. For this comprehensive grasp of stagecraft he is studied today by aspiring dramatists. Yet his plays, which were chiefly inventions, have not endured. However, he did much to emancipate the drama of his day and imbue it with new spirit.

About the middle of the nineteenth century another coterie of thinkers developed, first in France, whence their tenets spread into other lands. They were known as realists. They held that there should be less invention and keener observation; less idealizing and more revealing. We know their work perhaps best through fiction; Balzac was one of the most eminent advocates of these principles in France and was followed in other countries by those of similar ideas. Finally, towards the close of the century just passed, the naturalistic school appeared, carrying the principles of the realists to an extreme. This school maintained that poet, painter, sculptor and playwright should produce pictures of life with the veracity of a photographer. Those taking their stand beneath this banner sought out no pleasing models or scenes or characters.

Instead, they depicted the gross and ugly, the crude and repulsive until in derision it was said that the naturalists were artists who would not paint your portrait unless you were pitted with smallpox. The most prominent exponent of this school has been Zola.

PIERRE CORNEILLE.

Creator of the French Drama is the noble title awarded to Pierre Corneille, of Normandy. In chronological justness, this title should be bestowed upon Étienne Jodelle (1532-1573), one of the famous Pléiade. Jodelle had imitated Seneca. Corneille's "Le Cid," which was to represent to Victor Hugo the extreme of classicism, did not seem truly classical enough to Corneille's own contemporaries. To them "Le Cid" was highly romantic in both theme and treatment. Jodelle's tragedies had better pleased the scholars who, in celebration of one of his dramas, had actually held an ancient fête champêtre and crowned a stag with ivy and flowers in honor of Thespis. But Jodelle's tragedy never flourished outside of college and court. It was Corneille who was to make, in spite of the censure of Cardinal Richelieu's new Academy, the supreme appeal to the people of Paris. It was not, however, until Corneille had written eight dramas of small value that he found his true province. Indeed, in one of his earliest tragedies, that of "Clitandre, or Innocence Delivered" (1632), Dorise, the heroine, had her "innocence delivered" by stabbing her would-be seducer with a hair-pin—after which followed, of course, the inevitable philosophic meditation.

But in 1636, when Corneille was thirty years old, he gave to the French stage its great masterpiece, "The Cid." The theme was romantic, instead of classic, being based on Spain's chivalric romances. The especial source of Corneille's drama was a work by Guillen de Castro on "The Youth of the Cid." In the drama of both writers the Cid is a gallant young Castilian hero of twenty, and the plot celebrates his

love-episode with Chimène. Tragic in its opening involve-
ment, its happy outcome renders this love affair highly
romantic. Its Spanish code of honor, its almost demigod
type of chivalry, and its interminably pompous declamations
alone make it seem classical, instead of romantic in spirit, to
Victor Hugo and the passionate young bards of the opening
nineteenth century.

The character of the Cid, Don Rodrigue (in Spanish,
Roderigo), is almost legendary, and typifies, above even its
historical aspects, the patriotism and heroism of embattled
Spain against the Moors. The old folk-ballads recounted
how the youthful Cid avenged an insult to his father, Don
Diego, by the duel to death with Don Gomez, Count of
Gormas, father of Chimène (Ximenez or Ximena). Corneille's play begins, after a revelation of the mutual love
of Don Rodrigue and Chimène, with the fatal affront given
by Chimène's sire to Don Diego. The lover, after a severe
mental struggle between love and honor, avenges his father.
Chimène then agonizes in a like struggle, at the end of
which she hastens to the king to demand Rodrigue's
blood in vengeance—vowing to herself to die as soon as
this atonement is achieved. Meanwhile a raid of infidels
has been repulsed, and the invading host crushed by Rodrigue at the head of the nobles. The king feels compelled
to confer on him the title of Le Cid (in Arabic, el Seid,
"the Lord"), which he has won for himself among the Sara-
cens. Rodrigue's description of the combat is a splendid
piece of Corneille's rhetoric. Chimène, deserted by the king,
now accepts Don Sancho as a champion. But previously
Chimène has swooned on a false report of the Cid's death,
and when, as a subtle ruse, Rodrigue sends his sword by Don
Sancho, as if conquered, Chimène pours out her love-wrath
on the unlucky knight. The lovers are thus reunited, after
all, in a manner which struck Corneille's classical critics as
decidedly unheroic. Chapelain, encouraged by the jealous
Richelieu, complained that the dramatist could not "please
the learned;" Corneille was said to rank below Scudéry, and
to have degraded tragedy to melodrama. But to the Pari-
sian public all such classical fastidiousness was caviare : to the

people Chimène was more lovely because of her very humanity, her feminine inconsistency, and yet faithfulness to the great passion of love. As Boileau declared,

> In vain 'gainst the Cid a minister makes league;
> All Paris for Chimène has the eyes of Rodrigue.

And throughout France it became a proverb, "Cela est beau comme le Cid" (beautiful as "The Cid").

Corneille himself realized, in the condemnation of his master work by the Academy, that he had broken the Aristotelian unities and laws of the classical drama. In his three essays on the dramatic art—"On the Utility of Dramatic Poetry," "On Tragedy," and "On the Three Unities"—he shows that he did not himself perceive the vital essence of his own reform. In "Horatius," dedicated with a dry satire to his arch-enemy, Richelieu, and in "Cinna," which he wrote as an answer to his critics to show his power to invent an original drama, he returned more to the classic model. And he took pride, in fact, that "as the verses of 'Horatius' are more appropriate and less strained for the expression of thought than those of the 'Cid,' so those of 'Cinna' are more finished than the verses of 'Horatius.'" After two defeats, he was finally crowned an Immortal in the boastful Academy. In "Horatius," Corneille contrasts the characters of Sabine and Camille, and paints an old-time Roman in old Horatius. In "Cinna," he depicts a fruitless conspiracy against the forgiving Cæsar Augustus. In "Polyeucte" he composed "a Christian tragedy," as he himself styled it. His other dramas call for no mention here, save that it may be remarked that he wrote a comedy-ballet, Psyche, in conjunction with Molière, and a comedy, "Le Menteur" (The Liar), which has caused him to be styled the Father of French Comedy.

Pierre Corneille was born at Rouen in 1606, the son of a king's advocate at the court of Normandy. He was educated by the Jesuits and was destined for the bar. Strange to say, it was an impediment of speech that rescued him for the stage. Before his death (in 1684) he had been surpassed by Racine and beheld with sadness his own decline. Corneille, once the pride of Paris, died neglected and almost forgotten.

DON DIEGO AND HIS SON, THE CID.

DON DIEGO, formerly a valiant warrior of Castile, but now infirm
through age, was appointed by King Ferdinand tutor of his son. Count
de Gormas is jealous of this mark of favor, and meeting Don Diego quarrels with him and strikes him on the cheek with his glove. This insult
is worse than death to the aged warrior, who appeals to his assailant
to slay him, but the Count derides him. Diego's rage and shame find
vent in the following outburst:

> O rage, despair! O age, thou traitor-foe!
> Have I not lived too long to bear a blow?
> To see, grown grey in martial toils and fame,
> So many laurels fade in one day's shame?
> My arm, so long by Spain in honor held—
> My arm, that hath so oft the realm upheld,
> So oft the king upon his throne sustained,
> Now to betray my quarrel, leave me stained!
> O cruel memory of my glories gone,
> So many days thus one by one undone!
> New dignity by which my peace is ta'en,
> Precipice whence my honor fallen is slain,
> Must my foe triumph in your light, while I
> Disgraced must live, or unavenged must die?
> Count, take my office: near my prince must be
> In this high rank no man disgraced like me.
> Thy jealous rage by such affront hast brought
> To me unfitness, the king's choice to nought.
> And thou, the instrument of glorious deeds,
> Thou sword which icy age no longer needs,
> Once dreaded, but which in this last offence
> Hast been a thing of show, not of defence—
> Go, leave the last and lowest of mankind,
> And to avenge me better master find.

Diego then calls upon his son Roderigo, the Cid, to avenge the
affront, but Roderigo is in love with Chimène (Ximena), the daughter
of Count de Gormas. The struggle in his soul between the demands
of honor and the passion of love is shown in his soliloquy.

> Struck to the depths of my sad heart
> By blow so unforeseen, a mortal thrust;
> Avenger of a quarrel stern and just,

Victim of an unjust and deadly dart,
Silent I stand.—My soul, in sad amaze,
    Yields to the blow that slays.
So near, so near to recompense so tender,
    O God, the wondrous pain!
My father's name insulted, and the offender
    The father of Chimène.

What bitter strife within me burns!
Against my honor my affections move.
I must avenge my sire—and lose my love.
    One stirs my soul, my arm the other turns.
O bound to such sad choice!—*her* heart to break,
    Or bear shame for her sake.
On either side my woe is infinite.
    O God, the bitter pain!
Accept the insult, and refrain to slay
    The father of Chimène.

My father—my betrothed; honor or love.
O noble tyranny, O high constraint!
My pleasures all are dead, my glories faint.
    Unworthy or unhappy I must prove.
What dear and cruel hope dost thou discover
    To generous son and lover,
O noble enemy of all my joy,
    Sword that bring'st nought but pain!
To 'venge my sire must I thy blade employ,
    And lose by thee Chimène?

THE CID AND CHIMÈNE.

RODERIGO, the Cid, having vindicated his father's honor by slaying the Count de Gormas in a duel, makes his way to his betrothed Chimène, the Count's daughter, and offers her his sword that she may take vengeance for the death of her father. But she rejects the proposal with horror. Roderigo declares that he has justly incurred her wrath, and cannot live to hear her reproach him. Then Chimène replies:

    Chimène. Ah, Roderigo, though thy foe I be,
I blame thee not to have fled this infamy;
And howsoe'er my misery outwards flows,
Without accusing thee I weep my woes.

I know for such a wrong what cruel art
Honor demands from every generous heart.
Thou hast done only what the brave must do,
But in the act I learn my part from you:
Thy fatal valor and sad victory show
What to my father and my house I owe.

Mine the same care:
bound for my misery
T' avenge my sire, and
win my fame in thee.
Alas! thy part in this is
my despair.
Had I from other hand
such woe to bear,
My soul had found in
thee the sole relief,
The only solace for her
bitter grief.
What help, what strength
in sorrow's evil day
If thy dear hand had
wiped my tears away!
But think not in my heart
that love has room
With coward thoughts
to save thee from thy
doom,
Although affection fain
would break thy bonds,
My courage, generous too, to thine responds.
Thou prov'st thee worthy me in wounding me;
And by thy death I'll prove me worthy thee.

Roderigo. Do not borrow another arm, O my Chimène! believe
me, this is not a fit return. My arm alone avenged my offence;
thy hand alone should take vengeance for thine.

Chim. Cruel! why torture me with this persistence? You
avenged yourself without aid, but you would help me to my vengeance. No, I will follow your example; I have too much courage
to share my glory with thee.

Rod. Can I not obtain this last favor? For the sake of your
dead father, for the sake of our love, strike me, for vengeance or
for pity!

Chim. Go! I hate you not.

Rod. But I deserve your hatred.

Chim. Go! I cannot give it.

Rod. Care you so little for blame and public reproach? When it is known that you love me still, what will envy and malice say? Silence them, and slay me for your good fame.

Chim. My good fame shall shine the brighter that I let thee live. The blackest envy will applaud me and lament my sorrows when they see that I adore thee, yet pursue thee.

Rod. Let me die!

Chim. Go! go!

Rod. What purpose is in thy mind?

Chim. To avenge my father in spite of our love. But notwithstanding the rigor of this cruel duty, my only hope is to fail in it.

Rod. O miracle of love!

Chim. O crown of misery!

Rod. What grief and tears will our fathers cost us!

Chim. Roderigo, who could have believed it?

Rod. Chimène, who would have uttered it?

Chim. That our joy so nigh was so soon lost!

Rod. That close to port, unlikely as it seemed,
A sudden storm should shipwreck all our hopes!

Chim. Ah! fatal griefs!

Rod. Ah! profitless regrets!

ÆMILIA.

CORNEILLE considered his "Cinna" the finest of his classical dramas. It relates to the plots in the household of the Emperor Augustus. He had, beyond his usual generosity to former enemies, been liberal to Cinna, the grandson of Pompey, and to Æmilia, the daughter of Toranius. Yet Æmilia cannot forgive him for causing the death of her father Toranius, who had been proscribed during the Triumvirate. She persuades her lover Cinna to engage in a conspiracy against the Emperor. The following soliloquy in the opening of the play expresses her feeling, and gives the keynote to the drama.

> Ye impatient longings for a signal revenge,
> Whose origin is due to my father's death,
> Headstrong children of my resentment,
> Whom my misguided grief blindly embraces,
> Ye assume too potent sway over my soul.

Suffer me to breathe yet for a few moments,
And to consider, in this state where I am,
Both what I venture and what I pursue.
When I behold Augustus in the midst of his glory,
And when you reproach my sad memory
That my father, slain by his own hand,
Was the first step to the throne where I see him—
When you offer me this picture of blood,
The cause of my hatred, the result of his fury,
I abandon myself to your burning transports,
I feel that for one death, I owe him a thousand.
And yet, amidst a rage so founded on reason,
Still more love I Cinna than I hate Augustus,
And I feel this seething passion grow cool,
When to effect it, I must expose my lover.

THE TRAITOR LOVERS.

THE Emperor Augustus, having been informed of Cinna's conspiracy, sends for him and rehearses all its details. He shows that
from it no good can result for Cinna or for Rome. The conspirator
admits his guilt and professes his readiness to suffer the extreme
penalty, but Augustus allows him to choose his own punishment.
Then Livia, the emperor's wife, enters with Æmilia, his adopted
daughter. The latter, to his astonishment, declares that she alone is
responsible for Cinna's crime.

Livia. You know not yet all his accomplices.
Your Æmilia is one of them; behold her.
Cinna. O heavens! It is herself.
Augustus. And you, my daughter, too!
Æmilia. Yes; all that he did, he did to please me;
Of it, my lord, I was the cause and the reward.
Aug. What! Does the love which yesterday I caused to
　　　spring
Move you already to die for him to-day?
Your soul yields itself too much to that passion,
It is too soon to love the lover that I gave you.
Æmil. This love which subjects me to your resentment
Is not the prompt effect of your commands;
Without your order these flames arose in our hearts,
They are the secret of more than four years.
But though I loved him, and he burned for me,

A hatred still stronger made the law for both.
I would never give him the least hope of love
Till he had assured me of vengeance for my father.
I made him swear it; he sought out his friends;
Heaven destroys the success that I had promised myself,
And I come, my lord, to offer you a victim,
Not to save his life by charging myself with crime.
After his attempt his fault is too clear,
And in a crime of state every excuse is vain.
To die in his presence and regain my sire,
'Tis that brings me here, and that is my hope.
   Aug. Until when, O Heaven! and for what reason
Will you direct against me attacks in my house?
Julia I have driven from it for her debauchery;
In her place my love had made choice of Æmilia,
And her likewise I see unworthy of that rank.
The one robbed me of honor, the other thirsts for my blood,
Both took their guilty passions as their guides;
The one became wanton, the other a parricide.
O my daughter! Is this the reward of my favors?
   Æmil. My father's produced the like effect in you.
   Aug. Think with what affection I nourished your youth.
   Æmil. He nourished yours with the same tenderness;
He was your tutor, and you were his assassin;
You have already shown me the path to crime.
Mine differs from yours in this point alone,
That your ambition sacrificed my father,
And that a just wrath with which I still burn
Resolved to slay you for his innocent blood.

Livia then interrupts to declare that, by the law of Heaven, the
emperor cannot be punished for crimes committed by him as a private
person, that he is surrounded with an inviolable sanctity. Æmilia
assents to this doctrine, and declares that she is not seeking to defend
herself.

   Æmil. Punish then, lord, these pampered criminals
Who of your favorites make conspicuous ingrates.
Cut off my sad days to assure your own.
If I seduced Cinna, I will seduce many another.
I am more to be feared, and you are more in danger,
If love and blood together call me to avenge them.
   Cin. Have I been seduced by you? Can I endure still

To be dishonored by her whom I adore?
My lord, the truth must here be fully told.
Before I loved her I had formed that plot.
To my pure desires finding her immovable,
I thought that to other feelings she would yield.
I spoke of her father and of your severity,
And the offer of my arm followed that of my heart.
How sweet is vengeance to a woman's soul!
By that means I attacked, by that I won her soul.
For my small merit she might neglect me,
She could not neglect the arm that would avenge her.
She did not conspire save by my artifice;
I was the sole author, she but an accomplice.

 Æmil. Cinna, what dare you say? Is it to cherish me
To rob me of honor when I must die?

 Cin. Die, but in dying tarnish not my glory.

 Æmil. Mine would wither, should Cæsar believe you.

 Cin. And mine is lost, if you draw to yourself
All that follows from such powerful strokes.

 Æmil. Well then, take your part of it, and leave me mine;
To weaken it would be to weaken thine.
Glory and pleasure, shame and torments,
All should be common between true lovers.
(*To Augustus.*) The souls of both, my lord, are Roman souls;
Uniting our loves, we united our hates,
The quick desire to avenge our lost relatives
Taught us our duties at the same moment.
In that noble plot our hearts were joined,
Our generous spirits formed it together;
Together we sought the honor of a fair crime.
You wished to unite us, separate us not.

JEAN BAPTISTE RACINE.

JEAN RACINE, the second of the classic tragedists of France, was the son of a controller of the salt office at Ferté Milon, and was born in 1639, three years after the triumphant production of Corneille's "Le Cid." He commenced writing twenty years before Corneille's death, and his earliest verses are a palpable imitation of his predecessor's poetry. The principles enunciated by Corneille served as the guide for Racine in the dramatic art.

The themes of Racine's classical tragedies were taken directly from the Greek tragedies. "Andromaque," based on Euripides, is a picture of pure motherhood; "Iphigénie en Aulide," the drama of rivalry between Eriphile and Iphigenia over Achilles, and "Phédre," the passion of the wife of Theseus for her step-son Hippolytus. The flat reception of this last-named piece nearly drove Racine to become a Carthusian friar.

Racine's famous comedy is "Les Plaideurs" (The Litigants), written in 1668. It is virtually a farce, after the manner of Aristophanes, dealing with the mania of an old judge, Dandin, for pronouncing sentence, and with the fondness of the Countess de Pimbesche and Chicaneau for lawsuits.

The amiable and friendly Racine was more religious in temperament than Corneille. Corneille had been educated by the Jesuits, and translated Thomas á Kempis's "De Imitatione Christi." Racine, though in early life somewhat licentious, was essentially, however, of a religious type, and to the last he remained attached to the Port Royal school of his day. He composed, indeed, a series of "Cantiques

Spirituels" (sacred canticles). He was admitted to the
French Academy in 1673, and died in Paris in 1699.

Racine drew from the Bible the plots for his "Esther"
(1689), and his crowning masterpiece, "Athalie" (1691). The
poet follows the sacred narrative so faithfully that hardly
anything more than a general reference to the sources is
necessary; and yet the playwright felt himself called upon
to give a summary of the biblical story in his own prologue.
The central character of Athaliah is painted in powerful
colors. She is the daughter of the wicked Jezebel, who had
been thrown to the dogs as a punishment for her bloody per-
secution of the prophets. Athaliah is "another Jezebel"—
cruel and bloody-minded, but even in her wickedness always
a queen. She has married Joram, King of Judah, but on his
death she seeks to extirpate the royal house of David for the
sake of Baal. In a dream her mother appears to her and warns
her, and she also sees the vision of a young priest. Hastening
to the temple she finds the living image, who is in reality the
hidden heir to the throne, Joash. Determined to pierce the
mystery, she holds a forced interview with the nine-year-old
prince. This scene, in which the young Joash is brought into
the presence of Athaliah, is full of a high beauty. The child-
ish yet wise simplicity with which he replies to the queen's
pressing inquiries, at every step unconsciously foiling her
purpose and throwing her into confusion and rage, are exhibited with consummate art. "It is the first and only time,"
remarked La Harpe in his day, "that one has been inspired
to draw from the charm of childhood all the interest of a
tragic scene. There is nothing more touching, as witness the
effect at the theatre where this scene has affected deliciously
every soul." Athaliah's narration of her terrible dream of
prophecy, with its picture of the dogs gnawing and snarling
over her mother's bones, is stirringly dramatic. The queen's
attack on the temple, the arming of the Levites, and Athaliah's
tragic death ensue. The tragedy opens on Pentecost, or the
Feast of Weeks—the day the giving of the law on Mount
Sinai was commemorated, and ends with the anointing and
crowning of Joash. Racine declared his choice of this time of
action since its features "furnished such variety for the chants

of the chorus." This chorus is composed of young maidens of the tribe of Levi, headed by a niece of the high priest. Racine's object was to imitate the ancients in thus preserving a continuity of action unbroken by intervals. However undramatic to the present view, these hymns of the chorus are superb triumphs of devotional lyricism, pregnant with majesty and beauty. Both these scriptural plays were performed (without the aid of scenery) by the female pupils of the school at Saint Cyr, founded by Madame de Maintenon. Even the male characters were, according to Racine, "represented by the young ladies, with all the decorum of their sex, which was the easier for them as in ancient times the Persians and the Jews wore long dresses which reached to the ground." This prudish remark emphasizes the effeminate nature of Racine's genius. In contra-distinction to the severity of tone of his great predecessor, who is styled "le grand Corneille," the author of "Athalie" is affectionately known as "le tendre Racine." Racine was—aside from his two sacred tragedies— the painter of love. Despite his formal classicism we can still appreciate his tenderness. But this trait was accompanied by a lack of virile qualities. Appointed, along with his intimate friend Boileau, as historiographer to the Grand Monarque, he was somewhat too king-worshiping to the last, and his death has even been attributed to over-sensitiveness at the loss of royal favor. In "Esther" he is said to have represented Madame de Maintenon as Esther and the King as Ahasuerus ; while Madame de Montespan was put to scorn as the haughty Vashti—a strange use to which to subject a sacred theme truly. But in "Athalie" Racine made the high priest caution the youthful King Joash :

> You are ignorant of the intoxication of absolute power
> And of the bewitching voice of cowardly flatterers.
> Soon they'll tell you that the holiest laws
> Rule the vile people, but obey the kings,
> That a king has no other restraint than his own will ;
> That he ought to sacrifice everything to his supreme grandeur ;
> That the people is condemned to tears, to labor,
> And must be governed with a rod of iron ;
> That unless they are oppressed they will oppress sooner or later.

This sentiment must have sounded somewhat discordantly in the Grand Monarque's ear, and it is small wonder "Athalie" had no favor at court. Later Madame de Maintenon persuaded Racine to write out some of his ideas on social reform. "Because he can make verses," exclaimed the irritated king, "does he want to be a minister of state?"

ORESTES AND HERMIONE.

(From the Tragedy of "Andromaque.")

Hermione. WHAT have I done? Where am I? Where is
    Pyrrhus?
Ye gods! what mean these horrors? I'm undone!
My soul is on the rack! I cannot bear it!
Why do I wander like some guilty ghost?
What brought me to this place? What keeps me here?
The court of Pyrrhus has no room for me!
Do I still doubt if I should love or hate him?
Hard-hearted man! how unconcerned he left me!
Did he once sigh? bestow one pitying look?
Once shed a tear? or speak one soft, kind word?
Did he so much as feign one moment's sorrow,
To calm my griefs, and mitigate his falsehood?
Why am I still thus anxious for his life?
Why do I start at his impending fate?
Shall he, then, live? Shall the base traitor live
To laugh at my distress? No, let him perish!
Be quick, Orestes! Execute my orders!
Alas! my orders! O preposterous guilt!
Can I decree the death of him I love?
Was it for this my soul delighted in him?
Was it for this I left my father's court?
Have I, then, crossed so many realms and seas
To murder Pyrrhus?—   *[Cleone enters.*
O Cleone, help me!
What have I done? Is Pyrrhus yet alive?
What say'st thou? Answer me: where is the king?
    Cleone. Madam, I saw the cruel prince set forward,
Triumphant in his looks, and full of joy.
Still as he walked, his ravished eyes were fixed
On the fair captive; while through shouting crowds

She passed along with a dejected air,
And seemed to mourn her Hector to the last.

Herm. Insulting tyrant! I shall burst with rage!
But say, Cleone, didst thou mark him well?
Was his brow smooth? Say did there not appear
Some shade of grief, some little cloud of sorrow?
Did he not stop? Did he not once look back?
Didst thou approach him? Was he not confounded?
Did he not —— Oh, be quick, and tell me all!

Cle. Madam, the tumult of his joy admits
No thought but love. Unguarded he marched on,
'Midst a promiscuous throng of friends and foes.
His cares all turn upon Astyanax,
Whom he has lodged within the citadel,
Defended by the strength of all his guards.

Herm. Enough! he dies! the traitor! Where's Orestes?

Cle. He's in the temple with his whole retinue.

Herm. Is he still resolute? Is he still determined?

Cle. Madam I fear ——

Herm. How! Is Orestes false? Does he betray me, too?

Cle. A thousand doubts
Perplex his soul, and wound him with remorse:
His virtue and his love prevail by turns.
He told me Pyrrhus should not fall ignobly,—
Pyrrhus, the warlike son of great Achilles.
He dreads the censure of the Grecian states,—
Of all mankind, and fears to stain his honor.

Herm. Poor timorous wretch! 'Tis false! He basely
    fears
To cope with dangers, and encounter death;
'Tis that he fears! Am I bright Helen's daughter?
To vindicate her wrongs all Greece conspired;
For her, confederate nations fought, and kings were slain
Troy was o'erthrown, and a whole empire fell:
My eyes want force to raise a lover's arm
Against a tyrant that has dared to wrong me!

Cle. Madam, like Helen, trust your cause to Greece.

Herm. No! I'll avenge myself: I'll to the temple;
I'll overturn the altar, stab the priest;
I'll hurl destruction like a whirlwind round me!
They must not wed! they must not live! they shall not!
Let me begone! I have no time to lose!

Stand off! hold me not! I am all distraction!
O Pyrrhus, tyrant! traitor! thou shalt bleed!

> [*Orestes enters.*

Orestes. Madam, 'tis done; your orders are obeyed:
The tyrant lies expiring at the altar.

Herm. Is Pyrrhus slain?

Or. Even now he gasps in death.
Our Greeks, all undistinguished in the crowd,
Flocked to the temple and dispersed themselves
On every side the altar.   I was there:
Pyrrhus observed me with a haughty eye,
And, proud to triumph over Greece in me,
From his own brows he took the diadem,
And bound it on the temples of his captive:
"Receive," said he, "my crown! receive my faith,
Mine and my people's sovereign reign, forever!
From this blessed hour, a father to your son,
I'll scourge his foes: henceforth be he styled
The Trojan king: I swear it at the altar.
And call the gods to ratify my vows!"
His subjects with loud acclamations shook
The spacious dome.   Our Greeks, enraged, cried out,
"Revenge! revenge!" broke through the thronging press,
And rushed tumultuous on the unguarded king:
Their eager fury left no work for me.
Pyrrhus awhile opposed their clashing swords,
And dealt his fatal blows on every side
With manly fierceness; till, oppressed by numbers,
Streaming with blood, all over gashed with wounds,
He reeled, he groaned, and at the altar fell.
Haste, Madam, let us fly!   Haste to our ships!
They lie unmoored,—our friends attend us there.

Herm. What have they done?

Or. Madam, forgive their rage!
I own your vengeance had been more complete
Had Pyrrhus fallen by me, and had he known
Hermione chastised him by my arm.

Herm. Peace, monster, peace!   Go, tell thy horrid tale
To savages, and howl it in the deserts!
Wouldst thou impute to me thy barbarous guilt?
Me wouldst thou make the accomplice of thy crimes?
Hence to thy Greeks, and boast thy foul exploits!

My soul abhors them! I disclaim the deed!
Begone! I know thee not, thou fell barbarian?
What had he done? What could provoke thy madness
To assassinate so great, so brave a man?
Who set thee on?

    Or. Oh, grant me patience, Heaven!
With your own lips did you not curse the tyrant,
Pronounce his death, and urge me to destroy him?

    Herm. What if, transported by my boundless passion,
I could not bear to see him wed another,—
Were you to obey a jealous woman's frenzy?
You should have div'd into my inmost thoughts:
My heart, though full of rage, was free from malice;
And all my anger was excess of love.
Why did you take me at my word? You saw
The struggles of my soul; you heard me rave:
You should have questioned me a thousand times,
Yet still have doubted, and still questioned on,
Before you ventured on a life so precious.

    Or. Hear me but speak: Heaven knows, against my
       will ——

    Herm. Why did you not return? why not consult me
A second time? and, undetermined still,
Again return, and still find new delays?
What had your rash, officious Greeks—dire bloodhounds!
To do with my revenge? What drew you hither?
To bring on me the vengeful woes that haunt you?
Are these the fruits of your detested love?
Your fatal embassy, your hateful presence,

Drove Pyrrhus to my rival, and destroys
Both him and me. He might have loved me still,
Had you ne'er interposed. Avaunt! Begone!
And leave me in Epirus. I renounce
My friends, my country, Greece, and all mankind:
But, chiefly, I renounce thee, monster! thee!   [*Exit.*
    Or. Am I awake? Where am I? Soft, my soul!
Be not too rash. —— Was that Hermione?
Why should her anger thunder against me?
Was not this blood shed all by her command?
I am, indeed, a most outrageous monster!
A ruffian, murderer, a base assassin!
And all to please a false, ungrateful woman.
Henceforward let the laws of nations cease;
And let the pale that severs right and wrong,
Things sacred and profane, be broken down:
Gods in their temples, kings upon their thrones,
Are not in safety while Orestes lives.
Oh, never more shall my torn mind be healed,
Nor taste the gentle comforts of repose;
A dreadful band of gloomy cares surround me,
And lay strong siege to my distracted soul!

ATHALIAH AND JOASH.

RACINE's drama "Athalie" is founded on II Kings, chapter xi., and II Chronicles, chapters xxii., xxiii. Athaliah, the daughter of Ahab and Jezebel, was the wife of Joram, King of Judah. On learning that Jehu had slain the sons of Ahab, she resolved to destroy all the royal race of David, putting to death even the children of her own son Ahaziah. But one of them, Joash, was saved by his aunt Jehosheba, and brought up under the name Eliakim, by Jehoiada, the high priest. The queen at last meets the boy, attended by Jehosheba, Zechariah, and others, in the temple. She is startled by his resemblance to one whom she had seen in a dream.

Athaliah. Wife of Jehoiada, is that your son?
Jehosheba. I am not his mother; (*pointing to Zechariah*), this is my son.
Ath. And you, child, who is your father? Answer me.
Jehosh. Heaven, till to-day.
Ath. Why should you answer for him? Let him speak.
Jehosh. At so tender an age, what explanation can he give?

Ath. At his age he is innocent: he has no craft to alter the truth. Let him answer for himself.

. *Jehosh.* (*aside*). Great God, put wisdom in his mouth!

Ath. What is your name?

Joash. I am called Eliakim.

Ath. And who is your father?

Jo. I am, they tell me, an orphan, thrown since my birth into God's paternal arms.

Ath. Are you without parents?

Jo. They have forsaken me.

Ath. But you know at least where your home is?

Jo. This temple is my home; I never knew any other.

Ath. But who, then, cared for you in your infant years?

Jo Does God ever let his little children want? He feeds the birds, and everywhere his hand is seen. I pray to him every day, and every day at his altar he gives me food.

Jehosheba would now take the child away; but Athaliah calls him back.

Ath. What is your daily occupation?

Jo. I worship God. I am taught his Law. In his divine Book I learn to read. And already I begin to write it with my own hand.

Ath. And what does this law teach you?

Jo. That God desires us to love him; that he will avenge, sooner or later, those who blaspheme his holy name; that he is the defender of the timid orphan; that he will crush the proud man, and punish the murderer.

Ath. I understand; but all the people in that place, what are they doing?

Jo. Praising God.

Ath. Does God desire that they should always pray?

Jo. Other exercises are banished from his temple.

Ath. What! have you no other pastime? I pity the sad fate of such a child as you. Come into my palace and see my splendor.

Jo. No; for I should then forget the goodness of God.

Ath. I will not ask you to forget him.

Jo. But you do not pray to him.

Ath. You may do so if you like.

Jo. I should see you kneeling before another god.

Ath. I have my god whom I worship, and you may worship yours: they are both powerful gods.

Jo. You must fear him too. Mine only is God, madam. Yours is nothing.

Ath. If you come with me I will give you every kind of pleasure.

Jo. The happiness of wicked people flows away like a torrent.

Ath. And who are the wicked?

Jehosh. Excuse him, madam; he is but a child.

Ath. (*to Jehosheba*). I love to see how you train him. Now, Eliakim, you have known how to please me. You are not an ordinary child. You see I am a queen, and have no heir. Put off these clothes; abandon this vile office; I wish you to share in all my riches. Try this very day if I keep my promise. Seated at my table, standing at my side, I will treat you as my son.

Jo. As your son?

Ath. Yes. You say nothing.

Jo. What a father should I leave! And for—

Ath. Well?

Jo. And for what a mother!

Ath. (*to Jehosheba*). His memory is faithful, and in all he says I see the teaching of Jehoiada and your own. You employ the quiet in which I leave you to corrupt this simple childhood: you cultivate hate and fury in them—you make my name a horror to them!

Jehosh. In all you have done you have triumphed. But God sees, and is our judge.

Ath. This God, who has so long been your hope, what will become of his prophecies? Let him send you your promised king —this son of David in whom you trust. . . . But we shall meet again. Adieu! I have seen what I wished to see, and I am satisfied.

The queen retires, and Jehoiada enters attended by his Levites. He thanks Abner for his protection to Joash, and prepares to cleanse with blood the spots which Athaliah's unholy footsteps had polluted. Then the choir comes in and sings.

CHORUS. What star of lustre strikes our eyes?
How bright does this young wonder rise?
With what a noble scorn
He dares seduction's charms despise,
To high achievements born!

ONE VOICE. Whilst at the impious queen's decree
Thousands to Baal basely bend the knee,

An infant's voice has dared proclaim
The one adorable eternal name.
Thus before Jezebel, defiled with blood,
Denouncing vengeance, great Elijah stood.

Cho. Happy, thrice happy, must he prove
The child who shares his heavenly Father's love,
Who in a blessed hour His voice has heard
And yields obedience to the sacred word!
'Tis his within the hallowed shrine,
By impious footsteps never trod,
To own the bounteous hand divine,
The guardian care of Israel's God.
O happy youth, so early blest,
On Heaven's eternal truth forever rest!

THE AGE OF LOUIS XIV.

It is not baseless flattery which has given to the reign of
Louis XIV. the glorious title of the Golden Age of French
literature. The greatest genius of that time, whose power
was acknowledged, though his true greatness was not fully
recognized in his own day, must here be discussed and exemplified. Molière, in spite of the hundred obstacles thrown in
his way by the authorities of the Church and State, by the
prejudices of society and literature, succeeded by pure force of
wit and fidelity to nature in achieving a glorious triumph.
Palpable as was his success in his lifetime, it was not equal
to that which his works have since accomplished. The supreme tribunal of the Academy, which refused to admit him
to a seat in its sacred precincts, has since acknowledged that
this failure was no loss to his glory, but the absence of his
name is a perpetual reproach to its judgment. Molière won
victories not only on the French stage, but even on the English, for his style of play-writing has practically prevailed
since it was introduced into English by his imitators. His
success was due to the fact that he "held the mirror up to
nature; showed virtue her own feature, scorn her own image,
and the very age and body of the time his form and pressure."

MOLIÈRE.

MOLIÈRE, the great French dramatist
of real life and contemporary man-
ners, was born plain Jean Baptiste Poquelin in 1622. He
has been pronounced by Professor Ward "the foremost of all
modern masters of comedy, whether of character or of manners." The French stage has no greater name, and on the
English stage, from the days of Dryden, Molière's wit has
reigned even to the exclusion of Shakespeare's joyous romance.
Like Shakespeare, Molière was himself an actor, as well as a
playwright; and like Shakespeare, too, he managed a troupe
and theatre. He had an unhappy marriage with a young
actress who led him a jealous career. Molière's father was a
well-to-do upholsterer, "tapissier valet de chambre du Roy,"
and secured for his son succession to his own Court office.
But Molière's stage career ruined his social status. After his
death he was almost denied a Christian burial. His death
itself was strikingly pathetic. From the start of his work as
a playwright he had never tired of scathing the ignorant
leeches and apothecaries of his age. During the period of his
provincial tours he wrote "Le Médecin volant," "Le Docteur
amoureux," and other farces directed against them. In the
heyday of his glory he aimed the formidable artillery of his
wit at them in "L'Amour Médecin" and "M. de Pourceaugnac," and especially in "Le Médecin malgré lui" ("The
Physician in Spite of Himself"). His last play was entitled
"Le Malade Imaginaire" (The Imaginary Illness), a biting
satire on the whole craft of doctors. As if Apollo became at
last aroused to vengeance on behalf of the sons of Æsculapius,
Molière was seized with a convulsion during the third per-

formance. He had been coughing and spitting blood before the comedy had been produced. Carried home, he died within a few hours. He died, as he had lived, faithful to his art. He was then fifty-one years old, a year and a half younger than Shakespeare at his death.

Molière's father sought to make his heir an upholsterer, but the boy had a grandfather who liked comedy, and who took him sometimes to the plays at the Hôtel de Bourgogne. When Francis I. (in 1543) had ordered the demolition of this Hôtel, the old Fraternities of the Passion had bought the site. Although these players were no longer allowed to act religious mysteries, they had some old farces—among them Patelin, born in the fifteenth century, and destined to be forefather of Tartuffe. They had also translations from Plautus and Terence, from Seneca and from the early Italians. These old farces were written almost altogether in octosyllabics. Professor Morley has declared: "It remained for Molière not only to perfect the form of comic dialogue in verse, but also to show how wit and wisdom could point every phrase in lightest dialogue of prose." His greatest comedies are, however, almost all in verse. Molière was only fourteen when Corneille produced his Cid; and when Molière scored his hit with "Les Précieuses Ridicules" (in 1659), Racine was only twenty years old. Later Racine fell in love with Madame Duparc, a pretty widow, who was leading lady in Molière's troupe. Racine induced her to leave Molière, and play the heroine in his "Andromaque," which led to a quarrel between the two dramatists. Racine's friend, Boileau, was led to pass this criticism: "Perchance Molière might have reaped the meed of his art if, less friendly to the people, he had not often made his figures grimace in his learned pictures, neglected the pleasant and the refined for the burlesque, and shamelessly allied Terence with Tabarin."

Molière was never poor like Shakespeare, it must be borne in mind. At the age of fourteen he was sent to a Jesuit College, and polished in philosophy. At the age of nineteen he took his father's place in the retinue of Louis XIII., during that king's visit to Languedoc. But when he came back from that courtly trip his natural bent for the stage asserted itself. He

joined a band of young associates, who called themselves
L'Illustre Théâtre. From 1646 to 1658 he was in the pro-
vinces, acting at Grenoble, Lyons and Rouen. At Lyons he
and his troupe performed with success his first regular five-
act comedy in verse, "L'Etourdi," adapted by Dryden as
"Sir Martin Marr-all." Molière also wrote, about that time,
"Le Dépit Amoureux," made English by Sir John Vanbrugh
as "The Mistake." Emboldened by his successes, Molière returned in 1658 (at the age of thirty-six) to Paris, where through
an introduction from the Prince of Conti, he won the patronage of Louis XIV., then a youth of twenty. Molière's company acted that year before his majesty on a stage built in a
guard-room of the old palace of the Louvre. The king's
brother allowed Molière to entitle his company "La Troupe
de Monsieur," and in 1660 they established themselves in the
Palais Royal, on a stage built by Richelieu for the acting of
a tragedy to which Richelieu himself had contributed five
hundred verses. A year later, at the age of forty, Molière
unhappily married Armande Béjart.

For the purpose of brevity Molière's comedies after
"L'Étourdi" may be thus chronologically enumerated: "Les
Précieuses Ridicules" (1659), a satire in one act on the exag-
gerations of the Hôtel de Rambouillet; "Sganarelle, ou le Cocu
Imaginaire" (1660); "L'École des Maris" (School for Hus-
bands), (1661), a satire on unreasonable jealousy; "L'École des
Femmes" (School for Women), (1662), showing the danger
of ill-assorted marriages and of bringing up girls in too strict
a manner, and its sequel, "Critique de l'École des Femmes;"
"Don Juan" (1665), on libertinism in nobles; "Tartuffe ou
l'Imposteur," a scathing satire on the vice of hypocrisy (1669);
"L'Amour Médecin" (1665), his first attack on the doctors;
"Le Misanthrope" (1666), the portrait of a cynic disgusted
in the extreme with the pretenses of society; "Médecin
Malgré Lui" (1666); "L'Avare" (1668), with its famous portrait of the miser Harpagon; "Monsieur de Pourceaugnac"
a farcical comedy in three acts, with a masterly sketch of a
consultation of doctors in Molière's time; "Bourgeois Gen-
tilhomme" (1670), the folly of aping noblemen, pictured in
poor M. Jourdain, who did not know when he was talking

MRS. SIDDONS AS THE TRAGIC MUSE.—REYNOLDS.

prose; "Femmes Savantes" (Learned Ladies), a sort of sequel to the "Précieuses Ridicules" (1672); and, finally, "Malade Imaginaire," the fatal comedy. As M. Van Laun declares, "Molière placed upon the stage nearly all the human passions which lend themselves to comedy or farce. Sordid avarice, lavish prodigality, shameless vice, artless coquetry, greed for money, hypocrisy, would-be gentility, self-sufficient vanity, fashionable swindling, misanthropy, jealousy, heartlessness, roguery, affectation, pedantry, arrogance. The language which they employ is always natural to them. . . . His verse has none of the stiffness of the ordinary French rhyme. . . . And how remarkable and delicate is the nuance between his different characters, even though they may represent the same profession or general type. . . . A remarkable characteristic of Molière is, that he does not exaggerate. . . . His satire is always kept within bounds. . . . His claim to distinction is based on strong common sense, good manners, sound morality, real wit, true humor."

In the "Précieuses Ridicules" Molière laughed to jest the pedantic conceits of the salon of "Arthénice"—Catherine de Vivonne, at the Hôtel de Rambouillet. Mascarille, the hero, is a scurvy knave, who masquerades with a brother lackey as one of the wits of this affected coterie. In "Tartuffe" Molière "gives us the hypocrite by nature, who cannot help being so." Tartuffe seeks to seduce his benefactor's wife and marry the daughter, and failing in this he tries to cheat him of his property and drive him out homeless. He does all this under a cunning mask of the most humble saintliness, and has even the sublime audacity in the moment of supreme rascality to compare himself to Jesus Christ. In "Le Misanthrope" Molière paints a cynic with whom we are forced greatly to sympathize. Alceste's cynicism grows out of his own intense honesty. He hates shams, intrigue, bribery, flattery, and law. He neglects his lawsuit, tells brutal truths to a noble patron, and, despite his cynicism, loses just such a wife as he would esteem through his unhappy infatuation for a heartless coquette.

Molière's first comedy was produced seventy-seven years after the first play of Jodelle. Professor Ward adds: "In comedy Molière borrowed much from the Spaniards and Italians, who thus reached English literature at second-hand; and his debts to Latin comedy have probably been under-rated rather than over-rated."

Molière confessed to Boileau his great indebtedness to Corneille, whose comedy, "Le Menteur" (the Liar), was produced when Molière was only twenty-two years old. "My ideas were still confused," declared Molière, who had been adapting the old *sotties*, "but this piece determined me. But for 'Le Menteur,' I should no doubt have written comedies of intrigue, like my first plays." He would perhaps never have written "The Misanthrope," which is in many respects his chef-d'œuvre. In Alceste, Molière has painted himself in perhaps the same way that Shakespeare seems to have revealed his inner self in "Hamlet." Unhappy love and jealousy furnished Molière dramatic themes time and again, as though there were such torments at the bottom of his own heart—and we know as a fact that they were. "Mlle." Molière certainly resembled the coquette Célimène. As Alceste exclaims in the comedy, "Reason does not give the law to love."

Molière's influence on English literature has been tremendous. At the Restoration, in 1660, courtiers who came from Paris knew Molière as actor and dramatist, chief of a troupe which had been in Paris two years. Molière was then thirty-eight; Dryden twenty-nine. Dryden wanted Molière's refinement. In pleasing the roistering court of Charles II. he lacked the necessary light touch of the fashionable libertine. He strove to borrow the comedy of Molière, which so pleased the court of the Grand Monarque. But his version of "L'Étourdi," as "Sir Martin Marr-all," produced in London while Molière was bringing out "Tartuffe" in Paris, was really Molière in a coarse disguise, and is a horrible mixture of blank verse and prose. William Wycherley made a version of "Le Misanthrope" as "The Plain Dealer," with Alceste as Manly. Dryden glanced at this hero in his praise of "the satire, wit. and strength of Manly Wycherley." Wycherley also hurt Molière's comedy, but succeeded better than Dryden had done, and became, in fact, the father of the British "Prose Comedy of Manners." In "The Plain Dealer" he introduced a litigious Widow Blackacre, evidently suggested by Racine's "Les Plaideurs." Sir John Vanbrugh adapted "Le Dépit Amoureux" as "The Mistake." Henry Fielding, author of "Tom Jones," adapted both "Le Médecin Malgré Lui," as "The Mock Doctor," and "L'Avare" as "The Miser." "One pleasure I enjoy," he declared, "from the success of my attempt, is a prospect of transplanting some others of Molière's pieces of great value." Colley Cibber, born two years after Molière's death, made a highly-triumphant version of "Tartuffe," as "The Non-Juror." As Professor Morley remarks: "This version applied, with Whig bitterness of party feeling, a general satire on hypocrisy in sacred things to the religion of political opponents. It was directed against Roman Catholics and Non-Jurors, who had sympathized with the Jacobite insurrection of 1715. Pope was of Roman Catholic family, and Cibber's play contained an insult to Roman Catholics. Its factious loyalty obtained for Colley Cibber the office of poet-laureate, and its intolerance secured for him the highest gibbet in the 'Dunciad.'" Colley's brother-laureate, Shadwell, borrowed from "Les Précieuses Ridicules" for his "Bury Fair." Sir William D'Avenant used "Sganarelle" in his "Playhouse to be Let." Sir Charles Sedley founded his "Mulberry Garden" on "L'École des Femmes." "Tartuffe" also suggested Croune's "English Friar." Indeed, the list might be much farther extended.

Professor Brander Matthews goes so far as to assert that "the influence of Shakespeare on modern English comedy, on the comic plays acted during the past two centuries, is indisputable, of course, but it is less in quantity and less in quality than the influence of Molière. It would be easy to pick out the plays, like Tobin's 'Honeymoon,' and Knowles's 'Hunchback,' written consciously in the imitation—however remote—of Shakespeare. It would not be easy to name half the English comedies whose form and substance had been unconsciously molded by the example of Molière. . . . Modern English comedy is not made on the model of Elizabethan comic drama, and it is made— immorality apart—on the model of the Restoration comic drama. The comic dramatists of the Restoration . . . were the children of Molière. . . . Unfortunately for themselves, when they borrowed the point of view of the great Frenchman, they forgot to borrow his sobriety and his self-respect. . . . The reason why the influence of Molière is more potent on the form of English comedy than the influence of Shakespeare . . . is, that Molière represents a later stage of the development of play-making. . . . Molière began to write half a century after Shakespeare ceased to write ; and in that half century many and marked changes had taken place in the arrangement and constitution of the theatre. . . . In fact, the difference between the theatre as organized in the time of Shakespeare and as organized in the time of Molière is enormous and radical; whereas the difference between the theatre of Molière and of to-day is unessential and insignificant."

First Lesson in Philosophy.

(From "The Bourgeois Gentleman.")

Philosophy-Master. What have you a mind to learn ?

M. Jourdain. Everything I can, for I have all the desire in the world to be a scholar, and it vexes me that my father and mother had not made me study all the sciences when I was young.

Master. That's a very reasonable feeling. *Nam sine doctrina vita est quasi mortis imago.* You understand that, and are acquainted with the Latin, of course ?

M. Jour. Yes; but act as if I were not acquainted with it. Tell me what it means.

Master. It means that "without learning life is as it were an image of death."

M. Jour. That same Latin's in the right.

Master. Don't you know some principles, some rudiments of science ?

M. Jour. Oh, yes ! I can read and write. . . . But now I must confide a secret to you. I'm in love with a person of quality, and I should be glad if you would help me to write something to her in a short billet-doux, which I'll drop at her feet.

Master. Very well.

M. Jour. That will be gallant, won't it ?

Master. Undoubtedly. Is it verse you wish to write to her ?

M. Jour. No, no; none of your verse.

Master. You would only have prose?

M. Jour. No, I would neither have verse nor prose.

Master. It must be one or the other.

M. Jour. Why so?

Master. Because, sir, there's nothing to express oneself by but prose or verse.

M. Jour. Is there nothing, then, but verse or prose?

Master. No, sir; whatever is not prose is verse, and whatever is not verse is prose.

M. Jour. And when one talks what may that be, then?

Master. Prose.

M. Jour. How? When I say, " Nicole, bring me my slippers and give me my nightcap,'' is that prose?

Master. Yes, sir.

M. Jour. On my conscience, I have spoken prose above these forty years without knowing it; and I am hugely obliged to you for informing me of this.

M. Jour. (*to his wife*). I am ashamed of your ignorance. For example, do you know what it is you now speak?

Mme. Jour. Yes, I know that what I speak is right, and that you ought to think of living in another manner.

M. Jour. I don't talk of that. I ask you what the words are that you now speak?

Mme. Jour. They are words that have a good deal of sense in them, and your conduct is by no means such.

M. Jour. I don't talk of that, I tell you. I ask you what it is that I now speak to you, which I say this very moment?

Mme. Jour. Mere stuff.

M. Jour. Pshaw, no, it is not that. That which we both of us say, the language we speak this instant?

Mme. Jour. Well?

M. Jour. How is it called?

Mme. Jour. It's called just what you please to call it.

M. Jour. It's prose, you ignorant creature.

Mme. Jour. Prose?

M. Jour. Yes, prose. Whatever is prose is not verse, and whatever is not verse, is prose. Now, see what it is to study.

ALCESTE'S LOVE FOR CÉLIMÈNE.

(From "The Misanthrope," Act IV., Scene 3.)

Alceste.   O Heaven! how can I control here my passion?
Célimène (aside). Ah! (*To Alceste*). What's this trouble which
          you clearly show?
          And what's the meaning of those long-drawn sighs,
          And those black looks which you direct on me?
Alceste.   That all the horrid deeds one can conceive
          Will not compare to your perfidious conduct;
          That neither fate, nor hell, nor heaven in wrath
          Has e'er produced a thing so false as you are.
Célimène. These pretty things I surely much admire.
Alceste.   Ah! do not jest, this is no time for laughing.
          Indeed, blush rather; for you've cause to do so!
          And of your treachery I've the clearest proofs.
          That's what the emotions of my heart forebode;
          'Twas not in vain my love was seized with fear;
          You thought it odious when I oft suspected
          And sought that evil which my eyes have seen;
          Spite all your care and your deceitful skill,
          My star foretold me what I had to fear;
          But don't imagine that, without revenge,
          I'll bear the slight of being thus insulted.
          I know we cannot rule our inclinations;
          That love spontaneously springs everywhere;
          That there's no entering a heart by force,
          And that each soul may freely name its victor.
          Thus I'd no reason to complain at all,
          If you had spoken to me openly,
          And had disdained my love when it sprang up;
          My heart would then have only blamed its luck.
          But to fan my affection by deceit,
          Is such a treachery, such perfidy,
          That nothing I can do is too severe;
          And my resentment may do anything:
          Yes, yes, dread everything for such an outrage.
          I am beside myself; I'm mad with rage.
          Pierced by the deadly blow which you have dealt me
          My senses are no longer swayed by reason;

I yield to th' outbursts of a righteous wrath,
And do not answer what I may not do.

Célimène. Whence comes, I pray you, such a fit of passion?
Tell me, are all your senses wholly gone?

Alceste. Yes, yes, I lost them when I first beheld you,
And thus, to my misfortune, took the poison,
And when I thought to find sincerity
In those deceitful charms that have bewitched me.

Célimène. And of what treach'ry have you to complain?

Alceste (aside). Ah! what deceit! how well she can dissemble!
But, to confound her, I've the means at hand.
(*Aloud.*) Cast your eyes here, and recognize your writing
This picked-up note suffices to condemn you,
And such proof cannot lightly be refuted. . . .

Célimène. If this note to a woman be addressed,
How can it hurt you, and where is the guilt?

Alceste. Ah! this is good, the excuse is marvellous.
I must confess this turn is unexpected,
And now I am convinced, and wholly so.
Dare you employ such ordinary tricks?
And do you think me so bereft of sense?
Come, let us hear how far, and with what air,
You will support so palpable a falsehood;
And how you can apply to any woman
Those loving words found in this very note?
Explain away, to hide your broken vows,
What I will read. . . .

Célimène. It does not suit me now.
'Tis most ridiculous to lord it thus,
And to my face say what you dare to me!

Alceste. No, don't fly in a rage, but take some pains,
To justify the words which I see here.

Célimène. No, I shall not act thus; on this occasion
It matters nought to me what you believe.

Alceste. Pray, show me, and I shall be satisfied,
If this note can be meant for any woman.

Célimène. No, it was for Oronte; you may believe so;
All his attentions gladly I accept,
I admire what he says, I like him much;
And shall agree to whatever you please.
Do what you will; let nothing hinder you,
But let my thoughts be undisturbed by you.

Alceste (aside). O, Heavens! can aught more cruel be conceived?
Was e'er a heart treated in such a way?
What! with just anger I am moved against her,
I come to blame, and am myself attacked!
My grief and my suspicions are excited,
I credit all; she boasts of everything;
And yet my heart is cowardly enough
Not to tear off the bonds which hold it fast,
Not to put on a generous contempt
For the ungrateful object of its flame.
(*To Célimène.*) Ah, treacherous woman! but too well
    you know
To take advantage of my utmost weakness,
And to employ the excessive, fatal love,
So wondrously born of your treach'rous eyes.
Defend yourself from this o'erwhelming crime,
And cease to feign that you are culpable.
Prove, if you're able, that this note is blameless;
My love consents to lend a helping hand.
Though without faith yet put its semblance on,
And I'll endeavor to believe you such.

Célimène. Bah! you are mad with all these jealous frenzies,
And don't deserve the love I have for you.
I should much like to know what could compel me
To stoop for you to such a base pretence;
Why, if my heart inclined towards another,
Should I not say so with sincerity?
What! I avow the love I feel for you,
Yet your suspicions are not all allayed!
They ought to have no weight, with such a warrant
Does it not wrong me to attend to them?
And since we hardly dare confess our love,
And since our sex, hostile to lovers' passion,
To such avowals is so much opposed,
Should not a lover suffer who can doubt
When such an obstacle is overcome?
And is his guilt not clear, who is not sure
That we speak truth, at such a bitter cost?
Go! these suspicions well deserve my anger;
And you're not worthy I should care for you.
I wrong myself in my simplicity,
Still to preserve the smallest kindness for you;

I ought elsewhere to place all my affections,
And give you lawful cause for your complaints.
Alceste. Ah, traitress! strange the weakness you inspire;
Your sweet expressions are no doubt deceptive;
It matters not, I must accept my fate;
My very soul is wholly wrapt in you;
And to the very end I'll prove your heart,
And see if it be black enough to cheat me.
Célimène. No, you don't love me as you ought to love.
Alceste. Nothing can be compared to my deep love;
And, in its haste to show itself to all,
It e'en forms wishes 'gainst your lovely self.
Yes, I could wish no one to think you handsome,
That you were plunged in abject misery;
That Heaven had given you nothing, at your birth;
That you had had nor rank, nor birth, nor wealth;
So that the public proffer of my heart
Might make amends for so unjust a lot;
That I might then possess the joy and glory
To see you owe it all to my affection.

The Amenities of Authors.

(From "The Learned Ladies," Act III., scene 5.)

Trissotin (introducing Vadius). This is the man that is dying to see you. When I introduce him to you, I do not fear being blamed for having admitted a profane person to you, Madame; he may hold his place amongst the Beaux Esprits.

Philaminte. The hand that introduces him is sufficient guarantee of his worth.

Tris. He has a perfect knowledge of the ancient authors, and understands Greek, Madam, as well as any man in France.

Phil. (to Bélise). Greek, oh, heavens! Greek. He understands Greek, sister.

Bélise (to Armande). Ah, niece, Greek.

Armande. Greek! How delightful!

Phil. What, does the gentleman understand Greek? Ah! pray let me embrace you, sir, for Greek's sake.

> [*Vadius embraces both Bélise and Armande.*

Henriette (to Vadius, who would embrace her likewise). Excuse me, sir, I do not understand Greek.   [*They sit down.*

Phil. I have a wonderful respect for Greek books.

Vad. I fear my intrusion, caused by the great desire I had to see you, madam, has disturbed some learned discourse.

Phil. Sir, with your Greek you can spoil nothing ——

Tris. He likewise does wonders in verse as well as prose, and could, if he would, show you something.

Vad. The fault of authors is to bore people by talking about their own works; to be at the palace, in courts, streets, or at table, indefatigable readers of their own tiresome verses. For my part I see nothing more ridiculous than an author who goes everywhere mumping for praise, and, seizing the ears of the first comers, makes them martyrs to his lucubrations. They never saw me such a conceited fool; and in this I am of the opinion of a certain Greek, who, by an express injunction, forbids all his wise men the unbecoming forwardness of reading their own works.

. . . .

Tris. (*to Vadius*). Have you seen a little sonnet upon the Princess Urania's fever?

Vad. Yes, it was read to me yesterday.

Tris. Do you know the author?

Vad. No; but I know very well that, not to flatter him, his sonnet's worth nothing.

Tris. A great many people, however, think it admirable.

Vad. That doesn't hinder it's being miserable; and if you had seen it you would be of my opinion.

Tris. I know I should not be so at all; and that few are capable of such a sonnet.

Vad. Heaven preserve us from making such!

Tris. I maintain that a better can't be made, and I ought to know, since I am the author.

Vad. You?

Tris. I.

Vad. I can't tell then how the thing was.

Tris. It was, that I was unfortunate enough not to be able to please you.

Vad. I could not have been paying attention when I heard it, or else the reader spoiled the sonnet. But let's leave this subject and see my ballad.

Tris. A ballad, in my opinion, is an insipid thing; it's no longer in fashion; it smells of antiquity.

Vad. A ballad, however, pleases a great many people.

Tris. That doesn't hinder its displeasing me.

Vad. It may be none the worse for that.

Tris. It has a wonderful charm for pedants.

Vad. And yet it does not please you.

Tris. You gratuitously assign your own faults to others.

[*They all rise.*

Vad. You very impertinently cast yours upon me.

Tris. Go, you school-boy paper-blotter.

Vad. Go, pitiful rhymer; disgrace to the profession!

Tris. Begone, verse-stealer, impudent plagiarist.

Vad. Begone, pedant——

Phil. O gentlemen, what do you mean?

Tris. (*to Vadius*). Go, go; restore the shameful thefts you have made from the Greeks and Latins.

Vad. Go, go, and do penance on Parnassus for having lamed Horace in your verses.

Tris. Remember your book, and the little stir it made.

Vad. Remember your publisher, reduced to the workhouse.

Tris. My reputation is established; in vain you endeavor to mangle it.

Vad. My pen shall teach you what sort of a man I am.

Tris. And mine shall make you know your master.

Vad. I defy you in verse, prose, Greek and Latin.

THE HYPOCRITE MAKES LOVE.

(From " Tartuffe," Act III.)

IN this act Tartuffe first appears upon the scene, but there has already been sufficient mention of him to enable the audience to understand his character. Damis is the son of Orgon, upon whose generosity Tartuffe has imposed, and Dorine is the faithful servant of the family.

Damis. May Heaven this moment crush me; may everybody take me forever for the greatest fool alive, if there is any respect or any power able to stop me, and if I do not ——

Dorine. Pray moderate your anger; your father only just mentioned the matter; people do not always do what they propose, and it's a long way from the project to the execution.

Da. I will put a stop to the intrigues of that scoundrel, and will tell him in his ear a word or two which——

Dor. Gently, gently; allow your stepmother to act first upon him and your father. She has a certain power over Tartuffe. He is very amiable towards her, and may have a real affection for her. Would to Heaven it were possible! It would be a fine thing! In short, she has sent for him on your account; she wants to sound him about this marriage, which makes you so furious, to know what he thinks, and to make him understand what unpleasantness it would cause in the family, if he encourages it at all. His servant says that he is at his prayers, so that I have not been able to see him; but he added that he will soon come down. Go, then, I beg of you, and leave me to wait for him.

Da. But I can be present at this interview.

Dor. No, no; better leave them alone.

Da. I should say nothing to him.

Dor. You think so; but we know what a state of anger you are put in at times; it is the surest way to spoil everything. You must go.

Da. No, I will listen without getting into a rage.

Dor. How tiresome you are! There he is coming. Go away. (*Damis hides himself.*)　　　　　　　　. [*Enter Tartuffe.*

Tartuffe (as soon as he sees Dorine speaks to his servant, who is inside). Laurent, lock up my hair-shirt and my scourge, and pray Heaven ever to enlighten you with grace. If anybody comes to see me, say that I am gone to the prisons to distribute my alms.

Dor. (aside.) What boasting and affectation!

Tar. What is it you want?

Dor. To tell you ——

Tar. (taking a handkerchief out of his pocket). Ah! Heaven! Before you speak to me, take this handkerchief, pray.

Dor. What's the matter?

Tar. Cover your bosom, of which I cannot endure the sight. Such objects hurt the soul, and are conducive to sinful thoughts.

Dor. You are very susceptible to temptation, it seems, and the flesh makes great impression on you. I don't know why you should burn so quickly; but, as for me, I am not so easily moved, and were I to see your hide from top to toe, I know pretty well that I should in no way be tempted.

Tar. Put more modesty into your speech, or I will leave you at once.

Dor. You need not, for I shall soon leave you in peace, and all I have to say is, that my lady is coming in this room, and would be glad to have a moment's talk with you.

Tar. Alas! With all my heart.

Dor. (aside). How sweet we are! In good troth, I still abide by what I said.

Tar. Will she soon be here?

Dor. **Directly.** I hear her, I believe; yes, here she is. I leave you together. [*Exit. Enter Elmire.*

Tar. May Heaven, in its great goodness, ever bestow on you health of body and of mind, and shower blessings on your days, according to the prayer of the lowest of its servants.

Elmire. I am much obliged to you for this pious wish; but let us sit down a moment to talk more comfortably.

Tar. (*seated*). Have you quite recovered from your indisposition?

El. (*seated*). Quite. That fever soon left me.

Tar. My prayers have not merit sufficient to have obtained this favor from Heaven; but I have not offered up one petition in which you were not concerned.

El. Your anxious zeal is really too great.

Tar. We cannot have too great anxiety for your dear health; and to give you back the full enjoyment of it, I would have sacrificed my own.

El. You carry Christian charity very far, and I am under much obligation to you for all this kindness.

Tar. I do only what you deserve.

El. I wished to speak to you in private on a certain matter, and I am glad that nobody is here to hear us.

Tar. And I also am delighted. It is very sweet for me, madam, to find myself alone with you. —— I have often prayed Heaven to bestow this favor upon me, but till now it has been in vain.

El. For my part, all I want is, that you should speak frankly, and hide nothing from me. (*Damis, without being seen, half opens the door of the room to hear the conversation.*)

Tar. And my wish is also, that you will allow me the cherished favor of speaking openly to you, and of giving you my word of honor, that if I have said anything against the visits which are paid here to your charms, it has never been done out of hatred to you, but rather out of an ardent zeal which carries me away, and from a sincere feeling of ——

El. I quite understand it to be so, and I feel sure that it all proceeds from your anxiety for my good.

Tar. (*taking her hands and pressing them*). It is really so, madam, and my fervor is such ——

El. Ah! you press my hand too much.

Tar. It is through an excess of zeal. I never intended to hurt you, I had much rather —— (*He puts his hand on Elmire's knees.*)

El. Why do you put your hand there?

Tar. I was feeling your dress; the stuff is very soft.

El. I beg you to leave off, I am very ticklish.

(Elmire draws back her chair, and Tartuffe follows her with his.)

Tar. (*handling Elmire's collar*). Heaven! how marvelous this point lace is! The work done in our days is perfectly wonderful, and never has such perfection been attained in everything.

El. It is true. But let us speak of what brings me here. I have been told that my husband intends to break his word, and to give you his daughter in marriage. Is that true? Pray tell me.

Tar. He has merely alluded to it. But, madam, to tell you the truth, that is not the happiness for which my soul sighs; I find elsewhere the unspeakable attractions of the bliss which is the end of all my hopes.

El. That is because you care not for earthly things.

Tar. My bosom, madam, does not enclose a heart of flint.

El. I know, for my part, that all your sighs tend towards Heaven, and that you have no desire for anything here below.

Tar. Our love for the beauty which is eternal stifles not in us love for that which is fleeting and temporal; and we can easily be charmed with the perfect works Heaven has created. Its reflected attractions shine forth in such as you; but it is in you alone that its choicest wonders are centred. It has lavished upon you charms which dazzle the eye, and which touch the heart; and I have never gazed on you, perfect creature, without admiring the Creator of the universe, and without feeling my heart seized with an ardent love for the most beautiful picture in which He has reproduced Himself. At first I feared that this secret tenderness might be a skillful assault of the Evil One; I even thought I would avoid your presence, fearing you might prove a stumbling-block to my salvation. But I have learned, O adorable beauty, that my passion need not be a guilty one; that I can reconcile it with modesty; and I have given up my whole soul to it. I know that I am very presumptuous in making you the offer of such a heart as mine; but in my love I hope everything from you, nothing from the vain efforts of my unworthy self. In you is my hope, my happiness, my peace; on you depends my misery or bliss; and by your verdict I shall be forever happy, if you wish it; unhappy, if it pleases you.

El. Quite a gallant declaration. But you must acknowledge that it is rather surprising. It seems to me that you might have fortified your heart a little more carefully against temptation, and have paused before such a design. A devotee like you, who is everywhere spoken of as ——

Tar. Ah! Although a devotee, I am no less a man. When your celestial attractions burst upon the sight, the heart surrenders, and reasons no more. I know that such language from me seems somewhat strange; but after all, madam, I am not an angel; and, if you condemn the confession I make, you have only your own attractions to blame for it. As soon as I beheld their more than human beauty, my whole being was surrendered to you. The unspeakable sweetness of your divine charms forced the obstinate resistance of my heart; it overcame everything—fasting, prayers, and tears—and fixed all my hopes in you. A thousand times my eyes and my sighs have told you this; to-day I explain myself with words. Ah! if you consider with some kindness the tribulations and trials of your unworthy slave, if your goodness has compassion on me, and deigns to stoop so low as my nothingness, I shall ever have for you, O marvelous beauty, a devotion never to be equalled. With me your reputation runs no risk, and has no disgrace to fear. All those court gallants upon whom women dote, are noisy in their doings, boastful in their talk. Ever vain of their success, they never receive favors without divulging them; and their indiscreet tongues dishonor the altar on which their hearts sacrifice. But men like me burn with a hidden flame, and secrecy is forever assured. The care which we take of our own reputation is a warrant to the woman who accepts our heart, that she will find love without scandal, and pleasure without fear.

El. I have listened to you, and your rhetoric expresses itself in terms strong enough. Are you not afraid that I might be disposed to tell my husband of this passionate declaration, and that its sudden disclosure might influence the friendship which he has towards you?

Tar. I know that your tender-heartedness is too great, and that you will excuse, because of human frailty, the violent transports of a love which offends you, and will consider, when you look at yourself, that people are not blind, and that flesh is weak.

El. Others might take all this differently; but I will endeavor to show my discretion. I will tell nothing to my husband of what has taken place; but, in return, I must require one thing of you, which is to forward honestly and sincerely the marriage which has been decided between Valère and Marianne, and renounce the unjust power which would enrich you with what belongs to another ——

Damis. (*coming out of concealment*). No, madam, no; all this must be made public. I was in that place and overheard everything. Heaven in its goodness seems to have directed my steps hither, to confound the pride of a wretch who wrongs me, and to guide me to a sure revenge for his hypocrisy and insolence. I will undeceive my father, and will show him in a clear, strong light the heart of the miscreant who dares to speak to you of love.

El. No, Damis, it is sufficient if he promises to amend, and endeavors to deserve the forgiveness I have spoken of. Since I have promised it, let me abide by my word. I have no wish for scandal. A woman should despise these follies, and never trouble her husband's ears with them.

Da. You have your reasons for dealing thus with him, and I have mine for acting otherwise. It is a mockery to try to spare him. In the insolent pride of his canting bigotry he has already triumphed too much over my just wrath, and has caused too many troubles in our house. The impostor has governed my father but too long, and too long opposed my love and Valère's. It is right that my father's eyes should be opened to the perfidy of this villain. Heaven offers me an easy opportunity, and I am thankful for it. Were I not to seize it, I should deserve never to have another.

THE HYPOCRITE UNMASKED.

(From "Tartuffe," Act IV.)

Orgon. Ah! I am delighted to find you all here. (*To Marianne.*) In this contract I bring wherewith to please you. You know, do you not, what I mean?

Marianne (*at Orgon's feet*). Father! in the name of Heaven, which is a witness of my grief; in the name of all that can move your heart, forego the rights my birth gives you, and do not exact this obedience from me. Do not by such a harsh law compel me to complain to Heaven of my duty to you, and do not, alas! render most miserable the life I owe you. If, contrary to the sweet hopes which I had cherished, you now forbid me to belong to the man I love, I beseech you on my knees at least to save me from the wretchedness of belonging to him I abhor. Do not drive me to despair by making use of all your power over me.

Org. (*aside*). Stand firm, my heart! No human weakness!

Mar. I do not feel aggrieved by your tenderness for him; you can act as your heart prompts you—give him all you possess, and join to it what is mine. I consent, and give it up to him with all my heart. But do not dispose in the same way of my person; suffer me to wear out the rest of my wretched life in the austere discipline of a convent.

Org. Ah, yes, you are, I see, one of those would-be nuns, because your father crosses your forbidden love. Stand up! The more your heart recoils from the match, the better it will be for your salvation. Mortify your senses by this marriage and trouble me no longer on the subject.

Dorine. But what ——

Org. Hold your tongue; speak to people of your own set. I forbid you once for all to say a word.

Cléante. If you will allow me to speak and advise ——

Org. Brother, your advice is of the best possible kind; it is full of truth and good sense, and I value it highly. You will, however, allow me not to avail myself of it.

Elmire (to her husband). I hardly know what to say in the face of all this, and I really admire you in your blindness. You must be bewitched with the man and altogether prepossessed in his favor for you to deny the truth of what we tell you took place today!

Org. I am your humble servant, but I judge by appearances. I know how lenient you are towards my rascal of a son, and see that you were afraid of disowning the trick he would have played on the poor fellow. In short, you took the matter too easily for me to believe you; you would have been more moved had the thing been true.

El. Is it necessary for our honor, to take up arms so furiously at a simple declaration of love? Is it not possible to give a fitting answer without anger in our eyes and invectives in our mouth? For my part, I listen with mere indifference to such talk, and I care not to make any ado about it. I prefer to show that virtue can be accompanied by gentleness, and I have no respect for those savage prudes who defend their honor with tooth and nail, and who at the slightest word are ready to tear a man's eyes out. Heaven preserve me from such discretion! I prefer a virtue with nothing of the tigress about it, for I believe that a quiet and cold rebuff is quite as efficient.

Org. In short, I know all about this business, and no words of yours can alter my conviction.

El. I wonder more and more at your strange weakness. But
VII—17

what answer would your credulity give, if I made you see that
we have told you the truth?

Org. See?

El. Yes.

Org. Rubbish.

El. But, still, suppose I find a way of showing it to you, so
that you cannot mistake it?

Org. Moonshine.

El. What a strange man you are! Yet at least answer me. I
do not ask you to believe us; but suppose we could find a place
where you can see and hear all about what we have told you,
what would you say then of your pious man?

Org. In that case, I should say that —— I should say nothing; for, in short, it is impossible.

El. Your error lasts too long, and you have taxed me too long
with falsehood. You must, to satisfy me, without delay, be a
witness of what I have said.

Org. Be it so; I take you at your word. We will see how far
you can make your promise good.

El. (to Dorine). Get him to come in here.   [*Exit Dorine.*

El. Now bring the table here, and get under it.

Org. Get under it?

El. It is important that you should be well concealed.

Org. But why under the table?

El. Ah! never mind; do what I tell you. I have my plan
quite ready in my head, and you shall judge. Place yourself
where I tell you, and then be careful that you are neither seen
nor heard.

Org. I must say that my condescension is very great. However, I will see you through your scheme.   [*Gets under.*

El. You will have nothing to answer me. Mind! I'm going
to speak on a strange subject, and you must not be shocked. I
have a right to say whatever I choose, since it is to convince you,
as I have promised to do. I will, by coaxing speeches, make the
hypocrite drop his mask, will flatter the insolent desires of his
love, and leave free room to his audacity. As it is only because
of you, and the better to confound him, that I shall affect to return
his love, I will cease as soon you feel convinced, and things need
go no further than you please. It is for you to spare your wife,
to stop his mad purpose when you think matters have been carried far enough, and to suffer me to be exposed to his insolence
only as far as is necessary to disabuse you. This is your concern,

you can act when you like, and —— He is coming.—— Do not move, and be careful that you do not show yourself. [*Enter Tartuffe.*

Tar. I am told that you wish to speak with me here.

El. Yes, I have important things to reveal to you. But shut this door before I begin, and look everywhere to see if any one can overhear us (*Tartuffe shuts the door and returns*); it will never do to risk having over again such an affair as that of this morning. Never in my life was I so taken by surprise, and Damis put me in a terrible fright on your account. You saw how I tried all I could to baffle his design and to calm his anger. My confusion was so great, it is true, that the thought of denying his accusations never came to my mind. But, thank Heaven, it is all for the best, and things are through it on a much safer footing. The esteem in which you are held has dispersed the storm; and my husband can have no suspicion of you, for, in order to set at defiance ill-natured comments, he wishes us to be constantly together. I can therefore be locked up here alone with you without fear of incurring blame; and thus I feel authorized to open to you a heart too forward perhaps in answering your love.

Tar. This language, madam, is somewhat hard for me to understand, and you spoke but lately in a very different strain.

El. Ah! if such a refusal has offended you, how little you know the heart of woman, and how little you understand what we mean when we so feebly defend ourselves! At such times our modesty always struggles against any tender feelings a lover inspires. Whatever reasons we may find to justify the love that conquers us, there is always a certain shame attached to the avowal of it. At first we try to avoid this avowal, but from our manner it is easy to see that our heart surrenders; that, simply for the sake of honor, our lips refuse to give words to our wishes; and that, while refusing, we promise everything.—I feel that I am making a very free confession to you, and not sparing woman's modesty; but I have begun, and will continue.—Should I have been so anxious to restrain Damis; should I have listened, think you, with so much calmness to your declaration throughout, and have taken the thing as you know I did, if the offer of your heart had not been a pleasure to me? When I tried to make you renounce the match which had just been proposed, what could you infer from such an action, if it was not that I felt interested in you, and that I should have experienced great sorrow if by such a marriage you had divided that affection which I wanted wholly to be mine!

Tar. It is certainly, madam, an extreme delight to hear such words from the lips of one we love; and their honey diffuses through all my senses a soothing softness I never knew till now. To please you is the supreme study of my life, and to be sure of your love my greatest happiness. Yet, forgive me, madam, if my heart somewhat doubts its felicity, and fancies that these words may be a specious artifice to make me break off the marriage which is soon to take place; and, if I may speak openly to you, I shall not trust such sweet language unless some of the favors after which I sigh have assured me of their sincerity, and fix in my mind a sure belief in the enchanting goodness you bear for me.

El. (*after coughing*). What! would you proceed so fast, and from the first exhaust the tenderness of my heart? I do myself violence to make you a sweet declaration of love; yet this is not enough for you, and to satisfy you the affair must be pushed even to the last extreme.

Tar. The less we deserve a blessing, the less we dare to hope for it. Love cannot feel secure with words only. We easily suspect a lot brimful of happiness, and we must enjoy the possession of it, before we can believe in it. I feel myself so unworthy of your favors that I doubt the success of my boldness, and I will believe nothing, madam, before you give real proofs.

El. Alas! how tyrannical your passion is! How it bewilders my mind! With what fierce sway it takes possession of my heart! and with what violence it exacts what it desires! Is there no avoiding your pursuit? and will you not allow me time to breathe? Is it right that you should persist so peremptorily? Should you exact what you desire with such tenacity, and thus abuse by your pressing ardor the weakness that you see I have for you?

Tar. But if you receive my love with kindness, why refuse me convincing proof?

El. But how can I consent to what you ask without offending Heaven, of which you are always speaking?

Tar. If it is only Heaven you can oppose to my wishes, it is nothing for me to remove such an obstacle; and that ought not to be a restraint to your love.

El. But they make us so terribly afraid of the judgments of Heaven.

Tar. I can, madam, dissipate these ridiculous terrors, and I understand the art of allaying scruples. It is true that Heaven forbids certain gratifications, but there are means of compounding with it upon such matters, and of rectifying the evil of the act by the purity of the intention. We shall be able to initiate you into all those secrets, madam; all you have to do is to suffer yourself to be led by me. Satisfy my wishes, and be without fear. I will be answerable for everything and take the sin upon myself. (*Elmire coughs louder.*) You cough very much, madam.

El. Yes, I am suffering torture.

Tar. Will you accept a piece of this liquorice?

El. It is an obstinate cold, and I see plainly that all the liquorice in the world will do no good in this case.

Tar. That is certainly very trying.

El. Yes, more than can be expressed.

Tar. In short, your scruples, madam, are easy to remove. You are sure of an inviolable secrecy with me, and it is only publicity which makes the wrong. The scandal is what constitutes the offence, and to sin in secret is not to sin at all.

El. (*coughing and knocking the table*). Well, I see that I have no alternative but to yield, that I must consent to grant you everything, and that unless I do so I must not expect to satisfy or to convince. It is surely very hard to come to this, and I give way much against my will; but since it seems a settled thing that I should be driven to it, since I cannot be believed without more convincing proofs, in spite of all I may say, I must perforce make up my mind to it and give satisfaction. If my thus consenting carries any offence with it, so much the worse for him who forces me to do this violence to myself. The fault certainly cannot be accounted mine.

Tar. No, madam, I take it entirely upon myself, and the thing in itself ——

El. Just open this door, I pray you, and see if my husband is not in the passage.

Tar. There is no need, madam, to trouble about him. Between ourselves, he is a man to be led by the nose. He is more likely to be proud of finding us together, and I have brought him to the point of seeing everything without believing in anything.

El. All the same, go for a moment and look everywhere very carefully, I beg of you.

Org. (*coming from under the table*). We have here, I acknowledge, an abominable scoundrel. I cannot get over it; I feel stunned.

El. What! you come out so soon! You are jesting. Go under the table again; it is not time yet; wait to see the end in order to feel quite sure, and don't trust to mere surmises.

Org. No, never did hell produce anything more wicked.

El. Nonsense! you should not believe things too lightly. Be sure that you feel quite convinced before you surrender, and be in no hurry, for fear of a mistake. (*She hides Orgon behind her.*)

Tar. (*returning*). Everything is propitious to me. I have searched every room, there is no one there; and my delighted soul —— (*Tartuffe goes to embrace Elmire; she draws back and he sees Orgon.*)

Org. (*stopping Tartuffe*). Gently, gently, you yield too freely to your amorous transports, and you should be less imperious in your desires. Oh! oh! you saint, you wanted to make a fool of me! How you give way to temptation! You marry my daughter, and covet my wife! For a long time I doubted if you were in earnest, and I expected every moment that you would change your tone, but this is carrying the proof far enough; I am satisfied, and I require no further test.

El. (*to Tartuffe*). It is much against my inclination that I have done all this, but I have been driven to the necessity of treating you thus.

Tar. (*to Orgon*). What! can you believe ——

Or. Come, no noise, out of this house, and without ceremony.

Tar. My intention ——

Org. Your speeches are no longer in season; leave this house at once.

Tar. It is for you to leave the house, you who speak as if you were master here. The house belongs to me, and I will make you know it. I will soon show you that it is vain for you to resort to these base falsehoods to quarrel with me. You little know what you do when you insult me. I can confound and punish imposture, avenge offended Heaven, and make those repent who speak of driving me hence.   [*Exit.*

El. What language is this? What does he mean?

Org. I am, in truth, all confused. This is no laughing matter.

El. How so?

Org. I perceive my mistake by what he says. The deed of gift troubles my mind.

El. The deed of gift!

Org. Yes. The thing is done. But something else disturbs me.

THE MODERN DRAMA.

The first thing that strikes us in the drama of the day is the decay, one might almost say the creeping paralysis, of external action. Next we note a very pronounced desire to penetrate deeper and deeper into human consciousness, and place moral problems upon a high pedestal; and finally the search, still very timid and halting, for a kind of new beauty, that shall be less abstract than was the old.

It is certain that, on the actual stage, we have fewer extraordinary and violent adventures. Bloodshed has grown less frequent, passions less turbulent; heroism has become less unbending, courage less material and less ferocious. People still die on the stage, it is true, as in reality they still must die, but death has ceased—or will cease, let us hope, very soon—to be regarded as the indispensable setting, the *ultima ratio*, the inevitable end, of every dramatic poem. In the most formidable crises of our lives which, cruel though it may be, is cruel in silent and hidden ways—we rarely look to death for a solution; and for all that the theatre is slower than the other arts to follow the evolution of human consciousness, it will still be at last compelled, in some measure, to take this into account. . . .

Should a youth of our own time love, and meet obstacles not unlike those which, in another order of ideas and events, beset Romeo's passion, we need no telling that his adventure will be embellished by none of the features that gave poetry and grandeur to the episode of Verona. Gone beyond recall is the entrancing atmosphere of a lordly, passionate life; gone the brawls in picturesque streets, the interludes of bloodshed and splendour, the mysterious poisons, the majestic, complaisant tombs! And where shall we look for that exquisite summer's night, which owes its vastness, its savour, the very appeal that it makes to us, to the shadow of an heroic, inevitable death that already lay heavy upon it? Divest the story of Romeo and Juliet of these beautiful trappings and we have only the very simple and ordinary desire of a noble-hearted, unfortunate youth for a maiden whose obdurate parents deny him her hand.

All the poetry, the splendour, the passionate life of this desire, result from the glamour, the nobility, tragedy, that are proper to the environment wherein it has come to flower; nor is there a kiss, a murmur of love, a cry of anger, grief or despair, but borrows its majesty, grace, its heroism, tenderness—in a word, every image that has helped it to visible form —from the beings and objects around it; for it is not in the kiss itself that the sweetness and beauty are found, but in the circumstance, hour and place, wherein it was given. Again, the same objections would hold if we chose to imagine a man of our time who should be jealous as Othello was jealous, possessed of Macbeth's ambition, unhappy as Lear; or, like Hamlet, restless and wavering, bowed down beneath the weight of a frightful and unrealizable duty.

Where are we to look, then, for the grandeur and beauty that we find no longer in visible action, or in words, stripped as these are of their attraction and glamour? For words are only a kind of mirror which reflects the beauty of all that surrounds it; and the beauty of the new world wherein we live does not seem as yet able to project its rays on these somewhat reluctant mirrors. Where shall we look for the horizon, the poetry, now that we no longer seek it in a mystery which, for all that it still exists, does yet fade from us the moment we endeavour to give it a name?

The modern drama would seem to be vaguely conscious of this. Incapable of outside movement, deprived of external ornament, daring no longer to make serious appeal to a determined divinity or fatality, it has fallen back on itself, and seeks to discover, in the regions of psychology and of moral problems, the equivalent of what once was offered by exterior life. It has penetrated deeper into human consciousness; but has encountered difficulties there no less strange than unexpected.

To penetrate deeply into human consciousness is the privilege, even the duty, of the thinker, the moralist, the historian, novelist, and to a degree, of the lyrical poet; but not of the dramatist. Whatever the temptation, he dare not sink into inactivity, become mere philosopher or observer.

Do what one will, discover what marvels one may, the

sovereign law of the stage, its essential demand, will always
be *action*. With the rise of the curtain, the high intellectual
desire within us undergoes transformation; and in place of
the thinker, psychologist, mystic or moralist, there stands the
mere instinctive spectator, the man electrified negatively by
the crowd, the man whose one desire it is to see something
happen. This transformation or substitution is incontestable,
strange as it may seem; and is due, perhaps, to the influence
of the *human polypier,* to some undeniable faculty of our soul,
which is endowed with a special, primitive, almost unimprov-
able organ, whereby men can think and feel, and be moved,
en masse. And there are no words so profound, so noble
and admirable, but they will soon weary us if they leave the
situation unchanged, if they lead to no action, bring about no
decisive conflict, or hasten no definite solution.—*Maeterlinck.*

BREAD   MILK   WATER   FIRE

CHAPTER XVI.

MODERN DRAMA IN FRANCE.

Within the last few years a kind of symbolism has permeated the writings of poets and dramatists, as it has also manifested itself in art. It is not easy to explain definitely, and yet it is possible for all to grasp something of its meaning. It is essentially a reaction against the materialism of the past few decades. Science has held sway for two or three generations, and the scientific spirit has made itself felt in every field of human thought.

It appeared as though science had classified everything and stated it in definite terms. Newton discovered the law of gravitation that tends to draw all bodies toward the center of the earth and then every schoolboy could explain what it was. Yet who, today, knows anything of that unseen and irresistible force that thus attracts? People are fast finding out that having named and defined, the secret lies still beyond them.

The average person professes to believe that the body is the temporary abode of the mind, or soul; that at death the mind is set free and passes on to other and more ideal conditions. Then, with delicious inconsistency, each fills his life to the brim with interests which pertain alone to the material needs and spends little or no time in silent meditation. The more material the age, the more do people flee from their own thoughts, the more do they seek diversion outside of their own minds, and the more do they welcome the companionship of their fellowmen. Symbolistic writers are not afraid of silence and solitude. Emerson was a mystic to some extent, and each age has produced minds that have found greatest consolation in reaching out to the world just beyond our grasp, and which we feel rather than see.

> "The infinite always is silent—
> 'Tis only the finite speaks;
> Our words are the idle wave-caps
> On a deep that never breaks.

"We question with wand of silence,
Explain, decide, discuss,
But only in meditation
The infinite speaks to us."

Written before the present symbolist movement manifested itself in an avowed way, the lines nevertheless embody similar ideas. Maeterlinck says: "Speech is never the medium of communication of real and inmost thoughts. Silence alone can transmit them from soul to soul. We talk to fill up the blanks of life. Silence is so truth-telling, so illuminative, that few have the courage to face it. Mankind fears silence more than the dark."

The so-called realities of life are after all temporary, and the *real* and abiding seldom remembered; those relations in which mankind thinks to touch reality closest are very transitory and a wider view throws into strange relief the true realities of our being.

Symbolism in literature is an attempt to spiritualize it— to dismiss the material and come to the contemplation of the soul. No longer is the visible world a reality or the invisible world a dream. It reaches its culmination today in the writings of Maeterlinck.*

"He has realized, better than any one else, the significance, in life and art, of mystery. He has realized how unsearchable is the darkness out of which we have but just stepped, and the darkness into which we are about to pass. And he has realized how the thought and sense of that twofold darkness invade the little space of light in which, for a moment, we move; the depth to which they shadow our steps, even in that moment's partial escape. . . . All that he says we know already; we may deny it, but we know it. It is what we are often at leisure enough with ourselves, sincere enough with ourselves, to realize; but, when he says it, we know that it is true, and our knowledge of it is his warrant for saying it. He is what he is precisely because he tells us nothing which

*Although of Belgian birth and training, Maeterlinck has latterly made France his home, and writes in the French language.

we do not already know, or it may be, what we have known and forgotten."†

Maurice Maeterlinck was born at Ghent in 1862. He early developed, or perhaps it would be truer to say, satisfied a liking for the mystic writers, and his earliest poems gave evidence of this mental bent.

He has written poems, essays and plays, all pervaded by the mysticism with which he is imbued.

La Princesse Maleine, Pelleas et Melisande, Mona Vanna, Mary Magdalene and *L'Oiseau Bleu* are among his best known plays. Most generally known beyond a question is *L'Oiseau Bleu—The Blue Bird.*

Tyltyl and Mytyl, two little peasant children, lie dreaming in bed on Christmas Eve. They appear to waken and watch a party in the great house across the street. A knock comes at the door and what seems to be the neighbor woman, Madame Berlingot, enters. Presently she looks less like the neighbor and more like a fairy. Her little daughter is ill and wants the Blue Bird and she asks the children to go in search of it. To assist them, she gives Tyltyl a green hat and a magical diamond. Turn it once, it reveals the inside of things; one more, the past; a third, and it shows the future. The simple things which one would need: bread, milk, water, sugar, together with light and the dog and the cat, prepare to accompany the children.

Of course fairy palaces are easily evolved and many obstacles that would ordinarily confront mortals do not disturb the children because they do not expect them. They journey to the past, through a misty forest. It really is difficult for most of us to remember clearly what happened when we were young; and in time they arrive at the Land of Memory. They find their grandmother and their grandfather, whom they supposed were dead, but who it appears are only sleeping. They make quite a discovery when they find that "there are no dead." Granny's blackbird seems to be blue and thinking they have found the object of their search, they start away; but soon this bird is blue no longer and so they know this cannot be the one they were sent to find. They visit the kingdom of the Future and all the little beings that shall be; they

†Symons: The Symbolist Movement in Literature.

wander here and wander there and at last return without the coveted bird. When they arrive home, they discover that their own little bird is quite blue, and they give it to the old woman for her sick child—and some way she appears to be a fairy no longer.

To the children this is a delightful fairy story, pure and simple. "And to think they had the blue bird at home all the time!" is their exultant cry. To those who look beneath, the children symbolize the whole world, on its ceaseless quest for happiness—the blue bird—and at last it must be sought, not far away, but each must find it in his own heart.

The Blue Bird.

Act IV. Scene 2. *The Palace of Happiness.*

Tyltyl. Who are those fat gentlemen enjoying themselves and eating such a lot of good things?

Light. They are the biggest Luxuries of the Earth, the ones that can be seen with the naked eye. It is possible, though not very likely, that the Blue Bird may have strayed among them for a moment. That is why you must not turn the diamond yet. For form's sake, we will begin by searching this part of the hall.

Tyltyl. Can we go up to them?

Light. Certainly. They are not ill-natured, although they are vulgar, and usually rather ill-bred.

Tyltyl. What beautiful cakes they have! . . . How pleased and happy they look! . . . And they are shouting! And laughing! And singing! . . . I believe they have seen us.

[*A dozen of the biggest Luxuries have risen from table and now advance laboriously towards the Children.*

Light. Have no fear, they are affable. . . . They will probably invite you to dinner. . . . Do not accept, do not accept anything, lest you should forget your mission.

The Biggest of the Luxuries (*holding out his hand to Tyltyl*). How do you do, Tyltyl?

Tyltyl (*surprised*). Why, do you know me? . . . Who are you?

The Luxury. I am the biggest of the Luxuries, the Luxury of Being Rich; and I come, in the name of my brothers, to beg you and your family to honor our endless repast with your presence. You will find yourself surrounded by all that is best among the real, big Luxuries of this Earth. Allow me to introduce to you the chief of them. Here is my son-in-law, the Luxury of Being a Landowner, who has a stomach shaped like a pear. This is the Luxury of Satisfied Vanity, who has such a nice, puffy face. (*The Luxury of Satisfied Vanity gives a patronizing nod.*) These are the Luxury of Drinking When You Are Not Thirsty and the Luxury of Eating When You Are Not Hungry: they are twins and their legs are made of macaroni. (*They bow, staggering.*) Here are the Luxury of Knowing Nothing, who is as deaf as a post, and the Luxury of Understanding Nothing, who is as blind as a bat. Here are the Luxury of Doing Nothing and the Luxury of Sleeping More than Necessary; their hands are made of bread-crumbs and their eyes of peach-jelly. Lastly, here is Fat Laughter: his mouth is split from ear to ear and he is irresistible. (*Fat Laughter bows, writhing and holding his sides.*)

Light. Here come some amiable and curious Joys who will direct us. . . .

Tyltyl. Do you know them?

Light. Yes, I know them all; I often come to them, without their knowing who I am. . . .

Tyltyl. Oh, what a lot of them there are! . . . They are crowding from every side!

Light. There were many more of them once. The Luxuries have done them great harm.

Tyltyl. No matter, there are a good few of them left. . . .

Light. You will see plenty of others, as the influence of the diamond spreads through the halls. . . . There are many more Happinesses on Earth than people think; but the generality of men do not discover them. . . .

Tyltyl. Here are some little ones; let us run and meet them.

Light. It is unnecessary; those which interest us will pass this way. We have no time to make the acquaintance of all the rest. . . .

[*A troop of little Happinesses, frisking and bursting with laughter, run up from the back of the halls and dance round the Children in a ring.*

Tyltyl. How pretty, how very pretty they are! . . . Where do they come from? Who are they? . . .

Light. They are the Children's Happinesses.

Tyltyl. Can one speak to them?

Light. It would be no use. They sing, they dance, they laugh, but they do not talk yet. . . .

Tyltyl (*skipping about*). How do you do? How do you do? . . . Oh look at that fat one laughing! . . . What pretty cheeks they have, what pretty frocks they have! . . . Are they all rich here?

Light. Why, no, here as everywhere, there are many more poor than rich.

Tyltyl. Where are the poor ones?

Light. You can't distinguish them. . . . A Child's Happiness is always arrayed in all that is most beautiful in Heaven and upon Earth.

Tyltyl (unable to restrain himself). I should like to dance with them.

Light. It is absolutely impossible, we have no time. . . . I see that they have not the Blue Bird. . . . Besides, they are in a hurry; you see, they have already passed. They, too, have no time to waste, for childhood is very short.

[*Another troop of Happinesses, a little taller than the last, rush into the hall, singing at the top of their voice, "There they are! There they are! They see us! They see us!" and dance a merry fling around the Children, at the end of which the one who appears to be the chief of the little band goes up to Tyltyl with hand outstretched.*

The Happiness. How do you do, Tyltyl?

Tyltyl. Another one knows me! (*To Light.*) I am getting known wherever I go! . . . (*To the Happiness.*) Who are you?

The Happiness. Don't you recognize me? I'll wager that you don't recognize any one here!

Tyltyl (a little embarrassed). Why, no. . . . I don't know. . . . I don't remember seeing any of you.

The Happiness. There, do you hear? . . . I was sure of it! He has never seen us! (*All the Happinesses burst out laughing.*) Why, my dear Tyltyl, we are the only things you do know! . . . We are always around you! We eat, drink, wake up, breathe and live with you!

Tyltyl. Oh, yes, just so, I know, I remember. . . . But I should like to know what your names are.

The Happiness. I can see that you know nothing. . . . I am the chief of the Happinesses of your home; and all these are the other Happinesses that live there.

Tyltyl. Then there are Happinesses in my home?

The Happiness. You heard him! Are there Happinesses in his home! Why, you little wretch, it is crammed with Happinesses in every nook and cranny! We laugh, we sing, we create enough joy to knock down the walls and lift the roof, but do what we may, you see nothing and you hear nothing. I hope

that, in the future, you will be a little more sensible. . . .
Meantime, you shall shake hands with the more noteworthy of us
. . . . then, when you reach home again, you will recognize them more easily and, at the end of a fine day, you will
know how to encourage them with a smile, to thank them with
a pleasant word, for they really do all they can to make your
life easy and delightful. . . . Let me introduce myself first:
the Happiness of Being Well, at your service. . . . I am not
the prettiest, but I am the most important. Will you know me
again? . . . This is the Happiness of Pure Air, who is almost transparent. . . . Here is the Happiness of Loving
One's Parents, who is clad in grey and always a little sad because no one ever looks at him. . . . Here are the Happiness of the Blue Sky, who, of course, is dressed in blue, and the
Happiness of the Forest, who also of course is clad in green:
you will see him every time you go to the window. . . .
Here, again, is the good Happiness of Sunny Hours, who is dia-
mond-colored, and this is the Happiness of Spring, who is bright
emerald.

Tyltyl. And are you as fine as that every day?

The Happiness of Being Well. Why, yes, it is Sunday every
day, in every house, when people open their eyes. And then,
when evening comes, here is the Happiness of the Sunsets, who
is grander than all the kings in the world and who is followed
by the Happiness of Seeing the Stars Rise, who is gilded like a
god of old. . . . Then, when the weather breaks, here are
the Happiness of the Rain, who is covered with pearls, and the
Happiness of the Winter Fire, who opens his beautiful purple
mantle to frozen hands. . . . And I have not mentioned the
best among us, because he is nearly a brother of the great limpid
Joys who you will see presently; his name is the Happiness of
Innocent Thoughts, and he is the brightest of us all. And then
here are—but really there are too many of them! We should
never have done; and I must first send word to the Great Joys,
who are right at the back, near the gates of Heaven, and who
have not yet heard of your arrival. . . . I will send the
Happiness of Running Barefoot in the Dew, who is the nimblest
of us. (*To the Happiness of Running Barefoot in the Dew, who
comes forward capering.*) Off you go!

Light (to Tyltyl). In the meantime, you might enquire about
the Blue Bird. It is just possible that the chief Happiness of
your home knows where he is.

Tyltyl. Where is he?

The Happiness. He doesn't know where the Blue Bird is!
(*All the Happinesses of the Home burst out laughing.*)

Tyltyl (*vexed*). No, I do not know. There's nothing to
laugh at. (*Fresh bursts of laughter.*)

The Happiness. Come, don't be angry. . . . and let us
be serious. He doesn't know: well, what do you expect? He is
no more absurd than the majority of men. . . . But little
Happiness of Running Barefoot in the Dew has told the Great
Joys and they are coming towards us.

[*All and beautiful angelic figures, clad in shimmering dresses,
come slowly forward.*

Tyltyl. How beautiful they are! Why are they not laughing? Are they not happy?

Light. It is not when one laughs that one is really happy.

Tyltyl. Who are they?

The Happiness. They are the Great Joys.

Tyltyl. Do you know their names?

The Happiness. Of course; we often play with them. . . .
Here, first of all, before the others, is the Great Joy of Being
Just, who smiles each time an injustice is repaired. I am too
young: I have never seen her smile yet. Behind her is the Joy
of Being Good, who is the happiest, but the saddest; and it is
very difficult to keep her from going to the Miseries, whom she
would like to console; for, if she left us, we should be almost as
miserable as the Miseries themselves. On the right is the Joy
of Fame, next to the Joy of Thinking. After her comes the Joy
of Understanding, who is always looking for her brother, the
Luxury of Understanding Nothing.

Tyltyl. And there, far away, far away, in the golden clouds,
the one whom I can hardly see when I stand as high as I can
on tip-toe?

The Happiness. That is the Great Joy of Loving. . . .
But, do what you will, you are ever so much too small to see
her altogether.

Tyltyl. And over there, right at the back, those who are
veiled and who do not come here.

The Happiness. Those are the Joys whom men do not yet
know.

ROSTAND.

Of a very different type is the symbolism of Rostand—who did not use it in his earlier plays, *Cyrano de Bergerac*, *L'Aiglon*, and others—in his recent production *Chanticleer*. Reviving the plan carried out by the Greek comedy writer, Aristophanes, he has brought birds and beasts on the stage to satirize human foibles.

Rostand has called his play "a symbolic pastoral," and says that he conceived the idea of it while watching a scene in a farmyard. Having noticed a blackbird hopping around, he observed that its attitude changed when the cock appeared—as though it were ridiculing him, if such a thing could be imagined.

Chanticleer has been widely produced and has called forth all measure of praise and criticism. The cock represents the artist, the creative genius, the apostle of light and beauty, the champion of the weak. The ode it sings to the sun just rising over the horizon is one of the most beautiful poems written in recent times. The impossibility of adequately rendering it in another language will be apparent:

> "Je t'adore! Soleil! ô toi dont la lumière,
> Pour bénir chaque front et mûrir chaque miel,
> Entrant dans chaque fleur et dans chaque chaumière,
> Se divise et demeure entière
> Aussi que l'amour maternel!
> Je t'adore le Soleil! Tu mets dans l'air des roses,
> Des fleures dans la source, un dieu dans le buisson,
> Tu prends un arbre obscure et tu l'apothéose!
> O Soleil! tois sans qui les choses,
> Ne seraient que ce qu'elles sont!"

L'Aiglon has for its subject the weakling son born to Napoleon and named by him the King of Rome. *Cyrano de Bergerac* was a historical character who himself wrote certain productions that have been revived since Rostand's play became popular.

In certain particulars the dramatist has held to the historic Cyrano; in others he has developed him to suit his needs.

"Cyrano is a type—a type of the largest class of people in the world (for it includes every one) namely, those who do not get what they know they deserve, who find no chance to do what they know they could do, who are so much greater to themselves than to the cold world. . . . With him it is a nose; with us fortunately a something else, that prevents our standing forth to the world for all we are worth."

CYRANO DE BERGERAC.

Montefleury. Come to my aid, gentlemen!

A Marquis. Well, then, play!

Cyrano. You big fellow, if you play, I shall be obliged to slap your face!

Marquis. Enough!

Cyrano. Let the Marquises be silent in their seats, or their ribbons will feel my cane!

All the Marquises (standing). This is too much!—Montefleury—

Cyrano. Let Montefleury go, or I will cut off his ears and rip him open!

A Voice. But—

Cyrano. Let him go!

Another Voice. And yet?

Cyrano. Hasn't he gone yet? (*Turning up his sleeves.*) Good! I am going to the stage as if it were a sideboard to cut up this Italian sausage.

Montefleury. When you insult me, sir, you insult Thalia!

Cyrano. If this Muse, to whom, sir, you are nothing, had the honor of your acquaintance, believe me, when she saw you as fat and stupid as an urn, she would lay her buskin on you soundly.

The Pit. Montefleury!—Montefleury!—Give us Baro's play!

Cyrano. Have pity on my scabbard; if you go on, it will give up its blade!

The Crowd. Take care! There!

Cyrano (to Montefleury). Leave the stage!

The Crowd. Oh! oh!

Cyrano (turning suddenly). Does any one object?

A Voice (singing at the back).

> Monsieur de Cyrano,
> This tyranny must cease.
> Despite the blade you show,
> They *shall* play "Le Clorise."

Entire Audience (singing).   La Clorise, La Clorise!

Cyrano.   If I hear that song once more I will knock you down, every one of you!

A Bourgeois.   You are not Samson!

Cyrano.   Will you lend me your jaw, sir?

A Lady (in one of the boxes).   This is unheard of!

A Nobleman.   It is scandalous!

A Bourgeois.   It is vexatious!

A Page.   What a waste of time!

The Pit.   Hss—Montefleury!—Cyrano.

Cyrano.   Silence!

The Pit (in a frenzy).   He-haw! Baa! Bow-wow! Cock-a-doodle-doo!

Cyrano.   I command you!

A Page.   Miaou!

Cyrano.   I command you to be silent! And I challenge the pit collectively. I will write down your names! Draw near, young heroes! Each in his turn. I am going to number you. Come, who will open the list? You, sir? No! You? No! I will despatch the first duellist with all the honors due him. Let all who wish to die raise their finger! Does modesty forbid you from looking on my naked sword? Not one name? Not one finger? Very good. I will go on. *(Turning toward stage.)* Then, I desire to see the theater cured of this swelling. If not—*(his hand on his sword)* the scalpel!

Montefleury.   I—

Cyrano.   I am going to clap three times, you full moon! At the third you will be eclipsed.

The Pit (amused).   Ah!

Cyrano.   One!

Montefleury.   I—

A Voice (from one of the boxes).   Stay!

The Pit.   He will stay!—He will not stay!

Montefleury.   I believe, gentlemen—

Cyrano.   Two!

Montefleury.   I am sure that it would be better—

Cyrano.   Three!

[*Montefleury disappears as if through a trap-door. Tempest of laughter, whistles, and hoot.*

The Audience.   Coward! Come back!

Cyrano.   Let him come back, if he dares!

A Tradesman.   The orator of the troop!

[*Bellerose comes forward and bows.*

The Boxes. Ah! There is Bellerose!

Bellerose. Noble Lords—

The Pit. No! no! Jodelet!

Jodelet (*comes forward*). Pack of calves!

The Pit. Ah! Bravo! Very good. Bravo!

Jodelet. No bravos! The big tragedian whose paunch you take delight in has felt—

The Pit. He's a coward!

Jodelet. He was obliged to leave!

The Pit. Let him come back!

Some of them. No!

Others. Yes!

A Young Man (*to Cyrano*). But really, sir, what reason have you to hate Montefleury?

Cyrano. Young gosling, I have two reasons, either of which is sufficient alone. Primo: He is a wretched actor, who bawls and grunts like a water-carrier, over the verses that he ought to let soar away on wings! Secundo: That is my secret!

The Old Tradesman. But you are depriving us unscrupulously of "La Clorise." I object!

Cyrano. You donkey, old Baro's verses are worth less than nothing. I have no scruples in interrupting them.

The Precieuses (*in the boxes*). Ah! Oh! Our Baro! My dear! Is it possible? Oh Heavens!

Cyrano. Lovely ladies, shine, bloom, be the cup-bearers of our dreams, with a smile make death enchanting, inspire us to write verses—but do not criticize them!

Bellerose. But the money that must be given back!

Cyrano. Bellerose, you have made the only intelligent remark. I make no holes in the cloak of Thespis. (*Throws a bag on the stage.*) Catch this purse on the fly and hold your tongue!

The Audience. Ah! Oh!

Jodelet. At this price, sir, I authorize you to come every day to stop "La Clorise."

The Audience. Hoo! Hoo!

Jodelet. We should all be hooted together!

Bellerose. The hall must be cleared.

Jodelet. Clear it!

[*The crowd begins to go out, while Cyrano looks on with an air of satisfaction. But the crowd soon stops on hearing the following scene, and the going out ceases.*

Le Bret (*to Cyrano*). It's madness!

A Bore. The actor Montefleury! How scandalous! But he is protected by the Duke de Candale! Have you a patron?

Cyrano. No!

The Bore. You have not?

Cyrano. No!

The Bore. What, no great nobleman to protect you with his name?

Cyrano. No, I have told you so twice. Must I say it thrice? No, no protector (*his hand on his sword*) but a protectoress!

The Bore. But are you going to leave the town?

Cyrano. That depends.

The Bore. The Duke de Candale has a long arm!

Cyrano. Not so long as mine (*pointing to his sword*) when lengthened by this!

The Bore. But you do not dream of pretending—

Cyrano. I do dream of it.

The Bore. But—

Cyrano. Now start your boots.

The Bore. But—

Cyrano. Start! Or tell me why you are looking at my nose?

The Bore (bewildered). I—

Cyrano (going towards him). What is there surprising about it?

The Bore (drawing back). Your grace is mistaken—

Cyrano. Is it flabby and swaying like a trunk?

The Bore. I did not—

Cyrano. Or hooked like an owl's beak?

The Bore. I—

Cyrano. Do you notice a wart on the end of it?

The Bore. But—

Cyrano. Or a fly slowly taking its walk over it? What is there so uncommon about it?

The Bore. Oh!

Cyrano. Is it a phenomenon?

The Bore. But I knew how to keep my eyes from it.

Cyrano. And why, if you please, should you keep your eyes from it?

The Bore. I had—

Cyrano. Then you find it disgusting?

The Bore. Sir!

Cyrano. Does its color seem unwholesome to you?

The Bore. Sir!

Cyrano. Its shape obscene?

The Bore. Not at all!

Cyrano. Why, then, do you put on such a sneering air? Perhaps you find it a little too large?

The Bore (*stammering*). I find it small, very small—minute—

Cyrano. Eh! What? You accuse me of being ridiculous? My nose small?

The Bore. Heavens!

Cyrano. My nose is enormous; mean flat-nose, stupid flat-nose. Dullard, I would have you know that I pride myself on such an appendage, inasmuch as a big nose is, properly speaking, the sign of an affable, kind, courteous, witty, liberal, courageous man, such as I am, and such as you can never think of being! Miserable rascal! for the inglorious face that my hand is going to seek above your collar, is as bare— (*He slaps his face.*)

The Bore. Ow!

Cyrano. Of pride, of inspiration, of lyricism, of picturesqueness, of sparkle, of sumptuosity, of even a nose, as that where my boot is going to seek below your back!

The Bore (*escaping*). ·Help, guard!

Cyrano. Let this be a warning to the boobies, who might find the middle of my face amusing, and if the jester is of noble birth, my treatment is, before letting him escape, to apply the steel instead of leather, in front and higher up!

De Guiche. At last he grows tiresome!

The Viscount de Valvert. He is boastful!

De Guiche. Is no one going to reply to him?

The Viscount. No one? Wait! I am going to shoot an arrow at him. (*He approaches Cyrano, who is watching him.*) You—you have a very—very—large nose.

Cyrano (*gravely*). Very.

The Viscount. Ha!

Cyrano. Is that all?

The Viscount. But—

Cyrano. Ah! no! That is a little short, young man. One might make—oh, my Lord, many remarks, on the whole, by varying the tone, for example; listen:—

Aggressive: "Sir, if I had such a nose, I should have it amputated at once."

Friendly: "It must dip into your cup; in order to drink you must have a goblet made for you."

Descriptive. "It is a rock! It is a peak! It is a cape! What did I say? A cape? It is a peninsula!"

Curious: "For what do you use that oblong capsule? For an inkstand or a scissors-case?"

Gracious. "Do you love the birds so well that you take fatherly interest in holding out that perch for their little feet?"

Savage. "When you enjoy your pipe, sir, does the smoke ever come out of your nose without some neighbour crying that the chimney is on fire?"

Warning. "With such a weight dragging on your head, take care that you do not fall forward on the ground!"

Tender. "Have a little parasol made for it, for fear its color might fade in the sun."

Pedantic. "Only the animal, sir, called by Aristophanes the Hippocampelephant ocamelos, could have had so much flesh and bone under its forehead."

Flippant. "What, my friend, is this hook in style? To hang one's hat on, it is surely very convenient."

Emphatic. "No wind, except the mistral, could make you catch cold entirely, O magisterial nose!"

Dramatic. "When it bleeds it is the Red Sea!"

Admirer. "What a sign for a perfumer!"

Lyrical. "Is it a couch? Are you a triton?"

Naïve. "When can this monument be visited?"

Respectful. "Allow me, sir, to salute you; that is what is called having a house of one's own."

Rustic. "Hallo, there! Is that a nose? It is a giant turnip or a dwarf melon."

Military. "Point against the cavalry!"

Practical. "Will you put it in a lottery? Surely, sir, it will win the first prize."

      [Finally taking off Pyramus, with a sob.
There is that nose which has destroyed the harmony of it's master's features. It makes him blush, the traitor!

That is very nearly, my dear, what you would have said to me if you had a little knowledge of letters and a little wit; but of wit, Oh most lamentable of all beings, you never had an atom, and of letters, you have only the four which form the word: Fool! Moreover, if you had the invention necessary to make it possible for, before these noble galleries, to serve me with all these mad pleasantries, you would not have uttered the quarter of the half of the beginning of one, because I serve them out to myself with enthusiasm, but I allow no one else to serve them to me.

De Guiche (trying to lead away the petrified Viscount). Viscount, what nonsense!

The Viscount. Such grand arrogant airs! A country bumpkin, who—who—doesn't even wear gloves! And who goes without ribbons, without bows, and without frogs.

Cyrano. I keep my elegance to adorn my morals. I do not deck myself out like a coxcomb, but I am more careful, if I am less vain. I would not go out through neglect, leaving an insult not washed away, with my conscience still yellow from sleep in the corner of its eye, my honor crumbled, my scruples in mourning. But I walk along with nothing upon me that does not shine, plumed with independence and sincerity; it is not a fine figure, it is my soul that I restrain as in a corset, all covered with exploits, fastened on like ribbons, curling my wit like a mustache, as I pass through the crowd I make truths ring like spurs.

The Viscount. But, sir—

Cyrano. I have no gloves?—A serious matter! I have just one remaining of a very old pair, which was once very troublesome to me. I threw it in some one's face.

The Viscount. Knave, rascal, ridiculous flat-footed clown!

Cyrano (*taking off his hat and bowing down as if the Viscount had just introduced himself*). Ah? And I am Cyrano-Savinien-Hercule-de-Bergerac.

The Viscount (*exasperated*). Buffoon!

Cyrano (*crying out as if seized with the cramp*). Ay!—

The Viscount. Did he say something more?

Cyrano (*making up faces as if in pain*). It must be exercised or it will grow numb. This comes of leaving it idle!—

The Viscount. What is the matter?

Cyrano. I have a tingling in my sword!

The Viscount (*drawing his own*). So be it!

Cyrano. I will give you a charming little thrust.

The Viscount (*scornfully*). Poet!

Cyrano. Yes, sir, poet! and such a one that while fencing I am going to compose you a ballad, improvising.

The Viscount. A ballad?

Cyrano. You know what that is, I suppose?

The Viscount. But—

Cyrano (*as if reciting a lesson*). The ballad is composed of three stanzas, of eight lines—

The Viscount (*stamping*). Oh!

Cyrano. And of an envoi of four.

The Viscount. You—

Cyrano. I am going to compose one and fight you at the same time, and hit you, sir, at the last line.

The Viscount. No!

Cyrano. No? (*declaiming*). "Ballad of the duel which Monsieur de Bergerac fought with a rascal in the Hotel de Bourgogne!"

The Viscount. What is the meaning of that, if you please?

Cyrano. That is the title.

The Audience (*excited to the highest pitch*). Make room! Very amusing! Clear the way! No noise!

CHAPTER XVII.

RECENT ITALIAN DRAMA.

Since the drama in a larger measure than any other form of literature mirrors the life of the people, their ideas and ideals, their traditions and ambitions, it would naturally be expected that a survey of the dramatic writings of various nations, however limited, would reveal certain of their characteristic resemblances and differences. And such we find to be the case.

For ages the word *Italy* was a mere geographical expression. It signified a collection of petty states, each seeking its own aggrandizement at the expense of the rest. Some of the states were free and independent; others were ruled by princes or potentates; still others belonged to the Church. For centuries Italy suffered deeper injury than any other European country by the strife waged for supremacy between the emperor and pope. As the temporal power of the pope lessened, the strife merged into one between people and princes. So if we would familiarize ourselves with the political history of this peninsula we must follow the course of events in the Kingdom of Naples, the Republic of Venice, the Duchy of Tuscany, and so on. Each of these states had its leading city —the residence of the ruler or the seat of popular government—and around this center literature and culture flourished.

When during the last century a united Italy was born, the prejudices of these centers could not at once be obliterated. The very question of which Italian city should become the capital of the united kingdom excited the keenest jealousy, and only the prestige of Immortal Rome was sufficient to make a permanent choice possible. Slowly Rome is becoming the center of thought as well as government, but even today the feeling of one city towards her sister cities is so intense that dramatic companies passing from one place to another do not know what attitude may be shown in regard to their productions. A play which elicits the heartiest applause in Milan may be hissed and deserted by an audience in Naples. The movement to establish a national theater in Rome which shall stand in the relation to Italy that the theaters of London do to England, and that those of Paris do to France, is well under way; when it is realized the success of such plays as have won the plaudits of the capital city will doubtless be greeted favorably elsewhere.

There is no Italian word which corresponds to our word *play;* rather, four words are used, each indicating the kind of production which is offered. The *farsa* corresponds to our word farce; it depends largely upon buffoonery for its humor. *Commedia* is of a higher order, but no matter how serious the issue, so long as it does not end in death, dramas are thus classified. *Dramma* and *tragedia* both end in death; the first is concerned with personal and domestic matters; the second, with broader questions.

The Italian cares little for boisterous fun; he may be reached through the intellect or through his passions. Comedy is popular and holds its audiences in spite of the monotony of its theme, which is usually the relations of husband and wife, with such opportunities as mistress and lover afford for intrigue and ridiculous situation. *Dramma* is almost always characterized by a clumsy beginning and, like *tragedia,* gives indication by argument rather than acting of its dismal end. As one writer has aptly said: "There is a perpetual hauling in the sheet to fetch sail past the islands of the Blest into the wide sea of Misery," in spite of the fact that repeated chances seem to be offered for those involved to extricate themselves.

Gabriele d'Annunzio is today the leading playwright of Italy. While his marked ability is widely acknowledged throughout the theater-loving world, it would appear doubtful whether any large number of people springing from Teutonic origin could ever become devoted to his writings. Probably he will always be best understood by his own countrymen who possess with him certain temperamental feelings and susceptibilities that lie outside the range of any but Latin peoples.

He was born in 1864, belonging to an old aristocratic branch of the nobility. During his university life at Rome he gave promise of his poetic genius, evincing early that perfection of form which is peculiar to the artist. Using the medium of verse and fiction, he has more recently turned to the writing of plays, which are regarded generally as inferior to his former works. They lack action and the characters are statuesque.

Before discussing any of his plays, an enumeration of some of his predominating tendencies may help to explain his style. In the first place, D'Annunzio is always the aristocrat; the masses are not included at all in his world. Having made an extended study of abnormal psychology, he appears to understand the morbid workings of the mind far better than he understands *man;* again, finding his ideals in the Renaissance rather than the present, he shows a capacity for depicting gross cruelty that is staggering to our generation, which, nurtured in humanitarian precepts and developing in times of comparative peace, finds physical pain abhorrent. Love of sensuality characterizes all his heroes, who are ever superior beings; his women are viewed from this standpoint alone. Lacking the slightest sense of humor, he possesses a love of nature which relieves pages otherwise too full of gloom and depression, terror and nightmare to charm, although they may fascinate. However, it should be remembered that D'Annunzio is an artist, with an artist's delicate perceptions. Reflecting the glorious hues of Italian skies "his imagination is steeped in the gorgeous colorings of the semi-tropical south, and all the products of his pen are tinged with the colors of deep vermillion and glowing red and resplendent blue." He makes poetry sing like music and from the narration of dire deeds, falls into a description of sea or sunset that captivates by its rare beauty.

In studying his plays, one should take for granted the dramatist's limitations and be receptive to his treatment of such subjects as he offers. Several of his plays are given historical settings and sometimes the theme has been treated by various writers—as, for example, *Franscesca da Rimini,* a story of tumultuous times in Italy when a sister is offered in marriage for political reasons and is led to believe that she is pledged to one, only to be betrayed by her family to a brother of her lover. The effect of this deceit upon her and the man she loved, their subsequent intrigue which works their ruin, is treated by Leigh Hunt and other writers.

La Gioconda, La Citta Morta, La Figlia di Joria, La Nave and *Fedra* are known to theater-goers, although the last two were not successful on the stage. Eleonora Duse for some time played the leading role in D'Annunzio's productions until it came to be said that his success was due to her personal charm and talent.

Speaking of the world wherein this dramatist lives, peopled by creatures of his fancy, these appreciatory comments have been made by one who has seen these plays as they have been produced upon the Italian stage: "The ordinary landscape of life seems replaced by a world wherein thoughts take the place of persons, emotions supplant light and shade, and where, thinking to enter earthly caverns underground, we find ourselves wandering through the coils of the brain, where strange lights and weird shadows delight and delude us. Where poverty and riches cease to be felt, where the common fruits, either of the earth or the mind, do not ripen, where reality is represented by things which to our everyday eyes seem transcendental and absurd; but which here become as actual and visible facts as the vapour of the sky precipitates into clouds, or held in a solid of momentary miracle on the point of a blade of grass."

Next in importance to D'Annunzio among Italian playwrights is Giuseppe Giacosa. From the commonplace and trivial he has chosen subjects of general interest. His greatest play is *Come le Foglio; Tristi Amori* and *Il Piu Forte* are also favorably known.

Roberto Brocco writes in a style too laboured to please those who are ever captivated by spontaneity. Realizing how all society is hampered by the social standards that confront the Italian woman, Brocco has championed her right to go forth into the world as it is, and share whatever joy and sorrow it metes out to those who are a part of it—not held aloof.

One of the most attractive plays produced in modern Italy, from the standpoint of American readers,—for it is known here only as literature and it is not likely to be shown on stages outside its native land,— is *Romanticismo*, which portrays the Italian struggle for independence. It could only be appreciated fully by one who had known the condition of his native land endangered by foreign enslavement and appropriation. Yet the citizens of freedom everywhere rejoiced in the successful struggle for Italian unity and can feel the exultation in the sentence of Lamberti, who in the third act of his play answers the officers who would find out the names of those who are involved in a plot for freedom.

"I will tell you—and mind you remember them well. They are the names of all who have hearts and heads, of all who remember and hate. Go out in the streets and the squares. Go into the theaters, the churches; everywhere where people are pretending to amuse themselves or to pray; everywhere where people are suffering and hiding their torn coats. *Name . . . the Names!* (*he laughs aloud*) Aha, first enlarge your prisons, make them as big as our cities are, and take us there. . . . The name is the name of all. It is the hour —the hour has come! We are all conspirators and rebellious."

Francesca Da Rimini.

Francesca. Bring me a garland of March violets.
Today 'tis the March calends.
   Biancofiore. Madonna, you shall have one, and a fair
      one. . . .
[*Garsenda enters followed by the merchant and his boy
      carrying a pack.*
   Garsenda. Madonna, here is the merchant with his
      goods.
May he come in? He is the Florentine,
Who came to Rimini yesterday with the escort
Of Messer Paolo.
[*Francesca, her face suddenly flushing, shakes off her
      gloomy thoughts, and seems eager to seek forgetful-
      ness of her mortal anguish; but a kind of painful ten-
      sion accompanies her volubility.*
   Francesca. Come in, come in, we are minded to renew
Our robes with the new season.
Come in, come in. I would have something made
Of sarcenet woven of many coloured threads,
Of many colours, of a hundred colours,
So that at each turn and return of light
And of sight the aspect changes; O Smaragdi,
A raiment of pure joy!
                    [*The merchant inclines humbly.*
Good merchant, what have you to offer me?

  Merchant. Noble Madonna, everything that suits
With your nobility; light tattetas,
Highly embroidered, circlet upon circlet,
Sarcenct, samite, and damask,
Grogram and bombasin,
Camlet, barracan, fustian,
Serge, Neapolitan doublets,
Sicilian tunics,
Watered silk, high or low, watered with gold
And silver thread, and waved. . . .
  Francesca. Enough, enough! And have you found a
  warehouse
In Rimini for so many goods?
  Merchant.   I am
Giotto di Bernarduccio Boninsegni,
The agent of the Company of Piero
Di Miccalaio degli Oricellari,
That has its thousand samples in the warehouses
Of Calimala and of Calimaruzza,
And sends its agents over all the west,
As far as Ireland, and, in the Levant,
As far as the Cattaio, noble Madonna. . . .
  Francesca.   This is good,
Brocade with golden pomegranates. And how,
Giotto, did you come here to Rimini?
  Merchant. Noble Madonna, full of perils is
The life of merchants. Needs must be we take
Every occasion that is offered us.
I, by good fortune, chanced to come upon
The escort of the noble Messer Paolo,
And had good leave to follow it in safety.
So swift a journey may I never make
Again; with Messer Paolo you ride
The whole day long, and never sleep at all.
[*Francesca feels over the stuffs, outwardly calm, but an*
  unconquerable smile burns in her eyes.
  Francesca. You rode so swiftly?
  Merchant.   Without rest or stay,
With tightened bridles, if I might so put it;
And every stream they forded, could not wait
Until the flood had ebbed. And Messer Paolo
Laboured his horse with spur in such a haste
That there was always between him and us,
A mile or so of distance. I should say

He has some urgent business here. He asked
The Commune leave of absence
After two months, or little more, that he
Had entered into office; truth it is
That the whole city sorrows at it, never
A more accustomed and more civil knight
Was Captain of the People there in Florence.
   Francesca. I will take this brocade.
   Merchant. Good, very good,
Madonna. And Bernardino della Porta
Of Parma, they have chosen
To take his place, is worth,
Why not so much as one hair of the head
 Of Messer Paolo.
   Francesca. And this samite, too.
   Merchant. Madonna, this with patterns all of gold?
   Francesca. Yes, I like this one, too. It seems to me
You Florentines keep feast on feast, and make
The year a holiday, and care for nothing
Except for games and sports and banquetings
And dances.
   Merchant.   Yes, Madonna, 'tis a sweet
And blessed land, our Florence: 'tis the flower
Of the others, Fiorenza!
   Francesca. I will take this silk, too, with the silver
    lines.
And the Captain of the People,
Was he well liked by all the companies
Of knights and ladies?
   Merchant. Each rivaled with each
Of all the companies
To have his presence, as the most well-spoken
And gallant man he indeed is; but he,
By what I know, would hold himself apart,
A trifle haughtily, and rare it was
To see him at their suppers. And in time
Of Carnival, in Santa Felicita
Beyond the Arno, I know by Messer Betto
De' Rossi that they made a company,
A thousand men or more, all dressed in white,
And Messer Paolo by this company
Was chosen Lord of Love,
But he would not consent.
VII—19

Francesca.   Here, this shot sarcenet
And this buff-coloured cotton. You were saying,
Giotto—
[*Garsenda takes the stuffs selected, and puts them aside,
     first holding them up to the light. The musicians be-
     gin a prelude. Those standing near go to the back,
     so as to leave room for the dance.*
Alda.   Fresh, fresh, in the calends of March,
O swallows, coming home
Fresh from the quiet lands beyond the sea;
First to bring back the great good messages
Of joy, and first to taste the good wild scent.
O creature of pure joy,
Come in your garments white and black, fly hither,
And bring your springtide gladness to our dance!
   Altichiara.   March comes, and February
Goes with the wind today;
Bring out your taffety
And put the vair away.
And come with me, I pray,
Across the streams in flood,
Under the branching wood that leans along,
With dancing and with song in company
With fleet-foot lovers, or upon the lea
Gather the violets,
Where the grass smells more sweet because her feet
Have passed that way, the naked feet of Spring!
   Garsenda.   Today the earth appears
New-wedded like a girl;
The face that the sea wears
Today is like a pearl.
Hark, hark, is that the merle
Deep in the thicket? Hark,
How swift upsoars the lark into the sky!
The cruel wind goes by, and in his mouth
Bears ravished nests! O Swallow of the south,
Thy tail's an arrow feather,
And like the twanging of a bow thy cry
Whereby the spring will strike, the hands of Spring!
   Biancofiore.   O creature of delight,
Lead thou the dancing feet,
In robe of black and white,
As is thy usage sweet.
Make here thy stay, O fleet

Swallow, here in this room
Wherein is seen, in gloom or light of day,
The tale of Iseult, the fair flower of Ireland,
As here thou seest, and this shall be thy garland;
Thy nest, no prison-mesh,
Seeing that the fresh fair lady seated here
Is not Francesca, but the very—
  All. Spring!
  Francesca (impetuously). Biancofiore, Althichiara,
    Alda, Adonella,
Garsenda, for the new
Delight of this new dance,
I must give you something new;
These dresses, take them, each!
[*She picks up some of the scattered goods and gives them.*
Here's for you and for you! . .
Now go, I have given you something, all of you,
For the March calends' sake. Go now, and going,
Sing in the court the song of the March swallows.
You must come back again, Merchant; Garsenda
Will bring you word. You may leave your wares here
  now.
Go, and be merry, until vesper-time;
Adonella, lead the way into the court.
A happy spring to you!
[*After a few minutes, a hand raises the curtain, and Paolo
    Malatesta appears. The door closes behind him. As
    Paolo and Francesca gaze at one another, for a mo-
    ment, without finding words, both change color. The
    sound of music dies away through the palace. The
    room is gilded by the rays of the setting sun, which
    shines through the long window.*
  Francesca. Welcome, my lord and kinsman.
  Paolo.   I have come
Hearing a sound of music, to bring greetings,
My greetings of return.
  Francesca.   You have come back
Speedily, sir; indeed, with the first swallow.
My women even now
Were singing a new song that they have made
To welcome March. And there was also here
A merchant out of Florence, who had come
Among your following. Of him I had
Tidings of you.

Paolo.   But I, of you, no tidings,
None, I heard nothing there,
Nothing of you at all,
From that day onward, when, one perilous night
You put a cup of wine into my hands,
And said to me, "farewell!"
And said to me, "God-speed!"
   Francesca. I have no memory,
My lord, concerning this. I have prayed much.
   Paolo. You have forgotten then?
   Francesca. I have prayed much.
   Paolo. And I have suffered much.
If it be true that he who suffers conquers,
I think I must needs conquer—
   Francesca. What?
   Paolo. My fate, Francesca.
   Francesca.
And yet you have come back?
   Paolo.   I have come back
To live.
   Francesca. Not to die now?
   Paolo.   Ah, you remember
The death I was to die,
And you that would not! So much, at the least,
You have remembered.
[*She draws back toward the window, as if withdrawing
      herself from his scarcely repressed violence.*
   Francesca.   Paolo, give me peace!
It is so sweet a thing to live forgetting.
But one hour only, and be no more tossed,
Out of the tempest.
Do not call back, I pray,
The shadow of that time in this fresh light
That slacks my thirst at last
Like that long draught
That at the ford I drank,
Out of the living water.
And now, I desire now
To think my soul has left
That shore to come unto this sheltering shore,
Where music and where hope are sisters; so
To forget all the sorrow that has been
Yesterday, and shall be
Tomorrow, and so let

All of my life, and all the veins of it,
And all the days of it,
And all old things in it, far-away things,
But for one hour, one hour,
Slip away quietly, a quiet tide,
Unto that sea,
Even these eyes might behold smilingly,
Were it not hidden by the tears that tremble
And do not fall. O peace, peace in that sea
That was so wild with waves
Yesterday, and today is like a pearl.
Give me peace.

    Paolo. It is the voice of spring
I hear, and from your lips the music runs
Over the world, that I have seemed to hear,
Riding against the wind,
Sing in the voice of the wind,
At every turn of the way,
At every glade, and high
On the hilltops, and on the edges of the woods,
And under them the streams,
When my desire bent back,
Burning with breath, the mane of my wild horse,
Over the saddle-bow, and the soul lived,
In the swiftness of that flight,
On swiftness,
Like a torch carried in the wind, and all
The thoughts of all my soul, save one, save one;
Were all blown backward, spent
Like sparks behind me.

    Francesca.   Ah, Paolo, like sparks
All your words are, and still they take no rest,
And all your soul lives still
In the strong wind and swiftness of your coming,
And drags me with it, and I am full of fear.
I pray you, I pray you now,
That you will give me peace
For this hour only,
My fair friend, my sweet friend,
That I may quiet and put to sleep in me
The old sick pain, and forget all the rest;
Only bring back into my eyes the first
Look that took hold on me out of your face,

Unknown to me; for these dry eyelids have
No need of any healing but that dew,
Only to bring back and to have in them
Again the miracle of that first look;
And they will feel the grace that has come to them
As they felt once, out of the heart of a dream,
The coming near of the dawn;
And feel that they are to be comforted,
Perhaps in the shade
Of the new garland.

    Paolo. Why do you take the garland from your head?
    Francesca. Because it was not you who gave it me.
I gave you once a rose
From that sarcophagus.
But now, poor flowers, I feel
Your freshness is all spent!

[*Paolo rises, and goes up to the reading desk and touches
    the violets.*

    Paolo. 'Tis true! Do you remember? on that night
Of fire and blood, you asked of me the gift
Of a fair helmet; and I gave it you:
'Twas finely tempered.
The steel and gold of it have never known
What rust is, soiling. And you let it fall.
Do you remember?
I picked it up, and I have held it dear
As a king's crown.
Since then, when I have set it on my head,
I feel twice bold, and there is not a thought
Within my heart that is not a flame.

                  [*He bends over the book.*
Ah, listen, the first words that meet my eye!
"Made richer by that gift than had you given him
The gift of all the world."
What book is this?
    Francesca.   The famous history
Of Lancelot of the Lake.
          [*She rises and goes over to the reading desk.*
    Paolo.   And you have read
The book all through?
    Francesca.   I have but
Come in my reading to this point.
    Paolo.   To where?

Here, where the mark is?

[He reads.

" . . . but you ask of me
Nothing . . . " Will you go on?

   Francesca. Look how the sea is growing white with
    light!

   Paolo. Will you not read the page with me, Francesca?

   Francesca. Look yonder, how a flight
Of swallows comes, and coming sets a shadow
On the white sea!

   Paolo.   Will you not read, Francesca?

   Francesca. And there is one sail, and so red it seems
Like fire.

   Paolo (reading). " 'Assuredly, my lady,' says
Thereat Galeotto, 'he is not so hot
He does not ask you any single thing
For love of you, because he fears, but I
Make suit to you for him; and know that I
Had never asked it of you, but that you
Were better off for it, seeing it is
The richest treasure you shall ever compass.'
Whereat says she—"

[Paolo draws Francesca gently by the hand.
But now, will you not read

What she says? Will you not be Guenevere?
See now how sweet they are,
Your violets
That you have cast away! Come, read a little.

[Their heads lean together over the book.

   Francesca (reading). "Whereat says she: 'This know
    I well, and I
Will do whatever thing you ask of. me.'
And Galeotto answers her: 'Much thanks,
Lady! I ask you that you give to him
Your love.' . . . "

[She stops.

   Paolo. But read on.

   Francesca.   No, I cannot see
The words.

   Paolo. Read on. It says: "Assuredly . . . "

   Francesca. " 'Assuredly,' says she, 'I promise it,

But let him be mine own and I all his,
And let there be set straight all crooked things
And evil.' . . . " Enough, Paolo.
   Paolo (*reading, hoarsely and tremulously*) " 'Lady!
   says he, 'much thanks, but kiss him then
Now, and before my face, for a beginning
Of a true love. . . ' " You, you! what does she say?
Now, what does she say? Here.
[*Their white faces lean over the book, until their cheeks
   almost touch.*
   Francesca (*reading*). "Says she: 'For what
Shall I be then entreated. But I will it
More than he wills it. . . . "
   Paolo (*following brokenly*). "And they draw apart
And the queen looks on him and sees that he
Cannot take heart on him to do aught more.
Thereat she takes him by the chin, and slowly
Kisses him on the mouth . . . "
[*He makes the same movement toward Francesca and
   kisses her. Francesca staggers and falls back on the
   cushions.*
   Francesca (*faintly*). No, Paolo!

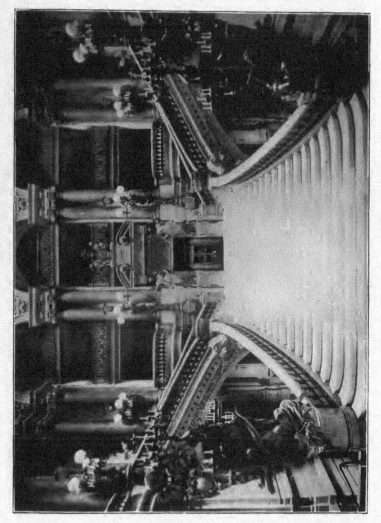

STAIRWAY OF HONOR.—PARIS OPERA HOUSE.

NORWEGIAN DRAMA.

CHAPTER XVIII.

HENRIK IBSEN.

HENRIK IBSEN, the greatest Norwegian dramatist and poet of modern times, was born in Skien, Norway, March 20, 1828. In 1850 he published his first drama, Catiline. In 1857 he became the director of the Christiania Theater, remaining in this capacity until 1864. During these years he wrote many plays which were produced on this stage. After the failure of this theatrical enterprise, Ibsen went to Rome where he wrote his greatest play, Peer Gynt.

In spite of long absences abroad, Ibsen remained first of all a Norwegian. He was a satirist who attacked in a merciless vein conventionalities and affectations. His plays in turn satirize social pretences, treatment of women, and conventionalities demanded by society at large. They have to do with the middle class rather than the wealthy or the smart set. Always a realist, Ibsen is perhaps best known by The Doll House, Hedda Gabler and Peer Gynt. His poems, while beautiful, are not so familiar to American readers.

A DOLL'S HOUSE.

Nora. Hide the Christmas-tree carefully, Ellen; the children mustn't see it before this evening, when it's lighted up. *(To the Porter, taking out her purse.)* How much?

Porter. Fifty öre.

Nora. There is a crown. No, keep the change. *(The Porter thanks her and goes out. Nora takes from her pocket a bag of macaroons, eats one or two, and goes to her husband's door and listens.)*

Nora. Yes, he is at home. *(Begins humming.)*

Helmer (in his room). Is that my lark twittering there?

Nora (busy opening her parcels). Yes, it is.

Helmer. Is it the squirrel skipping about?

Nora. Yes!

Helmer. When did the squirrel get home?

Nora. Just this minute. *(Hides the bag of macaroons.)* Come here, Torvald, and see what I've bought.

Helmer. Don't disturb me. (*A little later he opens the door and looks in*). "Bought," did you say? What! All that? Has my little spendthrift been making the money fly again?

Nora. Why, Torvald, surely we can afford to launch out a little now. It's the first Christmas we haven't had to pinch.

Helmer. Come, come; we can't afford to squander money.

Nora. Oh yes, Torvald, do let's squander a little—just the least little bit, won't you? You know you'll soon be earning heaps of money.

Helmer. Yes, from New Year's Day. But there's a whole quarter before my first salary is due.

Nora. Never mind; we can borrow in the meantime.

Helmer. Nora! Thoughtless as ever! Supposing I borrowed a thousand crowns today, and you spent it during Christmas week, and then on New Year's Eve a tile blew off the roof and knocked my brains out—

Nora. Hush! How can you talk so horridly?

Helmer. But supposing it were to happen—what then?

Nora. If anything so dreadful happened, I shouldn't care whether I was in debt or not.

Helmer. But what about the creditors?

Nora. They! Who cares for them? They're only strangers.

Helmer. Nora, Nora. What a woman you are! But seriously, Nora, you know my principles on these points. No debts! No credit! Home-life ceases to be free and beautiful as soon as it is founded on borrowing and debt. We two have held out bravely till now, and we won't give in at the last.

Nora (*going to the fireplace*). Very well—as you please, Torvald. . . .

Helmer. It's a sweet little lark; but it gets through with a lot of money. No one would believe how much it costs a man to keep such a little bird as you.

Nora. For shame! How can you say so? Why, I save as much as ever I can.

Helmer (*laughing*). Very true—as much as you can—but you can't. . . . You're a strange little being! Just like your father—always eager to get hold of money, but the moment you have it, it seems to slip through your fingers; you never know what becomes of it. Well, one must take you as you are. It's in the blood. Yes, Nora, that sort of thing is inherited.

Nora. I wish I had inherited many of my father's qualities.

Helmer. And I don't wish you anything but just what you are, my own sweet little song-bird. But, I say—it strikes me—you look so, so—what shall I call it?—so suspicious today—

Nora. Do I?

Helmer. You do, indeed. Look me full in the face.

Nora (looking at him). Well?

Helmer. Hasn't the little sweet-tooth been breaking the rules today?

Nora. No; how can you think of such a thing!

Helmer. Didn't she just look in at the confectioner's?

Nora. No, Torvald; really—

Helmer. Hasn't she even nibbled a macaroon or two?

Nora. No, Torvald, indeed!

Helmer. Well, well, well; of course I'm only joking.

Nora. I shouldn't think of doing what you disapprove of.

Helmer. No, I'm sure of that; and, besides, you've given me your word. Well, keep your little Christmas secrets to yourself, Nora darling. The Christmas-tree will bring them all to light, I daresay. . . .

[*Helmer retires to his study. Ellen ushers in Mrs. Linden, with whom Nora converses.*

.   .   .   .

Nora. And you're proud to think of what you have done for your brothers.

Mrs. Linden. Have I not the right to be?

Nora. Yes, surely. But now let me tell you, Christiana—I, too, have something to be proud and glad of.

Mrs. Linden. I don't doubt it. But what do you mean?

Nora. Hush! Not so loud. Only think, if Torvald were to hear! He mustn't—not for worlds! No one must know about it, Christiana—no one but you.

Mrs. Linden. What can it be?

Nora. Come over here (*draws her down on the sofa beside her*). Yes—I, too, have done something to be proud and glad of. *I* saved Torvald's life!

Mrs. Linden. Saved his life? How?

Nora. I told you about our going to Italy. Torvald would have died but for that.

Mrs. Linden. Yes—and your father gave you the money.

Nora (smiling). Yes, so Torvald and every one believes; but—

Mrs. Linden. But—?

Nora. Father didn't give us one penny. I found the money.

Mrs. Linden. You? All that money?

Nora. Twelve hundred dollars. Four thousand eight hundred crowns. What do you say to that?

Mrs. Linden. My dear Nora, how did you manage it? Did you win it in the lottery?

Nora (*contemptuously*). In the lottery? Pooh! Any fool could have done that!

Mrs. Linden. Then wherever did you get it from?

Nora (*hums and smiles mysteriously*). Hm; tra-la-la-la.

Mrs. Linden. Of course you couldn't borrow it.

Nora. No? Why not?

Mrs. Linden. Why, a wife can't borrow without her husband's consent.

Nora. Oh! when the wife knows a little of business, and how to set about things, then—

Mrs. Linden. But, Nora, I don't understand.

Nora. Well, you needn't. I never said I borrowed the money. Perhaps I got it another way. I may have got it from some admirer. When one is so—attractive as I am—

Mrs. Linden. You're too silly, Nora.

Nora. Now I'm sure you're dying of curiosity, Christiana—

Mrs. Linden. Listen to me, Nora dear: haven't you been a little rash?

Nora (*sitting upright*). Is it rash to save one's husband's life?

Mrs. Linden. I think it was rash of you, without his knowledge—

Nora. But it would have been fatal for him to know! Can't you understand that? He was never to suspect how ill he was. The doctors came to me privately and told me his life was in danger—that nothing could save him but a trip to the South. Do you think I didn't try diplomacy first? I told him how I longed to have a trip abroad, like other young wives; I wept and prayed; I said he ought to think of my condition, and not to thwart me; and then I hinted that he could borrow the money. But then, Christiana, he got almost angry. He said I was frivolous, and that it was his duty as a husband not to yield to my whims and fancies—so he called them. Very well, thought I, but saved you must be; and then I found the way to do it.

Mrs. Linden. And did your husband never learn from your father that the money was not from him?

Nora. No, never, father died at that very time. I meant to have told him all about it, and begged him to say nothing. But he was so ill—unhappily, it wasn't necessary.

Mrs. Linden. And you've never confessed to your husband?

Nora. Good heavens! What can you be thinking of? Tell him, when he has such a loathing of debt! And besides—how painful and humiliating it would be for Torvald, with his manly self-reliance, to know that he owed anything to me! It would utterly upset the relation between us; our beautiful, happy home would never again be what it is.

Mrs. Linden. Will you never tell him?

Nora (*thoughtfully*). Yes, some time perhaps—after many years, when I'm not so pretty. You mustn't laugh at me. Of course I mean when Torvald is not so much in love with me as he is now; when it doesn't amuse him any longer to see me skipping about, and dressing up and acting. Then it might do well to have something in reserve. (*Breaking off.*) Nonsense! nonsense! That time will never come. Now, what do you say to my grand secret, Christiana? Am I fit for nothing now? You may believe it has cost me a lot of anxiety. It has been no joke to meet my engagements punctually. You must know, Christiana, that in business there are things called installments, and quarterly interest, that are terribly hard to provide for. So I had to pinch a little here and there, wherever I could. I couldn't save anything out of the housekeeping, for of course Torvald had to live well. And I couldn't let the children go about badly dressed; all I got for them, I spent on them, the darlings.

Mrs. Linden. Poor Nora! So it had to come out o your own pocket-money.

Nora. Yes, of course. After all, the whole thing was my doing. When Torvald gave me money for clothes and so on, I never spent more than half of it; I always bought the simplest things. It's a mercy that everything suits me so well, Torvald never noticed anything. But it was often very hard, Christiana dear. For it's nice to be beautifully dressed—now, isn't it?

Mrs. Linden. Indeed it is.

Nora. Well, and besides that, I made money in other ways. Last winter I was so lucky—I got a heap of copying to do. I shut myself up every evening and wrote far into the night. And yet it was splendid to work in that way and earn money. I almost felt as if I was a man. . . Oh, Christiana, how glorious it is to think of! Free from cares! Free, quite free. To be able to play and romp about with the children; to have things tasteful and pretty in the house, exactly as Torvald likes it! And then the spring is coming, with the great blue sky. Perhaps then we shall have a short holiday. Perhaps I shall see the sea again. Oh, what a wonderful thing it is to live and to be happy! . . .

[*Mrs. Linden leaves, the children soon appear and Nora gives herself up to romping with them. The door is half opened and Krogstad appears. He waits a little, while the game goes on.*]

Krogstad. I beg your pardon, Mrs. Helmer—

Nora (with a suppressed cry turns around and half jumps up). Ah! What do you want?

Krogstad. Excuse me, the outer door was ajar—somebody must have forgotten to shut it—

Nora (standing up). My husband is not at home.

Krogstad. I know it.

Nora. Then what do you want here?

Krogstad. To say a few words to you.

Nora. To me? (*To the children, softly.*) Go in to Anna. What? No, the strange man won't hurt mamma. When he's gone we'll go on playing. (*Shuts the door behind them.*) It's with me you wish to speak?

Krogstad. Yes.

Nora. Today? But it's not the first yet—

Krogstad. No, today is Christmas Eve. It will depend upon yourself whether you have a merry Christmas. . . .

Nora. You won't tell my husband that I owe you money?

Krogstad. Suppose I were to.

Nora. It would be shameful of you. This secret, which is my joy and my pride—that he should learn it in such an ugly, coarse way—and from you! It would involve me in all sorts of unpleasantness. . .

Krogstad. Listen, Mrs. Helmer; either you have a weak memory, or you don't know much about business. I must make the position clear to you.

Nora. How so?

Krogstad. When your husband was ill, you came to me to borrow twelve hundred dollars.

Nora. I knew of nobody else.

Krogstad. I promised to find you the money under certain conditions. You were then so much taken up about your husband's illness, and so eager to have the wherewithal for your journey, that you probably didn't give much thought to the details. Let me remind you of them. I promised to find you the money in exchange for a note of hand which I drew up.

Nora. Yes, and I signed it.

Krogstad. Quite right. But then I added a few lines, making your father security for the debt. Your father was to sign this.

Nora. Was to? He did sign it!

Krogstad. I had left the date blank. That is to say, your father was himself to date his signature. Do you recollect that?

Nora. Yes, I believe—

Krogstad. Then I gave you the paper to send to your father. Is not that so?

Nora. Yes.

Krogstad. And of course you did so at once? For within five or six days you brought me back the paper, signed by your father; and I gave you the money.

Nora. Well, haven't I made my payments punctually?

Krogstad. Fairly—yes. But to return to the point. You were in great trouble at the time, Mrs. Helmer.

Nora. I was indeed!

Krogstad. Your father was very ill, I believe?

Nora. He was on his death-bed.

Krogstad. And died soon after?

Nora. Yes.

Krogstad. Tell me, Mrs. Helmer, do you happen to recollect the day of his death? The day of the month, I mean?

Nora. Father died on the 29th of September.

Krogstad. Quite correct. I have made inquiries. And here comes in the remarkable point—(*produces a paper*) which I cannot explain.

Nora. What remarkable point? I don't know—

Krogstad. The remarkable point, madam, that your father signed this paper three days after his death!

Nora. What! I don't understand—

Krogstad. Your father died on the 29th of September. But look here: he has dated his signature October 2nd. Is not that remarkable, Mrs. Helmer? (*Nora is silent*). Can you explain it? It is noteworthy, too, that the words "October 2nd" and the year are not in your father's handwriting, but in one which I believe I know. Well, this may be explained; your father may have forgotten to date his signature; and somebody may have added the date at random, before the date of your father's death was known. There's nothing wrong in that. Everything depends on the signature. Of course it is genuine, Mrs. Helmer? It was really your father who, with his own hand, wrote his name here?

Nora. No; *I* wrote father's name there.

Krogstad. Ah! Are you aware, madam, that that is a dangerous admission?

Nora. Why? you'll soon get your money.

Krogstad. May I ask you one more question? Why did you not send the paper to your father?

Nora. It was impossible. Father was ill. If I had asked him for his signature I should have had to tell him why I wanted the money; but he was so ill I really could not tell him that my husband's life was in danger. It was impossible.

Krogstad. Then it would have been better to have given up the tour.

Nora. No, I couldn't do that; my husband's life depended on that journey. I couldn't give it up. . . .

Krogstad. The law takes no account of motives.

Nora. Then it must be a very bad law.

Krogstad. Bad or not, if I lay this document before a court of law you will be condemned according to law.

Nora. I don't believe that. Do you mean to tell me that a daughter has no right to spare her dying father anxiety?— that a wife has no right to save her husband's life? I don't know much about the law, but I'm sure you'll find somewhere or other, that *that* is allowed. And you don't know that—you, a lawyer! You must be a bad one, Mr. Krogstad.

Krogstad. Possibly. But business—such business as ours— I do understand. You believe that? Very well; now do as you please. But this I may tell you, that if I'm flung into the gutter a second time, you shall keep me company. (*Bows and goes out.*)

Nora. Never! He wants to frighten me. I'm not so foolish as that. (*Pauses.*) But—? No, it's impossible; I did it for love.

Children (at the door). Mamma, the strange man has gone now.

Nora. Yes, yes, I know. But don't tell any one about the strange man. Do you hear? Not even papa!

Children. No, mamma; and now will you play with us again.

Nora. No, no, not now.

Children. Oh do, mamma; you know you promised.

Nora. Yes, but I can't just now. Run to the nursery; I've so much to do. Run along, run along, and be good, my darlings! (*Closes the door behind them*). Ellen, bring in the Christmas-tree! (*Again pauses.*) No, it's quite impossible!

Ellen. Where shall I stand it, ma'am?

Nora. There, in the middle of the room.

Ellen. Shall I bring in anything else?

Nora. No, thank you, I have all I want. (*Ellen goes out.*)

Nora (busy dressing the tree). There must be a candle here, and flowers there. That horrid man! Nonsense! Nonsense! There's nothing in it. The Christmas tree shall be beautiful. I'll do everything to please you, Torvald. . . . (*In the interim Helmer enters*).

HELMER—Just see how they've accumulated. *(Turning them over.)* Why, what's this?

NORA—*(At the window.)* The letter! Oh no, no, Torvald!

HELMER—Two visiting-cards—from Rank.

NORA—From Doctor Rank?

HELMER—*(Looking at them.)* Doctor Rank. They were on the top. He must have just put them in.

NORA—Is there anything on them?

HELMER—There's a black cross over the name. Look at it. What an unpleasant idea! It looks just as if he were announcing his own death.

NORA—So he is.

HELMER—What? Do you know anything? Has he told you anything?

NORA—Yes. These cards mean that he has taken his last leave of us. He is going to shut himself up and die.

HELMER—Poor fellow! Of course I knew we couldn't hope to keep him long. But so soon——! And to go and creep into his lair like a wounded animal——

NORA—When we must go, it is best to go silently. Don't you think so, Torvald?

HELMER—*(Walking up and down.)* He had so grown into our lives, I can't realize that he is gone. He and his sufferings and his loneliness formed a sort of cloudy background to the sunshine of our happiness. Well, perhaps it's best as it is—at any rate for him. *(Stands still.)* And perhaps for us, too. Now we two are thrown entirely upon each other. *(Takes her in his arms.)* My darling wife! I feel as if I could never hold you close enough. Do you know, Nora, I often wish some danger might threaten you, that I might risk body and soul, and everything, everything, for your dear sake.

NORA—*(Tears herself from him and says firmly:)* Now you shall read your letters, Torvald.

HELMER—No, no; not to-night. I want to be with you, my sweet wife.

NORA—With the thought of your dying friend——?

HELMER—You are right. This has shaken us both. Unloveliness has come between us—thoughts of decay and death. We must seek to cast them off. Till then—we will remain apart.

NORA—*(Her arms around his neck.)* Torvald! Good-night! good-night!

HELMER—*(Kissing her forehead.)* Good-night, my little song-bird. Sleep well. Now I shall go and read my letters. *(He goes with the letters in his hand into his room and shuts the door.)*

NORA—*(With wild eyes, gropes about her, seizes Helmer's domino, throws it round her, and whispers quickly, hoarsely and brokenly.)* Never to see him again. Never, never, never. *(Throws her shawl over her head.)* Never to see the children again. Never, never—— Oh, that black, icy water! Oh, that bottomless——! If it were only over! Now he has it, he's reading it. Oh, no, no, no, yet. Torvald, good-bye——! Good-bye, my little ones——! *(She is rushing out by the hall; at the same moment Helmer flings his door open, and stands there with an open letter in his hand.)*

HELMER—Nora!

NORA—*(Shrieks.)* Ah——!

HELMER—What is this? Do you know what is in this letter?

NORA—Yes, I know. Let me go! Let me pass!

HELMER—*(Holds her back.)* Where do you want to go?

NORA—*(Tries to break away from him.)* You shall not save me, Torvald.

HELMER—*(Falling back.)* True! Is what he writes true? No, no, it is impossible that this can be true.

NORA—It is true. I have loved you beyond all else in the world.

HELMER—Pshaw—no silly evasions!

NORA—*(A step nearer him.)* Torvald——!

HELMER—Wretched woman—what have you done?

NORA—Let me go—you shall not save me! You shall not take my guilt upon yourself!

HELMER—I don't want any melodramatic airs. *(Locks the outer door.)* Here you shall stay and give an account of yourself. Do you understand what you have done? Answer! Do you understand it?

NORA—*(Looks at him fixedly, and says with a stiffening expression:)* Yes; now I begin fully to understand it.

HELMER—*(Walking up and down.)* Oh! what an awful awakening! During all these eight years—she who was my pride and my joy—a hypocrite, a liar—worse, worse—a criminal. Oh, the unfathomable hideousness of it all! Ugh! Ugh!

(Nora says nothing and continues to look fixedly at him.)

HELMER—I ought to have known how it would be. I ought to have foreseen it. All your father's want of principle—be silent!—all your father's want of principle you have inherited—no religion, no morality, no sense of duty. How I am punished for screening him! I did it for your sake; and you reward me like this.

NORA—Yes—like this.

HELMER—You have destroyed my whole happiness. You have ruined my future. Oh, it's frightful to think of! I am in the power of a scoundrel; he can do whatever he pleases with me, demand whatever he chooses; he can domineer over me as much as he likes, and I must submit. And all this disaster and ruin is brought upon me by an unprincipled woman!

NORA—When I am out of the world, you will be free.

HELMER—Oh, no fine phrases. Your father, too, was always ready with them. What good would it do if you were "out of the world," as you say? No good whatever! He can publish the story all the same; I might even be suspected of collusion. People will think I was at the bottom of it all and egged you on. And for all this I have you to thank—you whom I have done nothing but pet and spoil during our whole married life. Do you understand now what you have done to me?

NORA—*(With cold calmness.)* Yes.

HELMER—The thing is so incredible, I can't grasp it. But we must come to an understanding. Take that shawl off. Take it off, I say! I must try to pacify him in one way or another—the matter must be hushed up, cost what it may.— As for you and me, we must make no outward change, you understand. Of course, you will continue to live here. But the children cannot be left in your care. I dare not trust them to you.—Oh, to have to say this to one I have loved so tenderly—whom I still——! But that must be a thing of the past. Henceforward there can be no question of happiness, but merely of saving the ruins, the shreds, the show—— *(A ring; Helmer starts.)* What's that? So late. Can it be the worst? Can he——? Hide yourself, Nora; say you are ill. *(Nora stands motionless. Helmer goes to the door and opens it.)*

ELLEN—*(Half dressed, in the hall.)* Here is a letter for you, ma'am.

HELMER—Give it to me. *(Seizes the letter and shuts the door.)* Yes, from him. You shall not have it. I shall read it.

NORA—Read it!

HELMER—*(By the lamp.)* I have hardly the courage to. We may both be lost, both you and I. Ah! I must know. *(Hastily tears the letter open; reads a few lines, looks at an enclosure; with a cry of joy:)* Nora! *(Nora looks inquiringly at him.)*

HELMER—Nora!—Oh, I must read it again.—Yes, yes, it is so. I am saved! Nora, I am saved!

NORA—And I?

HELMER—You, too, of course; we are both saved; both of us. Look here—he sends you back your promissory note. He writes that he regrets and apologizes; that a happy turn in his life—— Oh, what matter what he writes. We are saved, Nora! No one can harm you. Oh, Nora, Nora——; but first to get rid of this hateful thing. I'll just see—— *(Glances at the I. O. U.)* No, I will not look at it; the whole thing shall be nothing but a dream to me. *(Tears the I. O. U. and both letters in pieces. Throws them into the fire and watches them burn.)* There! it's gone!—— He said that ever since Christmas Eve—— Oh, Nora, they must have been three terrible days for you!

NORA—I have fought a hard fight for the last three days.

HELMER—And in your agony you saw no other outlet but—— No; we won't think of that horror. We will only rejoice and repeat—it's over, all over! Don't you hear, Nora? You don't seem able to grasp it. Oh, my poor Nora, I understand; you cannot believe that I have forgiven you. But I have, Nora; I swear it. I have forgiven everything. I know that what you did was all for love of me.

NORA—That is true.

HELMER—You loved me as a wife should love her husband. It was only the means that, in your inexperience, you misjudged. But do you think I love you the less because you cannot do without guidance? No, no. Only lean on me; I will counsel you, and guide you. I should be no true man if this very womanly helplessness did not make you doubly dear in my eyes. You mustn't dwell upon the hard things I said in my first moment of terror, when the world seemed to be tumbling about my ears. I have forgiven you, Nora—I swear I have forgiven you.

NORA—I thank you for your forgiveness. *(Goes out, to the right.)*

HELMER—No, stay——! *(Looking through the doorway.)* What are you going to do?

NORA—*(Inside.)* To take off my masquerade dress.

HELMER—*(In the doorway.)* Yes, do, dear. Try to calm down, and recover your balance, my scared little songbird. You may rest secure. I have broad wings to shield you. *(Walking up and down near the door.)* Oh, how lovely—how cozy our home is, Nora! Here you are safe; here I can shelter you like a hunted dove whom I have saved from the claws of the hawk. I shall soon bring your poor beating heart to rest; believe me, Nora, very soon. To-morrow all this will seem quite different—everything will be as before. I shall not need to tell you again that I forgive you; you will feel for yourself that it is true. How could you think I could find it in my heart to reproach you? Oh, you don't know a true man's heart, Nora. There is something indescribably sweet and soothing to a man in having forgiven his wife—honestly forgiven her, from the bottom of his heart. She becomes his property in a double sense. She is as though born again; she has become, so to speak, at once his wife and his child. That is what you shall henceforth be to me, my bewildered, helpless darling. Don't be troubled about anything, Nora; only open your heart to me, and I will be both will and conscience to you. *(Nora enters in everyday dress.)* Why, what's this? Not gone to bed? You have changed your dress?

NORA—Yes, Torvald; now I have changed my dress.

HELMER—But why now, so late——?

NORA—I shall not sleep to-night.

HELMER—But, Nora dear——

NORA—*(Looking at her watch.)* It's not so late yet. Sit down, Torvald; you and I have much to say to each other. *(She sits down at one side of the table.)*

HELMER—Nora—what does this mean? Your cold, set face——

NORA—Sit down. It will take some time. I have much to talk over with you. *(Helmer sits at the other side of the table.)*

HELMER—You alarm me, Nora. I don't understand you.

NORA—No, that is just it. You don't understand me, and I have never understood you—till to-night. No, don't interrupt. Only listen to what I say.—We must come to a final settlement, Torvald.

HELMER—How do you mean?

NORA—*(After a short silence.)* Does not one thing strike you as we sit here?

HELMER—What should strike me?

NORA—We have been married eight years. Does it not strike you that this is the first time we two, you and I, man and wife, have talked together seriously?

HELMER—Seriously? What do you call seriously?

NORA—During eight whole years, and more—ever since the day we first met—we have never exchanged one serious word about serious things.

HELMER—Was I always to trouble you with the cares you could not help me bear?

NORA—I am not talking of cares. I say we have never yet set ourselves seriously to get to the bottom of anything.

HELMER—Why, my dearest Nora, what have you to do with serious things?

NORA—There we have it! You have never understood me.—I have had great injustice done me, Torvald; first by father, and then by you.

HELMER—What! By your father and me?—By us, who have loved you more than all the world?

NORA—*(Shaking her head.)* You have never loved me. You only thought it amusing to be in love with me.

HELMER—Why, Nora, what a thing to say!

NORA—Yes, it is so, Torvald. While I was at home with father he used to tell me all his opinions, and I held the same opinions. If I had others I said nothing about them, because he wouldn't have liked it. He used to call me his doll-child, and played with me as I played with my dolls. Then I came to live in your house——

HELMER—What an expression to use about our marriage!

NORA—*(Undisturbed.)* I mean I passed from father's hands into yours. You arranged everything according to your taste; and I got the same tastes as you; or I pretended to—I don't know which—both ways, perhaps; sometimes the other. When I look back on it now, I seem to have been living here like a beggar, from hand to mouth. I lived by performing tricks for you, Torvald. But you would have it so. You and father have done me a great wrong. It is your fault that my life has come to nothing.

HELMER—Why, Nora, how unreasonable and ungrateful you are! Have you not been happy here?

NORA—No, never. I thought I was; but I never was.

HELMER—Not—not happy?

NORA—No; only merry. And you have always been so kind to me. But our house has been nothing but a play-room. Here I have been your doll-wife, just as at home I used to be papa's doll-child. And the children, in their turn, have been my dolls. I thought it fun when you played with me, just as the children did when I played with them. That has been our marriage, Torvald.

HELMER—There is some truth in what you say, exaggerated and overstrained though it be. But henceforth it shall be different. Play-time is over; now comes the time for education.

NORA—Whose education? Mine, or the children's?

HELMER—Both, my dear Nora.

NORA—Oh, Torvald, you are not the man to teach me to be a fit wife for you.

HELMER—And you can say that?

NORA—And I—how have I prepared myself to educate the children?

HELMER—Nora!

NORA—Did you not say yourself, a few minutes ago, you dared not trust them to me?

HELMER—In the excitement of the moment! Why should you dwell upon that?

NORA—No—you were perfectly right. That problem is beyond me. There is another to be solved first—I must try to educate myself. You are not the man to help me in that. I must set about it alone. And that is why I am leaving you.

HELMER—*(Jumping up.)* What—do you mean to say——?

NORA—I must stand quite alone if I am ever to know myself and my surroundings; so I cannot stay with you.

HELMER—Nora! Nora!

NORA—I am going at once. I daresay Christina will take me in for to-night——

HELMER—You are mad! I shall not allow it! I forbid it!

NORA—It is of no use your forbidding me anything now. I shall take with me what belongs to me. From you I will accept nothing, either now or afterwards.

HELMER—What madness this is!

NORA—To-morrow I shall go home—I mean to what was my home. It will be easier for me to find some opening there.

HELMER—Oh, in your blind inexperience——

NORA—I must try to gain experience, Torvald.

HELMER—To forsake your home, your husband, and your children! And you don't consider what the world will say.

NORA—I can pay no heed to that. I only know that I must do it.

HELMER—This is monstrous! Can you forsake your holiest duties in this way?

NORA—What do you consider my holiest duties?

HELMER—Do I need to tell you that? Your duties to your husband and your children.

NORA—I have other duties equally sacred.

HELMER—Impossible! What duties do you mean?

NORA—My duties toward myself.

HELMER—Before all else you are a wife and a mother.

NORA—That I no longer believe. I believe that before

all else I am a human being, just as much as you are—or at least that I should try to become one. I know that most people agree with you, Torvald, and they say that in books. But henceforth I can't be satisfied with what most people say, and what is in books. I must think things out for myself, and try to get clear about them.

HELMER—Are you not clear about your place in your own home? Have you not an infallible guide in questions like these? Have you not religion?

NORA—Oh, Torvald, I don't really know what religion is.

HELMER—What do you mean?

NORA—I know nothing but what Pastor Hansen told me when I was confirmed. He explained that religion was this and that. When I get away from all this and stand alone, I will look into that matter too. I will see whether what he taught me is right, or, at any rate, whether it is right for me.

HELMER—Oh, this is unheard of. And from so young a woman! But if religion cannot keep you right, let me appeal to your conscience—for I suppose you have some moral feeling? Or, answer me, perhaps you have none?

NORA—Well, Torvald, it's not easy to say. I really don't know—I am all at sea about these things. I only know that I think quite differently from you about them. I hear, too, that the laws are different from what I thought; but I can't believe that they are right. It appears that a woman has no right to spare her dying father, or to save her husband's life! I don't believe that.

HELMER—You talk like a child. You don't understand the society in which you live.

NORA—No, I do not. But now I shall try to learn. I must make up my mind which is right—society or I.

HELMER—Nora, you are ill; you are feverish; I almost think you are out of your senses.

NORA—I have never felt so much clearness and certainty as to-night.

HELMER—You are clear and certain enough to forsake husband and children?

NORA—Yes, I am.

HELMER—Then there is only one explanation possible.

NORA—What is that?

HELMER—You no longer love me.

NORA—No; that is just it.

HELMER—Nora! Can you say so?

NORA—Oh, I'm sorry, Torvald; for you've always been so kind to me. But I can't help it. I do not love you any longer.

HELMER—(*Mastering himself with difficulty.*) Are you clear and certain on this point too?

NORA—Yes, quite. That is why I will not stay here any longer.

HELMER—And can you also make clear to me how I have forfeited your love?

NORA—Yes, I can. It was this evening, when the miracle did not happen, for then I saw you were not the man I had imagined.

HELMER—Explain yourself more clearly; I don't understand.

NORA—I have waited patiently all these eight years; for, of course, I saw clearly enough that miracles don't happen every day. When this crushing blow threatened me, I said to myself so confidently, "Now comes the miracle!" When Krogstad's letter lay in the box, it never for a moment occurred to me that you would think of submitting to that man's conditions. I was convinced that you would say to him, "Make it known to all the world"; and that then——

HELMER—Well? When I had given my own wife's name up to disgrace and shame——?

NORA—Then I firmly believed that you would come forward, take everything upon yourself, and say, "I am the guilty one."

HELMER—Nora——!

NORA—You mean I would never have accepted such a sacrifice? No, certainly not. But what would my assertions have been worth in opposition to yours? That was the miracle that I hoped for and dreaded. And it was to hinder that that I wanted to die.

HELMER—I would gladly work for you night and day, Nora—bear sorrow and want for your sake. But no man sacrifices his honor, even for one he loves.

NORA—Millions of women have done so.

HELMER—Oh, you think and talk like a silly child.

NORA—Very likely. But you neither think nor talk like the man I can share my life with. When your terror was over—not for what threatened me, but for yourself—when there was nothing more to fear—then it seemed to you as though nothing had happened. I was your lark again, your doll, just as before—whom you would take twice as much care of in the future, because she was so weak and fragile. (*Stands up.*) Torvald—in that moment it burst upon me that I had been living here these eight years with a strange man, and had borne him three children. Oh, I can't bear to think of it! I could tear myself to pieces!

HELMER—(*Sadly.*) I see it, I see it; an abyss has opened between us. But, Nora, can it never be filled up?

NORA—As I now am, I am no wife for you.

HELMER—I have strength to become another man.

NORA—Perhaps—when your doll is taken away from you.

HELMER—To part—to part from you! No, Nora, no; I can't grasp the thought.

NORA—(*Going into room on the right.*) The more reason for the thing to happen. (*She comes back with outdoor things and a small traveling bag, which she places on a chair.*)

HELMER—Nora, Nora, not now! Wait till to-morrow.

NORA—(*Putting on cloak.*) I can't spend the night in a strange man's house.

HELMER—But can we not live here, as brother and sister——?

NORA—(*Fastening her hat.*) You know very well that wouldn't last long. (*Puts on the shawl.*) Good-bye, Torvald. No, I won't go to the children. I know they are in better hands than mine. As I now am, I can be nothing to them.

HELMER—But some time, Nora, some time——?

NORA—How can I tell? I have no idea what will become of me.

HELMER—But you are my wife, now and always!

NORA—Listen, Torvald; when a wife leaves her husband's house, as I am doing, I have heard that in the eyes of the law he is free from all duties toward her. At any rate, I release you from all duties. You must not feel yourself bound, any more than I shall. There must be perfect freedom on both sides. There, I give you back your ring. Give me mine.

HELMER—That too?

NORA—That too.

HELMER—Here it is.

NORA—Very well. Now it is all over. I lay the keys here. The servants know about everything in the house—better than I do. To-morrow, when I have started, Christina will come to pack up the things I brought with me from home. I will have them sent after me.

HELMER—All over! all over! Nora, will you never think of me again?

NORA—Oh, I shall often think of you, and the children, and this house.

HELMER—May I write to you, Nora?

NORA—No, never. You must not.

HELMER—But I must send you——

NORA—Nothing, nothing.

HELMER—I must help you if you need it.

NORA—No, I say. I take nothing from strangers.

HELMER—Nora, can I never be more than a stranger to you?

NORA—(*Taking her traveling bag.*) Oh, Torvald, then the miracle of miracles would have to happen——

HELMER—What is the miracle of miracles?

NORA—Both of us would have to change so that—oh, Torvald, I no longer believe in miracles.

HELMER—But *I* will believe. Tell me! We must so change that——?

NORA—That communion between us shall be a marriage. Good-bye. (*She goes out by the hall door.*)

HELMER—(*Sinks into a chair by the door with his face in his hands.*) Nora! Nora! (*He looks round and rises.*) Empty. She is gone. (*A hope springs up in him.*) Ah! The miracle of miracles——?

(*From below is heard the reverberation of a heavy door closing.*)

CHAPTER XIX.
GERMAN DRAMA.
LESSING.

SAXONY, the heart of Germany, gave
birth to Gotthold Ephraim Lessing (1729-
1781), who wrote the first German national comedy ("Minna
von Barnhelm"), the first great German drama of serious import
("Nathan der Weise"), and laid the solid foundations of
modern German literary and æsthetic criticism in his "Laokoon,"
a critical inquiry into artistic principles written in reply to
Winckelmann's antiquarian theories. Lessing was a fine type
of the clear-headed German truth-seeker. There was no mysticism nor etherealism in his intellectuality. He turned a keen
searchlight on all questions, and applied a calmly logical mind
to all his creative efforts. He was also the first to secure to
Germany due estimation for the vocation of a man of letters.
Lessing spoke of himself as a David who went out to slay the
Goliath of Philistinism. Goethe afterwards thus sang of the
departed master:

While thou wast living we honored thee as one of the gods:
Now thou art dead thy spirit over our spirits presides.

Lessing's calmly critical spirit was early revealed in his
religious tolerance, or, perhaps, indifferentism. In a youthful
work on "The Jew" he foreshadowed the charity for a despised race that he was so triumphantly to preach in "Nathan
the Wise." In later years he enjoyed the friendship of one
of the noblest Jews of his age, Moses Mendelssohn, a broad-
minded leader of rare intellect and character. He determined
to represent this man on the stage in a drama that should
inculcate the necessity for mutual tolerance of creed to creed.
A suitable plot was found in the story of "The Three Rings,"
already told in the old "Gesta Romanorum" and in Boccac-

cio's "Decameron." In "Nathan der Weise" (1779), when
Saladin seeks a pretext whereby to extort money from the
rich son of Israel, the Jew outwits the Sultan by reciting this
parable of the rings. Saladin is led to see that there may
be as much doubt and need for charity regarding the true
religion as concerning the magic ring of this parable. Not
only in this central motive, but in the love romance and incidental scenes as well, Lessing has admirably contrasted narrow
dogmatism and prejudice in all its ascending shades through
the brutal fanaticism of the Patriarch, the conventionalism of
Daja, the independence of the Templar, the humble piety of
the Friar, the worldly contempt of the Dervis, the generosity
of Saladin, to the enlightened virtue of Nathan.

Before "Nathan," however, Lessing had made his bow
as a dramatist. In "Miss Sara Sampson," a curious tragedy
founded on "Clarissa Harlowe," he had, as one critic says,
"cracked the egg of Columbus for German dramatic art."
In the comedy of "Minna von Barnhelm," he produced a
national military drama, in which he typified German honor
and valor in the hero—a veteran of the Prussian wars—and
German womanhood of the best type in Minna, his sweetheart.
His "Emilia Galotti" is a sort of Italian Virginia, and the
play is directed against the tyranny of petty princelings.

"Lessing," says Professor Francke, "while combining in
himself the enlightenment, the idealism, the universality of the
best of his age, added to this an intellectual fearlessness and a
constructive energy which have made him the champion destroyer of despotism and the master builder of lawful freedom."

NATHAN AND THE TEMPLAR.

Nathan. I'm almost shy of this strange fellow, almost
Shrink back from his rough virtue. That one man
Should ever make another man feel awkward!
And yet—He's coming—ha!—by God, the youth
Looks like a man. I love his daring eye,
His open gait. May be the shell is bitter;
But not the kernel surely. I have seen
Some such, methinks. Forgive me, noble Frank.

Templar. What?

Nath. Give me leave.

Temp. Well, Jew, what wouldst thou have?

Nath. The liberty of speaking to you.

Temp. So—can I prevent it? Quick then, what's your
business?

Nath. Patience—nor hasten quite so proudly by
A man, who has not merited contempt,
And whom, for evermore, you've made your debtor.

Temp. How so? Perhaps I guess—No—Are you then—

Nath. My name is Nathan, father to the maid
Your generous courage snatched from circling flames,
And hasten—

Temp. If with thanks, keep, keep them all.
Those little things I've had to suffer much from:
Too much already, far. And, after all,
You owe me nothing. Was I ever told
She was your daughter? 'Tis a templar's duty
To rush to the assistance of the first
Poor wight that needs him; and my life just then
Was quite a burden. I was mighty glad
To risk it for another; tho' it were
That of a Jewess.

Nath. Noble, and yet shocking!
The turn might be expected. Modest greatness
Wears willingly the mask of what is shocking
To scare off admiration : but, altho'
She may disdain the tribute, admiration,
Is there no other tribute she can bear with?
Knight, were you here not foreign, not a captive,
I would not ask so freely. Speak, command,
In what can I be useful?

Temp. You—in nothing.

Nath. I'm rich.

Temp. To me the richer Jew ne'er seemed
The better Jew.

Nath. Is that a reason why
You should not use the better part of him,
His wealth?

Temp. Well, well, I'll not refuse it wholly,
For my poor mantle's sake—when that is threadbare,
And spite of darning will not hold together,

I'll come and borrow cloth or money of thee,
To make me up a new one.   Don't look solemn;
The danger is not pressing; 'tis not yet
At the last gasp, but tight and strong and good,
Save this poor corner, where an ugly spot
You see is singed upon it.   It got singed
As I bore off your daughter from the fire.
 Nath. (*taking hold of the mantle*). 'Tis singular that such an
  ugly spot
Bears better testimony to the man
Than his own mouth.   This brand—Oh, I could kiss it!
Your pardon—that I meant not.
 Temp. What?
 Nath. A tear
Fell on the spot.
 Temp. You'll find up more such tears—
(This Jew methinks begins to work upon me).
 Nath. Would you send once this mantle to my daughter?
 Temp. Why?
 Nath. That her lips may cling to this dear speck;
For at her benefactor's feet to fall,
I find, she hopes in vain.
 Temp. But, Jew, your name
You said was Nathan—Nathan, you can join
Your words together cunningly—right well—
I am confused—in fact—I would have been—
 Nath. Twist, writhe, disguise you, as you will, I know you,
You were too honest, knight, to be more civil;
A girl all feeling, and a she-attendant
All complaisance, a father at a distance—
You valued her good name, and would not see her.
You scorned to try her, lest you should be victor;
For that I also thank you.
 Temp. I confess,
You know how templars ought to think.
 Nath. Still templars—
And only *ought* to think—and all because
The rules and vows enjoin it to the *order*—
I know how good men think—know that all lands
Produce good men.
 Temp. But not without distinction.
 Nath. In color, dress, and shape, perhaps, distinguished.

Temp. Here more, there fewer sure?

Nath.. That boots not much.

The great man everywhere has need of room.
Too many set together only serve
To crush each others' branches.   Middling good,
As we are, spring up everywhere in plenty.
Only let one not scar and bruise the other !
Let not the gnarl be angry with the stump;
Let not the upper branch alone pretend
Not to have started from the common earth.

Temp. Well said: and yet, I trust, you know the nation.
That first began to strike at fellow men,
That first baptised itself the chosen people—
How now if I were—not to hate this people,
Yet for its pride could not forbear to scorn it,
The pride which is to Mussulman and Christian
Bequeathed, as were its God alone the true one.
You start, that I, a Christian and a templar,
Talk thus.   Where, when, has e'er the pious rage
To own the better God—on the whole world
To force this better, as the best of all—
Shown itself more, and in a blacker form,
Than here, than now?   To him, whom, here and now,
The film is not removing from his eye—
But be he blind that wills!   Forget my speeches
And leave me.

Nath. Ah ! indeed you do not know
How closer I shall cling to you henceforth.
We must, we shall be friends.   Despise my nation—
We did not choose a nation for ourselves.
Are we our nations?   What's a nation then?
Were Jews and Christians such, ere they were men?
And have I found in thee one more, to whom
It is enough to be a man?

Temp. That hast thou.

Nathan, by God, thou hast.—Thy hand.   I blush
To have mistaken thee a single instant.

Nath. And I am proud of it.   Only common souls
We seldom err in.

Temp. And uncommon ones
Seldom forget.   Yes, Nathan, yes, we must.
We shall be friends.

Nath. We are so. And my Racha—
She will rejoice. How sweet the wider prospect .
That dawns upon me! Do but know her—once.

NATHAN THE WISE BEFORE SALADIN.

SCENE.—*An Audience Room in the Sultan's Palace.*

Saladin (giving directions at the door). Here, introduce the
     Jew, whene'er he comes,—
He seems in no great haste.
     Sittah. May be, at first
He was not in the way.
     Sal. Ah, sister, sister!
     Sit. You seem as if a combat were impending.
     Sal. With weapons that I have not learned to wield.—
Must I disguise myself? I use precautions?
I lay a snare? When, where gained I that knowledge?
And this, for what? To fish for money,—money,—
For money from a Jew. And to such arts
Must Saladin descend, at last, to come at
The least of little things?
     Sit. Each little thing,
Despised too much, finds methods of revenge.
     Sal. 'Tis but too true. And if this Jew should prove
The fair, good man, as once the dervis painted—
     Sit. Then difficulties cease. A snare concerns
The avaricious, cautious, fearful Jew;
And not the good, wise man: for he is ours
Without a snare. Then the delight of hearing
How such a man speaks out; with what stern strength
He tears the net, or with what prudent foresight
He one by one undoes the tangled meshes!
That will be all to boot.
     Sal. Then I shall joy in.
     Sit. What, then, should trouble thee? For if he be
One of the many only, a mere Jew,
You will not blush, to such a one to seem
A man as he thinks all mankind to be.
One that to him should bear a better aspect
Would seem a fool,—a dupe.
     Sal. So that I must
Act badly, lest the bad think badly of me?

Sit. Yes; if you call it acting badly, brother,
To use a thing after its kind.

Sal. There's nothing,
That woman's wit invents, it can't embellish.

Sit. Embellish?—

Sal. But their fine-wrought filagree
In my rude hand would break. It is for those
That can contrive them to employ such weapons:
They ask a practised wrist. But chance what may,
Well as I can—

Sit. Trust not yourself too little.
I answer for you, if you have the will.
Such men as you would willingly persuade us
It was their swords, their swords alone, that raised them.
The lion's apt to be ashamed of hunting
In fellowship of the fox;—'t is of his fellow,
Not of the cunning, that he is ashamed.

Sal. You women would so gladly level man
Down to yourselves!—Go, I have got my lesson.

Sit. What! must I go?

Sal. Had you the thought of staying?

Sit. In your immediate presence not, indeed;
But in the by-room.

Sal. You would like to listen.
Not that, my sister, if I may insist.
Away! the curtain rustles,—he is come.
Beware of staying,—I'll be on the watch.—
[*Sittah retires through one door; Nathan enters at another.*
Draw nearer, Jew; yet nearer; here, quite by me,
Without all fear.

Nathan. Remain that for thy foes!

Sal. Your name is Nathan?

Nath. Yes.

Sal. Nathan the Wise?

Nath. No.

Sal. If not thou, the people calls thee so.

Nath. May be, the people.

Sal. Fancy not that I
Think of the people's voice contemptuously;
I have been wishing much to know the man
Whom it has named the Wise.

Nath. And if it named

Him so in scorn? If wise meant only prudent;
And prudent, one who knows his interest well?

Sal. Who knows his real interest, thou must mean.

Nath. Then were the interested the most prudent;
Then wise and prudent were the same.

Sal. I hear
You proving what your speeches contradict.
You know man's real interests, which the people
Knows not,—at least, have studied how to know them.
That alone makes the sage.

Nath. Which each imagines
Himself to be.

Sal. Of modesty enough!
Ever to meet it, where one seeks to hear
Dry truth, is vexing. Let us to the purpose:—
But, Jew, sincere and open—

Nath. I will serve thee
So as to merit, Prince, thy further notice.

Sal. Serve me?—how?

Nath. Thou shalt have the best I bring,—
Shalt have them cheap.

Sal. What speak you of?—your wares?
My sister shall be called to bargain with you
For them. (*Aside.*) So much for the sly listener;—I
Have nothing to transact now with the merchant.

Nath. Doubtless, then, you would learn what, on my journey,
I noticed of the motions of the foe,
Who stirs anew. If unreserved I may—

Sal. Neither was that the object of my sending:
I know what I have need to know already.
In short, I willed your presence——

Nath. Sultan, order.

Sal. To gain instruction quite on other points.
Since you are a man so wise,—tell me, which law,
Which faith, appears to you the better?

Nath. Sultan,
I am a Jew.

Sal. And I a Mussulman:
The Christian stands between us. Of these three
Religions only one can be the true.
A man like you remains not just where birth

Has chanced to cast him, or, if he remains there,
Does it from insight, choice, from grounds of preference.
Share, then, with me your insight,—let me hear
The grounds of preference, which I have wanted
The leisure to examine,—learn the choice
These grounds have motived, that it may be mine.
In confidence I ask it. How you startle,
And weigh me with your eye! It may well be
I'm the first sultan to whom this caprice,
Methinks not quite unworthy of a sultan,
Has yet occurred. Am I not? Speak, then,—speak.
Or do you, to collect yourself, desire
Some moments of delay? I give them you.—
(*Aside.*) Whether she's listening?—I must know of her
If I've done right.—Reflect,—I'll soon return.

        [*Saladin steps into the room to which Sittah had retired.*
  Nath. Strange! How is this? What wills the sultan of me?
I came prepared with cash,—he asks truth. Truth?
As if truth, too, were cash,—a coin disused,
That goes by weight,— indeed, 't is some such thing;—
But a new coin, known by the stamp at once,
To be flung down and told upon the counter,
It is not that. Like gold in bags tied up,
So truth lies hoarded in the wise man's head,
To be brought out.—Which, now, in this transaction,
Which of us plays the Jew? He asks for truth,—
Is truth what he requires, his aim, his end?
That this is but the glue to lime a snare
Ought not to be suspected,—'t were too little.
Yet what is found too little for the great?
In fact, through hedge and pale to stalk at once
Into one's field beseems not,—friends look round,
Seek for the path, ask leave to pass the gate.—
I must be cautious. Yet to damp him back,
And be the stubborn Jew, is not the thing;
And wholly to throw off the Jew, still less.
For, if no Jew, he might with right inquire,
Why not a Mussulman?—Yes,—that may serve me.
Not children only can be quieted
With stories.—Ha! he comes;—well, let him come.

  Sal. (*returning*). So there the field is clear.—I'm not too
    quick?

Thou hast bethought thyself as much as need is?—
Speak, no one hears.

 Nath. Might the whole world but hear us!

 Sal. Is Nathan of his cause so confident?
Yes, that I call the sage,—to veil no truth;
For truth to hazard all things, life and goods.

 Nath. Ay, when 't is necessary, and when useful.

 Sal. Henceforth I hope I shall with reason bear
One of my titles,—"Betterer of the world
And of the law."

 Nath. In truth, a noble title.
But, Sultan, ere I quite unfold myself,
Allow me to relate a tale.

 Sal. Why not?
I always was a friend of tales well told.

 Nath. Well told,—that's not precisely my affair.

 Sal. Again so proudly modest?—Come, begin.

 Nath. In days of yore, there dwelt in East a man
Who from a valued hand received a ring
Of endless worth : the stone of it an opal,
That shot an ever-changing tint: moreover,
It had the hidden virtue him to render
Of God and man beloved, who, in this view,
And this persuasion, wore it. Was it strange
The Eastern man ne'er drew it off his finger,
And studiously provided to secure it
For ever to his house? Thus he bequeathed it,
First, to the most beloved of his sons,—
Ordained that he again should leave the ring
To the most dear among his children,—and,
That without heeding birth, the favorite son,
In virtue of the ring alone, should always
Remain the lord o' th' house.—You hear me, Sultan?

 Sal. I understand thee,—on.

 Nath. From son to son,
At length this ring descended to a father
Who had three sons alike obedient to him;
Whom, therefore, he could not but love alike.
At times seemed this, now that, at times the third
(Accordingly as each apart received
The overflowings of his heart), most worthy
To heir the ring, which, with good-natured weakness,

He privately to each in turn had promised.
This went on for a while.   But death approached,
And the good father grew embarrassed.   So
To disappoint two sons, who trust his promise,
He could not bear.   What's to be done?   He sends
In secret to a jeweller, of whom,
Upon the model of the real thing,
He might bespeak two others, and commanded
To spare nor cost nor pains to make them like,
Quite like the true one.   This the artist managed.
The rings were brought, and e'en the father's eye
Could not distinguish which had been the model.
Quite overjoyed, he summons all his sons,
Takes leave of each apart, on each bestows
His blessing and his ring, and dies.—Thou hear'st me?
   Sal. I hear, I hear.   Come, finish with thy tale;—
Is it soon ended?
   Nath. It is ended, Sultan;
For all that follows may be guessed of course.
Scarce is the father dead, each with his ring
Appears, and claims to be the lord o' th' house.
Come questions, strife, complaint,—all to no end;
For the true ring could no more be distinguished
Than now can—the true faith.
   Sal. How, how?—is that
To be the answer to my query?
   Nath. No,
But it may serve as my apology,
If I can't venture to decide between
Rings which the father got expressly made,
That they might not be known from one another.
   Sal. The rings,—don't trifle with me: I must think
That the religions which I named can be
Distinguished, e'en to raiment, drink, and food.
   Nath. And only not as to their grounds of proof.
Are not all built alike on history,
Traditional or written?   History
Must be received on trust,—is it not so?
In whom now are we likeliest to put trust?
In our own people surely, in those men
Whose blood we are, in them who from our childhood
Have given us proofs of love, who ne'er deceived us,

Unless 't were wholesomer to be deceived.
How can I less believe in my forefathers
Than thou in thine?   How can I ask of thee
To own that thy forefathers falsified,
In order to yield mine the praise of truth?
The like of Christians.
 Sal. By the living God!
The man is in the right,—I must be silent.
 Nath. Now let us to our rings return once more.
As said, the sons complained.   Each to the judge
Swore from his father's hand immediately
To have received the ring, as was the case;
After he had long obtained the father's promise
One day to have the ring, as also was.
The father, each asserted, could to him
Not have been false: rather than so suspect
Of such a father, willing as he might be
With charity to judge his brethren, he
Of treacherous forgery was bold to accuse them.
 Sal. Well, and the judge,—I 'm eager now to hear
What thou wilt make him say.   Go on, go on.
 Nath. The judge said, "If ye summon not the father
Before my seat, I cannot give a sentence.
Am I to guess enigmas?   Or expect ye
That the true ring should here unseal its lips?
But hold,—you tell me that the real ring
Enjoys the hidden power to make the wearer
Of God and man beloved: let that decide.
Which of you do two brothers love the best?
You're silent.   Do these love-exciting rings
Act inward only, not without?   Does each
Love but himself?   Ye're all deceived deceivers,—
None of your rings is true.   The real ring,
Perhaps, is gone.   To hide or to supply
Its loss, your father ordered three for one."
 Sal. Oh, charming, charming!
 Nath. "And," the judge continued,
"If you will take advice, in lieu of sentence,
This is my counsel to you,—to take up
The matter where it stands.   If each of you
Has had a ring presented by his father,
Let each believe his own the real ring.

'Tis possible the father chose no longer
To tolerate the one ring's tyranny;
And certainly, as he much loved you all,
And loved you all alike, it could not please him,
By favoring one, to be of two the oppressor.
Let each feel honored by this free affection
Unwarped of prejudice; let each endeavor
To vie with both his brothers in displaying
The virtue of his ring; assist its might
With gentleness, benevolence, forbearance,
With inward resignation to the Godhead;
And if the virtues of the ring continue
To show themselves among your children's children
After a thousand thousand years, appear
Before this judgment-seat,—a greater one
Than I shall sit upon it, and decide."—
So spake the modest judge.

   Sal. God!

   Nath. Saladin,
Feel'st thou thyself this wiser, promised man?

   Sal. I, dust,—I, nothing,—God?
          [*Casts himself upon Nathan and takes hold of his hand,
                        which he does not quit.*

   Nath. What moves thee, Sultan?

   Sal. Nathan, my dearest Nathan, 't is not yet
The judge's thousand thousand years are past,—
His judgment seat 's not mine. Go, go, but love me.

   Nath. Has Saladin, then, nothing else to order?

   Sal. No.

   Nath. Nothing?

   Sal. Nothing in the least,— and wherefore?

   Nath. I could have wished an opportunity
To lay a prayer before you.

   Sal. Is there need
Of opportunity for that? Speak freely.

   Nath. I have come from a long journey, from collecting
Debts, and I've almost of hard cash too much;—
The times look perilous,—I know not where
To lodge it safely;—I was thinking thou—
For coming wars require large sums—couldst use it.

   Sal. Nathan, I ask not if thou saw'st Al-Hafi,—
I'll not examine if some shrewd suspicion

Spurs thee to make this offer of thyself.

Nath. Suspicion?—

Sal. I deserve this offer.   Pardon!
For what avails concealment?   I acknowledge
I was about——

Nath. To ask the same of me?

Sal. Yes.

Nath. Then 't is well we 're both accommodated.
That I can't send thee all I have of treasure
Arises from the templar;—thou must know him;—
I have a weighty debt to pay to him.

Sal. A templar?   How? thou dost not with thy gold
Support my direst foes?

Nath. I speak of him
Whose life the sultan——

Sal. What art thou recalling?
I had forgot the youth.   Whence is he? know'st thou?

Nath. Hast thou not heard, then, how thy clemency
To him has fallen on me?   He, at the risk
Of his new-spared existence, from the flames
Rescued my daughter.

Sal. Ha! Has he done that?
He looked like one that would.   My brother, too,
Whom he's so like, had done it.   Is he here still?
Bring him to me.   I have so often talked
To Sittah of this brother, whom she knew not,
That I must let her see his counterfeit.
Go, fetch him.   How a single worthy action,
Though but of whim or passion born, gives rise
To other blessings!   Fetch him.

Nath. In an instant.
The rest remains as settled.

JOHANN WOLFGANG GOETHE.

GOETHE is the great Olympian of the German Parnassus, the giant representative of Teutonic literature at the Court of the Muses. His only approximate compeer in German poetry is Schiller, with whom his friendship became so close and reciprocally beneficial that their memories are inseparably linked in fame. In their personal relations at Weimar these noble poets were like twin stars. Both lie entombed together in the ducal mausoleum of that little court of their living glory, and in the square of Weimar their statues stand side by side, their perfect friendship thus symbolized in bronze. There they hold a laurel wreath between them, as though each were crowning the other. As Goethe once remarked: "Instead of arguing as to which of us, Schiller or Goethe, is the greater genius, the Germans should be proud that they have two such men."

Schiller is the more loved of the two; Goethe the more admired. Schiller was the more human in his art; Goethe the more universal. As it has been pithily expressed: "Goethe strove for æsthetic universality, Schiller strove for moral freedom." Both poets were idealists; but while Schiller's flight was winged towards the dawn of an ideal liberty and humanity, Goethe's genius gazed aloft and far away to the all-illuminating sun of universal culture. In art Schiller has himself thus defined their differentiation: "The naïve poet is nature; the sentimental poet seeks nature. The one imitates the natural, the other the ideal."

In a word, the world to-day speaks of these great brother spirits as the good Schiller and the great Goethe.

As for Goethe's life, it would be a vain task to seek to analyze it here. The earnest student may well follow it in the elaborately minute biography by the German scholar, Dr. Düntzer, in Lewes's popular English biography, and in the poet's own charming autobiography. Johann Wolfgang Goethe was born on August 28, 1749, in the proud commercial city of Frankfort, the grandson of a tailor and innkeeper, the son of an imperial councillor and a magistrate's daughter. He studied first at Leipsic, fell seriously ill, recovered at home, and went to Strasburg, where he studied jurisprudence and graduated. But he also met and was inspired by Herder, who played a vital part in the young man's literary development. While at Strasburg Goethe had the love affair with Friederike Brion, which was later to supply him with the basis of the Gretchen romance. At Wetzlar, whither he went to practice law, he met Charlotte Buff, the Lotte of Werther. Meanwhile he had felt the influence of the Storm and Stress movement, and when only twenty-four years old he made himself famous in a day by his revolutionary drama, "Götz von Berlichingen." In this earliest drama he presented an idealized portrait of the old robber-knight of the sixteenth century, the Knight of the Iron Hand. Goethe chose this "noblest of Germans," not as a national type, but as one who foreshadowed the modern struggle for individualism.

Passing quickly to the languidly sentimental vein, he told the story of his hopeless love for Charlotte Buff in "The Sorrows of Young Werther." In a series of letters the hero relates how, enamored of a married woman, he flees from temptation and at last determined on suicide. Under the pretext of starting on a journey, he borrows the husband's pistols, reflecting that Charlotte will take them down and dust them before sending them to him. Despite its remarkable beauties of style, the mawkish and false character of this prose novel of passion and suicide has been cleverly revealed by Thackeray's bald and doggerel relation of the incidents themselves. Goethe himself had not loved Lotte to the point of despair, and the suicide was suggested by the self-murder of a more sentimental lover, young Jerusalem at Wetzlar. Nevertheless, "The Sorrows of Werther" struck a sentimental chord all over the Europe of that day. Even the unsentimental Napoleon carried the book with him on his Egyptian campaign, and read of Werther's sorrows under the shadow of the Sphinx. Later in life he discussed the work with Goethe, who eventually outgrew its mood and mocked his early indiscretion. But at the time Goethe sent a copy to Lotte, declaring: "I have kissed it a hundred times." Mme. de Staël asserted that the book was responsible for more suicides than the most beautiful woman had ever been. It may here be repeated of Goethe that in love matters he was always "both the patient and the physician." Soon after he had a new spell of romance with Anna Elizabeth Schönemann, who figures as the Lili of many of his lyrics.

But in 1775 Goethe was suddenly summoned to the Court of Weimar, to become the Apollo of modern German literature. Until his death he dwelt there with honors, public esteem and literary glory. Another woman, Frau von Stein, became a factor in his life. Her influence and the inspiration of his Italian journey (1786-7) are to be seen in his dramas of "Iphigenie" and "Tasso." The works produced at Weimar may be briefly characterized.

"Egmont" is a drama of the Netherlands' struggle for liberty, in which Goethe's hero is not the Egmont of history, but an unmarried, high-minded patriot standing almost alone against relentless despotism and bigotry, personified in Alva. The Brussels mob refuse to stand by him. Egmont has been styled as "Götz's weak, aristocratic twin-brother." His love romance with Clärchen is exquisite. "Iphigenie" is a drama in noble iambic verse, in which Goethe, like his heroine, "sought Greece with all his soul." "Iphigenie" typifies the classic spirit of idealism conquering man's passions, the Furies of Orestes. It is his first great dramatic work free from the early impetuosity and revolutionary bitterness. The drama of "Torquato Tasso" was founded upon the Italian poet's unhappy love for the Princess Leonora. Tasso represents the idealist, as opposed to Antonio, a realist.

The remarkable "Reineke Fuchs" is the definitive High German poetic version of the Low German Willem's fox fable.

"Wilhelm Meister's Apprenticeship" and "Wilhelm Meister's Wander-year" are novels in which Goethe presents on the surface a realistic picture of life, ending in a rosy-hued romance. The hero's development of culture is, however, the underlying motive. In Wilhelm's experience with a troupe of actors, Goethe reviewed his own entire theatrical studies, from his youthful puppet shows to his ripest Shakespearean criticism. "Hamlet" is analyzed in this first book in almost classical style. In the sequel Wilhelm passes through an experience of coquetry with the vivacious and worldly actress, Philine, to find a little pearl of womanhood in the waif Mignon (rendered still more familiar through Ambroise Thomas's opera). Her songs express well Goethe's longing for Italy. The character of the mysterious Harper is also highly romantic. The "Italian Journey," "Roman Elegies" and "Venetian Epigrams" are the critical and lyrical fruits of Goethe's travels.

"Hermann and Dorothea" is the chief German idyllic epic. Goethe founded this tender hexameter tale on an incident of the expulsion of a band of Protestants from Salzburg in 1731, but he transplanted it to the time of the French Revolution. A band of German emigrants leave their homes beyond the Rhine to escape the French pillagers. Among them is the orphaned Dorothea, whom Hermann, the son of the host of "The Golden Lion," leads home as his bride. Dorothea is Goethe's type of woman, helpful and pure. This idyll has well been pronounced a "hymn to the family" and "the pearl of Germany's art." The "West-Easterly Divan" is a series of Oriental lyrics, inspired by Hafiz. In one of these, "Timur," Napoleon's invasion of Russia is noticed. Goethe's "Pages from My Life: Poetry and Truth," is one of the most fascinating autobiographies ever written. In it he has described the most impressionable period of his life, but has presented many episodes in a fanciful rather than realistic way. Thus, in his retrospect of his love intrigue with Friederike Brion, he has undoubtedly idealized her remembrance and painted his relations with her in darker and more romantic colors than the facts, soberly related, would warrant. But through a long life of deep meditation, the aged Goethe had come to look upon that early indiscretion as a sad episode. He possessed to the last a distinct vein of sentimentality in regard to all women, and a study of his life reveals one feminine influence after another. It is scarcely possible to see in Friederike more than a mere suggestion of the Gretchen of "Faust." The poet utilized many events of his experience for an artistic purpose, idealizing and transmuting them by the alchemy of his genius. Indeed, no truer characterization of his entire art and life could have been invented than his own expression of ": Poetry and Truth" or "Fact and Fancy."

Goethe was less noble and pure than Schiller in his personal life. His multitude of love affairs ended in a liaison with an uneducated Gretchen of Weimar (Christiane Vulpius), whom he only married after the birth of a son. He was a pantheist in religion, believing that evil exists in appearance only, and in many of his actions he justified Heine's caustic description of him as "the great heathen." Perhaps this gives us the key to the inner significance of Heine's other saying, that "Nature wanted to see how she looked, and she created Goethe." Despite the languid sentimentality of his youthful "Sorrows of Werther" and the artificial note of some of his later writings, Goethe was what Schiller called a naïve poet, a poet of Nature. Thus, in his lyrics, he mirrored her true self. In "Hermann and Dorothea" he achieved a genuine pastoral idyl. In "Götz" he could be violent and headlong as a mountain torrent; in "Faust" as varied and bafflingly incongruous as life and humanity.

Personally he passed through a whole category of changes. His autobiography shows him as the typical, even if precocious, child of the commercial classes of the old "Free cities," such as his native Frankfort was. To Herder he seemed "a good fellow, somewhat frivolous and sparrowlike." On his arrival at the court of Weimar, in the strength and beauty of youth, he enjoyed a period of luxurious indulgence before settling down into the sedate and titled councillor of the kingdom.

As to his egoism, Goethe stood as the confessed champion and apostle of self-culture. German culture had reached, in his day, the state described in his own words: "Germany as a whole is nothing, the individual German is everything." It was in this spirit that Goethe composed his "West-Easterly Divan," his Oriental songs, during that stirring period when Körner and other patriotic poets were hymning the hopes of the Fatherland and the great War of Liberation was being waged against Napoleon. Goethe had a high admiration for the wonderful individual greatness of the French Emperor, and he thought the struggle would be in vain. He was not indifferent to the ideals of Freedom, Fatherland, People. "Germany is dear to my heart," he once wrote to Luden; but he wrote to Eckermann: "As a man and citizen, the poet will love his fatherland, but the fatherland of his poetic strength and his poetic activity is the good, noble and beautiful, which is confined to no special province or land, which he seizes and forms where he finds it." Of his lyrics, it is only necessary to add that no other German poet has equaled him, save only Heine. Many of his finest songs were set to music by Schubert. Goethe's world masterpiece, "Faust," is analyzed in a separate article. The commendation which the poem has received far and near may be perhaps owing to this quality, that it permanently preserves the period of development of a human soul which is tormented by all that afflicts mankind, shaken also by all that disturbs it, repelled by all that it finds repellant and made happy by all that it desires.

As a slight testimony to the universality of Goethe's genius, a word may be added concerning his scientific researches. He deserves the title of Father of Comparative Anatomy. He suggested the study of the morphology of plants and recognized in the human skull the highest type of vertebra. He also opposed Newton's corpuscular hypothesis of light, and originated a theory of colors which Tyndall has refuted.

MONA LISA.—LEONARDO.

FAUST.

THE drama of Faust is the world-masterpiece of Goethe, the crowning literary form of an oft-treated and highly popular legend, based upon a genuine historical personage. Dr. Johann Faustus was born at Knittlingen, Würtemburg, or at Roda, near Weimar, toward the last quarter of the fifteenth century, and died in 1538. During Goethe's long residence at Weimar he may have himself visited the historic structure on a rocky eminence near Roda, in which Dr. Faustus once dwelt. For a time, too, history tells us that Faustus sojourned in Poland. Whatever his actual professions may have been, he acquired, even in his own lifetime, a widespread fame as an astrologer, alchemist, soothsayer and magician. It was said that he even boasted of being able to perform all the Biblical miracles. So renowned a professor of the Black Art was sure to be considered in league with hell, and it is small wonder that folk began to believe implicitly that he was finally carried off by the devil, who had lived all along with him as a black dog. The multiplied host of legends concerning him was at last gathered together in a little chap-book first hawked at the fair at Frankfort-on-Main in 1587. Goethe was thus linked to this legend by both his birthplace and the scene of his glory.

This Frankfort chap-book professed to give a veracious account (Historia) of " Dr. Faustus, the Notorious Magician

VII—2

and Master of the Black Art." It had evidently been written by a Lutheran, and was aimed probably to reflect also on the late lamented Aureolus Theophrastus Bombastus Paracelsus (1493-1541), the celebrated Swiss alchemist and mystic. It was intended to curb the rising desire to pierce beyond orthodox limits of personal investigation of the human and divine Faust himself was the contemporary of Luther, and indeed, this legend makes him Luther's counterpart, in that, son of a peasant, he achieves great distinction at the University or Wittenberg. But, unlike the Reformer, he seeks to deepen his knowledge by magic. He signs in blood a compact with the devil, by which Mephistopheles becomes his servant for twenty-four years, at the end of which Faust shall belong to the Evil One. Faust has a famulus, Wagner, whom the devil amuses as well as Faust. After all manner of revels on earth, Faust visits hell and the stars. Returning to earth he flies on his magic cloak everywhere, bewildering emperors with his wonderful feats, and finally conjuring up the Grecian Helen herself, whom he takes for a concubine, and by whom he has a sooth-saying child, Euphorion. Goethe later accepted all these details, and yet transmuted them into high allegorical symbols. The great German genius not only transformed Faust from a common necromancer (which others, from Marlowe down, really accomplished before him), but he likewise read new meanings into Mephisto, into Helen and her elf-child, into Wagner and the students' revel. But in the old legend all these matters are seriously regarded as actual events, and after his quarter-century of world-astonishing magic Faust is carried off to hell by the devil.

This crude and medieval relation of Dr. Faustus's career was eagerly imbibed by the German peasantry, and in the same year a metrical version appeared in England. Christopher Marlowe, father of English blank verse and "famous gracer of tragedians," must have been instantly attracted to the subject. Fired by the daring aspiration of Faust for knowledge beyond the stars, this brilliant young rhapsodist seized upon this legend with true poetic instinct, and in his

"Tragical History of Dr. Faustus" (1588) he depicted with all his peerless power the central thought of man in his Promethean pride of knowledge turning from his God. Marlowe followed almost exactly the original legend and his comical prose scenes are fit only for clownish laughter; but in the soliloquies of Faust—ending with that tremendous monologue which Swinburne pronounces to be "without parallel in all the range of tragedy"—Marlowe has turned all to gold by his fiery imagination. And when Faust beholds the radiant vision of Helen, the poetry itself becomes as exquisite as Helen's beauty. Goethe gave generous praise to the genius of Marlowe as displayed in this dramatic poem (for it can now be scarcely styled a play), and exclaimed: "How greatly it is all planned!" He even thought of translating this passionate masterpiece.

But about the beginning of the seventeenth century Marlowe's "Dr. Faustus" had been translated in an inferior fashion for German audiences, and the English actors had by this time added a miserable lot of cheap diablerie to Marlowe's splendid original. So much more pleasing was such treatment of the legend to the groundlings that by Lessing's time "Dr. Faustus" had degenerated into a mere puppet-play. Lessing recognized in it, however, one of the deepest problems, and with his usual critical insight wrote in 1759: "Dr. Faust has a number of scenes in it that only a genius akin to Shakespeare could have conceived." Lessing even drafted two different versions of a "Faust" tragedy—neither of them ever finished. Faust attracted, too, the Stormsters after Lessing, as a type of rebellious individualism. Besides the plays already mentioned, twenty-nine different Faust plays by various authors were produced in Germany during the sixty years (1772–1831) in which Goethe remained employed upon his masterpiece.

One of these twenty-nine may be more particularly noted. Adelbert von Chamisso's dramatic sketch, "Faust" (1803) represents the learned doctor as one who will no longer endure doubt. His good and bad angels alternately plead with him, but he finally breaks the Staff of Judgment on his own doom, exclaiming that, whatever the punishment to come, he welcomes "certainty at last." The whole scene occurs in his cresset-lit study. Other efforts worthy at least of mention are Heine's ingenious ballet, "Der Doktor Faust" and Lenau's epic.

Goethe approached the legend with a rich world of emotions and ideas. In his youth he had witnessed "Faust" as a puppet-play, and the story itself appealed to him. But he also saw in it a perfect cosmos of human problems. And eventually he determined to make it the symbolical vehicle for all his views on art and culture, and, above all, idealism. He commenced work upon the poem in 1772, had numerous relapses of interest, published a fragment in 1790, Part One as "a tragedy" by itself in 1808, and Part Two in 1831. Thus, in this long-meditated, slowly maturing poem are to be found all manner of styles, ideas, modifications, and even contradictions. It is like some wonderful old cathedral solemnly built part by part through centuries, and revealing in the very heterogeneity of its architecture the multifarious inspirations, vicissitudes, and shifting sentiments of its upbuilding. Once he entirely lost his grasp of the plans of his early inspiration, but he rediscovered the thread, and connected the human tragedy of Gretchen with the allegory of Helen by means of a serio-comic, half-human and half-divine Witches' Kitchen scene. To Schiller he spoke of his great work as his "tragelaph," or goat-stag—a fantastic creature. On another occasion he styled it a rhapsodical drama.

Goethe set out, in the first place, to make of the Faust legend a modern tragedy of Job. Faust was to be tempted by the desire for all knowledge, but he was not utterly to fall. In the boldly familiar Prologue in Heaven, in which the devil converses with God in a naïve style worthy of Hans Sachs, it is made emphatically clear that Faust is God's servant, as Job was, and that although momentarily "confused" he would attain in due time to "clearness." Mephisto himself cares less for Faust's soul than to prove his Satanic contention of negation, denial, and pessimism. Goethe then introduces us to Faust in his study, an aged, wise scholar who has dropped his plummet into all the seas of human knowledge, but not yet—as he feels—into the deep well of truth.

So disillusioned of human learning is he that he is even about
to commit suicide. The joy of the common throng singing Easter carols restrains him from this fell purpose, and
later Mephisto, disguised as an uncanny black dog, follows
him to his study. He then reveals himself to Faust as a sort
of reflection of Faust's own pessimism, as "the spirit that
denies," and declares that "all that exists is worthy of
perishing." Faust is so completely oppressed with the vanity
of all things (Solomon's oft-reëchoed *Vanitas Vanitatum*) that
he makes this blood-compact with the tempter:

> When on an idler's bed I stretch myself in quiet,
>   There let at once my record end.
> Canst thou with lying flattery rule me,
>   Until self-pleased myself I see,—
> Canst thou with rich enjoyment fool me,
>   Let that day be the last for me.

Now, according to this induction of the work Goethe
should, in the opinion of many of his later critics, have
appealed entirely to Faust's higher aspirations. But Mephisto
immediately begins an appeal to the grossest and most sensual
appetites of Faust. After all, does this not seem to be the
most natural thing for the cynical, mocking devil to have
done? Faust is first of all treated to a bacchanalian orgy of
students in Auerbach's cellar in Leipsic, which he quits
in disgust. Thereupon Mephisto introduces him to the
"Witches' Kitchen," a grotesquely uncanny scene, in which
Goethe has a lot of apes gibber a lot of what Goethe himself
afterwards labeled as "dramatic-humoristic nonsense." Faust
drinks a magic potion, and becomes a young man again.
Helena, the ideal of womanly beauty, is shown him in a glass,
and it is foretold that "with this drink in his veins he shall
soon see Helena in every woman." And now Mephisto brings
Faust back to earth and Gretchen appears—the Marguerite of
Gounod's popular opera, which has rendered this love-
romance familiar to many who have never read a line of
Goethe's "Faust." Gretchen is a neat young German girl of
the lower walks of life, such as Goethe had himself had liai-
sons with. This theme had been treated already in "Götz,"

in "Clavigo," and in 'Egmont." The whole episode, in its delineation of character, and in its tragic development, is a masterpiece hardly equalled, save by Shakespeare, in the range of literature. It is thoroughly popular, universally comprehensible, and thus it fixed itself immediately in the public mind as *the* Faust drama, while the higher unity of the whole was perceived only by the thoughtful few.

Of this episode Charles Lamb once indignantly asked, "What has Gretchen to do with Faust?" But what, either, the students' revel? The original Faust was perplexed by intellectual problems; the Faust of Goethe's First Part is simply tempted by sensual delights. Yet such is often the case of the poet and scholar in real life, and as Goethe has already been quoted as saying, the chief merit of his Faust is that he passes through all the various temptations of all men. Goethe himself was irresistibly impelled to distort this romance, which should have been a mere episode, into its disproportionate length, but who can regret it?

Faust implores Mephisto to aid him, but that mocker answers contemptuously, "I have no power over souls so green." But he fetches Faust the jewels, which, left in Gretchen's chamber, prove the first step to her ruin. In Martha's garden the lovers meet and Gretchen falls. A poisonous sleep-potion kills her mother. Gretchen's shame finds her out, and her brother Valentin returns from the wars only to be slain in a duel by Faust. In the Cathedral the poor betrayed woman seeks comfort as a penitent, but, during the Judgment Hymn, an evil spirit goads her with thoughts of despair and she falls fainting. Faust seeks relief for his guilty conscience, and Mephisto transports him to the witches' carnival on Walpurgis Night (May 1) on the Brocken, the highest peak of the Harz mountains. (Goethe here introduces a fantastic satire, "Oberon's Wedding"). But Gretchen, convicted of infanticide, is imprisoned, and Faust flies to her rescue. Her mind wanders, and she dies pardoned by angel voices, while Mephisto commands Faust to speed away.

Gretchen is repelled and yet attracted to Faust. And after he has worked out the problem of humanity in Part II., he is bidden to rise to Gretchen and follow her spirit in a new life.

PROLOGUE IN HEAVEN.

GOETHE's drama of "Faust" opens with a Prologue in Heaven, that shows the design of the entire work, though not its action. Here the Archangels Raphael, Gabriel and Michael address God in adoration, but Mephistopheles follows in mockery. The idea is taken from Satan's appearing among the angels in the opening of the Book of Job.

Raphael. The Sun-orb sings in emulation
   'Mid brother-spheres his ancient round:
His path predestined through creation
   He ends with a lip of thunder-sound.
The angels from his visage splendid
   Draw power, whose measure none can say:
The lofty works, uncomprehended,
   Are bright as on the earliest day.
Gabriel. And swift and swift beyond conceiving,
   The splendor of the world goes round,
Day's Eden-brightness still relieving
   The awful night's intense profound:
The ocean-tides in foam are breaking,
   Against the rocks' deep bases hurled,
And both, the spheric race partaking,
   Eternal, swift, are onward whirled.
Michael. And rival storms abroad are singing,
   From river to land, from land to sea,
A chain of deepest action forging
   Round all, in wrathful energy.
There flames a desolation, blazing
   Before the thunder's crashing way:
Yet Lord, Thy messengers are praising
   The gentle movement of Thy day.
The Three. Though still by them uncomprehended,
   From these the angels draw their power,
And all Thy works, sublime and splendid,
   Are bright as in creation's hour.
Mephistopheles. Since Thou, O Lord, deign'st to approach again,
   And ask us how we do, in manner kindest,
And heretofore to meet myself wert fain,
   Among Thy menials now my face Thou findest.

Pardon, this troop I cannot follow after
  With lofty speech, though by them scorned and spurned!
My pathos certainly would move Thy laughter
  If Thou hadst not all merriment unlearned.
Of suns and worlds I've nothing to be quoted;
How men torment themselves is all I've noted;
The little god o' the world sticks to the same old way,
And is as whimsical as on Creation's day.
Life somewhat better might content him
But for the gleam of heavenly light which Thou hast lent
    him:
He calls it Reason—thence his power's increased,
To be far beastlier than any beast.
Saving Thy Gracious Presence, he to me
A long-legged grasshopper appears to be,
That springing flies, and flying springs,
And in the grass the same old ditty sings.
Would he still lie among the grass he grows in,
Each bit of dung he seeks, to lay his nose in.

   THE LORD. Hast thou then nothing more to men-
    tion?
Com'st ever thus with ill intention?
Find'st nothing right on earth eternally?
   Meph. No, Lord! I find things there still bad as they
    can be.
Man's misery even to pity moves my nature;
I've scarce the heart to plague the wretched creature.
   THE LORD. Know'st thou Faust?
   Meph. The Doctor Faust?
   THE LORD. My servant he!
   Meph. Forsooth! He serves you after strange devices:
No earthly food or drink the fool suffices:
His spirit's ferment far aspireth;
Half conscious of his frenzied, crazed unrest,
The fairest stars of Heaven he requireth,
From Earth the highest raptures and the best,
And all the Near and Far that he desireth
Fails to subdue the tumult of his breast.
   THE LORD. Though still confused his service unto Me,
I soon shall lead him to a clearer morning.
Sees not the gardener, even while he buds his tree,
Both flower and fruit the future years adorning?

Meph. What will you bet? There's still a chance to
    gain him,
If unto me full leave you give
Gently upon *my* road to lead him !
    THE LORD. As long as he on earth shall live,
So long I make no prohibition.
While Man's desires and aspirations stir,
He cannot choose but err.
    Meph. My thanks! I find the dead no acquisition,
And never cared to have them in my keeping.
I much prefer the cheeks whose ruddy blood is leaping,
And when a corpse approaches, close my house:
It goes with me as with the cat the mouse.
    THE LORD. Enough! What thou hast asked is granted.
    Turn off this spirit from his fountain-head;
To trap him let thy snares be planted,
    And him with thee be downward led;
Then stand abashed, when thou art forced to say ;
    A good man, through obscurest aspiration,
Has still an instinct of the one true way.
    Meph. Agreed! but 'tis a short probation.
About my bet I feel no trepidation.
If I fulfill my expectation,
You'll let me triumph with a swelling breast:
Dust shall he eat, and with a zest,
As did a certain Snake—my near relation.
    THE LORD. Therein thou'rt free, according to thy
      merits;
    The like of thee have never moved My hate.
Of all the bold denying Spirits,
    The waggish knave least trouble doth create.
Man's active nature, flagging, seeks too soon the level;
    Unqualified repose he learns to crave;
    Whence, willingly, the comrade him I gave,
Who works, excites and must create, as Devil.
Be ye God's sons in love and duty,
Enjoy the rich, the ever-living Beauty!
Creative Power, that works eternal schemes,
    Clasp you in bonds of love, relaxing never,
    And what in wave inconstant gleams,
Fit in its place with thoughts that stand forever !
            [*Heaven closes: the Archangels separate.*

Meph. (*alone*), I like at times to hear The Ancient's word,
And have a care to be most civil :
It's really kind of such a noble Lord
So humanly to gossip with a Devil.

FAUST AND MARGARET.

(Translated by Bayard Taylor.)

Margaret on Faust's arm; Martha with Mephistopheles walking up and down.

Margaret. I feel it, you but spare my ignorance,
To shame me, sir, you stoop thus low ;
A traveler from complaisance
Still makes the best of things ; I know
Too well, my humble prattle never can
Have power to entertain so wise a man.

Faust. One glance, one word of thine doth charm me more,
Than the world's wisdom or the sage's lore.

[He kisses her hand.

Mar. Nay ! trouble not yourself ! A hand so coarse,
So rude as mine, how can you kiss ?
What constant work at home must I not do perforce !
My mother too exacting is.   [*They pass on.*

Martha. Thus, sir, unceasing travel is your lot ?

Mephistopheles. Traffic and duty urge us ! With what pain
Are we compelled to leave full many a spot,
Where yet we may not once remain !

Martha. In youth's wild years, with vigor crowned,
'Tis not amiss thus through the world to sweep ;
But ah, the evil days come round !
And to a lonely grave as bachelor to creep,
A pleasant thing has no one found.

Meph. The prospect fills me with dismay.

Martha. Therefore, in time, dear sir, reflect, I pray.

[*They pass on.*

Mar. Ay, out of sight is out of mind !
Politeness easy is to you ;
Friends everywhere, and not a few,
Wiser than I am, you will find.

Faust. Trust me, my angel, what doth pass for sense
Full oft is self-conceit and blindness !

Mar. How?

Faust. Simplicity and holy innocence,—

When will ye learn your hallowed worth to know!
Ah! when will meekness and humility,
Kind and all-bounteous nature's loftiest dower—
   Mar. Only one little moment think of me!
To think of you I shall have many an hour.
   Faust. You are perhaps much alone?
   Mar. Yes, small our household is, I own,
Yet must I see to it. No maid we keep,
And I must cook, sew, knit and sweep,
Still early on my feet and late;
My mother is in all things, great and small,
So accurate!
Not that for thrift there is such pressing need;
Than others we might make more show indeed;
My father left behind a small estate,
A house and garden near the city-wall.
Quiet enough my life has been of late;
My brother for a soldier gone;
My little sister's dead; the babe to rear
Occasioned me some care and fond annoy;
But I would go through all again with joy,
The darling was to me so dear.
   Faust. An angel sweet, if it resembled thee!
   Mar. I reared it up, and it grew fond of me.
After my father's death it saw the day;
We gave my mother up for lost, she lay
In such a wretched plight, and then at length
So very slowly she regained her strength.
Weak as she was, 'twas vain for her to try
Herself to suckle the poor babe, so I
Reared it on milk and water all alone;
And thus the child became as 'twere my own;
Within my arms it stretched itself and grew,
And smiling, nestled in my bosom too.
   Faust. Doubtless the purest happiness was thine.
   Mar. But many weary hours, in sooth, were also mine.
At night its little cradle stood
Close to my bed; so I was wide awake
If it but stirred;
One while I was obliged to give it food,
Or to my arms the darling take;
From bed full oft must rise, whene'er the cry I heard,

And, dancing it, must pace the chamber to and fro;
Stand at the wash-tub early; forthwith go
To market, and then mind the cooking too—
To-morrow like to-day, the whole year through.
Ah, sir, thus living, it must be confessed
One's spirits are not always of the best;
Yet it a relish gives to food and rest.   [*They pass on.*
  Martha. Poor women! we are badly off, I own;
A bachelor's conversion's hard, indeed!
  Meph. Madam, with one like you it rests alone,
To tutor me a better course to lead.
  Martha. Speak frankly, sir, none is there you have met?
Has your heart ne'er attached itself as yet?
  Meph. One's own fireside and a good wife are gold
And pearls of price, so says the proverb old,
  Martha. I mean, has passion never stirred your breast?
  Meph. I've everywhere been well received, I own.
  Martha. Yet hath your heart no earnest preference known?
  Meph. With ladies one should ne'er presume to jest.
  Martha. Ah! you mistake!
  Meph. I'm sorry I'm so blind!
But this I know—that you are very kind.   [*They pass on.*
  Faust. Me, little angel, didst thou recognize,
When in the garden first I came?
  Mar. Did you not see it? I cast down my eyes.
  Faust. Thou dost forgive my boldness, dost not blame
The liberty I took that day,
When thou from church didst lately wend thy way?
  Mar. I was confused. So had it never been,
No one of me could any evil say.
Alas, thought I, he doubtless in thy mien,
Something unmaidenly or bold hath seen?
It seemed as if it struck him suddenly,
Here's just a girl with whom one may make free!
Yet I must own that then I scarcely knew
What in your favor here began at once to plead;
Yet I was angry with myself indeed,
That I more angry could not feel with you.
  Faust. Sweet love!
  Mar. Just wait a while!
               [*She gathers a star-flower and plucks off the
                  leaves one after another.*

Faust. A nosegay may that be?

Mar. No! It is but a game.

Faust. How?

Mar. Go, you'll laugh at me!

       [She plucks off the leaves and murmurs to herself.

Faust. What murmurest thou?

Mar. (half aloud). He loves me,—loves me not.

Faust. Sweet angel, with thy face of heavenly bliss!

Mar. (continues) He loves me—not—he loves me—not—

       [Plucking off the last leaf with fond joy.

He loves me!

Faust. Yes!

And this flower-language, darling, let it be,

A heavenly oracle! He loveth thee!

Knowest thou the meaning of, He loveth thee?

       [He seizes both her hands.

Mar. I tremble so!

Faust. Nay! do not tremble, love!

Let this hand-pressure, let this glance reveal

Feelings, all power of speech above;

To give oneself up wholly and to feel

A joy that must eternal prove!

Eternal!—Yes, its end would be despair.

No end!—It cannot end!

   [Margaret presses his hand, extricates herself and runs away.

     He stands a moment in thought, and then follows her.

Mar. (approaching). Night's closing.

Meph. Yes, we'll presently away.

Martha. I would entreat you longer yet to stay;

But 'tis a wicked place, just here about;

It is as if the folk had nothing else to do,

Nothing to think of too,

But gaping watch their neighbors, who goes in and out;

And scandal's busy still, do whatsoe'er one may.

And our young couple?

Meph. They have flown up there,

The wanton butterflies!

Martha. He seems to take to her.

Meph. And she to him. 'Tis of the world the way!

     [A Summer-house. Margaret runs in, hides behind

       the door, holds the tip of her finger to her lip,

       and peeps through the crevice.

Mar. He comes!

Faust. Ah, little rogue, so thou
Thinkest to provoke me! I have caught thee now!

> [*He kisses her.*

Mar. (*embracing him and returning the kiss*). Dearest of men!
I love thee from my heart!   [*Mephistopheles knocks.*

Faust (*stamping*). Who's there?

Meph. A friend!

Faust. A brute!

Meph. 'Tis time to part.

Martha (*comes*). Ay, it is late, good sir.

Faust. Mayn't I attend you, then?

Mar. Oh, no—my mother would—adieu!

Faust. And must I really then take leave of you?
Farewell!

Martha. Good-bye!

Mar. Ere long to meet again!

> [*Exeunt Faust and Mephistopheles.*

Mar. Good heavens! how all things far and near
Must fill his mind,—a man like this!
Abashed before him I appear,
And say to all things only, yes.
Poor simple child, I cannot see,
What 'tis that he can find in me.   [*Exit.*

ADMISSION TO HEAVEN.

THE Tragedy of Faust ends with the admission of the hero's soul to
heaven, and a vision of the Glorious Mother adored by blessed penitents,
among whom is Gretchen. Part only of the scene is given.

> *Angels* (*bearing the immortal part of Faust*). Saved is
>   this noble soul from ill,
> Our spirit-peer. Whoever
> Strives forward with unswerving will,—
> Him can we aye deliver;
> And if with him celestial love
> Hath taken part,—to meet him
> Come down the angels from above;
> With cordial hail they greet him. . . .
>   *Blessed Boys.* Him as a chrysalis
> Joyful receive we:

Pledge of angelic bliss
In him achieve we.
Loosen the flakes of earth
That still enfold him!
Great through the heavenly birth,
And fair, now behold him. . . .
    Doctor Marianus. Here is the prospect free,
The soul subliming.
Yonder fair forms I see,
Heavenward they're climbing;
In starry wreath is seen,
Lofty and tender,
Midmost the heavenly Queen,
Known by her splendor.
(*Enraptured.*) In thy tent of azure hue,
Queen supremely reigning,
Let me now thy secret view,
Vision high obtaining!
With the holy joy of love,
In man's breast, whatever
Lifts the soul to thee above,
Kind one, foster ever!
All invincible we feel,
If our arm thou claimest;
Suddenly assuaged our zeal
If our breast thou tamest.
Virgin, pure from taint of earth,
Mother, we adore thee,
With the Godhead one by birth,
Queen, we bow before thee!
              [*The Glorious Mother soars forward.*
  Chorus of Female Penitents. To realms eternal
        Upward art soaring;
        Peerless, supernal,
        Hear our imploring,
        Thy grace adoring.
  The Magdalen. By the love, warm tears outpouring,
Laving as with balsam sweet,
Pharisaic sneers ignoring,
Of thy godlike Son the feet;
By the vase, rich odor breathing,
Lavishing its costly store;

By the locks, that gently wreathing,
Dried his holy feet once more—
    The Samaritan woman. By the well, whereto were
        driven
Abram's flocks in ancient days;
By the cooling draught thence given,
Which the Saviour's thirst allays;
By the fountain, still outsending
Thence its waters, far and wide,
Overflowing, never-ending,
Through all worlds it pours its tide—
    Mary of Egypt. By the hallowed grave, whose portal
Closed upon the Lord of yore;
By the arm, unseen by mortal,
Back which thrust me from the door;
By my penance, slowly fleeting,
Forty years amid the waste;
By the blessèd farewell greeting,
Which upon the sand I traced—
    The Three. Thou unto the greatly sinning
Access who dost not deny,
By sincere repentance winning
Bliss throughout eternity,
So from this good soul thy blessing,
Who but once itself forgot,
Sin who knew not, while transgressing,
Gracious One, withhold thou not!
    A Penitent (*formerly named Gretchen, pressing towards*
        her). Incline, oh, incline,
All others excelling,
In glory are dwelling,
Unto my bliss thy glance benign!
The loved one, ascending,
His long trouble ending,
Comes back, he is mine!
    Blessed Boys (*hovering in a circle*). Mighty of limb,
        he towers
E'en now above us,
He for this care of ours
Richly will love us.
Dying, ere we could reach
Earth's pain or pleasure;

SEA NYMPH.—BURNE JONES.

What he hath learned he'll teach
In ample measure.

The Penitent. Encircled by the choirs of heaven,
Scarcely himself the stranger knows;
Scarce feels the existence newly given,
So like the heavenly host he grows.
See, how he every band hath riven!
From earth's old vesture freed at length,
Now clothed upon by garb of heaven,
Shines forth his pristine youthful strength,
To guide him, be it given to me;
Still dazzles him the new-born day.

The Glorious Mother. Ascend, thine influence
   feeleth he,
He'll follow on thine upward way.

Doctor Marianus (adoring, prostrate on his face).
Penitents, her Saviour-glance
Gratefully beholding
To beatitude advance,
Still new powers unfolding!
Thine each better thought shall be
To thy service given!
Holy Virgin, gracious be,
Mother, Queen of Heaven!

THE MYSTIC CHORUS.

All of mere transient date
As symbol showeth;
Here, the inadequate
To fulness groweth;
Here the ineffable
Wrought is in love;
The ever-womanly
Draws us above.

FRIEDRICH VON SCHILLER.

SCHILLER was Goethe's junior by ten years. When their close friendship began Goethe was forty-four, Schiller thirty-four. Both had already passed under the influence of the Storm and Stress period, Schiller having given in his wild drama of "The Robbers" an even fiercer apostrophe to individual liberty than had Goethe in his "Götz." Both afterwards renounced these early follies. Goethe's ripe culture also tended to calm and harmonize, to chasten and refine Schiller's intense love of liberty into a truly classical championship of moral freedom. Schiller stands to-day preeminently as the great Apostle of Freedom. His "Wilhelm Tell" is a noble clarion of liberty. Nor can Schiller's greatest ideal be better expressed than in these words of his own, in the preface to his "Bride of Messina:" "Art has for its object not merely to excite to a momentary dream of liberty; its aim is to make us truly free. And this it accomplishes by awakening, exercising and perfecting in us the power of removing to an objective distance the world of the senses, which otherwise only burdens us as formless matter and presses us down with a brute influence; of transforming it into the free working of our spirit, and of thus acquiring a dominion over the material world by means of ideas."

The wholesomeness of Schiller's nature, mind and art—the purity and nobility of his ideals—impress us conspicuously at the very outset of our acquaintance with him. In "Wilhelm Tell" we breathe the mountain air of liberty, we tread the Alps of lofty personal freedom, we feel the thrill of the eternal glaciers in the moonlight scene of the oath at Rütli. In "The Maid of Orleans" we enter into a spiritual sympathy with Joan of Arc, we are convinced of her purity and sincerity, and in the wonderful accusation scene at Rheims, with the thunder pealing above the solemn organ chant, the Lily of France becomes idealized out of earthly matter into the grand symbol of suffering innocence and oppressed truth. In the "Song of the Bell" we hear an echo of the holiest, sweetest, purest joys of honest toil and wedlock and hymeneal faith—a worthy epithalamium to Goethe's "Hermann and Dorothea."

Johann Christoph Friedrich Schiller was born in 1759 at Marbach, the son of a military surgeon who had served in the War of the Austrian Succession. At an early age he was "gently kidnapped" by Duke Karl Eugene of Würtemburg and forced into his military academy as a student. Here the boy, suffering under this petty despotism and feeling like a stork in his old Prussian uniform, gave vent to his woes in his drama of "The Robbers." In this play the hero is a social anarchist, who would shake the pillars of the world. Schiller wrote it by stealth, under cover of a medical book and under pretense of headaches, in his room. When he later deserted his post as medical officer of the grenadiers to witness a performance of his drama, the Duke threatened to imprison him without trial. Schiller resolved to flee. The story of that elopement with a single comrade, two flintless pistols and a few guilders presents a curiously romantic contrast to the terrible bombast of Karl Moor in "The Robbers."

In this drama Schiller cried out for a German republic, but his hero, Karl Moor, was a social Ishmaelite, defrauded by his brother and believing himself betrayed by his affianced love. He becomes a ferocious robber with store of great plunder in the Bohemian forest. His horses bathe in wine; he stabs his supposed false love and there is a glut of horrors. At last, tired of life, he delivers himself up to a starving workman, in order to help him secure the price offered for the bandit's head. Moor is thus the type of a noble greatness perverted by injustice—a frightful example, so to speak. The motto of the play was "In tyrannos." In his world-agony

Karl exclaimed: "Two such men as I would shatter the whole structure of the moral world." This ranting Karl became at once a rival in popularity of the sentimental Werther, Schiller's great dramatic strength was recognized, and until the orgies of the French Revolution Karl remained a hero of the German burghers.

The despotism of the petty German courts was next depicted by Schiller under an Italian guise in the drama, "Fiesco," which proved a failure; but he succeeded again in "Kabale und Liebe" (Love and Intrigue), in which he openly attacked the vice and inhumanity of the German courts. The heroine, Luise Miller, is a fiddler's daughter, who wins the love of the Chancellor's son; but their lives are ruined by the unscrupulous court intrigues. As an example of citizen tragedy, this piece excelled Lessing's "Miss Sara Sampson." In this play Schiller also satirized the traffic in Hessian soldiers as mere chattels of a prince.

In his next tragedy, "Don Carlos," the titular hero, son of King Philip II. of Spain, perishes a victim to the Inquisition and court intrigue, while his friend, the Marquis Posa, also dies for him in vain. In the Marquis Schiller portrayed just such an ideal dreamer as he himself was, and ever remained—"a citizen of a time yet to be."

And now Schiller passed through a transitional period of professorship of history at the University of Jena; wrote "The Rise of the Netherlands" and the "History of the Thirty Years' War;" became a fellow-spirit of Goethe, who had hitherto misunderstood him; was invited to Weimar, where he was ultimately ennobled, and produced, under Goethe's influence and encouragement, the great dramatic masterpieces that have crowned him with world-wide fame.

In his study of the Thirty Years' War Schiller had found the impressive character of Wallenstein, the general who betrayed his Emperor in order to secure his own aggrandisement, an earlier Napoleon, worshipped by his soldiers and believing in destiny. He has painted this colossal figure in enduring colors against a wonderful background, reproducing the social anarchy that reigned in Germany of that day. Wallenstein is the greatest dramatic character of German literature, and probably of all European literature since Shake-speare. The man is first felt as an unseen power amid the unruly hosts of soldiers, controlled only by his will. Then among his generals he is seen a very Cæsar, an actual emperor. All this Schiller achieved in his "Camp of Wallenstein," the first drama of the Trilogy, called by him the "Vorspiel" (prelude). This portion is highly realistic, with the Capuchin friar's quaint camp sermon and the Cuirassier's stirring song, which has become nationally famous as "Schiller's Trooper's Song." In "The Piccolomini," the second drama, Max Piccolomini, the hero, loves Wallenstein's daughter Thekla, but will remain true to the Emperor. At last, to vindicate his honor, he perishes in a wild charge against the Swedes. He represents the opposite to Wallenstein, the principle of honor as opposed to unscrupulous ambition. His love romance is beautifully touching. In the third drama, "Wallenstein's Death," the general who betrays is himself betrayed by Max's father, Octavio, whom he had trusted. He is murdered, after having acknowledged the better part played in life by the noble Max.

In "Mary Stuart," which followed the Wallenstein trilogy, Schiller makes us sympathize with the purely personal tragedy of the unhappy Queen of Scots, purified by her sufferings. Queen Elizabeth is sacrificed to this idealized Mary. The most famous scene of the play is that of the garden at Fotheringay, in which Mary, overjoyed at her unexpected liberty, is unexpectedly confronted by the Queen, and so insults Elizabeth as to lead to the death sentence.

Similarly in "The Maid of Orleans" he idealizes the character of Joan of Arc. She is no longer the peasant maid of Domremy, but the romantic warrior maid of Schiller's ideal vision. The critics have severely criticized his treatment of the character; yet, as Baumgart has well expressed it, this is a tragedy of moral idealism. In this play Joan dies victorious on the battlefield, and not as a martyr at the stake; but she is also represented (quite unhistorically, it must be admitted), as yielding for a disastrous moment to a prompting of love for the English soldier, Talbot. For this falling away for even the moment from her lofty ideals, the Virgin chas-

tises herself by remaining silent under false accusation, and
seeks vindication only in a heroic death.   Schiller has here
once more revised history to create an ideal.

From these quasi-historical dramas Schiller turned to a
new and less popular method in his "Bride of Messina,"
a melodramatic, Greek-like tragedy of evil destiny.   In this
work he introduced a chorus, but he was warned by its partial
failure to return to his true field, and in "Wilhelm Tell,"
finished in the year before that of his death, he left a masterpiece as a farewell legacy.   The idea had been suggested by
Goethe, who had intended to write an epic on the legend, but
who abandoned the notion.   From Goethe's own recollections
and from Tschudi, the Swiss chronicler, Schiller acquired
such a grasp of his theme that its local color is remarkable;
one is transported to the Alps with all their sights and
sounds.   The heroic characters of the book have a broad
nobility of patriotism.   The legends of the hat and apple-
shooting are skillfully used, and the murder of the tyrant
Gessler is splendidly vindicated.   The apostrophes to freedom
are inspiring, and Arnold von Melchthal's outburst on learning of the cruel blinding of his father, is Shakespearean.

WALLENSTEIN'S DAUGHTER.

(From "The Piccolomini."   Act I., Scene 8.   Translated by S. T.
Coleridge.)

*Enter the Countess Tertsky leading the Princess Thekla, richly
adorned.*

Countess. How, sister!   What, already upon business!
                                        [*Observing the Duchess.*
And business of no pleasing kind I see,—
Ere he has gladdened at his child.   The first
Moment belongs to joy.   Here, Friedland!   Father!
This is thy daughter.
                    [*Thekla approaches and bends as if about to kiss his
                    hand.   He receives her in his arms.*
    Wallenstein. Yes, pure and lovely hath hope risen on me:
I take her as the pledge of greater fortune.

    Duchess. 'Twas but a little child when you departed
To raise up that great army for the Emperor:
And after, at the close of the campaign,
When you returned home out of Pomerania,

Your daughter was already in the convent,
Wherein she has remained till now.
   Wal. The while
We in the field here gave our cares and toils
To make her great and fight her a free way
To the loftiest earthly good; lo! mother Nature
Within the peaceful, silent convent walls,
Has done her part, and out of her free grace
Hath she bestowed on the beloved child
The godlike! and now leads her, thus adorned,
To meet her splendid fortune and my hope.
   Duch. (*to Thekla*). Thou wouldst not have recognized thy
      father,
Wouldst thou, my child? She counted scarce eight years
When last she saw your face.
   Thek. O yes, yes, mother!
At the first glance!—My father is not altered.
The form that stands before me falsifies
No feature of the image that hath lived
So long within me!
   Wal. The voice of my child!   [*Then after a pause*
I was indignant at my destiny
That it denied me a man-child, to be
Heir of my name and of my prosperous fortune,
And re-illume my soon extinguished being
In a proud line of princes.
I wronged my destiny. Here upon this head,
So lovely in its maiden bloom, will I
Let fall the garland of a life of war,
Nor deem it lost, if only I can wreathe it
Transmuted to a regal ornamen'
Around these beauteous brows.   [*He clasps her in his arms.*

WALLENSTEIN'S TREASON.

(From "The Piccolomini." Act V., Scene 2.)

   Max. Piccolomini (*advancing*). My General!
   Wallenstein. That am I no longer, if
Thou styl'st thyself the Emperor's officer.
   Max. Then thou wilt leave the army, General?
   Wal. I have renounced the service of the Emperor.
   Max. And thou wilt leave the army?

Wal. Rather hope I
To bind it nearer still and faster to me.   [*He seats himself.*
Yes, Max., I have delayed to open it to thee,
Even till the hour of acting 'gins to strike.
Youth's fortunate feeling doth seize easily
The absolute right, yea, and a joy it is
To exercise the single apprehension
Where the sums square in proof;
But where it happens that of two sure evils
One must be taken, where the heart not wholly
Brings itself back from out the strife of duties,
There 'tis a blessing to have no election,
And blank necessity is grace and favor.
—This is now present: do not look behind thee—
It can no more avail thee.   Look thou forwards:
Think not! judge not! prepare thyself to act!
The court—it hath determined on my ruin,
Therefore I will to be beforehand with them.
We'll join the Swedes—right gallant fellows are they
And our good friends.

> [*He stops himself, expecting Piccolomini's answer.*

I have ta'en thee by surprise.   Answer me not.
I grant thee time to recollect thyself.

> [*He rises and retires.   Max. remains motionless i·*
> *excessive anguish.   Wallenstein returns.*

Max. My general, this day thou makest me
Of age to speak in my own right and person,
For till this day I have been spared the trouble
To find out my own road.   Thee have I followed
With most implicit, unconditional faith,
Sure of the right path if I followed thee.
To-day, for the first time, dost thou refer
Me to myself, and forcest me to make
Election between thee and my own heart.

Wal. Soft cradled thee thy fortune till to-day;
Thy duties thou couldst exercise in sport,
Indulge all lovely instincts, act forever
With undivided heart.   It can remain
No longer thus.   Like enemies the roads
Start from each other.   Duties strive with duties.
Thou must needs choose thy party in the war

Which is now kindling 'twixt thy friend and him
Who is thy Emperor.

   Max. War! is that the name?
War is as frightful as Heaven's pestilence.
Yet it is good, is it Heaven's will as that is.
Is that a good war, which against the Emperor
Thou wagest with the Emperor's own army?
O God of heaven! what a change is this.
Beseems it me to offer such persuasion
To thee, who, like the fixed star of the pole,
Wert all I gazed at on life's trackless ocean?
Oh! what a rent thou makest in my heart!
The ingrained instinct of old reverence,
The holy habit of obediency,
Must I pluck live asunder from thy name?
Nay, do not turn thy countenance upon me—
It always was as a god looking at me.
Duke Wallenstein, its power is not departed:
The senses still are in thy bonds, although,
Bleeding, the soul hath freed itself.

   Wal. Max., hear me.

   Max. Oh! do it not; I pray thee, do it not!
There is a pure and noble soul within thee,
Knows not of this unblest, unlucky doing.
Thy will is chaste, it is thy fancy only
Which hath polluted thee—and innocence,
It will not let itself be driven away
From that world-awing aspect. Thou wilt not,
Thou canst not, end in this. It would reduce
All human creatures to disloyalty
Against the nobleness of their own nature.
'Twill justify the vulgar misbelief,
Which holdeth nothing noble in free will,
And trusts itself to impotence alone
Made powerful only in an unknown power.

   Wal. The world will judge me sternly! I expect it:
Already have I said to my own self
All thou canst say to me. Who but avoids
The extreme, can he by going round avoid it?
But here there is no choice. Yes—I must use
Or suffer violence. So stands the case,
There remains nothing possible but that,

Max. Oh, that is never possible for thee!
'Tis the last desperate resource of those
Cheap souls to whom their honor, their good name
Is their poor *saving*, their last worthless *Keep*,
Which having staked and lost, they stake themselves
In the mad rage of gaming.   Thou art rich
And glorious; with an unpolluted heart
Thou canst make conquest of whate'er seems highest;
But he, who once hath acted infamy,
Does nothing more in this world.

    Wal. (grasps his hand.) Calmly, Max!
Much that is great and excellent shall we
Perform together yet.   And if we only
Stand on the height with dignity, 'tis soon
Forgotten, Max., by what road we ascended.
Believe me, many a crown shines spotless now,
That was deeply sullied in the winning.
To the evil spirit doth the earth belong,
Not to the good.   All, that the Powers divine
Send from above, are universal blessings;
Their light rejoices us, their air refreshes,
But never yet was man enriched by them:
In their eternal realm no *property*
Is to be struggled for—all there is general.
The jewel, the all-valued gold we win
From the deceiving Powers, depraved in nature,
That dwell beneath the day and blessed sunlight;
Not without sacrifices are they rendered
Propitious, and there lives no soul on earth
That e'er retired unsullied from their service.

    Max. Whate'er is human, to the human being
Do I allow, and to the vehement
And striving spirit readily I pardon
The excess of action; but to thee, my General!
Above *all* others, make I large concession.
For thou must move a world, and be the master—
He kills thee, who condemns thee to inaction.
So be it then! maintain thee in thy post
By violence.   Resist the Emperor,
And if it must be, force with force repel:
I will not praise it, yet I can forgive it.
But not—not to the *traitor*—yes,—the word

Is spoken out——
Not to the *traitor* can I yield a pardon.
That is no mere excess! that is no error
Of human nature—that is wholly different;
Oh, that is black,—black as the pit of hell!

                  [Wallenstein betrays a sudden agitation.
Thou canst not hear it *named*, and wilt thou *do* it?
Oh, turn back to thy duty; that thou canst,
I hold it certain. Send me to Vienna.
I'll make thy peace for thee with the Emperor.
He knows thee not. But I do know thee. He
Shall see thee, Duke, with my unclouded eye,
And I bring back his confidence to thee.

    Wal. It is too late; thou know'st not what has happened.

    Max. Were it too late, and were things gone so far
That a crime only could prevent thy fall,
Then—fall! fall honorably, even as thou stood'st,
Lose the command. Go from the stage of war.
Thou canst with splendor do it—do it too
With innocence. Thou hast lived much for others,
At length live thou for thy own self. I follow thee;
My destiny I never part from thine.

    Wal. It is too late! Even now, while thou art losing
Thy words, one after the other are the mile-stones
Left fast behind by my post-couriers
Who bear the order on to Prague and Egra.
Yield thyself to it. We act as we are forced.
I cannot give assent to my own shame
And ruin. Thou—No!—*thou* canst not forsake me;
So let us do what must be done, with dignity,
With a firm step. What am I doing worse
Than did famed Cæsar at the Rubicon,
When he the legions led against his country,
The which his country had delivered to him?
Had he thrown down the sword he had been lost,
As I were, if I but disarmed myself.
I trace out something in me of his spirit.
Give me his luck, that other *thing* I'll bear.

                    [Max. quits him abruptly.

THE MAIDEN'S LAMENT.

(The two first Stanzas of this Poem are sung by Thekla, in Act III. of
"The Piccolomini.")

THE wind rocks the forest,
  The clouds gather o'er;
The girl sitteth lonely
  Beside the green shore;
The breakers are dashing with might, with might:
And she mingles her sighs with the gloomy night,
    And her eyes are hot with tears.

"The earth is a desert,
  And broken my heart,
Nor aught to my wishes
  The world can impart.
To her Father in Heaven may the Daughter now go;
I have known all the joys that the world can bestow—
    I have lived—I have loved."—

"In vain, oh! how vainly,
  Flows tear upon tear!
Human woe never waketh
  Dull Death's heavy ear!—
Yet say what can soothe for the sweet vanish'd love,
And I, the Celestial, will shed from above
    The balm for thy breast."

"Let ever, though vainly,
  Flow tear upon tear;
Human woe never waketh
  Dull Death's heavy ear;
Yet still when the heart mourns the sweet vanish'd love,
No balm for its wound can descend from above
    Like Love's own faithful tears!"

WILLIAM TELL LEAVING HOME.

(From "Wilhelm Tell," Act III., Scene 1.)

Hedwig. The boys begin to use the bow betimes.
Tell. 'Tis early practice only makes the master.
Hed. Ah! Would to Heaven they never learnt the art!

Tell. But they shall learn it, wife, in all its points.
Who'er would carve an independent way
Through life, must learn to ward or plant a blow.

    Hed. Alas, alas! and they will never rest
Contentedly at home.

    Tell. No more can I!
I was not framed by nature for a shepherd.
Restless I must pursue a changing course;
I only feel the flush and joy of life,
In starting some fresh quarry every day.

    Hed. Heedless the while of all your wife's alarms,
As she sits watching through long hours at home:
For my soul sinks with terror at the tales
The servants tell about your wild adventures.
Whenc'er we part, my trembling heart forbodes,
That you will ne'er come back to me again.
I see you on the frozen mountain steeps,
Missing, perchance, your leap from cliff to cliff.
I see the chamois, with a wild rebound,
Drag you down with him o'er the precipice.
I see the avalanche close o'er your head,—
The treacherous ice give way, and you sink down
Entombed alive within its hideous gulf.
Ah! in a hundred varying forms does death
Pursue the Alpine huntsman on his course.
That way of life can surely ne'er be blessed,
Where life and limb are peril'd every hour.

    Tell. The man that bears a quick and steady eye,
And trusts to God, and his own lusty sinews,
Passes with scarce a scar, through every danger.
The mountain cannot awe the mountain child.

                         [He lays aside his tools.
And now, methinks, the door will hold awhile.—
The axe at home oft saves the carpenter.   *[Takes his cap.*

    Hed. Whither away?

    Tell. To Altdorf, to your father.

    Hed. You have some dangerous enterprise in view—
Confess!

    Tell. Why think you so?

    Hed. Some scheme's on foot
Against the governors. There was a council
Held on the Rütli—that I know—and you

Are one of the confederacy, I'm sure.

Tell. I was not there.   Yet will I not hold back,
Whene'er my country calls me to her aid.

Hed. Wherever danger is, will you be placed.
On you, as ever, will the burden fall.

Tell. Each man shall have the post that fits his powers

Hed. You took—ay, 'mid the thickest of the storm—
The man of Unterwald across the lake.
'Tis a marvel you escaped.   Had you no thought
Of wife and children, then?

Tell. Dear wife, I had;
And therefore saved the father for his children.

Hed. To brave the lake in all its wrath !   'Twas not
To put your trust in God !   'Twas tempting him.

Tell. The man that's over cautious will do little.

Hed. Yes, you've a kind and helping hand for all:
But be in straits, and who will lend you aid?

Tell. God grant I ne'er may stand in need of it!
                    [*Takes up his crossbow and arrows.*

Hed. Why take your crossbow with you? Leave it here.

Tell. I want my right hand, when I want my bow.
                    [*The boys, Walter and Wilhelm, return.*

Walter. Where, father, are you going?

Tel. To grand-dad, boy—
To Altdorf.   Will you go?

Wal. Ay, that I will!

Hed. The Viceroy's there just now.   Go not to Altdorf!

Tell. He leaves to-day.

Hed. Then let him first be gone.
Cross not his path.—You know he bears us grudge.

Tell. His ill-will cannot greatly injure me.
I do what's right, and care for no man's hate.

Hed. 'Tis those who do what's right, whom most he hates.

Tell. Because he cannot reach them.   Me, I ween,
His knightship will be glad to leave in peace.

Hed. Ay !—are you sure of that?

Tell. Not long ago,
As I was hunting through the wild ravines
Of Shechenthal, untrod by mortal foot,—
There, as I took my solitary way
Along a shelving ledge of rocks, where 'twas
Impossible to step on either side;

For high above rose, like a giant wall,
The precipice's side, and far below
The Shechen thunder'd o'er its rifted bed;—
> [*The boys press towards him, looking upon him with
> excited curiosity.*

There, face to face, I met the Viceroy.   He
Alone with me—and I myself alone—
Mere man to man, and near us the abyss.
And when his lordship had perused my face,
And knew the man he had severely fined
On some most trivial ground, not long before;
And saw me, with my sturdy bow in hand,
Come striding towards him, then his cheek grew pale,
His knees refused their office, and I thought
He would have sunk against the mountain side.
Then, touch'd with pity for him, I advanced,
Respectfully, and said, "'Tis I, my lord."
But ne'er a sound could he compel his lips
To frame in answer.   Only with his hand
He beckoned me in silence to proceed.
So I pass'd on, and sent his train to seek him.

Hed. He trembled then before you?   Woe the while
You saw his weakness; that he'll ne'er forgive.

Tell. I shun him, therefore, and he'll not seek me.

Hed. But stay away to-day.   Go hunting rather!

Tell. What do you fear?

Hed. I am uneasy.   Stay.

Tell. Why thus distress yourself without a cause?

Hed. Because there is no cause.   Tell, Tell! stay here!

Tell. Dear wife, I gave my promise I would go.

Hed. Must you?—Then go; but leave the boys with me.

Wal. No, mother dear, I'm going with my father.

Hed. How, Walter! will you leave your mother then?

Wal. I'll bring you pretty things from grandpapa.
> [*Exit with his father*

Wilhelm. Mother, I'll stay with you!

Hed. (*embracing him.*)   Yes, yes! thou art
My own dear child.   Thou'rt all that's left to me.

WILLIAM TELL AND THE TYRANT.

SCENE—*The hollow way at Küssnacht.*

Tell (*among the rocks overhanging the pass*). Here through
    the hollow way he'll pass; there is
No other road to Küssnacht. Here I'll do it! . . .
The opportunity is good: the bushes
Of alder there will hide me; from that point
My arrow hits him; the strait pass prevents
Pursuit. Now, Gessler, balance thy account
With Heaven! Thou must be gone; thy sand is run! . . .
Remote and harmless I have lived; my bow
Ne'er bent save on the wild beast of the forest;
My thoughts were free of murder. Thou hast scared me
From my peace; to fell asp-poison hast thou
Changed the milk of kindly temper in me;
Thou hast accustomed me to horrors. Gessler!
The archer who could aim at his boy's head
Can send an arrow to his enemy's heart. . . .
Poor little boys! My kind, true wife! I will
Protect them from thee. Viceroy! when I drew
That bowstring and my hand was quivering,
And with devilish joy thou mad'st me point it
At the child, and I in fainting anguish
Entreated thee in vain; then, with a grim,
Irrevocable oath, deep in my soul,
I vowed to God in Heaven that the next aim
I took should be thy heart. The vow I made
In that despairing moment's agony,
Became a holy debt—and I will pay it.

[Various characters gradually appear upon the scene, among them
Stüssi, Frau Armgart, and the members of a wedding procession, who
come up the pass; at length Gessler (the Austrian Landvogt or Viceroy), and Rudolph der Harras approach, riding up the pass, while Tell
disappears among the rocks.]

Gessler. Say what you like, I am the Kaiser's servant,
And must think of pleasing him. He sent me,
Not to caress these hinds, to soothe or nurse them.
Obedience is the word! The point at issue is,
Shall Boor or Kaiser here be lord o' th' lands?

Armgart. Now is the moment! Now for my petition.

Gess. This Hat at Altdorf, mark you, I set up,
Not for the joke's sake, or to try the hearts
O' th' people—these I know of old—but that
They might be taught to bend their necks to me,
Which are too straight and stiff; and in thé way
Where they are hourly passing I have planted
This offence, so that their eyes may fall on't,
And remind them of their lord, whom they forgot.
   Rudolph. But the people have some rights—
   Gess. Which now
Is not a time for settling or admitting.
Mighty things are on the anvil. The House
Of Hapsburg must wax powerful; what the Father
Gloriously began, the Son must forward.
This people is a stone of stumbling, which
One way or t' other must be put aside.
   Arm. Mercy, gracious Viceroy! Justice! Justice!
   Gess. Why do you plague me here and stop my way
I' th' open road? Off! Let me pass!
   Arm. My husband
Is in prison; these orphans cry for bread.
Have pity, good your grace, have pity on us!
   Rud. Who or what are you, then? Who is your husband?
   Arm. A poor wild-hay-man of the Rigiberg,
Whose trade is, on the brow of the abyss,
To mow the common grass from craggy shelves
And nooks to which the cattle dare not climb.
   Rud. By Heaven, a wild and miserable life!
Do now! do let this poor drudge free, I pray you!—
Whatever be his crime, that horrid trade
Is punishment enough. You shall have justice;
In the castle there make your petition;
This is not the place.
   Arm. No, no! I stir not
From this spot till you give up my husband!
'Tis the sixth month he has lain i' th' dungeon,
Waiting for the sentence of some judge in vain.
   Gess. Woman! Would'st lay thy hands on me? Begone!
   Arm. Justice Viceroy! thou art judge o' th' land here,
I' th' Kaiser's stead and God's. Perform thy duty!
As thou expectest justice from above,
Show it to us.

VII—24

Gess. Off! take the mutinous rabble from my sight.

Arm. No, no! I now have nothing
More to lose. Thou shalt not move a step, Lord,
Till thou hast done me right. Ay, knit thy brows,
And roll thy eyes as sternly as thou wilt;
We are so wretched, wretched now, we care not
Aught more for thy anger.

Gess. Woman, make way!
Or else my horse shall crush thee.

Arm. Let it! there!
Here am I with my children. Let the orphans
Be trodden underneath thy horse's hoofs!
'Tis not the worst that thou hast done.

Rud. Woman, art mad?

Arm. 'Tis long that thou has trodden
The Kaiser's people under foot. Too long!
Oh, I am but a woman! Were I a man
I should find something else to do
Than lie here crying in the dust.

Gess. Where are my servants?
Quick! take her hence! I may forget myself,
And do the thing I shall repent.

Rud. My lord,
The servants cannot pass; the place above
Is crowded with a bridal company.

Gess. I've been too mild a ruler to this people;
They are not tamed as they should be; their tongues
Are still at liberty. This shall be altered!
I will break that stubborn humor. Freedom,
With its pert vauntings, shall no more be heard of.
I will enforce a new law in these lands;
There shall not—

[An arrow pierces him; he presses his hand on his heart, and slides from his horse into the arms of Rudolph, who has dismounted.]

Rud. Lord Viceroy—God! What is it? whence came it?

Gess. 'Tis Tell's arrow.

Tell (from a rock above). Thou hast found the archer;
Seek no other. Free are the cottages,
Secure is innocence from thee; thou wilt
Torment the land no more.

CHAPTER XX.

MODERN GERMAN DRAMATISTS.

It is difficult for Englishmen or Americans to comprehend at once the conditions confronting the present day German playwright. No play which criticizes the existing order of things can be produced in a public theater. A centralized empire claims absolute control over the intellectual and moral training of its subjects. The upholders of the monarchy resist with all their strength whatever may shatter popular faith in the unquestioned right of kings or may be instrumental in the propaganda of republican ideas. There are organized efforts to suppress free thought and its natural expression. We may judge to what an extent this surveillance over the morals of the people is carried by the fact that Ibsen's *Doll's House* is not permitted on a German stage with the ending which the dramatist originally gave it. Instead, lest the *hausfrau* in an unguarded moment might catch the spirit of Nora's awakening and leave the home where she feels she no longer belongs, the authorities have submitted a different conclusion. Nora—in Germany—goes for the last time to see her children and is so overcome with emotion that she has not the courage to depart.

The result of the inevitable clash between the established order and the course of progress has resulted in the rise of two schools of literature. One gives unbounded support to the monarchy and all it represents; the other, no less patriotic, stands for liberalism, free thought, free expression. For the most part those of the first school are today seekers after abstract truth: philosophers, scientists, mathematicians. Those who have attracted wide attention outside the boundaries of the Fatherland during the last few years have been ardent workers for the cause of the progressive party, both in its relations to society in general and to industry and education. They are Sudermann and Hauptmann.

This party has for its avowed purpose the bettering of conditions under which humanity exists and continues an unceasing struggle for existence. It does not ask whether or not life is good, but taking it for granted, seeks to make the circumstances surrounding human beings more tolerable. It proceeds on the theory that if life at present is ugly and cheerless, it is the duty, not alone of the philanthropist to labor for the regeneration of the age, but of writers as well to faithfully portray the truth, that all may see. If the result is depressing, so much the worse for society, which allows these conditions to exist and which, brought face to face with them, will the more speedily inaugurate a happier era. To dream pleasant dreams, to weave pretty tales, while the masses are hungry and weary and heartsick is not only idle but wrong.

The naturalistic school in the beginning, originating in France, set to work to portray life simply with the veracity of a photographer, eliminating all ideality; however, it developed that there was so much more misery than comfort, so much more sorrow than joy, so much more discord than harmony, that shortly the naturalistic school was confining its attention chiefly to the darker picture, either regarding the happier aspect as too commonplace or too rare to require portrayal.

Three questions or social problems have appealed to writers of this school: the hardness of life as the overshadowing fact in our social existence; the influence of environment and heredity as limiting the possibility of man to become what he will; the justice of extending to women, no longer slaves or playthings, equal chances with men in education and opportunity.

The fault which the conservative school finds with the naturalistic school—that it dwells upon the seamy side, that we are burdened by the harsh features it emphasizes and oppressed by the stern realities it sets forth—is just; and the naturalists find satisfaction in this public acknowledgment of their successful accomplishment. So much the worse for those thus depressed, they would reply, when they enjoy for themselves what they deny to their neighbors. So much more wrong the sin of those who profess a belief in the brotherhood of men and then by their selfishness and greed allow others around them to perish, or at best to drag out a miserable existence.

Sometimes the naturalists treat not of the poor and simple but of the crude and prosperous; sometimes of the well-fed upper class who by their conventionalities are hemmed in on every side and become puppets rather than free individuals.

We are too near to judge of contemporary schools and writers, but we may feel sure that the hope of the German people lies with its progressive party. The trend of human thought and deed has led to the unalterable belief that free thought, free action, an uncensored press and liberality in every walk of life must prevail. Although it is doubtful if a single play which nineteenth century playwrights in Germany have so far produced will endure, they have, notwithstanding, furnished pictures of contemporary life that will long be greatly appreciated. Furthermore, they have done much to stimulate thought upon these crucial questions which today hang in the balance in the Fatherland, and which will never disappear until they have been rightly settled.

SUDERMANN.

Hermann Sudermann, socialist, writer, dramatist, was born in 1860 in East Prussia. He first turned to novel writing but for some years has largely confined himself to producing plays. His mastery of stagecraft is remarkable and he pleases more in this particular than in depth of thought. Because of their socialistic tendencies, his earlier plays were refused in public theaters and he became known to his countrymen by means of the "free theater" which was opened in 1889, by a society created for the purpose of providing means whereby plays rejected by the censors might still be shown in private. No admission being charged, this project was practical in so far as it complied with the laws of the land. Ibsen's *Ghosts* was the first drama produced; others followed until popular sentiment permitted the general production of naturalistic plays.

Affected by the harsh criticism that greeted his writings, Sudermann became less radical in his dramatic works. *Honor, The Joy of Life, Magda, John the Baptist, The Battle of the Butterflies and Roses,* are among his best known plays.

THE JOY OF LIVING.

Baron Ludwig. What do you hear from Kellinghausen? He is still at Lengenfeld, I hear.

Beata. I have just had a letter. Now that the elections are over he means to take a day's shooting, and then he is coming home—free from his party-duties for the first time in years!

Baron Ludwig. And what does the Egeria of the party say to such a state of things?

Beata. Do you mean *me*, your Excellency?

Baron Ludwig. I mean the woman at whose delightful dinner-table the fate of more than one important bill has been decided. Now that Kellinghausen has retired into private life, do you mean to keep up the little political dinners we've always been so much afraid of?

Beata. I hope so, your Excellency. And if you care to beard the lion in his den, I shall be charmed to send you an invitation. You haven't dined with us in an age. I've always fancied that the estrangement between your brother and yourself might be the cause of our seeing so little of you.

Baron Ludwig. My dear Countess, those eyes of yours see through everything; and I read in them all the answers I might make to that question. Ah, well—Richard had the good luck, the unspeakable good luck, to win your friendship, and under your influence to develop into the man he is!

Beata. I know how to listen when clever men are talking. That is the secret of what you call my influence.

Baron Ludwig. You think so?—Well—there was Richard, dabbling in poetry and politics, in archæology and explorations, like the typical noble amateur. He had a fortune from his mother, while I was poor. But in one respect I was richer than he; for he married a fool who dragged him down to the level of her own silly snobbishness. But then you came—and lifted him up again. Then all his dormant powers awoke—he discovered his gift as a speaker, he became the mouthpiece of the party, he got into the Reichstag, and—

Beata. And dropped out again.

Baron Ludwig. Exactly. And the estrangement between us dates from that time. It was reported that the government had left him in the lurch, and I was thought to be more or less responsible.

Beata. At all events, his career was cut short. And he failed again at the next election.

Baron Ludwig. And now your friendship has helped him to success.

Beata. My husband's friendship, you mean.

Baron Ludwig. In my loveless household I know too little of the power of woman to pronounce definitely on that point.

Beata. You do well to suspend your judgment.

Baron Ludwig. Ah, now you are displeased with me. I am sorry. I might be of use to you.

Beata. If you wish to be of use to me you can do so by becoming your brother's friend. It was to ask this that I sent for you.

Baron Ludwig. Countess, I wonder at your faith in human nature!

Beata. Human nature has never deceived me.

Baron Ludwig. One would adore you for saying that if one hadn't so many other reasons for doing so!

Beata (*laughing*). Pretty speeches at our age?

Baron Ludwig. You may talk of *my* age, but not of yours.

Beata. Look at the grey hair—here, on my temples; and my medicine-bottles over there. I never stir without them now.

Baron Ludwig. I have been distressed to hear of your illness.

Beata. Yes, my heart bothers me—an old story. My heart is tired—and I—I'm not. And when I drive it too hard it grows a little restive now and then. But it doesn't matter! (*Enter Ellen.*) Is that you, Ellen? Come in, dear.

Ellen (*in skating dress*). Mother, dear, I didn't know you had a visitor. How do you do, your Excellency?

Baron Ludwig. How do you do, young lady? Dear me— dear me—what have you been growing into?

Ellen. Into life, your Excellency!

Baron Ludwig. Ha—very good—very neat. So many people grow past it.

Beata. And how was the skating, dear?

Ellen. Oh, heavenly. Norbert and I simply flew.

. . . .

[*Ellen enters.*

Ellen (*throwing her arms about her mother's neck*). Mother! You dear little mamma!

Beata. Well, madcap, what is it now?

Ellen. Oh, nothing, nothing. I'm so happy, that's all.

Beata. What are you happy about, dear?

Ellen. I don't know—does one ever?

Beata. Has anything in particular happened?

Ellen. No; nothing. That is—Norbert said—Oh, yes, to be sure; we met Uncle Richard.

Beata. Ah—where?

Ellen. In the Zoo. On horseback. He sent his love and said he would be in before dinner. Norbert is coming, too. Mother, is it true that Uncle Richard is such a wonderful speaker? Norbert says he can do what he likes with people.

Beata. Some people—but only those whose thoughts he can turn into feelings, or whose feelings he can turn into thoughts. Do you understand?

Ellen. Oh, yes! You mean, one can give only to those who have something to give in return?

Beata. Yes.

Ellen. But he must have great power—I am sure of it! He's always so quiet, and says so little—yet one feels there's a great fire inside—and sometimes it blazes up.

Beata (laughing). What do you know about it?

Ellen. Oh, I know. It's just the same with—mother, how can people *bear* life sometimes? It's so beautiful one simply can't breathe!

Beata (with emotion). Yes, it *is* beautiful. And even when it's nothing but pain and fear and renunciation, even then it's still beautiful, Ellen.

Ellen (alarmed). Mother—what is the matter?

Beata. Nothing, dear. I'm only a little tired. (*She goes to the door.*)

. . . .

Norbert. Oh, father, how happy you must be! How they cheered, how they fought to get near you and shake your hand! Oh, if only I could have one such hour in my life!

Richard (laying a hand on his shoulder). If you do, my son, may you pay for it less dearly!

Norbert. What do you mean?

Richard. Listen, Norbert. Have you heard anything of Aunt Beata?

Norbert. I went there, but they told me she wouldn't see any one.

Richard (musingly). H'm.

Norbert. The fact is, I wanted to see Uncle Michael.

Richard (who has walked toward the window). Uncle Michael? That reminds me that I wanted to tell you— How the sunset shines on the housetops over there! Everything is in a glow—we shall have glorious winter weather soon—

Norbert. You said you had something to tell me, father.

Richard. Yes, yes; to be sure. But first, haven't you something to tell *me?*

Norbert (with an embarrassed smile). Yes; but not today— when you're so—

Richard. The very day, dear boy! Tomorrow I may—but there's nothing to tell, after all. Aunt Beata and I have seen this coming and it has made us very happy.

Norbert (flinging his arms about his father). Father! Father!

Richard. Norbert! My dear lad! But we don't know what Uncle Michael will say—

Norbert. Uncle Michael? When I'm *your* son? Father, you've heard something. You wouldn't frighten me for nothing.

Richard. I have heard nothing. But, Norbert, listen. Whatever comes to you in after days I want you to remember one thing: it doesn't matter whether we succeed or not. What we need is the guiding note of a voice that seems the echo of our best hopes. It doesn't matter whether we are mistaken in the voice or not—the great thing is to hear it. And the worst thing is not to feel the need of it.

Norbert. Thank you, father. I'm not sure I understand— but you may be sure I shall listen for the voice.

. . . .

Baron Ludwig. Isn't your Highness's skepticism a little overdone? Surely society has made us the natural protectors of the social order. The order may change with the times—all we ask is that it should maintain the moral balance of power. (*Beata laughs.*) You are amused, Countess?

Beata (still laughing). I was only laughing to think how often I'd heard it before—the moral balance of power, and all the rest! I'm sure our ancestors sang the same song when they threw their victims to Moloch. And our souls are still thrown by the million to the Moloch of social expediency. We all expect to sacrifice our personal happiness to the welfare of the race! (*She laughs excitedly.*)

Kellinghausen (almost threateningly). Beata!

Baron Ludwig. Countess, you are conjuring up a phantom.

Beata. It may be a phantom, but it has us by the throat. (*To Richard.*) What are you thinking of, Volkerlingk? You are not going to refuse our celebrated game-pie?

Richard. I beg your pardon. I wasn't thinking. (*He helps himself to the dish.*)

Beata. You must know that that pie is an invention of my own!

Prince. Dear me, Countess, are you at home in every branch of learning?

Beata. Oh, I had the making of a great cook in me. I believe I'm the last of the old school—the model housekeeper, the domestic wife, the high priestess of the family! (*She goes on laughing excitedly, and Michael nervously echoes her laugh.*)

Richard (*making a perceptible effort to change the conversation*). My dear Countess, no one ever ventures to dispute your statements. But there is one family about which I want to say a word—that is the one we are in. (*Rising.*) I drink to the house of Kellinghausen!

Prince (*to Kellinghausen*). Is anything wrong with the Countess?

Kellinghausen. Beata!

Beata (*raising herself with a smile*). Yes?

Kellinghausen. Would you not rather go into the drawing-room? You look tired. (*She shakes her head.*)

Richard (*in a formal tone, with a glance at Michael*). We all beg of you, Countess—

Beata (*looking from one to the other with growing apprehension*). No—no—no I'm quite—quite—on the contrary—I have a toast to propose. (*Richard makes a startled gesture.*) Yes—a toast of my own! But please all sit down first—

Prince. Woman disposes!

Kellinghausen. Beata, you are overtaxing yourself. Be careful.

Beata. My dear friends, you all go on wishing each other a long life—but which of us is really alive? Which of us really dares to live? Somewhere, far off in the distance, we catch a glimpse of life—but we hide our eyes and shrink away from it like transgressors. And that's our nearest approach to living! Do you really think you're alive—any one of you? Or do you think I am? (*She springs up with an inspired look.*) But I, at least—I—whose whole life is one long struggle against death—I who never sleep, who hardly breathe, who barely stand—I at least know how to laugh, how to love life and be thankful for it. (*She staggers to her feet, raising her glass, her voice no more than a hoarse whisper.*) And as the only living soul among you, I drink to the joy of living!

The Others (*holding out their glasses*). Good! Good! Brave!

Beata (*draws a deep breath, sets down her glass, and looks about her confusedly. Her eyes rest on Richard, and then turn to Michael, to whom she speaks*). I think I will take your advice and go into the other room for a little while. (*She rises with an effort.*)

Kellinghausen. There, Beata! I warned you.

Baron Ludwig (*offering her his arm*). Won't you take my arm, Countess?

Beata. No, no—thanks! Michael, make my excuses. I shall be back in a few minutes. (*She lingers in the doorway with a last smile and a last look at Richard.*) Good-bye. I shall be back—in a few minutes. (*Goes out.*)

Kellinghausen (*to the others*). Don't be alarmed. My wife often breaks down in this way—I knew by her excitement that it was coming. Please sit down again. I assure you that in a few minutes she— (*A heavy fall is heard in the next room. Richard starts violently. Michael half springs from his seat, but controls himself with an effort. There is a short pause*)—she'll be coming back laughing as usual. (*Whispers are heard behind the door to the left. Richard is seen to listen intently.*) What are you listening to? What's the matter?

Richard (*agitated*). I beg your pardon — I thought I — (*Ellen is heard to utter a piercing shriek. The men start to their feet. Michael rushes out.*)

Baron Ludwig. Surely that was the Countess Ellen's voice?

Prince. It doesn't look as if the Countess were going to come back laughing as usual.

. . . .

Richard. Thank you, Michael—for letting me be with her—

Kellinghausen. Read this. (*Hands him Beata's letter.*)

Richard (*takes the letter, shudders at sight of the handwriting, tries to read it, and then hands it back*). I cannot—

Kellinghausen. Then I will read it to you. It's meant for both of us. (*He reads.*) "Dear Michael, even if the poison is found in me they will think I took it by mistake. To avoid suspicion I shall do it while we are all at luncheon. I see that some-one must pay the penalty—better I than he. He has his work be-fore him—I have lived my life. And so I mean to steal a march on him. Whatever you have agreed upon between you, my death will cancel the bargain—he cannot die now without causing the scandal you have been so anxious to avert. I have always loved happiness and I find happiness now in doing this for his sake, and the children and yours. Beata." As she says, this cancels our agreement. You see I must give you back your word.

Richard. And you see, Michael, that I live because I must—that I live—because I am dead—

CURTAIN.

HAUPTMANN.

Gerhart Hauptmann was born in Silesia in 1862. His life presents many contradictions and his philosophy is difficult for his critics to classify. Following the tenets of the naturalistic party, his first plays were as photographic as they could well be. Take for example *The Weavers,* called by someone "the modern dance of death." No more vivid picture of under-paid, under-fed workers has been produced by a pen. The one criticism which the reader feels upon concluding it is that the play is local; it lacks universality. Struggle, starvation and ruin have faced humanity for ages; but of these we may read in newspapers, journals, and stories. A play which would bring these conditions before us must reach beneath particular circumstances and make us feel that it is true of all time and in many countries wherein a similar life confronted men. *Before Dawn* is a play set in the mountains of his native country, wherein he represents the miners made suddenly rich by the discovery of rich coal deposits beneath their holdings. Having no conception of what use to make of money, they spend it in drunken carousals. The effects of excessive drinking upon them and the rising generation are plainly shown.

From these plays which picture the unhappiness and sordidness of life so faithfully, it is a relief to turn to Hauptmann's later play, *The Sunken Bell.* It is a symbolic drama, full of the folk and fairy lore of the German mountains. It is doubtful whether any writer of plays since the days of Shakespeare has introduced wood nymphs and water sprites with such charming results. There will always be critics and readers who, possessing the impulse to get at the root of a matter—acting much as the one who dissects a flower to understand its beauty—will wish to search out every elf and gnome and sprite to ascertain its origin and its faithful portrayal.

For the one who enjoys the general effect of fairy folk and cares not at all whence they came or whither they go, if only they act while before him as he should expect them to act could they unexpectedly materialize, few modern plays will satisfy so well. However, the play was not created for the fairy folk; they merely help to enable one mortal to set before his fellow mortals a symbolism or an allegory of life. It has been divined that Hauptmann herein reveals his own story to us; however this may be, it is evident that he shows us the probable fate of one who, having great ambitions and a fervent desire to accomplish a given purpose, and who, catching a vision of the wonderful possibilities that accomplishment offers, feels it imperative to sacrifice all else for the one coveted end. Such a person appears abnormal to his friends; they frequently reproach him bitterly for the omissions and commissions of his daily life. But they never can know, as he does, the tremendous force that has caught him in its power and draws him on, in spite of opposition and entreaties.

The play is usually interpreted as personifying the poet or writer who, having known the heights, cannot again adjust himself to the valley. It would be as true of the artist, the musician, of the adventurer who seeks buried treasure or new realms beyond the sea. For each one the beautiful play has its message and for that reason it is destined to endure longer than anything else Hauptmann has thus produced.

The scene is set back in the Middle Ages at a time when Christianity, having struggled long and grimly, has obtained a hold upon the people of Germany. Its victory, however, is not yet universal and in the recesses of the heights the mountain folk still hold out against the encroachments of mortals. Particularly distasteful to them are bells; at the sound of a church bell, it will be remembered, spirits of darkness fled in fear. Loving the wildness of an otherwise uninhabited world, they hate with undying hatred the spirit of industry which prompts the people of the valley to come into the mountains and hew out marble and disturb with their noise and worry and fret the peace of their former kingdom. Learning that Heinrich, the bell-founder, has fashioned a great bell which is to be hung up in the heights to chime abroad its message, a malicious spirit has wrenched loose a wheel from the wagon

whereon the bell is being carried and caused it to sink into
the lake. From the gnomes and wood-folk we learn of the
fate of the bell and its maker.

Rautendelein, a wood maiden, the embodied power which
beckons men on in their aspirations, discovers the unconscious
man where he has fallen in his struggle to recover himself.
Looking into her eyes, he sees his heart's desire, his one great
purpose. By her presence his fever is allayed and his anguish
soothed, in spite of tormenting pain of body and distress of
mind at his failure. Presently, well-disposed villagers come
in search of their loved neighbor, who has won from them
the name Master. They cross themselves trying thus to gain
protection against possible witches who may inhabit the
mountain and do them harm. They carry Heinrich home to
his anxious wife; she is alarmed by his condition but still
more alarmed by his words. His bell, he insists, was not
worthy of the heights and so he and it were cast down forever.
He has been changed by the vision he has caught and can
never more be as he was before; those around cannot understand him. Heinrich welcomes the thought of death as a
solution of his otherwise unsolvable problem. Yet the vision
of what he might achieve does not wholly abandon him; it
comes even to his home, in his despair, and he sees it face to
face. Transported by it, he wanders away to the mountains,
there to labor with the avowed purpose of building a church
worthy of the pure heights, whereon another and more perfect bell shall chime so appealingly that it will draw all men
upward. Of course he is utterly misunderstood by friends and
family. The kindly disposed vicar comes to labor with him
and when he finds it impossible to recall the wanderer, he
leaves him to what he considers his well-deserved ruin.

Worse for Heinrich than any imprecations of others are
the torments of his own soul, as now and then the fear creeps
into his consciousness that he may fail again; worse yet are
the memories of the past and those neglected. Finally, brought
face to face with the havoc he has wrought in other lives,
he curses the very hope that led him on and returns to the
valley. Still, in the end, before he dies, he stumbles back once
more in quest of the deserted aspiration and expires with its
vision before him.

THE SUNKEN BELL.

The Wood-Sprite.

  . . . Yesterday I cut
My first spring salad. It grew near my hut.
This morning, early, I went out,
And, roaming carelessly about,
Through brush and brier,
Then climbing higher,
At last I reached the topmost wood.
There I espied a hateful brood
Of mortals, who did sweat and stew,
And dig the earth, and marble hew.
A curse upon their church and creed—
Their chapels, and their clanging bells—

The Nickelmann.

Their bread they mix with cumminseed!

The Wood-Sprite.

They plague us in our woods and wells.
But vain is all our wrath and woe.
Beside the deep abyss 'twiss grow
With tower and spire, and, overhead,
The cross that you and I do dread.
Ay! . . . The noisy monster was all but hung
In the lofty steeple, and soon had rung.
But I was alert! We shall never hear
That bell! It is drowned in the mere!

              (Changing tone

By cock and pie!
A devil of a joke! . . . I stood on the brink
Of the cliff, chewing sorrel to help me think,
As I rested against a stump of birch,
'Mid the mountain grasses, I watched the church.
When, all of a sudden, I saw the wing
Of a blood-red butterfly, trying to cling
To a stone. And I marked how it dipped, and tipped,
As if from a blossom the sweet it sipped.
I called. It fluttered, to left and to right,
Until on my hand I felt it light.
I knew the elf. It was faint with fright.

We babbled o' that,
Of the frogs that had spawned
Ere the day had dawned,—
We babbled and gabbled, a-much, I wis:
Then it broke
Into tears!   .   .   .
I calmed its fears.
And it spoke.
"O, they're cracking their whips,
And they gee! and they whoa!
As they drag it aloft
From the dale below.
'Tis some terrible tub, that had lost its lid,
All of iron! Will nobody rid
Our woods of the horrible thing? 'Twould make
The bravest moss-mannikin shudder and quake.
They swear they will hang it, these foolish people,
High up in the heart of the new church steeple,
And they'll hammer, and bang, at its sides all day
To frighten good spirits of earth away!"

I hummed, and I hawed, and I said, ho ho!
As the butterfly fell to the earth: while I
Stole off in pursuit of a herd near by.
I guzzled my fill of good milk, I trow!
Three udders ran dry. They will seek in vain
So much as a drop of it more to drain.
Then, making my way to a swirling stream,
I hid in the brush, as a sturdy team
Came snorting, and panting, along the road—
Eight nags, tugging hard at their heavy load.
We will bide our time, quoth I—and lay
Quite still in the grass, till the mighty dray
Rumbled by:—when, stealing from hedge to hedge,
And hopping and skipping from rock to rock,
I followed the fools. They had reached the edge
Of the cliff when there came—a block!
With flank all a-quiver, and hocks a-thrill,
They hauled and they lugged at the dray until,
Worn out by the struggle to move the bell,
They had to lie down for a moment. Well—
Quoth I to myself, the Faun will play
Them a trick that will spare them more work today.

THE SHEPHERD'S CHIEF MOURNER.—LANDSEER.

One clutch at the wheel—I had loosened a spoke—
A wrench, and a blow, and the wood-work broke
A wobble, a crack, and the hateful bell
Rolled over—and into the gulf it fell!
And oh, how it sounded,
And clanged, as it bounded,
From crag to crag, on its downward way:
Till at last in the welcoming splash and the spray
Of the lake it was lost—for aye!

Heinrich.

Where am I? Maiden, wilt thou answer me?

Rautendelein.

Why, in the mountains.

Heinrich.

In the mountains? Ay—
But how . . . and why? What brought me here to-
    night?

Rautendelein.

Nay, gentle stranger, naught know I of that.
Why fret thyself about such trifles. See—
Here I have brought thee hay. So lay thy head
Down and take all the rest thou need'st.

Heinrich.

Yes! Yes!
'Tis rest I need. Indeed—indeed—thou'rt right.
But rest will come to me no more, my child!
                                        [*Uneasily.*
Now . . . tell me . . . what has happened?

Rautendelein.

Nay, if I knew . . .

Heinrich.

Meseems . . . methinks . . and . . then . .
    all ends in dreams.
Ay, surely, I am dreaming.

VII—25

Rautendelein.

Here is milk.
Thou must drink some of it, for thou art weak.

Heinrich (eagerly).

Thanks, maiden. I will drink. Give me the milk.
[*He drinks from a bowl which she offers him.*

Rautendelein (while he drinks).

Thou art not used to mountain ways. Thy home
Lies in the vale below, where mortals dwell.
And, like a hunter who once fell from the cliff
While giving chase to some wild mountain fowl,
Thou hast climbed far too high. And yet . . .
        that man
Was not quite fashioned as the man thou art.

Heinrich.

[*After drinking and looking ecstatically and fixedly at
    Rautendelein.*
Speak on! Speak on! Thy drink was very sweet.
But sweeter still thy voice . . .
                                [*Again becoming anxious.*
        She said—a man
Not fashioned like myself. A better man—
And yet he fell! . . . Speak on, my child.

Rautendelein.

        Why speak?
What can my words avail? I'll rather go
And fetch thee water from the brook, to wash
The blood and dust from off thy brow. . . .

Heinrich.

[*Pleading and grasping her by the wrist. Rautendelein
    stands undecided.*
        Ah, stay!
And look into mine eyes with thy strange eyes.
For lo, the world, within thine eyes renewed,
So sweetly bedded, draws me back to life!
Stay, child. O stay!

Rautendelein (uneasy).

        Then . . . as thou wilt. And yet . . .

Heinrich (fevered and imploring).

Ah, stay with me! Thou wilt not leave me so?
Thou dost not dream how dear to me thou art.
O wake me not, my child. I'll tell thee all.
I fell . . . yet—no. Speak thou; for thy dear voice
Has heaven's own music. God did give it thee.
And I will listen. Speak! . . . Wilt thou not speak?
Wilt thou not sing to me?. Why then . . . I must
I fell. I know not how—I've told thee that—
Whether the path gave way beneath my feet;
Whether 'twas willingly I fell, or no—
God wot. Enough. I fell into the gulf.

[More fevered.

And then I clutched at a wild cherry tree
That grew between the rocks. It broke—and I,
Still clasping a bough tightly, felt a shower
Of pale pink blossoms riot round my head;
Then swift was hurled to the abyss—and died!
And even now I'm dead. It must be so.
Let no one wake me!

Rautendelein (uncertainly).

Yet thou seem'st alive!

Heinrich.

I know—I know—what once I did not know:
That Life is Death, and only Death is Life.

. . . .

(*In the old-fashioned house of Heinrich the bellfounder.*)

Heinrich.

Strangely entangled seems the web of souls.

Magda (stroking his hair tenderly).

If I have ever been a help to thee—
If I have sometimes cheered thy working hours—
If favor in thine eyes I ever found . . .
Bethink thee, Heinrich: I, who would have given
Thee everything—my life—the world itself—
I had but that to pay thee for thy love:

Heinrich (uneasily).

I'm dying. That is best. God means it well.
Should I live on . . . Come nearer, wife, and hear
    me.
'Tis better for us both that I should die.
Thou think'st, because we blossomed out together,
I was the sun that caused thy heart to bloom.
But that the eternal Wonder-Worker wrought,
Who, on the wings of His chill winter-storms,
Rides through a million woodland flowers,
Slaying them, as He passes, in their Spring!
'Tis better for us both that I should die.
See: I was cracked and aging—all misshaped.
If the great Bellfounder who moulded me
Tosses aside His work, I shall not mourn.
When He did hurl me down to the abyss,
After my own poor, faulty, handiwork,
I did not murmur; for my work was bad!
Good—wife—the bell that sank into the mere
Was not made for the heights—it was not fit
To wake the answering echoes of the peaks!

Magda.

I cannot read the meaning of thy words.
A work so highly prized, so free from flaw,
So clear and true that, when it first rang out
Between the mighty trees from which it hung,
All marveled and exclaimed, as with one voice,
"The Master's bell sings as the Angels sing!"

Heinrich (fevered).

'Twas for the valley, not the mountain-top!

Magda.

That is not true! Hadst thou but heard, as I,
The Vicar tell the Clerk, in tones that shook,
"How gloriously 'twill sound upon the heights!"

Heinrich.

'Twas for the valley—not the mountain-top!
I only know't. The Vicar does not know. . . .
Well, let life go! The service of the valleys
Charms me no longer, and no more their peace

Calms my wild blood. Since on the peaks I stood,
All that I am has longed to rise, and rise,
Cleaving the mists, until it touched the skies!
I would work wonders with the power on high:
And, since I may not work them, being so weak;
Since, even could I, with much straining, rise,
I should but fall again—I choose to die.
[*Rautendelein has silently entered and is recognized by
the Vicar and Magda as a neighbor maiden.*

The Vicar (to Rautendelein).

Stand here, my child; or, if thou wilt, sit down,
Be good and do the very best thou canst.
Make thyself helpful, while they need thy help.
God will reward thee for the work thou dost.
Thou art greatly changed, dear child, since I last saw
    thee.
But keep thou honest—be a good, true maid—
For the dear Lord has blessed thee with much beauty.
In truth, my dear, now that I look at thee,
Thou art, yet art not, Anna. As a princess,
Stepp'd from the pages of some fairy book,
Thou seem'st. So quickly changed! Who would have
    thought
It possible! Well, well! . . . Thou'lt keep him cool?
He's burning! (*To Heinrich.*) May God bring thee back
    to health!
[*Rautendelein, who till now has seemed shy and meek,
changes suddenly and bustles about the hearth.*

Rautendelein.

Flickering spark in the ash of death,
Glow with life of living breath!
Red, red wind, thy loudest blow!
I, as thou, did lawless grow!
    Simmer, sing, and simmer.
                [*The flame leaps up on the hearth.*

.   .   .   .

[*Heinrich has opened his eyes, and lies staring at Rautendelein.*

Heinrich (amazed).

Tell me . . . who art thou?
    Rautendelein (quickly and unconcernedly).
        I? Rautendelein.

Heinrich.

Rautendelein? I never heard that name.
Yet somewhere I have seen thee once before.
Where was it?

Rautendelein.

Why, 'twas on the mountain-side.

Heinrich.

True. True. 'Twas there—what time I fevered lay.
I dreamt I saw thee there. . . . Again I dream.
At times we dream strange dreams! . . .

Rautendelein.

Thou art dreaming? Why?

Heinrich (in anguish).

Because . . . I must be dreaming.

Rautendelein.

Art thou so sure?

Heinrich.

Yes. No. Yes. No. I'm wandering. Let me dream
    on!
Thou asked if I am sure. I know not.
Ah, be it what it will; or dream, or life—
It is. I feel it, see it—thou dost live!
Real or unreal, within me or without,
Child of my brain, or whatsoe'er thou art,
Still I do love thee, for thou art thyself.
So stay with me, sweet spirit. Only stay!

Rautendelein.

So long as thou shalt choose.

    .   .   .   .

. . . But tell me whence thou'rt sprung and who has
    sent thee!
What would'st thou of a broken, suffering man,
A bundle of sorrow, drawing near the end
Of his brief pilgrimage . . . ?

Rautendelein.

I like thee.
Whence I did spring I know not—nor could tell
Whither I go. But Granny said one day
She found me lying in the moss and weeds.
A hind did give me suck. My home's the wood,
The mountain-side, the crag, the storm-swept moor—
Where the wind moans and rages, shrieks and groans,
Or purrs and mews, like some wild tiger-cat!
There thou wilt find me, whirling through the air;
There I laugh loud and shout for sheer mad joy;
Till faun and nixy, gnome and water-sprite,
Echo my joy and split their sides with laughter.
I'm spiteful when I'm vexed, and scratch and bite:
And who should anger me had best beware.
Yet—'tis no better when I'm left alone:
For good and bad in me's all mood and impulse.
I'm thus or thus, and change with each new whim.
But thee I'm fond of . . . Thee I would not scratch.
And, if thou wilt, I'll stay. Yet were it best
Thou camest with me to my mountain home.
Then thou should'st see how faithfully I'd serve thee.
I'd show thee diamonds, and rubies rare,
Hid at the bottom of unfathomed deeps.
Emeralds, and topazes, and amethysts—
I'd bring thee all—I'd hang upon thy lids!
Froward, unruly, lazy, I may be;
Spiteful, rebellious, wayward, what thou wilt!
Yet thou should'st only need to blink thine eye,
And ere thou'st time to speak, I'd nod thee—yes.

.   .   .   .

Rautendelein (with incantations).

Master, sleep is thine!
When thou wakest, thou art mine.
Happy dreams shall dull thy pain,
Help to make thee whole again.
Hidden treasures, now grow bright!
In the depths ye give no light.
Glowing hounds in vain do bark,
Whine and whimper in the dark!
We, who serve him, glad will be:

For the Master sets us free!
One, two, three. A new man be!
For the future thou art free!

Heinrich (awaking).

What's happened to me? . . . From what wondrous
    sleep
Am I aroused? . . . What is this glorious sun
That, streaming through the window, gilds my hand?
O breath of morning! Heaven, if 'tis thy will—
If 'tis thy strength that rushes through my veins—
If, as a token of thy power, I feel
This strange, new beating heart within my breast?
Then, should I rise again—again I'd long
To wander out into the world of life:
And wish, and strive, and hope and dare, and do. . .
And do . . . and do . . . !

THE BLUE BIRD.

NATURE STUDY

Since the dawn of human intelligence man has recognized to some degree a relationship existing between himself and nature. This frequently excited fear, and by various means he tried to propitiate forces which might otherwise work him harm. The Indian hunter, proud of his strength, fell down in humble attitude of worship before the stick that tripped him in the forest, regarding with awe the apparent power possessed by so slight an object. Each year the Indians in the vicinity of Niagara offered a young maiden to the spirit of the mighty waters, sending her over the Falls in a light canoe. Three thousand years before this custom was discovered among them, the Egyptians offered a victim yearly to the god of the Nile, hoping thereby to appease Hapi and insure a sufficient overflow to make good crops a certainty throughout the valley. The Greeks were never actuated by fear. It gratified them to feel that their divinities were ever in immediate association with them; salt and libations of wine were offered to them at every meal; they felt the presence of a nymph in each fountain and an unseen deity in every rustling leaf. Conscious of natural beauty as they always were, closely attuned to respond to its various changes, there was no attempt to interpret human life through nature. Man did not seek to reconcile himself with nature— he was identified with it. The classical poets extolled the glory of spring, but this was because the end of winter's damp and chill was welcomed and the farmer could once more break the soil and sow the seed and life start anew— not because spring was in itself regarded as an elixir.

Mythology is a great pæan to nature and yet it is less concerned with her varying moods than with the doings of the gods whose power was thus revealed to men. How important a place nature held among the ancients we realize only when we compare the thousand years before the advent of Christianity with the thousand that immediately succeeded.

The early Christians were concerned only with the spiritual. They fixed their hopes upon a future life, for which this was merely preparatory. All ties that tended to bind them to the earthly existence were viewed in the light of temptations. They renounced the joys of earth as enticements of evil. This feeling survived for centuries and was signally exemplified in the life of St. Bernard of Clairvaux of whom it was related with commendation that he walked all day by the side of a beautiful lake nor once raised his eyes to behold the glorious vision spread out before him.

St. Francis of Assisi did much to restore a love of nature in the hearts of men. He called the birds his little sisters and preached a sermon to them saying it well behooved them to sing the praises of their Creator who cared for them and provided for their maintenance though they toiled not. He tenderly removed the worm from the path lest it be crushed by a careless foot, and exulted in every natural beauty.

During the Renaissance this regard for nature was revived and intensified. The classics were read and Europe reveled in the learning of the ancients. Whatever had been favorably regarded by the Greeks was once more restored to favor. A reaction from the austerity of the Middle Ages set in; troubadours and minnesingers sang of love and dwelt upon the attractions of the garden, the beauties of the meadow, and compared the heroines of their songs to various flowers. Among English poets Chaucer found pleasure in the wonders about him and frequently mentioned his favorite flower, which he called "the day's eye." The rich robes of his ladies were "broidered like a flowery mead." Spenser was observant of nature, and Shakespeare manifested a familiarity with its manifold wonders.

Poets of the sixteenth and seventeenth centuries were primarily interested in man. Nature merely supplied them with similitudes. Figures of speech were borrowed one from another and often voiced the ignorance of the writer. The poet was always the lark; the fair maiden, a rose. If she faded early, she was like the blighted rose; if she wept, like the rose bathed in dew. Prosperity was likened to the rising sun; adversity to the sun receding. The Milky Way served many a turn. Swift satirized some of those trite comparisons:

> "No simile shall be begun
> With *rising* or with *setting* sun.
> No son of mine shall e'er dare say,
> *Aurora ushered-in the day,*
> Or even name the *Milky Way.*"

The eighteenth century witnessed a change in the attitude toward nature. The world was now regarded as beautiful and well worthy of study, but observations concerning it were still superficial. In the nineteenth century the unity between man and nature was thoroughly realized and Wordsworth was conspicuous as an exponent of this new conception.

It is interesting to trace a growing appreciation of mountains. Formerly, because of the danger and difficulty they engendered for travelers, they were disliked. In the Middle Ages the Alps were spoken of as "high and hideous." Even Addison, whose poetry testifies to a love of the night and the star-lit heavens referred to them as "irregular, misshapen scenes." Ruskin was probably the first among Englishmen to call attention to the wonder of the mountains in such a way that people were compelled to listen and observe.

The sea, also, was mentioned ever as a waste, its desolation being emphasized. Wild scenery was repellant to people in the Middle Ages and even to the Greeks and Romans. Winter was mentioned as the "inverted year" and its dreary gloom deplored. Modern facilities for travel and devices for general comfort have done much to free the mind from these earlier conceptions, wherein association played so large a share.

Even today people rarely stop to consider how vitally they are controlled by nature. Not only are the occupations of a region determined in advance for its inhabitants but the temperament of a nation is to quite an extent molded and modified by the natural conditions. Ruskin has considered this at length in his *Mountain Glory* and *Mountain Gloom*. A school of writers may develop characteristically influenced by the general aspect of the land, as the Lake Poets of England, and schools of painters controlled mainly by the appearance of a country, as the Landscape Painters of Holland.

It is significant that three great religions of the world developed among desert peoples. Life under desert skies, where stars shine with exceptional radiance and rocks change in the dawning light or appear as phantoms in the darkness; where man is not sheltered, as in civilization, but stands face to face with the primæval forces of the world—all this produces a mental vision unlike that stimulated elsewhere. Contemplation predominates in the place of activity and "creature comforts" do not impede spiritual expansion.

Life in the country should be the heritage of every child. Here wide spaces and extended views are restful to the sight. The full significance of storms or fair weather is brought home to a degree impossible in cities. The wind bows the grain and grasses; the rain revives a thirsty earth. Snow covers all with a beautiful mantle nor is this at once polluted and made unsightly. The frost and snow convert a forest into fairy land. Only those country-bred can comprehend to the full the poet's thought in the lines:

> "The rain had fallen; the poet arose;
>   He passed by the town and out of the street.
> A light wind blew from the gates of the sun
>   And waves of shadow went over the wheat."

Broad fields of ripening grain tossed into undulating waves, flecked with the shadows of fleeting clouds; swaying barley, nodding grasses, are called to mind by one accustomed to rural scenes.

One hundred years ago America boasted but few cities. Today there is a tendency for people to gather in populous centers. Fewer in proportion have the advantage of country life: the natural life for man. Already those satiated with the artificiality and killing pace of the city are turning back to the country for its restorative powers. The soil possesses healing properties and those who have lost health in the mad rush find themselves restored by contact with it. A certain sanity and mental poise prevail among those accustomed to the ways of nature; the farmer sows his seed and must needs wait calmly for the sun, the rain and dews of heaven to give him a plenteous harvest. The dignity of his life of toil is nowhere shown to better advantage than in Millet's pictures.

Ignorance rather than maliciousness explains the wanton destruction of forests, flora and fauna that has been permitted in the United States. John Muir has labored for many years to bring men into a rational mind regarding the preservation of our forests. Not only has he been compelled to work against the greed of those to whom a tree represents but so much lumber, but against the total indifference with which the great portion of the population have viewed the question. Burroughs has characterized with stinging rebuke those who continue to destroy the birds of the land with misdirected enthusiasm over the collection of them and their eggs—showing conclusively that this work has already been done sufficiently to enable all who wish to study each variety exhaustively. Nor this alone; every year the liquid notes of the meadow lark are jeopardized and only saved for the moment from those who would swell the list for the huntsman.

> "Hast thou named all the birds without a gun,
> Loved the wood-rose and left it on its stalk? . . .
> Then be my friend, and teach me to be thine."

Thoreau knew the flora of his New England region so well that he could tell the hour and the day of the month by the appearance of certain plants. While few are likely to understand them so thoroughly, greater familiarity and love of native plants and flowers would aid greatly in perpetuating species which now threaten to become shortly extinct. The arbutus, so fondly loved by those who have known it well, has already become a memory in regions that could have supplied blossoms each spring for generations had not the entire plant been ruthlessly torn up by those intent upon self-gratification and thoughtless of others to come in quest in future years.

How beautiful was the continent when first visited by discoverers we may know by reading their journals. Columbus joyed in the wonderful birds and flowers, unlike those known in Europe. In their zest to settle the country, little thought was given by colonists to the preservation of its resources nor was it thought these would ever be exhausted. Now, after four hundred years of destruction, societies in different localities are trying to save what remains. Those who know and delight in the haunts of nature are not the ones who destroy; only those unacquainted with the pleasures which communion with her ways and secrets bring are ready to do them harm. Thus the study of nature not only offers more from the æsthetic standpoint than study of all the fine arts, but it has for the present generation a practical aspect and every woodland and hamlet affords opportunity for the nature lover to aid in the protection of natural beauties. When Nature Study Clubs grow as abundant as Browning Societies and organizations for the purpose of directing proper living in its widest sense become as numerous as those for the promotion of good government, parks and national reserves will multiply and the appearance of the country become more gratifying to the citizen and the stranger within the borders.

JOHN MUIR.

John Muir, geologist and naturalist, was born April 21, 1838, in Scotland. He was educated there and in the University of Wisconsin. As a young man, being threatened with blindness, he set out to see the world before this calamity might overtake him. His attention became centered in the natural world and he has become world famed for his discovery of Muir Glacier in Alaska. For many years he has labored for the preservation of American forests, in the interest of which his books and many of his magazine articles have been written.

AMERICAN FORESTS.

The forests of America, however slighted by man, must have been a great delight to God; for they were the best he ever planted. The whole continent was a garden, and from the beginning it seemed to be favored above all the other wild parks and gardens of the globe. To prepare the ground, it was rolled and sifted in seas with infinite loving deliberation and forethought, lifted into the light, submerged and warmed over and over again, pressed and crumpled into folds and ridges, mountains, and hills, subsoiled with heaving volcanic fires, ploughed and ground and sculptured into scenery and soil with glaciers and rivers—every feature growing and changing from beauty to beauty, higher and higher. And in the fullness of time it was planted in groves, and belts, and broad, exuberant, mantling forests, with the largest, most varied, most fruitful, and most beautiful trees in the world. Bright seas made its border, with wave embroidery and ice-bergs; gray deserts were outspread in the middle of it, mossy tundras on the north, savannas on the south, and blooming prairies and plains; while lakes and rivers shone through all the vast forests and openings, and happy birds and beasts gave delightful animation. Everywhere, everywhere over all the blessed continent, there were beauty and melody and kindly, wholesome, foodful abundance.

These forests were composed of about five hundred species of trees, all of them in some way useful to man, ranging in size from twenty-five feet in height and less to one foot in diameter at the ground to four hundred feet in height and more than twenty feet in diameter,—lordly monarchs proclaiming the gospel of beauty like apostles. For many a century after the ice-ploughs were melted, nature fed them and dressed them every day,—working like a man, a loving, devoted, painstaking gardener; fingering every leaf and flower and mossy furrowed bole; bending, trimming, modeling, balancing; painting them with the loveliest colors; bringing over them now clouds with cooling shadows and showers, now sunshine; fanning them with gentle winds and rustling their leaves; exercising them in every fibre with storms, and pruning them; loading them with flowers and fruit, loading them with snow, and ever making them more beautiful as the years rolled by. Wide-branching oak and elm in endless variety, walnut and maple, chestnut and beech, ilex and locust, touching limb to limb, spread a leafy translucent canopy along the coast of the Atlantic over the wrinkled folds and ridges of the Alleghanies,—a green billowy sea in summer, golden and purple in autumn, pearly grey like steadfast, frozen mist of interlacing branches and sprays in leafless, restful winter.

To the southward stretched dark, level-topped cypresses in knobby tangled swamps, grassy savannas in the midst of them like lakes of light, groves of gay, sparkling spice-trees, magnolias and palms, glossy-leaved and blooming and shining continually.   To the northward, over Maine and Ottawa, rose hosts of spiry, rosiny evergreens,—white pine and spruce, hemlock and cedar, shoulder to shoulder, laden with purple cones, their myriad needles sparkling and shimmering, covering hills and swamps, rocky headlands and domes, ever bravely aspiring and seeking the sky; the ground in their shade now snow-clad and frozen, now mossy and flowery; beaver meadows here and there full of lilies and grass; lakes gleaming like eyes, and a silvery embroidery of rivers and creeks watering and brightening all the vast glad wilderness.

Thence westward were oak and elm, hickory and tupelo, gum and liriodendron, sassafras and ash, linden and laurel, spreading on ever wider in glorious exuberance over the great fertile basin of the Mississippi, over damp level bottoms, low dimpling hollows, and round dotting hills, embossing sunny prairies and cheery park openings, half sunshine, half shade; while a dark wilderness of pines covered the region around the Great Lakes.   Thence still westward swept the forests to right and left around grassy plains and deserts a thousand miles wide: irrepressible hosts of spruce and pine, aspen and willow, nut-pine and juniper, cactus and yucca, caring nothing for drought, extending undaunted from mountain to mountain, over mesa and desert, to join the darkening multitudes of glorious forests along the coast of the moist and balmy Pacific, where new species of pine, giant cedars and spruces, silver firs and Sequoias, kings of their race, growing close together like grass in a meadow, poised their brave domes and spires in the sky, three hundred feet above the ferns and lilies that enameled the ground; towering serene through the long centuries, preaching God's forestry fresh from heaven.

Here the forests reached their highest development. Hence they went wavering northward overy icy Alaska, brave spruces and fir, poplar and birch, by the coasts and the rivers, to within sight of the Arctic Ocean.   American forests! the glory of the world! Surveyed thus from the east to the west, from the north to the south, they are rich beyond thought, immortal, immeasurable, enough and to spare for every feeding, sheltering beast and bird, insect and son of Adam;   and nobody need have cared had there been no pines in Norway, no cedars and deodars on Lebanon and the Himalayas, no vine-clad selvas in the basin of the Amazon. With such variety, harmony and triumphant exuberance, even nature, it would seem, might have rested content with the forests of North America, and planted no more.

So they appeared a few centuries ago when they were rejoicing in wildness. The Indians with stone axes could do them no more harm than could gnawing beavers and browsing moose. Even the fires of the Indians and the fierce shattering lightning seemed to work together only for good in clearing spots here and there for smooth garden prairies, and openings for sunflowers seeking the light. But when the steel axe of the white man rang out on the startled air their doom was sealed. Every tree heard the bodeful sound, and pillars of smoke gave the sign in the sky.

I suppose we need not go mourning the buffaloes. In the nature of things they had to give place to better cattle, though the change might have been made without barbarous wickedness. Likewise many of nature's five hundred kinds of wild trees had to make way for orchards and cornfields. In the settlement and civilization of the country, bread more than timber or beauty was wanted; and in the blindness of hunger, the early settlers, claiming Heaven as their guide, regarded God's trees as only a larger kind of pernicious weeds, extremely hard to get rid of. Accordingly, with no eye to the future, their pious destroyers waged interminable forest wars; chips flew thick and fast; trees in their beauty fell crashing by millions, smashed to confusion, and the smoke of their burning has been rising to heaven more than two hundred years. After the Atlantic coast from Maine to Georgia had been mostly cleared and scorched into melancholy ruins, the overflowing multitude of bread and money seekers poured over the Alleghanies into the fertile middle West, spreading ruthless devastation ever wider and farther over the rich valley of the Mississippi and the vast shadowy pine region about the Great Lakes. Thence still westward, the invading horde of destroyers called settlers made its fiery way over the broad Rocky Mountains, felling and burning more fiercely than ever, until at last it has reached the wild side of the

VII—26

continent, and entered the last of the great aboriginal forests on the shores of the Pacific.

Surely, then, it should not be wondered at that lovers of their country, bewailing its baldness, are now crying aloud: "Save what is left of the forests!" Clearing has surely now gone far enough; soon timber will be scarce, and not a grove will be left to rest in or pray in. The remnant protected will yield plenty of timber, a perennial harvest for every right use, without further diminution of its area, and will continue to cover the springs of the rivers that rise in the mountains and give irrigating waters to the dry valleys at their feet, prevent wasting floods, and be a blessing to everybody forever.

FOUNTAINS AND STREAMS OF THE YOSEMITE.

The joyful, songful streams of the Sierra are among the most famous and interesting in the world, and draw the admiring traveler on and on through their wonderful cañons, year after year, unwearied. After long wanderings with them, tracing them to their fountains, learning their history and the forms they take in their wild works and ways throughout the different seasons of the year, we may then view them together in one magnificent show, outspread over all the range like embroidery, their silvery branches interlacing on a thousand mountains, singing their way home to the sea: the small rills, with hard roads to travel, dropping from ledge to ledge, pool to pool, like chains of sweet-toned bells, slipping gently over beds of pebbles and sand, resting in lakes, shining, spangling, shimmering, lapping the shores with whispering ripples, and shaking over-leaning bushes and grass; the larger streams and rivers in the cañons displaying noble purity and beauty with ungovernable energy, rushing down smooth inclines in wide foamy sheets fold over fold, springing up here and there in magnificent whirls, scattering crisp clashing spray for the sunbeams to iris, bursting with hoarse reverberating roar through rugged gorges and boulder dams, booming in falls, gliding, glancing with cool soothing murmuring, through long forested reaches richly embowered,—filling the grand cañons with glorious song, and giving life to all the landscape.

The present rivers of the Sierra are still young, and have made but little mark as yet on the grand cañons prepared for them by the ancient glaciers. Only a very short geological time ago they all lay buried beneath the glaciers they drained, singing in low smothered or silvery ringing tones in crystal channels, while the summer weather melted the ice and snow of the surface or gave showers. At first only in warm weather was any part of these buried rivers displayed in the . light of day; for as soon as frost prevailed the surface rills vanished, though the streams beneath the ice and in the body of it flowed on all the year. When, toward the close of the glacial period, the ice mantle began to shrink and recede from the lowlands, the lower portions of the rivers were developed, issuing from cavelike openings on the melting margin and growing longer as the ice withdrew; while for many a century the tributaries and upper portions of the trunks remained covered. In the fullness of time these also were set free in the sunshine, to take their places in the newborn landscapes; each tributary with its smaller branches being gradually developed like the main trunks, as the climatic changes went on. At first all of them were muddy with glacial detritus, and they became clear only after the glaciers they drained had receded beyond lake basins in which the sediments were dropped.

This early history is clearly explained by the present rivers of southeastern Alaska. Of those draining glaciers that discharge into arms of the sea, only the rills on the surface of the ice, and upboiling, eddying, turbid currents in the tide water in front of the terminal ice wall are visible. Where glaciers, in the first stage of decadence, have receded from the shore, short sections of the trunks of the rivers that are to take their places may be seen rushing out from caverns and tunnels in the melting front,—rough, roaring, detritus-laden torrents, foaming and stumbling over outspread terminal moraines to the sea, perhaps without a single bush or flower to brighten their raw, shifting banks. Again, in some of the warmer cañons and valleys from which the trunk glaciers have been melted, the main trunks of the rivers are well developed, and their banks planted with fine forests, while their upper branches, lying high on the snowy mountains, are still

buried beneath shrinking residual glaciers; illustrating every
stage of development, from icy darkness to light, and from
muddiness to crystal clearness.

Now that the hard grinding sculpture work of the glacial
period is done, the whole bright band of Sierra rivers run
clear all the year, except when the snow is melting fast in
the warm spring weather, and during extraordinary winter
floods and the heavy thunderstorms of summer, called cloud-
bursts. Even then they are not muddy above the foothill
mining region, unless the moraines have been loosened and
the vegetation destroyed by sheep; for the rocks of the upper
basins are clean, and the most able streams find but little to
carry save the spoils of the forests—trees, branches, flakes
of bark, cones, leaves, pollen dust, etc.,—with scales of mica,
sand grains, and boulders, which are rolled along the bottom
of the steep parts of the main channels. Short sections of a
few of the highest tributaries heading in glaciers are of course
turbid with finely ground rock mud, but this is dropped in
the first lakes they enter.

On the northern part of the range, mantled with porous
fissured volcanic rocks, the fountain waters sink and flow
below the surface for considerable distances, groping their
way in the dark like the draining streams of glaciers, and
at last bursting forth in big generous springs, filtered and
cool and exquisitely clear. Some of the largest look like
lakes, their waters welling straight up from the bottom of
deep rock basins in quiet massive volume giving rise to young
rivers. Others issue from horizontal clefts in sheer bluffs,
with loud tumultuous roaring that may be heard half a mile
or more. Magnificent examples of these great northern spring
fountains, twenty or thirty feet deep and ten to nearly a
hundred yards wide, abound on the main branches of the
Feather, Pitt, McCloud, and Fall rivers.

The springs of the Yosemite Park, and the high Sierra
in general, though many times more numerous, are comparatively small, oozing from moraines and snowbanks in thin,
flat, irregular currents which remain on the surface or near it,
the rocks of the south half of the range being mostly flawless
impervious granite; and since granite is but slightly soluble,
the streams are particularly pure. Nevertheless, though they

are all clear, and in the upper and main central forest regions delightfully lively and cool, they vary somewhat in color and taste as well as temperature, on account of differences, however slight, in exposure, and in the rocks and vegetation with which they come in contact. Some are more exposed than others to winds and sunshine in their falls and thin plume-like cascades; the amount of dashing, mixing, and airing the waters of each receive varies considerably; and there is always more or less variety in the kind and quality of the vegetation they flow through, and in time they lie in shady or sunny lakes and bogs. . . .

Excepting a few low, warm slopes, fountain snow usually covers all the Yosemite Park from November or December to May, most of it until June or July, while on the coolest parts of the north slopes of the mountains, at a height of eleven to thirteen thousand feet, it is perpetual. It seldom lies at a greater depth than two or three feet on the lower margin, ten feet over the middle forested region, or fifteen to twenty feet in the shadowy cañons and cirques among the peaks of the summit, except where it is drifted, or piled in avalanche heaps at the foot of long converging slopes to form perennial fountains.

The first crop of snow crystals that whitens the mountains and refreshes the streams usually falls in September or October, in the midst of charming Indian summer weather, often while the golden-rods and gentians are in their prime; but these Indian summer snows, like some of the late ones that bury the June gardens, vanish in a day or two, and garden work goes on with accelerated speed. The grand winter storms that load the mountains with enduring fountain snow seldom set in before the end of November. The fertile clouds, descending, glide about and hover in brooding silence, as if thoughtfully examining the forests and streams with reference to the work before them; then small flakes or single crystals appear, glinting and swirling in zigzags and spirals; and soon the thronging feathery masses fill the sky and make darkness like night, hurrying wandering mountaineers to their winter quarters. The first fall is usually about two to four feet. Then, with intervals of bright weather, not very cold, storm succeeds storm, heaping snow on snow, until from thirty to fifty or sixty feet has fallen; but on account of heavy settling and compacting, and the waste from evaporation and melting, the depth in the middle region rarely exceeds ten feet. Evaporation never wholly ceases, even in the coldest weather, and the sunshine between storms melts the surface more or less. Waste from melting also goes on at the bottom from summer heat stored in the rocks, as shown by the rise of the streams after the first general storm, and their steady, sustained flow all winter. . . .

In the spring, after all the avalanches are down and the snow is melting fast, it is glorious to hear the streams sing out on the mountains. Every fountain swelling, countless rills hurry together to the rivers at the call of the sun,—beginning to run and sing soon after sunrise, increasing until toward sundown, then gradually failing through the cold frosty hours of the night. Thus the volume of the upper rivers, even in flood time, is nearly doubled during the day, rising and falling as regularly as the tides of the sea. At the height of flood, in the warmest June weather, they seem fairly to shout for joy, and clash their upleaping waters together like clapping of hands; racing down the cañons with white manes flying in glorious exuberance of strength, compelling huge speaking boulders to wake up and join in the dance and song to swell their chorus.

Then the plants also are in flood; the hidden sap singing into leaf and flower, responding as faithfully to the call of the sun as the streams from the snow, gathering along the outspread roots like rills in their channels on the mountains, rushing up the stems of herb and tree, swirling in their myriad cells like streams in potholes, spreading along the branches and breaking into foamy bloom, while fragrance, like a finer music, rises and flows with the winds.

About the same may be said of the spring gladness of blood when the red streams surge and sing in accord with the swelling plants and rivers, inclining animals and everybody to travel in hurrahing crowds like floods, while exhilarating melody in color and fragrance, form and motion, flows to the heart through all the quickening senses.

In early summer the streams are in bright prime, running crystal clear, deep and full, but not overflowing their banks,—

about as deep through the night as the day, the variation so marked in spring being now too slight to be ——ed. Nearly all the weather is cloudless sunshine, and everything is at its brightest, lake, river, garden, and forest, with all their warm, throbbing life. Most of the plants are in full leaf and flower; the blessed ousels have built their mossy huts, and are now singing their sweetest songs on spray-sprinkled ledges beside the waterfalls.

In tranquil, mellow autumn, when the year's work is about done, when the fruits are ripe, birds and ——ts out of their nests, and all the landscape is glowing like a benevolent countenance at rest, then the streams are at their lowest ebb,— their wild rejoicing soothed to thoughtful calm. All the smaller tributaries whose branches do not reach back to the perennial fountains of the summit peaks shrink to whispering, tinkling currents. The snow of their ——, they are now fed ——

RUINS OF KENILWORTH CASTLE.

DURING the Middle Ages, when the peace and order of localities depended largely upon the aggressive action of knights, castles dotted the country—each being a seat of authority, a military center and a fortress. After comparative tranquility had settled over the land, the great lords continued to dwell in the castles, which gradually lost their significance as fortresses. Kenilworth has been made famous by Scott's well-known story, interesting especially in connection with the picture.

in mountain —— of their ——. —— are by no means in proportion to the height and extent of mountains. There are —— summit claims as high or higher than the Alps, which —— few and ——; if, indeed, they have any. In the Andes, the Rocky Mountains, the Pyrenees, the ——, the few glaciers —— from the great ice period are —— to the ——. The volcanic, cone-like shapes of the Andes give —— little chance for the formation of glaciers, though their summits are capped with snow. The glaciers of the Rocky Mountains have been little explored, but it is known that they are by no means extensive. In the Pyrenees there is —— glacier, though the height of their summits is ——

about as deep through the night as the day, the variation so marked in spring being now too slight to be noticed. Nearly all the weather is cloudless sunshine, and everything is at its brightest, lake, river, garden, and forest, with all their warm, throbbing life. Most of the plants are in full leaf and flower; the blessed ousels have built their mossy huts, and are now singing their sweetest songs on spray-sprinkled ledges beside the waterfalls.

In tranquil, mellow autumn, when the year's work is about done, when the fruits are ripe, birds and seeds out of their nests, and all the landscape is glowing like a benevolent countenance at rest, then the streams are at their lowest ebb,— their wild rejoicing soothed to thoughtful calm. All the smaller tributaries whose branches do not reach back to the perennial fountains of the summit peaks shrink to whispering, tinkling currents. The snow of their basins gone, they are now fed only by small moraine springs, whose waters are mostly evaporated in passing over warm pavements, and in feeling their way from pool to pool through the midst of boulders and sand. Even the main streams are so low they may be easily forded, and their grand falls and cascades, now gentle and approachable, have waned to sheets and webs of embroidery, falling fold over fold in new and ever changing beauty.

GLACIERS.

The first essential condition for the formation of glaciers in mountain ranges is the shape of their valleys. Glaciers are by no means in proportion to the height and extent of mountains. There are many mountain chains as high or higher than the Alps, which can boast of but few and small glaciers, if, indeed, they have any In the Andes, the Rocky Mountains, the Pyrenees, the Caucasus, the few glaciers remaining from the great ice period are insignificant in size. The volcanic, cone-like shape of the Andes gives indeed but little chance for the formation of glaciers, though their summits are capped with snow. The glaciers of the Rocky Mountains have been little explored, but it is known that they are by no means extensive. In the Pyrenees there is but one great glacier, though the height of these mountains is such that,

were the shape of their valleys favorable to the accumulation
of snow, they might present beautiful glaciers. In the Tyrol,
on the contrary, as well as in Norway and Sweden, we find
glaciers almost as fine as those of Switzerland, in mountain
ranges much lower than either of the above-named chains.
But they are of diversified forms, and have valleys widening
upward on the slope of long crests. The glaciers on the
Caucasus are very small in proportion to the height of the
range; but on the northern side of the Himalaya there are
large and beautiful ones, while the southern slope is almost
destitute of them. Spitzenberg and Greenland are famous
for their extensive glaciers, coming down to the seashore,
where huge masses of ice, many hundred feet in thickness,
break off and float away into the ocean as icebergs. At the
Aletsch in Switzerland, where a little lake lies in a deep cup
between the mountains with the glacier coming down to its
brink, we have these Arctic phenomena on a small scale; a
miniature iceberg may often be seen to break off from the
edge of the larger mass, and float out upon the surface of the
water. Icebergs were first the ice-land of which they are
always composed, and which is quite distinct in structure and
consistency from the marine ice produced by frozen sea water,
and called "ice-flow" by the Arctic explorers, as well as from
the pond or river ice, resulting from the simple congelation
of fresh water, the laminated structure of which is in striking
contrast to the granular structure of glacier ice.

Water is changed to ice at a certain temperature under
the same law of crystallization by which inorganic bodies in
a fluid state may assume a solid condition, taking the shape
of perfectly regular crystals, which combine at certain angles
with mathematical precision. The frost does not form a solid,
continuous sheet of ice over an expanse of water, but produces
crystals, little ice-blades as it were, which shoot into each other
at angles of thirty or sixty degrees, forming the closest network. Of course, under the process of alternate freezing and
thawing, these crystals lose their regularity, and soon become
merged into each other. But even then a mass of ice is not
continuous or compact throughout, for it is rendered completely porous by air-bubbles, the presence of which is easily
explained. Ice being in a measure transparent to heat, the

water below any frozen surface is nearly as susceptible to the elevation of the temperature without as if it were in immediate contact with it. Such changes of temperature produce air-bubbles, which float upward against the lower surface of the ice and are stranded there. At night there may come a severe frost; new ice is then formed below the air-bubbles, and they are thus caught and imprisoned, a layer of air-bubbles between two layers of ice, and this process may be continued until we have a succession of such parallel layers, forming a body of ice more or less permeated with air. These air-bubbles have the power also of extending their own area, and thus rendering the whole mass still more porous; for, since the ice offers little or no obstacle to the passage of heat, such an air-bubble may easily become heated during the day; the moment it reaches a temperature above thirty-two degrees, it melts the ice around it, thus clearing a little space for itself, and rises through the water produced by the action of its own warmth. The spaces so formed are so many vertical tubes in the ice, filled with water, and having an air-bubble at the upper extremity. . . .

Land-ice, of which both the ice fields of the Arctics and the glaciers consist, is produced by the slow and gradual trans-formation of snow into ice; and though the ice thus formed may eventually be as clear and transparent as the purest pond- or river-ice, its structure is nevertheless entirely distinct. We may compare these different processes during any mod-erately cold winter in the ponds and snow-meadows immedi-ately about us. We need not join an Arctic exploring expedi-tion, nor even undertake a more tempting trip to the Alps, in order to investigate these phenomena for ourselves, if we have any curiosity to do so. The first warm day after a thick fall of light, dry snow, such as occurs in the coldest of our winter weather, is sufficient to melt its surface. As this snow is porous, the water readily penetrates it, having also a ten-dency to sink by its own weight, so that the whole mass becomes more or less filled with moisture in the course of the day. During the lower temperature of the night, however, the water is frozen again, and the snow is now filled with new ice-particles. Let this process be continued long enough, and the mass of snow is changed to a kind of ice-gravel, or, if the grains adhere together, to something like what we call pudding-stone, allowing, of course, for the difference of material; the snow, which has been rendered cohesive by the process of partial melting and regelation, holding the ice globules to-gether, just as the loose materials of the pudding-stone are held together by the cement which unites them.

Within this mass, air is intercepted and held enclosed between particles of ice. The process by which snowflakes or snow-crystals are transformed into grains of ice, more or less compact, is easily understood. It is the result of a partial thawing, under a temperature maintained very nearly at thirty-two degrees, falling sometimes a little below, and then rising a little above the freezing point, and thus producing constant alternations of freezing and thawing in the same mass of snow. This process amounts to a kind of kneading of the snow, and when combined with the cohesion among the par-ticles more closely held together in one snowflake, it produces granular ice. Of course, the change takes place gradually, and is unequal in its progress at different depths in the same bed of recently fallen snow. It depends greatly on the amount of moisture infiltrating the mass, whether derived from the melting of its own surface, or from the accumulation of dew or the falling of rain or mist upon it. The amount of water retained within the mass will also be greatly affected by the bottom on which it rests and by the state of the atmosphere. Under a certain temperature, the snow may only be glazed at the surface by the formation of a thin, icy crust, an outer membrane as it were, protecting the mass below from a deeper transformation into ice; or it may be rapidly soaked through-out its whole bulk, the snow being thus changed into a kind of soft pulp, what we commonly call slosh, which, upon freez-ing, becomes at once compact ice; or, the water sinking rapidly, the lower layers only may be soaked, while the upper portion remains comparatively dry. Under all these various circumstances, frost will transform the crystalline snow into more or less compact ice, the mass of which will be composed of an infinite number of aggregated snow particles, very unequal in regularity of outline, and cemented by ice of another kind, derived from the freezing of the infiltrated moisture, the whole being interspersed with air. Let the temperature rise, and such a mass, rigid before, will resolve itself again into disconnected ice particles, like grains more or less rounded. The process may be repeated till the whole mass is transformed into very compact, almost uniformly transparent and blue ice, broken only by the intervening air-bubbles. Such a mass of ice, when exposed to a temperature sufficiently high to dissolve it, does not melt from the surface and disappear by a gradual diminution of its bulk like pond-ice, but crumbles into its original granular fragments, each one of which melts separately. This accounts for the sudden disappearance of icebergs, which, instead of slowly dissolving into the ocean, are often seen to fall to pieces and vanish at once.

Ice of this kind may be seen forming every winter on our sidewalks, on the edge of the little ditches which drain them, or on the summits of broad gate-posts when capped with snow. Of such ice glaciers are composed; but, in the glacier, another element comes in which we have not considered as yet—that of immense pressure in consequence of the vast accumulations of snow within circumscribed spaces. We see the same effects, produced on a small scale, when snow is transformed into a snowball between the hands. Every boy who balls a mass of snow in his hands illustrates one side of a glacial phenomenon. Loose snow, light and porous, and pure white from the amount of air contained in it, is in this way presently converted into hard, compact, almost transparent ice. This change will take place sooner if the snow be damp at first, but if dry, the action of the hand will presently produce moisture enough to complete the process. In this case, mere pressure produces the same effect which, in the cases we have been considering above, was brought about by alternate thawing and freezing, only that in the latter the ice is distinctly granular, instead of being uniform throughout, as when formed under pressure. In the glaciers we have the two processes combined. The investigators of glacial phenomena have considered too exclusively one or the other: some of them attributing glacial motion wholly to the dilation produced by the freezing of infiltrated moisture in the mass of snow; others accounting for it entirely by weight and pressure. There is yet a third class, who, disregarding the real properties of ice, would have us believe that because tar, for instance,

is viscid when it moves, therefore ice is viscid because it
moves. . . .

Thus far we have examined chiefly the internal structure
of the glacier; let us look now at its external appearance, and
at the variety of curious phenomena connected with the deposit
of foreign materials upon its surface, some of which seem
quite inexplicable at first sight. Among the most striking
of these are the large boulders elevated on columns of ice,
standing sometimes ten feet or more above the level of the
glacier, and the sand pyramids, those conical hills of sand
which occur not infrequently on the larger Alpine glaciers.
One is at first quite at a loss to explain the presence of these
pyramids in the midst of a frozen ice-field, and yet it has a
very simple cause.

I have spoken of the many little rills arising on the surface
of the ice in consequence of its melting. Indeed, the voice
of the waters is rarely still during the warm season on a
glacier, except at night. On a summer's day, a thousand
streams are born before noontide, and die again at sunset;
it is no uncommon thing to see a full cascade come rushing
out from the lower end of a glacier during the heat of the
day, and vanish again at its decline. Suppose one of these
rivulets should fall into a deep, circular hole, such as often
occur on the glacier, and the nature of which I shall presently
explain, and that this cylindrical opening narrows to a mere
crack at a greater or less depth within the ice, the water will
find its way through the crack and filter down into the deeper
mass; but the dust and sand carried along with it will be
caught there, and form a deposit at the bottom of the hole.
As day after day, throughout the summer, the rivulet is
renewed, it carries with it an additional supply of these light
materials, until the opening is gradually filled and the sand
is brought to a level with the surface of the ice. We have
already seen that, in consequence of evaporation, melting, and
other disintegrating causes, the level of the glacier sinks
annually at the rate of from five to ten feet, according to
stations. The natural consequence must be, that the sand is
left standing above the surface of the ice, forming a mound
which would constantly increase in height in proportion to the
sinking of the surrounding ice, had it sufficient solidity to

retain its original position. But a heap of sand, if unsupported, must very soon subside and be dispersed; and, indeed, these pyramids, which are often quite lofty and yet look as if they would crumble at a touch, prove, on nearer examination, to be perfectly solid, and are, in fact, pyramids of ice with a thin sheet of sand spread over them. A word will explain how this transformation is brought about. As soon as the level of the glacier falls below the sand, thus depriving it of support, it sinks down and spreads slightly over the surrounding surface. In this condition it protects the ice immediately beneath it from the action of the sun. In proportion as the glacier wastes, this protected area rises above the general mass and becomes detached from it. The sand, of course, slides down over it, spreading toward its base, so as to cover a wider space below, and an ever narrowing one above, until it gradually assumes the pyramidal form in which we find it, covered with a thin coating of sand. Every stage of this process may occasionally be seen upon the same glacier, in a number of sand piles raised to various heights above the surface of the ice, approaching the perfect pyramidal form, or falling to pieces after standing for a short time erect.

The phenomenon of the large boulders, supported on tall pillars of ice, is of a similar character. A mass of rock, having fallen on the surface of the glacier, protects the ice immediately beneath it from the action of the sun; and as the level of the glacier sinks all around it, in consequence of the unceasing waste of the surface, the rock is gradually left standing on an ice-pillar of considerable height. In proportion as the column rises, however, the rays of the sun reach its sides, striking obliquely upon them under the boulder and wearing them away, until the column becomes at last too slight to sustain its burden and the rock falls again upon the glacier; or, owing to the unequal action of the sun, striking of course with most power on the southern side, the top of the pillar becomes slanting and the boulder slides off. These ice-pillars, crowned with masses of rock, form a very picturesque feature in the scenery of the glacier, and are represented in many of the landscapes in which Swiss artists have endeavored to reproduce the grandeur and variety of Alpine views, especially in the masterly Aquarelles of Lory. The English reader will find them admirably described and illustrated in Dr. Tyndall's work upon the glaciers. They are known throughout the Alps as "glacier-tables." Many a time my fellow travelers and I have spread our frugal meal on such a table, erected, as it seemed, especially for our convenience.

Another curious effect is that produced by small stones or pebbles, small enough to become heated through by the sun in summer. Such a heated pebble will of course melt the ice below it, and so wear a hole for itself into which it sinks. This process will continue as long as the sun reaches the pebble with force enough to heat it. Numbers of such deep, round holes, like organ-pipes, varying in size from the diameter of a minute pebble or a grain of coarse sand to that of an ordinary stone, are found on the glacier, and at the bottom of each is the pebble by which it was bored. The ice formed by the freezing of water collecting in such holes and in the fissures of the surface is a pure crystallized ice, very different in color from the ice of the great mass of the glacier produced by snow; and sometimes, after a rain and frost, the surface of a glacier looks like a mosaic-work, in consequence of such veins and cylinders or spots of clear ice with which it is inlaid.

Indeed, the aspect of a glacier changes constantly with the different conditions of the temperature. We may see it in the early dawn, before the new ice of the preceding night begins to yield to the action of the sun, and then the surface of the glacier is veined and inlaid with the water poured into its holes and fissures during the day and transformed into pure fresh ice during the night; or we may see it when the noonday heat has wakened all its streams, and rivulets sometimes as large as rivers rush along its surface, find their way to the lower extremity of the glacier, or, dashing down some gaping crevasse or open well, are lost beneath the ice. We may see it when, during a long dry season, it has collected upon its surface all sorts of light floating materials, as dust, sand, and the like, so that it looks dull and soiled, or when a heavy rain has washed the surface clean from all impurities and left it bright and fresh. We may see it when the heat and other disintegrating influences have acted upon the ice to a certain superficial depth, so that its surface is covered with a decomposed crust of broken, snowy ice, so permeated with air that it has a dead-white color, like pounded ice or glass. Those who see the glacier in this state miss the blue tint so often described as characteristic of its appearance in its lower portion, and as giving such a peculiar beauty to its caverns and walls. Let them come again after a summer storm has swept away this loose sheet of broken, snowy ice above, and before the same process has had time to renew it, and they will find the compact, solid surface of the glacier of as pure a blue as if it reflected the sky above. —*Russell*.

A Good Word for Winter.

The love of Nature in and for herself, or as a mirror for the moods of the mind, is a modern thing. The fleeing to her as an escape from man was brought into fashion by Rousseau; for his prototype Petrarch, though he had a taste for pretty scenery, had a true antique horror for the grander aspects of nature. He got once to the top of Mont Ventoux, but it is very plain that he did not enjoy it. Indeed, it is only within a century or so that the search after the picturesque has been a safe employment. It is not so even now in Greece or Southern Italy. Where the Anglo-Saxon carves his cold fowl, and leaves the relics of his picnic, the ancient or mediæval man might be pretty confident that some ruffian would try the edge of his knife on a chicken of the Platonic sort, and leave more precious bones as an offering to the genius of the place. The ancients were certainly more social than we, though that, perhaps, was natural enough, when a good part of the world was still covered with forest. They huddled together in cities as well for safety as to keep their minds warm. The Romans had a fondness for country life, but they had fine roads, and Rome was always within easy reach. The author of the Book of Job is the earliest I know of who showed any profound sense of the moral meaning of the outward world; and I think none has approached him since, though Wordsworth comes nearest with the first two books of the "Prelude." But their feeling is not precisely of the kind I speak of as modern, and which gave rise to what is called descriptive poetry. Chaucer opens his Clerk's Tale with

a bit of landscape admirable for its large style, and as well
composed as any Claude.

"There is right at the west end of Itaille,
    Down at the root of Vesulus the cold,
A lusty plain abundant of vitaille,
    Where many a tower and town thou mayest behold,
    That founded were in time of fathers old,
    And many another delectable sight;
    And Saluces this noble country hight."

What an airy precision of touch there is here, and what a
sure eye for the points of character in landscape! But the
picture is altogether subsidiary. No doubt the works of
Salvator Rosa and Gaspar Poussin show that there must have
been some amateur taste for the grand and terrible in scenery;
but the British poet Thomson ("sweet-souled" is Wordsworth's
apt word) was the first to do with words what they had done
partially with colors. He was turgid, no good metrist, and
his English is like a translation from one of those poets who
wrote in Latin after it was dead; but he was a man of sincere
genius and not only English but European literature is largely
in his debt. He was the inventor of cheap amusement for
the million, to be had of all outdoors for the asking. It was
his impulse which unconsciously gave direction to Rousseau,
and it is to the school of Jean Jacques that we owe St. Pierre,
Cowper, Chateaubriand, Wordsworth, Byron, Lamartine,
George Sand, Ruskin—the great painters of ideal landscape.

So long as men had slender means, whether of keeping
out cold or checkmating it with artificial heat, Winter was an
unwelcome guest, especially in the country. There he was
the bearer of a *lettre de cachet,* which shuts its victims in
solitary confinement with few resources but to boose round
the fire and repeat ghost-stories, which had lost all their freshness and none of their terror. To go to bed was to lie awake
of cold, with an added shudder of fright whenever a loose
casement or a waving curtain chose to give you the goose-
flesh. Bussy Rabutin, in one of his letters, gives us a notion
how uncomfortable it was in the country, with green wood,
smoky chimneys, and doors and windows that thought it was
their duty to make the wind whistle, not to keep it out. With
fuel so dear, it could not have been much better in the city,

to judge by Menage's warning against the danger of our dressing-gowns taking fire, while we cuddle too closely over the sparing blaze. The poet of Winter himself is said to have written in bed, with his hand through a hole in the blanket; and we may suspect that it was the warmth quite as much as the company that first drew men together at the coffee-house. Coleridge, in January, 1800, writes to Wedgewood: "I am sitting by the fire in a rug great-coat. . . . It is most barbarously cold, and you, I fear, can shield yourself from it only by perpetual imprisonment." This thermometrical view of winter is, I grant, a depressing one; for I think there is nothing so demoralizing as cold. I know a boy who, when his father, a bitter economist, was brought home dead, said only, "Now we can burn as much wood as we like." I would not off-hand prophesy the gallows for that boy. I remember with a shudder a pinch I got from the cold once in a railroad-car. A born fanatic of fresh air, I found myself glad to see the windows hermetically sealed by the freezing vapor of our breath, and plotted the assassination of the conductor every time he opened the door. I felt myself sensibly barbarizing, and would have shared Colonel Jack's bed in the ash-hole of the glass-furnace with a grateful heart. Since then I have had more charity for the prevailing ill-opinion of winter. It was natural enough that Ovid should measure the years of his exile in Pontus by the number of winters.

> "Ut sumus in Ponto, ter frigore constitit Ister,
> Facta est Euxini dura ter unda maris:'"

> "Thrice hath the cold bound Ister fast, since I
> In Pontus was, thrice Euxine's wave made hard."

Jubinal has printed an Anglo-Norman piece of doggerel in which Winter and Summer dispute which is the better man. It is not without a kind of rough and inchoate humor, and I like it because old Whitebeard gets tolerably fair play. The jolly old fellow boasts of his rate of living with that contempt of poverty which is the weak spot in the burly English nature.

> "Now God forbid it hap to me
> That I make not more great display,
> And spend more in a single day
> Than you can do in all your life."

The best touch, perhaps, is Winter's claim for credit as a mender of the highways, which was not without point when every road in Europe was a quagmire during a good part of the year, unless it was bottomed on some remains of Roman engineering.

> "Master and lord I am, says he,
> And of good right so ought to be,
> Since I make causeways, safely crost,
> Of mud, with just a pinch of frost."

But there is no recognition of Winter as the best outdoor company. Even Emerson, an open-air man, and a bringer of it, if ever any, confesses,

> "The frost-king ties my fumbling feet,
> Sings in my ear, my hands are stones,
> Curdles the blood to the marble bones,
> Tugs at the heartstrings, numbs the sense,
> And hems in life with narrowing fence."

Winter was literally the "inverted year," as Thomson called him; for such entertainments as could be had must be got within doors. What cheerfulness there was in verse was that of Horace's *dissolve frigus ligna super foco large reponens*, so pleasantly associated with the cleverest scene in Roderick Random. This is the tone of that poem of Walton's friend Cotton, which won the praise of Wordsworth:

> "Let us home,
> Our mortal enemy is come;
> Winter and all his blustering train
> Have made a voyage o'er the main.
>
> .   .   .   .   .
>
> "Fly, fly, the foe advances fast;
> Into our fortress let us haste,
> Where all the roarers of the north
> Can neither storm nor starve us forth.
>
> "There underground a magazine
> Of sovereign juice is cellared in,

Liquor that will the siege maintain
Should Phœbus ne'er return again.

. . . . . .

"Whilst we together jovial sit
Careless, and crowned with mirth and wit,
Where, though belak winds confine us home,
Our fancies round the world shall roam," etc.

Thomson's view of winter is also, on the whole, a hostile
one, though he does justice to his grandeur.

"Thus Winter falls,
A heavy gloom oppressive o'er the world,
Through Nature shedding influence malign."

He finds his consolations, like Cotton, in the house, though
more refined:

"While without
The ceaseless winds blow ice, be my retreat
Between the groaning forest and by the shore
Beat by the boundless multitude of waves,
A rural, sheltered, solitary scene,
Where ruddy fire and beaming tapers join
To cheer the gloom. There studious let me sit
And hold high converse with the mighty dead."

Doctor Akenside, a man to be spoken of with respect,
follows Thomson. With him, too, "Winter desolates the
year," and

"How pleasing wears the wintry night
Spent with the old illustrious dead!
While by the taper's trembling light
I seem those awful scenes to tread
Where chiefs or legislators lie."

Akenside had evidently been reading Thomson. He had
the conceptions of a great poet with less faculty than many a
little one, and is one of those versifiers of whom it is enough
to say that we are always willing to break him off in the
middle with an etc., well knowing that what follows is but
the coming-round again of what went before, marching in a
circle with the cheap numerosity of a stage-army. In truth,
it is no wonder that the short days of that cloudy northern
climate should have added to winter a gloom borrowed of the

mind. We hardly know, till we have experienced the contrast, how sensibly our winter is alleviated by the longer daylight and the pellucid atmosphere. I once spent a winter in Dresden, a southern climate compared with England, and really almost lost my respect for the sun when I saw him groping among the chimney-pots opposite my windows as he described his impoverished arc in the sky. The enforced seclusion of the season makes it the time for serious study and occupations that demand fixed incomes of unbroken time. This is why Milton said "that his vein never happily flowed but from the autumnal equinox to the vernal," though in his twentieth year he had written, on the return of spring:

> "Err I? Or do the powers of song return
> To me, ard genius, too, the gifts of Spring?"

Goethe, so far as I can remember, was the first to notice the cheerfulness of snow in sunshine. His *Harz-reisse im Winter* gives no hint of it, for that is a diluted reminiscence of Greek tragic choruses and the Book of Job in nearly equal parts. In one of the singularly interesting and characteristic letters to Frau von Stein, however, written during the journey, he says: "It is beautiful, indeed; the mist heaps itself together in light snow-clouds, the sun looks through, and the snow over everything gives back a feeling of gayety." But I find in Cowper the first recognition of a general amiability in winter. The gentleness of his temper, and the wide charity of his sympathies, made it natural for him to find good in everything except the human heart. A dreadful creed distilled from the darkest moments of dyspeptic solitaries compelled him against his will to see in *that* the one evil thing made by a God whose goodness is over all his works. Cowper's two walks in the morning and noon of a winter's day are delightful, so long as he contrives to let himself be happy in the graciousness of the landscape. Your muscles grow springy, and your lungs dilate with the crisp air as you walk along with him. You laugh with him at the grotesque shadow of your legs lengthened across the snow by the just-risen sun. I know nothing that gives a purer feeling of outdoor exhilaration than the easy verses of this escaped hypochondriac. But Cowper also preferred his sheltered garden-walk to those robuster joys, and bitterly acknowledged the depressing influence of the darkened year. . . .

The preludings of winter are as beautiful as those of spring. In a gray December day, when, as the farmers say, it is too cold to snow, his numbed fingers will let fall doubtfully a few star-shaped flakes, the snowdrops and anemones that harbinger his more assured reign. Now, and only now, may be seen, heaped on the horizon's eastern edge, those "blue clouds" from forth which Shakespeare says that Mars "doth pluck the masoned turrets." Sometimes, also, when the sun is low, you will see a single cloud trailing a flurry of snow along the southern hills in a wavering fringe of purple. And when at last the real snow-storm comes, it leaves the earth with a virginal look on it that no other of the seasons can rival—compared with which they seem soiled and vulgar.

And what is there in nature so beautiful as the next morning after such confusion of the elements? Night has no silence like this of busy day. All the batteries of noise are spiked. We see the movement of life as a deaf man sees it, a mere wraith of the clamorous existence that inflicts itself on our ears when the ground is bare. The earth is clothed in innocence as a garment. Every wound of the landscape is healed; whatever was stiff has been sweetly rounded as the breasts of Aphrodite; what was unsightly has been covered gently with a soft splendor, as if, Cowley would have said, Nature had cleverly let fall her handkerchief to hide it. If the Virgin were to come back, here is an earth that would not bruise her foot nor stain it. It is

> "The fanned snow
> That's bolted by the northern blasts twice o'er."

packed so hard sometimes on hill-slopes that it will bear your weight. What grace is in all the curves, as if every one of them had been swept by that inspired thumb of Phidias's journeyman!

Poets have fancied the footprints of the wind in those light ripples that sometimes scurry across smooth water with a sudden blur. But on this gleaming hush the aerial deluge has left plain marks of its course; and in gullies through which it rushed torrent-like, the eye finds its bed irregularly scooped

like that of a brook in hard beach-sand, or, in more sheltered
spots, traced with outlines like those left by the sliding edges
of the surf upon the shore. The air, after all, is only an
infinitely thinner kind of water, such as I suppose we shall
have to drink when the state does her whole duty as a moral
reformer. Nor is the wind the only thing whose trail you
will notice on this sensitive surface. You will find that you
have more neighbors and night visitors than you dreamed of.
Here is the dainty footprint of a cat; here a dog has looked
in on you like an amateur watchman to see if all is right,
slumping about in the mealy treachery. And look! before
you were up in the morning, though you were a punctual
courtier at the sun's levee, here has been a squirrel zigzagging
to and fro like a hound gathering the scent, and some tiny
bird searching for unimaginable food—perhaps for the tinier
creature, whatever it is, that drew this slender, continuous trail
like those made on the wet beach by light borderers of the sea.
Poseidon traced his lines, or giant birds made their mark, on
preadamite sea-margins; and the thundergust left the tear
stains of its sudden passion there; nay, we have the signatures
of delicatest fern leaves on the soft ooze of æons that dozed
away their dreamless leisure before consciousness came upon
the earth with man. Some whim of nature locked them fast
in stone for us after-thoughts of creation. Which of us shall
leave a footprint as imperishable as that of the ornithorhyncus,
or much more so than that of these Bedouins of the snow-
desert? Perhaps it was only because the ripple and the rain-
drop and the bird were not thinking of themselves, that they
had such luck. The chances of immortality depend very much
on that. How often have we not seen poor mortals, dupes of
a season's notoriety, carving their names on seeming-solid
rock of merest beach-sand, whose feeble hold on the memory
shall be washed away by the next wave of fickle opinion!
Well, well, honest Jacques, there are better things to be found
in the snow than sermons.

The snow that falls damp comes commonly in larger flakes
from windless skies, and is the prettiest of all to watch from
under cover. This is the kind Homer had in mind; and Dante,
who had never read him, compares the *dilatate falde*, the
flaring flakes, of his fiery rain, to those of snow among the

mountains without wind. This sort of snowfall has no fight in it, and does not challenge you to a wrestle like that which drives well from the northward, with all moisture thoroughly winnowed out of it by the frosty wind. Burns, who was more out of doors than most poets, and whose barefoot Muse got the color in her cheeks by vigorous exercise in all weathers, was thinking of this drier deluge when he speaks of the "whirling drift," and tells how

> "Chanticleer
> Shook off the powthery snaw."

But the damper and more deliberate falls have a choice knack at draping the trees; and about eaves or stone walls; wherever, indeed, the evaporation is rapid, and it finds a chance to cling, it will build itself out in curves of wonderful beauty. I have seen one of these dumb waves, thus caught in the act of breaking, curl four feet beyond the edge of my roof and there hang for days, as if Nature were too well pleased with her work to let it crumble from its exquisite pause. After such a storm, if you are lucky enough to have even a sluggish ditch for a neighbor, be sure to pay it a visit. You will find its banks corniced with what seems precipitated light, and the dark current down below gleams as if with inward lustre. Dull of motion as it is, you never saw water that seemed alive before. It has a brightness, like that of the eyes of some smaller animals, which gives assurance of life, but of a life foreign and unintelligible. . . .

What a cunning silversmith is Frost! The rarest workmanship of Delhi or Genoa copies him but clumsily, as if the fingers of all other artists were thumbs. Fernwork and lacework and filigree in endless variety, and under it all the water tinkles like a distant guitar, or drums like a tambourine, or gurgles like the Tokay of an anchorite's dream. Beyond doubt there is a fairy procession marching along those frail arcades and translucent corridors.

> "Their oaten pipes blow wondrous shrill,
> The hemlock small blow clear."

And hark! is that the ringing of Titania's bridle, or the bells of the wee, wee hawk that sits on Oberon's wrist? This wonder of Frost's handiwork may be had every winter, but he can do better than this, though I have seen it but once in my life. There had been a thaw without wind or rain, making the air fat with gray vapor. Towards sundown came that chill, the avant-courier of a northwesterly gale. Then, though there was no perceptible current in the atmosphere, the fog began to attach itself in frosty roots and filaments to the southern side of every twig and grass stem. The very posts had poems traced upon them by this dumb minstrel. Wherever the moist seeds found lodgment grew an inch-deep moss, fine as cobweb, a slender coral-reef, argentine, delicate, as of some silent sea in the moon, such as Agassiz dredges when he dreams. The Frost, too, can wield a delicate graver, and in fancy leaves Piranesi far behind. He covers your window-pane with Alpine etchings, as if in memory of that sanctuary where he finds shelter even in midsummer.

Now look down from your hillside across the valley. The trees are leafless, but this is the season to study their anatomy, and did you ever notice before how much color there is in the twigs of many of them? And the smoke from those chimneys is so blue it seems like a feeder of the sky into which it flows. Winter refines it and gives it agreeable associations. In summer it suggests cookery or the drudgery of steam-engines, but now your fancy (if it can forget for a moment the dreary usurpation of stoves) traces it down to the fire-side and the brightened faces of children.　　*—Lowell.*

JOHN BURROUGHS.

JOHN BURROUGHS was born in Roxbury, New York, April 3, 1837. He received his schooling in district schools and academies nearby, teaching now and then to facilitate his progress. The habits of roaming about in the wide country, communing with nature and nature's fur and feathered creatures, were formed in boyhood.

The writings of Emerson, Thoreau, and Walt Whitman have had deep influence upon Burrough's literary productions —Emerson largely molding his style, Whitman affected more particularly his life and thought.

For some years Burroughs filled a position in the Treasury Department at Washington, and later became a bank examiner. It was his delight when leisure hours overtook him to get out of the city at once and into the country, where he was at once at home. Returning to his fireside, he gave the wealth of his discoveries to readers everywhere, who perhaps found fewer moments to revel in nature's obscure corners, and who generally speaking lacked Burroughs' eyes and ears had they been able to follow where he went. *Wake-Robin, Winter Sunshine, Fresh Fields, A March Chronicle*, are among his nature studies; *Notes on Walt Whitman, The Flight of the Eagle* and *Indoor Studies* are of a more purely literary character.

425

BIRD ENEMIES.

How surely the birds know their enemies! See how the wrens and robins and bluebirds pursue and scold the cat, while they take little or no notice of the dog! Even the swallow will fight the cat, and, relying too confidently upon its powers of flight, sometimes swoops down so near to its enemy that it is caught by a sudden stroke of the cat's paw. The only case I know of in which our small birds fail to recognize their enemy is furnished by the shrike; apparently the little birds do not know that this modest-colored bird is an assassin. At least, I have never seen them scold or molest him, or utter any outcries at his presence, as they usually do at birds of prey. Probably it is because the shrike is a rare visitant, and is not found in this part of the country during the nesting season of our songsters.

But the birds have nearly all found out the trick of the jay, and when he comes sneaking through the trees in May and June in quest of eggs, he is quickly exposed and roundly abused. It is amusing to see the robins hustle him out of the tree which holds their nest. They cry "Thief, thief!" to the top of their voices as they charge upon him, and the jay retorts in a voice scarcely less complimentary as he makes off.

The jays have their enemies also, and need to keep an eye on their own eggs. It would be interesting to know if jays ever rob jays, or crows plunder crows; or is there honor among thieves even in the feathered tribes? I suspect the jay is often punished by birds which are otherwise innocent of nest-robbing. One season I found a jay's nest in a small cedar on the side of a wooded ridge. It held five eggs, every one of which had been punctured. Apparently some bird had driven its sharp beak through their shells, with the sole intention of destroying them, for no part of the contents of the eggs had been removed. It looked like a case of revenge; as if some thrush or warbler, whose nest had suffered at the hands of the jays, had watched its opportunity, and had in this way retaliated upon its enemies. An egg for an egg. The jays were lingering near, very demure and silent, and probably ready to join a crusade against nest-robbers.

The great bugaboo of the birds is the owl. The owl

snatches them from off their roosts at night, and gobbles up their eggs and young in their nests. He is a veritable ogre to them, and his presence fills them with consternation and alarm.

One season, to protect my early cherries, I placed a large stuffed owl amid the branches of the tree. Such a racket as there instantly began about my grounds is not pleasant to think upon! The orioles and robins fairly "shrieked out their affright." The news instantly spread in every direction, and apparently every bird in town came to see that owl in the cherry-tree, and every bird took a cherry, so that I lost more fruit than if I had left the owl in-doors. With craning necks and horrified looks the birds alighted upon the branches, and between their screams would snatch off a cherry, as if the act was some relief to their outraged feelings.

The chirp and chatter of the young of birds which build in concealed or inclosed places, like the woodpeckers, the house wren, the high-hole, the oriole, is in marked contrast to the silence of the fledgelings of most birds that build open and exposed nests. The young of the sparrows,—unless the social sparrow be an exception,—warblers, fly-catchers, thrushes, never allow a sound to escape them; and on the alarm note of their parents being heard, sit especially close and motionless, while the young of chimney swallows, woodpeckers, and orioles are very noisy. The latter, in its deep pouch, is quite safe from birds of prey, except perhaps the owl. The owl, I suspect, thrusts its leg into the cavities of woodpeckers and into the pocket-like nest of the oriole, and clutches and brings forth the birds in its talons. In one case which I heard of, a screech-owl had thrust its claw into a cavity in a tree, and grasped the head of a red-headed woodpecker; being apparently unable to draw its prey forth, it had thrust its own round head into the hole, and in some way became fixed there, and had thus died with the woodpecker in its talons.

The life of birds is beset with dangers and mishaps of which we know little. One day, in my walk, I came upon a goldfinch with the tip of one wing securely fastened to the feathers of its rump, by what appeared to be the silk of some caterpillar. The bird, though uninjured, was completely crippled, and could not fly a stroke. Its little body was hot and

panting in my hands, as I carefully broke the fetter. Then
it darted swiftly away with a happy cry. A record of all the
accidents and tragedies of bird life for a single season would
show many curious incidents. A friend of mine opened his
box-stove one fall to kindle a fire in it, when he beheld in the
black interior the desiccated forms of two bluebirds. The
birds had probably taken refuge in the chimney during some
cold spring storm, and had come down the pipe to the stove,
from whence they were unable to ascend. A peculiarly touching little incident of bird life occurred to a caged female
canary. Though unmated, it laid some eggs, and the happy
bird was so carried away by her feelings that she would offer
food to the eggs, and chatter and twitter, trying, as it seemed,
to encourage them to eat! The incident is hardly tragic,
neither is it comic.

Certain birds nest in the vicinity of our houses and out-
buildings, or even in and upon them, for protection from their
enemies, but they often thus expose themselves to a plague of
the most deadly character.

I refer to the vermin with which their nests often swarm,
and which kill the young before they are fledged. In a state
of nature this probably never happens; at least I have never
seen or heard of it happening to nests placed in trees or under
rocks. It is the curse of civilization falling upon the birds
which come too near man. The vermin, or the germ of the
vermin, is probably conveyed to the nest in hen's feathers, or
in straws and hairs picked up about the barn or hen-house.
A robin's nest upon your porch or in your summer-house will
occasionally become an intolerable nuisance from the swarms
upon swarms of minute vermin with which it is filled. The
parent birds stem the tide as long as they can, but are often
compelled to leave the young to their terrible fate.

One season a phœbe-bird built on a projecting stone under
the eaves of the house, and all appeared to go well till the
young were nearly fledged, when the nest suddenly became a
bit of purgatory. The birds kept their places in their burning
bed till they could hold out no longer, when they leaped forth
and fell dead upon the ground.

After a delay of a week or more, during which I imagine
the parent birds purified themselves by every means known

to them, the couple built another nest a few yards from the first, and proceeded to rear a second brood; but the new nest developed into the same bed of torment that the first did, and the three young birds, nearly ready to fly, perished as they sat within it. The parent birds then left the place as if it had been accursed.

I imagine the smaller birds have an enemy in our native white-footed mouse, though I have not proof enough to convict him. But one season the nest of a chickadee which I was observing was broken up in a position where nothing but a mouse could have reached it. The bird had chosen a cavity in the limb of an apple-tree which stood but a few yards from the house. The cavity was deep, and the entrance to it, which was ten feet from the ground, was small. Barely light enough was admitted, when the sun was in the most favorable position, to enable one to make out the number of eggs, which was six, at the bottom of the dim interior. While one was peering in and trying to get his head out of his own light, the bird would startle him by a queer kind of puffing sound. She would not leave her nest like most birds, but really tried to blow, or scare, the intruder away; and after repeated experiments I could hardly refrain from jerking my head back when that little explosion of sound came up from the dark interior. One night, when incubation was about half finished, the nest was harried. A slight trace of hair or fur at the entrance led me to infer that some small animal was the robber. A weasel might have done it, as they sometimes climb trees, but I doubt if either a squirrel or a rat could have passed the entrance.

Probably few persons have ever suspected the catbird of being an egg-sucker; I do not know that she has ever been accused of such a thing, but there is something uncanny and disagreeable about her, which I at once understood, when I one day caught her in the very act of going through a nest of eggs.

A pair of the least fly-catchers, the bird which says *chebec, chebec,* and is a small edition of the pewee, one season built their nest where I had them for many hours each day under my observation. The nest was a very snug and compact structure placed in the forks of a small maple about twelve

feet from the ground.   The season before a red squirrel had
harried the nest of a wood-thrush in this same tree, and I was
apprehensive that he would serve the fly-catchers the same
trick; so, as I sat with my book in a summer-house near by, I
kept my loaded gun within easy reach.   One egg was laid,
and the next morning, as I made my daily inspection of the
nest, only a fragment of its empty shell was to be found.
This I removed, mentally imprecating the rogue of a red squirrel.   The birds were much disturbed by the event, but did
not desert the nest, as I had feared they would, but after
much inspection of it and many consultations together, con-
cluded, it seems, to try again.   Two more eggs were laid,
when one day I heard the birds utter a sharp cry, and on
looking up I saw a cat-bird perched upon the rim of the nest,
hastily devouring the eggs.   I soon regretted my precipitation
in killing her, because such interference is generally unwise.
It turned out that she had a nest of her own with five eggs,
in a spruce-tree near my window.

Then this pair of little fly-catchers did what I had never
seen birds do before; they pulled the nest to pieces and rebuilt
it in a peach-tree not many rods away, where a brood was
successfully reared.   The nest was here exposed to the direct
rays of the noon-day sun, and to shield her young when the
heat was greatest, the mother-bird would stand above them
with wings slightly spread, as other birds have been known to
do under like circumstances.

To what extent the cat-bird is a nest-robber I have no
evidence, but that feline mew of hers, and that flirting, flexible
tail, suggest something not entirely bird-like.   .   .   .

Among the worst enemies of our birds are the so-called
"collectors," men who plunder nests and murder their owners
in the name of science.   Not the genuine ornithologist, for no
one is more careful of squandering bird life than he; but the
sham ornithologist, the man whose vanity or affectation happens to take an ornithological turn.   He is seized with an
itching for a collection of eggs and birds because it happens
to be the fashion, or because it gives him the air of a man 'of
science.   But in the majority of cases the motive is a mercenary one; the collector expects to sell these spoils of the
groves   and   orchards.   Robbing   nests   and   killing   birds

becomes a business with him. He goes about it systematically, and becomes an expert in circumventing and slaying our songsters. Every town of any considerable size is infested with one or more of these bird highwaymen, and every nest in the country round about that the wretches can lay hands on is harried. Their professional term for a nest of eggs is "a clutch," a word that well expresses the work of their grasping, murderous fingers. They clutch and destroy in the germ the life and music of the woodlands. Certain of our natural history journals are mainly organs of communication between these human weasels. They record their exploits at nest-robbing and bird-slaying in their columns. One collector tells with gusto how he "worked his way" through an orchard, ransacking every tree, and leaving, as he believed, not one nest behind him. He had better not be caught working his way through my orchard. Another gloats over the number of Connecticut warblers—a rare bird—he killed in one season in Massachusetts. Another tells how a mocking-bird appeared in southern New England and was hunted down by himself and friend, its eggs "clutched," and the bird killed. Who knows how much the bird lovers of New England lost by that foul deed? The progeny of the birds would probably have returned to Connecticut to breed, and their progeny, or a part of them, the same, till in time the famous songster would have become a regular visitant to New England. In the same journal still another collector describes minutely how he outwitted three humming-birds and captured their nests and eggs,—a clutch he was very proud of. A Massachusetts bird harrier boasts of his clutch of the eggs of that dainty little warbler, the blue yellow-back. One season he took two sets, the next five sets, the next four sets, besides some single eggs, and the next season four sets, and says he might have found more had he had more time. One season he took, in about twenty days, three sets from one tree. I have heard of a collector who boasted of having taken one hundred sets of the eggs of the marsh wren in a single day; of another, who took, in the same time, thirty nests of the yellow-breasted chat; and of still another, who claimed to have taken one thousand sets of eggs of different birds in one season. A large business has grown up under the influence of this collecting craze. One dealer in eggs has those of over five hundred species. He says that his business in 1883 was twice that of 1882; in 1884 it was twice that of 1883, and so on. Collectors vie with each other in the extent and variety of their cabinets. They not only obtain eggs in sets, but aim to have a number of sets of the same bird, so as to show all possible variations. I hear of a private collection that contains twelve sets of king-birds' eggs, eight sets of house-wrens' eggs, four sets of mocking-birds' eggs, etc.; sets of eggs taken in low trees, high trees, medium trees; spotted sets, dark sets, plain sets, and light sets of the same species of bird. Many collections are made on this latter plan.

Thus are our birds hunted and cut off, and all in the name of science; as if science had not long ago finished with these birds. She has weighed and measured, and dissected, and described them, and their nests, and eggs, and placed them in her cabinet; and the interest of science and of humanity now demands that this wholesale nest-robbing cease. These incidents I have given above, it is true, are but drops in the bucket, but the bucket would be more than full if we could get all the facts. Where one man publishes his notes, hundreds, perhaps thousands, say nothing, but go as silently about their nest-robbing as weasels.

It is true that the student of ornithology often feels compelled to take bird-life. It is not an easy matter to "name all the birds without a gun," though an opera glass will often render identification entirely certain, and leave the songster unharmed; but once having mastered the birds, the true ornithologist leaves his gun at home. This view of the case may not be agreeable to that desiccated mortal called the "closet naturalist," but for my own part the closet naturalist is a person with whom I have very little sympathy. He is about the most wearisome and profitless creature in existence. With his piles of skins, his cases of eggs, his laborious feather-splitting, and his outlandish nomenclature, he is not only the enemy of the birds but the enemy of all those who would know them rightly.

Not the collectors alone are to blame for the diminishing numbers of our wild birds, but a large share of the responsibility rests upon quite a different class of persons, namely, the milliners. False taste in dress is as destructive to our feathered friends as are false aims in science. It is said that the traffic in the skins of our brighter plumaged birds, arising from their use by the milliners, reaches to hundreds of thousands annually. I am told of one middleman who collected from the shooters in one district, in four months, seventy thousand skins. It is a barbarous taste that craves this kind of ornamentation. Think of a woman or girl of real refinement appearing upon the street with her head gear adorned with the scalps of our songsters!

It is probably true that the number of our birds destroyed by man is but a small percentage of the number cut off by their natural enemies; but it is to be remembered that those he destroys are in addition to those cut off, and that it is this extra or artificial destruction that disturbs the balance of nature. The operation of natural causes keeps the birds in check, but the greed of the collectors and milliners tends to their extinction.

I can pardon a man who wishes to make a collection of eggs and birds for his own private use, if he will content himself with one or two specimens of a kind, though he will find any collection much less satisfactory and less valuable than he imagines, but the professional nest-robber and skin collector should be put down, either by legislation or with dogs and shot-guns.

A BUNCH OF HERBS.

The charge that was long ago made against our wild flowers by English travelers in this country, namely, that they were odorless, doubtless had its origin in the fact that, whereas in England the sweet-scented flowers are among the most common and conspicuous, in this country they are rather shy and withdrawn, and consequently not such as travelers would be likely to encounter. Moreover, the British traveler, remembering the deliciously fragrant blue violets he left at home, covering every grassy slope and meadow bank in spring, and the wild clematis, or traveler's joy, overrunning hedges and old walls with its white, sweet-scented blossoms, and finding the corresponding species here equally abundant but entirely scentless, very naturally inferred that our wild flowers were all deficient in this respect. He would be confirmed in this opinion when, on turning to some of our most beautiful and striking native flowers, like the laurel, the rhododendron, the columbine, the inimitable fringed gentian, the burning cardinal-flower, or our asters and golden-rod, dashing the roadsides with tints of purple and gold, he found them scentless also. "Where are your fragrant flowers?" he might well say; "I can find none." Let him look closer and penetrate our forests, and visit our ponds and lakes. Let him compare our matchless, rosy-lipped, honey-hearted trailing arbutus with his own ugly ground ivy; let him compare our sumptuous, fragrant pond-lily with his own odorless Nymphæa alba. In our northern woods he shall find the floors carpeted with the delicate linnæa, its twin rose-colored nodding flowers filling the air with fragrance. (I am aware that the linnæa is found in some parts of Northern Europe.) The fact is, we perhaps have as many sweet-scented wild flowers as Europe has, only they are not quite so prominent in our flora, nor so well known to our people or to our poets.

Think of Wordsworth's "Golden Daffodils":

"I wandered lonely as a cloud
    That floats on high o'er vales and hills,
When all at once I saw a crowd,
    A host of golden daffodils,
Beside the lake, beneath the trees,
Fluttering and dancing in the breeze.

"Continuous as the stars that shine
   And twinkle on the Milky Way,
They stretched in never-ending line
   Along the margin of a bay.
Ten thousand saw I at a glance,
Tossing their heads in sprightly dance."

No such sight could greet the poet's eye here. He might see ten thousand marsh marigolds, or ten times ten thousand houstonias, but they would not toss in the breeze, and they would not be sweet-scented like the daffodils.

It is to be remembered, too, that in the moister atmosphere of England the same amount of fragrance would be much more noticeable than with us. Think how our sweet bay, or our pink azalea, or our white alder, to which they have nothing that corresponds, would perfume that heavy, vapor-laden air!

In the woods and groves of England the wild hyacinth grows very abundantly in spring, and in places the air is loaded with its fragrance. In our woods a species of dicentra, commonly called squirrel corn, has nearly the same perfume, and its racemes of nodding whitish flowers, tinged with red, are quite as pleasing to the eye, but it is a shyer, less abundant plant. When our children go to the fields in April and May, they can bring home no wild flowers as pleasing as the sweet English violet, and cowslip, and yellow daffodil, and wall-flower; and when British children go to the woods at the same season, they can load their hands and baskets with nothing that compares with our trailing arbutus, or, later in the season, with our azaleas; and when their boys go fishing or boating in the summer, they can wreathe themselves with nothing that approaches our pond-lily. . . .

It is only for a brief period that the blossoms of our sugar maple are sweet-scented; the perfume seems to become stale after a few days; but pass under this tree just at the right moment, say at nightfall on the first or second day of its perfect inflorescence and the air is loaded with its sweetness; its perfumed breath falls upon you as its cool shadow does a few weeks later.

After the linnæa and the arbutus, the prettiest sweet-scented flowering vine our woods hold is the common mitchella vine, called squaw-berry and partridge-berry. It blooms in

June, and its twin flowers, light cream-color, velvety, tubular exhale a most agreeable fragrance.

Our flora is much more rich in orchids than the European, and many of ours are fragrant. The first to bloom in the spring is the showy orchis, though it is far less showy than several others. I find it in May, not on hills, where Gray says it grows, but in low, damp places in the woods. It has two oblong shining leaves, with a scape four or five inches high strung with sweet-scented, pink-purple flowers. I usually find it and the fringed polygala in bloom at the same time; the lady's-slipper is a little later. The purple fringed orchis, one of the most showy and striking of all our orchids, blooms in midsummer in swampy meadows and in marshy, grassy openings in the woods, shooting up a tapering column or cylinder of pink-purple fringed flowers, that one may see at quite a distance, and the perfume of which is too rank for a close room. This flower is, perhaps, like the English fragrant orchis, found in pastures.

Few fragrant flowers in the shape of weeds have come to us from the Old World, and this leads me to remark that plants with sweet-scented flowers are, for the most part, more intensely local, more fastidious and idiosyncratic, than those without perfume. Our native thistle—the pasture thistle—has a marked fragrance, and it is much more shy and limited in its range than the common Old World thistle that grows everywhere. Our little sweet white violet grows only in wet places, and the Canada violet only in high, cool woods, while the common blue violet is much more general in its distribution. How fastidious and exclusive is the cypripedium! You will find it in one locality in the woods, usually on high ground, and will look in vain for it elsewhere. It does not go in herds like the commoner plants, but affects privacy and solitude. When I come upon it in my walks, I seem to be intruding upon some very private and exclusive company. The large yellow cypripedium has a peculiar, heavy, oily color.

In like manner one learns where to look for arbutus, for pipsissewa, for the early orchis; they have their particular haunts, and their surroundings are nearly always the same. The yellow pond-lily is found in every sluggish stream and pond, but Nymphæa odorata requires a nicer adjustment of conditions, and consequently is more restricted in its range. If the mullein were fragrant, or toad-flax, or the daisy, or blueweed, or golden-rod, they would doubtless be far less troublesome to the agriculturist. There are, of course, exceptions to the rule I have here indicated, but it holds in most cases. Genius is a specialty; it does not grow in every soil; it skips the many and touches the few; and the gift of perfume to a flower is a special grace, like genius or like beauty, and never becomes common or cheap.

"Do honey and fragrance always go together in the flowers?" Not uniformly. Of the list of fragrant wild flowers I have given, the only ones that the bees procure nectar from, so far as I have observed, are arbutus, dicentra, sugar maple, locust, and linden. Non-fragrant flowers that yield honey are those of the raspberry, clematis, sumac, bugloss, ailanthus, golden-rod, aster, fleabane. A large number of odorless plants yield pollen to the bee. There is nectar in the columbine, and the bumble-bee sometimes gets it by piercing the spur from the outside, as she does with the dicentra. There ought to be honey in the honeysuckle, but I have never seen the hive bee make any attempt to get it.

AUTUMNAL TINTS.

Europeans coming to America are surprised by the brilliancy of our autumnal foliage. There is no account of such a phenomenon in English poetry, because the trees acquire but few bright colors there. The most that Thomson says on this subject in his "Autumn" is contained in the lines:

"But see the fading many-colored woods;
Shade deepening over shade, the country round
Imbrown; a crowded umbrage, dusk and dun,
Of every hue, from wan declining green to sooty dark;"

and the line in which he speaks of

"Autumn beaming o'er the yellow woods."

The autumnal change of our woods has not made a deep impression on our own literature yet. October has hardly tinged our poetry.

A great many, who have spent their lives in cities, and have never chanced to come into the country at this season, have never seen this, the flower, or rather the ripe fruit, of the year. I remember riding with one such citizen, who, though a fortnight too late for the most brilliant tints, was taken by surprise, and would not believe that there had been any brighter. He had never heard of this phenomenon before. Not only many in our towns have never witnessed it, but it is scarcely remembered by the majority from year to year.

Most appear to confound changed leaves with withered ones, as if they were to confound ripe apples with rotten ones. I think that the change to some higher color in a leaf is an evidence that it has arrived at a late and perfect maturity, answering to the maturity of fruits. It is generally the lowest and oldest leaves which change first. But as the perfect-winged and usually bright-colored insect is short-lived, so the leaves ripen but to fall.

Generally, every fruit, on ripening, and just before it falls, when it commences a more independent and individual existence, requiring less nourishment from any source, and that not so much from the earth through its stem as from the sun and air, acquires a bright tint. So do leaves. The physiologist says it is "due to an increased absorption of oxygen." That is the scientific account of the matter—only a reassertion of the fact. But I am more interested in the rosy cheek than I am to know what particular diet the maiden fed on. The very forest and herbage, the pellicle of the earth, must acquire a bright color, an evidence of its ripeness—as if the globe itself were a fruit on its stem, with ever a cheek toward the sun.

Flowers are but colored leaves, fruit but ripe ones. The edible part of most fruits is, as the physiologist says, "the parenchyma or fleshy tissue of the leaf," of which they are formed.

Our appetites have commonly confined our views of ripeness and its phenomena, color, mellowness, and perfectness, to the fruits which we eat, and we are wont to forget that an immense harvest which we do not eat, hardly use at all, is annually ripened by Nature. At our annual cattle shows and horticultural exhibitions we make, as we think, a great show of fair fruits, destined, however, to a rather ignoble end;

fruits not valued for their beauty chiefly. But round about and within our towns there is annually another show of fruits, on an infinitely grander scale, fruits which address our taste for beauty alone.

October is the month for painted leaves. Their rich glow now flashes round the world. As fruits and leaves and the day itself acquire a bright tint just before they fall, so the year near its setting. October is its sunset sky; November the later twilight.

I formerly thought that it would be worth the while to get a specimen leaf from each changing tree, shrub, and herbaceous plant, when it had acquired its brightest characteristic color, in its transition from the green to the brown state, outline it, and copy its color exactly, with paint, in a book, which should be entitled "October; or, Autumnal Tints"; beginning with the earliest reddening, woodbine and the lake of radical leaves, and coming down through maples, hickories, and sumacs, and many beautifully freckled leaves less generally known, to the latest oaks and aspens. What a memento such a book would be! You would need only to turn over its leaves to take a ramble through the autumn woods whenever you pleased. Or if I could preserve the leaves themselves, unfaded, it would be better still. I have made but little progress toward such a book, but I have endeavored, instead, to describe all these bright tints in the order in which they present themselves. The following are some extracts from my notes.

THE RED MAPLE.

By the 25th of September, the red maples generally are beginning to be ripe. Some large ones have been conspicuously changing for a week, and some single trees are now very brilliant. I notice a small one, half a mile off across the meadow, against the green woodside there, a far brighter red than the blossoms of any tree in summer, and more conspicuous. I have observed this tree for several autumns invariably changing earlier than its fellows, just as one tree ripens its fruit earlier than another. It might serve to mark the season, perhaps. I should be sorry if it were cut down. I know of two or three such trees in different parts of our town which might, perhaps, be propagated from, as early ripeners or September trees, and their seed be advertised in the market, as well as that of radishes, if we cared as much about them.

At present these burning bushes stand chiefly along the edge of the meadows, or I distinguish them afar on the hillsides here and there. Sometimes you will see many small ones in a swamp turned quite crimson when all other trees are still perfectly green and the former appear so much the brighter for it. They take you by surprise, as you are going by on one side, across the fields, thus early in the season, as if it were some gay encampment of the red men, or other foresters, of whose arrival you had not heard.

Some single trees, wholly bright scarlet, seen against others of their kind still freshly green, or against evergreens, are more memorable than whole groves will be by and by. How beautiful, when a whole tree is like one great scarlet fruit full of ripe juices, every leaf, from lowest limb to topmost spire, all aglow, especially if you look toward the sun! What more remarkable object can there be in the landscape? Visible for miles, too fair to be believed. If such a phenomenon occurred but once, it would be handed down by tradition to posterity, and get into the mythology at last.

The whole tree thus ripening in advance of its fellows attains a singular preëminence, and sometimes maintains it for a week or two. I am thrilled at the sight of it, bearing aloft its scarlet standard for the regiment of green-clad foresters around, and I go half a mile out of my way to examine it. A single tree becomes thus the crowning beauty of some meadowy vale, and the expression of the whole surrounding forest is at once more spirited for it.

A small red maple has grown, perchance, far away at the head of some retired valley, a mile from any road, unobserved. It has faithfully discharged the duties of a maple there, all winter and summer, neglected none of its economies, but added to its stature in the virtue which belongs to a maple, by a steady growth for so many months, never having gone gadding abroad, and is nearer heaven than it was in the spring. It has faithfully husbanded its sap, and afforded shelter to the wandering bird, has long since ripened its seeds and committed them to the winds, and has the satisfaction of knowing, perhaps, that a thousand little well-behaved maples are already settled in life somewhere. It deserves well of Mapledom. Its leaves have been asking it from time to time, in a whisper, "When shall we redden?" And now, in this month of September, this month of traveling, when men are hastening to the seaside, or the mountains, or the lakes, this modest maple, still without budging an inch, travels in its reputation, runs up its scarlet flag on that hillside, which shows that it has finished its summer's work before all other trees, and withdraws from the contest. At the eleventh hour of the year, the tree which no scrutiny could have detected here when it was most industrious is thus, by the tint of its maturity, by its very blushes, revealed at last to the careless and distant traveler, and leads his thoughts away from the dusty road into those brave solitudes which it inhabits. It flashes out conspicuous with all the virtue and beauty of a maple—*Acer Rubrum.* We may now read its title, or *rubric,* clear. Its *virtues,* not its sins, are as scarlet.

Notwithstanding the red maple is the most intense scarlet of any of our trees, the sugar maple has been the most celebrated, and Michaux in his "Sylva," does not speak of the autumnal color of the former. About the second of October these trees, both large and small, are most brilliant, though many still are green. In "sprout-lands" they seem to vie with one another, and ever some particular one in the midst of the crowd will be of a peculiarly pure scarlet, and by its more intense color attract our eye even at a distance, and carry off the palm. A large red-maple swamp, when at the height of its change, is the most obviously brilliant of all tangible things, where I dwell, so abundant is this tree with us. It varies much both in form and color. A great many are merely yellow; more, scarlet; others, scarlet deepening into crimson, more red than common. Look at yonder swamp of maples mixed with pines, at the base of a pine-clad hill, a quarter of a mile off, so that you get the full effect of the bright colors, without detecting the imperfections of the leaves, and see their yellow, scarlet, and crimson fires, of all tints, mingled and contrasted with the green. Some maples are yet green, only yellow or crimson-tipped on the edges of their flakes, like the edges of a hazelnut bur; some are wholly brilliant scarlet, raying out regularly and finely every way, bilaterally, like the veins of a leaf; others, of more irregular forms, when I turn my head slightly, emptying out some of its earthiness and concealing the trunk of the tree, seem to rest heavily flake on flake, like yellow and scarlet clouds, wreath upon wreath, or like snow-drifts driving through the air, stratified by the wind. It adds greatly to the beauty of such a swamp at this season that, even though there may be no other trees interspersed, it is not seen as a simple mass of color, but, different trees being of different colors and hues, the outline of each crescent treetop is distinct, and where one laps on to another. Yet a painter would hardly venture to make them thus distinct a quarter of a mile off.

As I go across a meadow directly toward a low rising ground this bright afternoon, I see, some fifty rods off toward the sun, the top of a maple swamp just appearing over the sheeny russet edge of the hill, a stripe apparently twenty rods long by ten feet deep, of the most intensely brilliant scarlet, orange and yellow, equal to any flowers or fruits, or any tints ever painted. As I advance, lowering the edge of the hill which makes the firm foreground or lower frame of the picture, the depth of the brilliant grove revealed steadily increases, suggesting that the whole of the inclosed valley is filled with such color. One wonders that the tithingman and fathers of the town are not out to see what the trees mean by their high colors and exuberance of spirits, fearing that some mischief is brewing. I do not see what the Puritans did at this season, when the maples blazed out in scarlet. They certainly could not have worshipped in groves then. Perhaps that is what they built meeting-houses and fenced them round with horse-sheds for.

THE ELM.

Now, too, the first of October, or later, the elms are at the height of their autumnal beauty — great brownish yellow masses, warm from their September oven, hanging over the highway. Their leaves are perfectly ripe. I wonder if there is any answering ripeness in the lives of the men who live beneath them? As I look down our street, which is lined with them, they remind me, both by their form and color, of yellowing leaves of grain, as if the harvest had indeed come to the village itself, and we might expect to find some maturity and flavor in the thoughts of the villagers at last. Under those bright rustling yellow piles just ready to fall on the heads of the walkers, how can any crudity or greenness of thought or act prevail? When I stand where half a dozen large elms droop over a house, it is as if I stood within a ripe pumpkin-rind, and I feel as mellow as if I were the pulp, though I may be somewhat stringy and seedy withal. What is the late greenness of the English elms, like a cucumber out of season, which does not know when to have done, compared with the early and golden maturity of the American tree? The street is the scene of a great harvest-home. It would be worth the while to set out these trees, if only for their autumnal value. Think of these great yellow canopies or parasols held over our heads and houses by the mile together, making the village all one and compact—an *ulmarium,* which is at the same time a nursery of men! And then how gently and unobserved they drop their burden and let in the sun when it is wanted, their leaves not heard when they fall on our roofs and in our streets; and thus the village parasol is shut up and put away. I see the market-man driving into the village, and disappearing under its canopy of elm-tops, with *his* crop, as into a great granary or barn-yard. I am tempted to go thither as to a husking of thoughts, now dry and ripe, and ready to be separated from their integuments; but, alas! I foresee that it will be chiefly husks and little thought, blasted pig-corn, fit only for cob-meal, for, as you sow, so shall you reap.

NATURAL SELECTION.

From a remote period, in all parts of the world, man has subjected many animals and plants to domestication or culture. Man has no power of altering the absolute conditions of life; he cannot change the climate of any country; he adds no new element to the soil; but he can remove an animal or plant from one climate or soil to another, and give it food on which it did not subsist in its natural state. It is an error to speak of man "tampering with nature" and causing variability. If organic beings had not possessed an inherent tendency to vary, man could have done nothing. He unintentionally exposes his animals and plants to various conditions of life, and variability supervenes, which he cannot even prevent or check. Consider the simple case of a plant which has been cultivated during a long time in its native country, and which consequently has not been subjected to any change of climate. It has been protected to a certain extent from the competing roots of plants of other kinds; it has generally been grown in manured soil, but probably not richer than that of many an alluvial flat; and lastly, it has been exposed to changes in its conditions, being grown sometimes in one district and sometimes in another, in different soils. Under such circumstances, scarcely a plant can be named, though cultivated in the rudest manner, which has not given birth to several varieties. It can hardly be maintained that during the many changes which this earth has undergone, and during the natural migrations of plants from one land or island to another, tenanted by different species, that such plants will not often have been subjected to changes in their conditions analogous to those which almost inevitably cause cultivated plants to vary. No doubt man selects varying individuals, sows their seeds, and again selects their varying offspring. But the initial variation on which man works, and without which he can do nothing, is caused by slight changes in the conditions of life, which must often have occurred under nature. Man, therefore, may be said to have been trying an experiment on a gigantic scale; and it is an experiment which nature during the long lapse of time has incessantly tried. Hence it follows that the principles of domestication are important for us. The main result of that organic beings thus treated have varied largely, and the variations have been inherited. This has apparently been one chief cause of the belief long held by some few naturalists that species in a state of nature undergo change. . . .

Although man does not cause variability and cannot prevent it, he can select, preserve, and accumulate the variations given to him by the hand of nature in any way which he chooses; and thus he can certainly produce a great result. Selections may be followed either methodically and intentionally, or unconsciously and unintentionally. Man may select and preserve each successive variation, with the distinct intention of improving and altering a breed, in accordance with a preconceived idea; and by thus adding up variations, often so slight as to be imperceptible by an uneducated eye, he has effected wonderful changes and improvements. It can, also, be clearly shown that man, without any intention or thought of improving the breed, by preserving in each successive generation the individuals which he prizes most, and by destroying the worthless individuals, slowly, though surely, induces great changes. As the will of man thus comes into play, we can understand how it is that domesticated breeds show adaptation to his wants and pleasures. We can further understand how it is that domestic races of animals and cultivated races of plants often exhibit an abnormal character, as compared with natural species; for they have been modified not for their own benefit, but for that of man. . . . .

It has truly been said that all nature is at war; the strongest ultimately prevail, the weakest fail; and we well know that myriads of forms have disappeared from the face of the earth. If then, organic beings in a state of nature vary even in a slight degree, owing to changes in the surrounding conditions, of which we have abundant geological evidence, or from any other cause; if, in the long course of ages, inheritable variations ever arise in any way advantageous to any being under its excessively complex and changing relations of life—and it would be a strange fact if beneficial variations did never arise, seeing how many have arisen which man has taken advantage of for his own profit or pleasure—if then these contingencies ever occur, and I do not see how the probability of their occurrence can be doubted, then the severe and often recurrent struggle for existence will determine that those variations, however slight, which are favourable shall be preserved or selected, and those which are unfavorable shall be destroyed.

This preservation, during the battle for life, of varieties which possess any advantage in structure, constitution, or instinct, I have called Natural Selection; and Mr. Herbert Spencer has well expressed the same idea by the Survival of the Fittest. The term "natural selection" is in some respects a bad one, as it seems to imply conscious choice: but this will be disregarded after a little familiarity. No one objects to chemists speaking of "elective affinity"; and certainly an acid has no more choice in combining with a base, than the conditions of life have in determining whether or not a new form be selected or preserved. The term is so far a good one, as it brings into connection the production of domestic races by man's power of selection, and the natural preservation of varieties and species in a state of nature. For brevity's sake I sometimes speak of natural selection as an intelligent power— in the same way as astronomers speak of the attraction of gravity as ruling the movements of the planets, or as agriculturists speak of man making domestic races by his power of selection. In the one case, as in the other, selection does nothing without variability, and this depends in some manner on the action of the surrounding circumstances on the organism. I have, also, often personified the word Nature; for I have found it difficult to avoid this ambiguity; but I mean by nature only the aggregate action and produce of many natural laws,— and by laws only the ascertained sequence of events. . . .

As all the inhabitants of each country may be said, owing to their high rate of reproduction, to be striving to increase in numbers; as each form is related to many other forms in the struggle for life,—for destroy any one and its place will be seized by others; as every part of the organization occasionally varies in some slight degree, and as natural selection acts exclusively by the preservation of variations which are advantageous under the excessively complex conditions to which each being is exposed, no limit exists to the number, singularity, and perfection of the contrivances and co-adaptations which may thus be produced. An animal or a plant may thus slowly become related in its structure and habits in the most intricate manner to many other animals and plants, and to the physical conditions of its home. Variations in the organization will in some cases be aided by habit, or by the use and disuse of parts, and they will be governed by the direct action of the surrounding physical conditions and by correlation of growth.

In scientific investigations it is permitted to invent any hypothesis, and if it explains various large and independent classes of facts it rises to the rank of a well-grounded theory.

The undulations of the ether and even its existence are hypothetical, yet every one now admits the undulatory theory of light. The principle of natural selection may be looked at as a mere hypothesis, but rendered in some degree probable by what we positively know of the variability of organic beings in a state of nature,—by what we positively know of the struggle for existence, and the consequent, almost inevitable, preservation of favourable variations,—and from the analogical formation of domestic race. Now this hypothesis may be tests,—and this seems to me the only fair and legitimate manner of considering the whole questions,—by trying whether it explains several large and independent classes of facts; such as the geological succession of organic beings, their distribution in past and present times, and their mutual affinities and homologies. If the principle of natural selection does explain these and other large bodies of facts, it ought to be received. On the ordinary view of each species having been independently created, we gain no scientific explanation of any one of these facts. We can only say that it has so pleased the Creator to command that the past and present inhabitants of the world should appear in a certain order and in certain areas; that He has impressed on them the most extraordinary resemblances, and has classed them in groups subordinate to groups. But by such statements we gain no new knowledge; we do not connect together facts and laws; we explain nothing.

When I visited the Galápagos Archipelago, situated in the Pacific Ocean about 500 miles from the shore of South America, I found myself surrounded by peculiar species of birds, reptiles, and plants, existing nowhere else in the world. Yet they nearly all bore an American stamp. In the song of the mocking-thrush, in the harsh cry of the carrion-hawk, in the great candlestick-like opuntias, I clearly perceived the neighborhood of America, though the islands were separated by so many miles of ocean from the mainland, and differed much from it in their geological constitution and climate. Still more surprising was the fact that most of the inhabitants of each separate island in this small archipelago were specifically different, though more closely related to each other. The archipelago, with its innumerable craters and bare streams of

lava, appeared to be of recent origin; and thus I fancied myself
brought near to the very act of creation. I often asked myself
how these many peculiar animals and plants had been produced: the simplest answer seemed to be that the inhabitants
of the several islands had descended from each other, undergoing modifications in the course of their descent; and that
all the inhabitants of the archipelago had descended from
those of the nearest land, namely, America, whence colonists
would naturally have been derived. But it long remained to
me an inexplicable problem how the necessary degree of
modification could have been effected, and it would have thus
remained forever, had I not studied domestic productions,
and thus acquired a just idea of the power of Selection. As
soon as I had fully realized this idea, I saw, on reading
Malthus on Population, that natural selection was the inevitable result of the rapid increase of all organic beings; for I
was prepared to appreciate the struggle for existence by having long studied the habits of animals.

Before visiting the Galápagos I had collected many animals whilst travelling from north to south on both sides of
America, and everywhere, under conditions of life as different
as it is possible to conceive, American forms were met with—
species replacing species of the same peculiar genera. Thus
it was when the Cordilleras were ascended, or the thick tropical forests penetrated, or the fresh waters of America searched.
Subsequently I visited other countries, which in all the
conditions of life were incomparably more like to parts of
South America than the different parts of that continent were
to each other; yet in these countries, as in Australia or Southern Africa, the traveller cannot fail to be struck with the
entire difference of their productions. Again the reflection
was forced on me that community of descent from the early
inhabitants or colonists of South America would alone explain
the wide prevalence of American types of structure throughout that immense area.

To exhume with one's own hands the bones of extinct and
gigantic quadrupeds brings the whole question of the succession of species vividly before one's mind; and I had found in
South America great pieces of tesselated armour exactly like,
but on a magnificent scale, that covering the pigmy armadillo;

Cologne.—General View with Bridge of Boats.

I had found great teeth like those of the living sloth, and bones like those of the cavy. An analogous succession of allied forms had been previously observed in Australia. Here then we see the prevalence, as if by descent, in time as in space, of the same types in the same areas; and in neither case does the similarity of the conditions by any means seem sufficient to account for the similarity of the forms of life. It is notorious that the fossil remains of closely consecutive formations are closely allied in structure, and we can at once understand the fact if they are likewise closely allied by descent. The succession of the many distinct species of the same genus throughout the long series of geological formations seems to have been unbroken or continuous. New species come in gradually one by one. Ancient and extinct forms of life often show combined or intermediate characters, like the words of a dead language with respect to its several offshoots or living tongues. All these and other such facts seemed to me to point to descent with modification as the method of production of new groups of species.

The innumerable past and present inhabitants of the world are connected together by the most singular and complex affinities, and can be classed in groups under groups, in the same manner as varieties can be classed under species and subvarieties, but with much higher grades of difference. . . . How inexplicable is the similar pattern of the hand of a man, the foot of a dog, the wing of a bat, the flipper of a seal, on the doctrine of independent acts of creation! How simply explained on the principle of the natural selection of successive slight variations in the diverging descendants from a single progenitor! So it is, if we look to the structure of an individual animal or plant, when we see the fore and hind limbs, the skull and vertebræ, the jaws and legs of a crab, the petals, stamens, and pistils of a flower, built on the same type or pattern. During the many changes to which in the course of time all organic beings have been subjected, certain organs or parts have occasionally become at first of little use, and ultimately superfluous; and the retention of such parts in a rudimentary and utterly useless condition, can, on the descent theory, be simply understood. On the principle of modifications being inherited at the same age in the child, at which each successive variation first appeared in the parent, we shall see why rudimentary parts and organs are generally well developed in the individual at a very early age. On the same principle of inheritance at corresponding ages, and on the principle of variations not generally supervening at a very early period of embryonic growth (and both these principles can be shown to be probable from direct evidence), that most wonderful fact in the whole round of natural history, namely, the similarity of members of the same great class in their embryonic conditions—the embryo, for instance, of a mammal, bird, reptile, and fish being barely distinguishable—becomes simply intelligible.

It is the consideration and explanation of such facts as these which had convinced me that the theory of descent with modifications by means of natural selection is in the main true. These facts have as yet received no explanation on the theory of independent creations; they cannot be grouped together under one point of view, but each has to be considered as an ultimate fact. As the first origin of life on this earth, as well as the continued life of each individual, is at present quite beyond the scope of science, I do not wish to lay much stress on the greater simplicity of the view of a few forms, or of only one form, having been originally created, instead of innumerable miraculous creations having been necessary at innumerable periods; though this more simple view accords well with Maupertuis's philosophical axiom "of least action." In considering how far the theory of natural selection may be extended,—that is, in determining from how many progenitors the inhabitants of the world have descended,—we may conclude that at least all the members of the same class have descended from a single ancestor. A number of organic beings are included in the same class, because they present, independently of their habits of life, the same fundamental type of structure, and because they graduate into each other. Moreover, members of the same class can in most cases be shown to be closely alike at an early embryonic age. These facts can be explained on the belief of their descent from a common form; therefore it may be safely admitted that all members of the same class have descended from one progenitor. But as the members of quite distinct classes have some-

thing in common in structure and much in common in constitution, analogy and the simplicity of the view would lead us
one step further, and to infer as probable that all living
creatures have descended from a single prototype.

The present action of natural selection may seem more or
less probable; but I believe in the truth of the theory, because
it collects under one point of view, and gives a national explanation of, many apparently independent classes of facts.

—*Darwin.*

Selection By Man.

The power of selection, whether exercised by man, or
brought into play under nature through the struggle for existence and the consequent survival of the fittest, absolutely depends on the variability of organic beings. Without variability nothing can be effected; slight individual differences, however, suffice for the work, and are probably the sole differences
which are effective in the production of new species. Hence
our discussion on the causes and laws of variability ought in
strict order to have preceded our present subject, as well as
the previous subjects of inheritance, crossing, etc.; but practically the present arrangement has been found the most convenient. Man does not attempt to cause variability; though
he unintentionally effects this by exposing organisms to new
conditions of life, and by crossing the breeds already formed.
But variability being granted, he works wonders. Unless
some degree of selection be exercised, the free commingling of
the individuals of the same variety soon obliterates, as we have
previously seen, the slight differences which may arise, and
gives to the whole body of individuals uniformity of character.
In separated districts, long-continued exposure to different
conditions of life may perhaps produce new races without the
aid of selection; but to this difficult subject of the direct action of the conditions of life we shall in a future chapter recur.

When animals or plants are born with some conspicuous
and firmly inherited new character, selection is reduced to the
preservation of such individuals, and to the subsequent pre-
vention of crosses; so that nothing more need be said on the
subject. But in the great majority of cases a new character,
or some superiority in an old character, is at first faintly pro-

nounced, and is not strongly inherited; and then the full difficulty of selection is experienced. Indomitable patience, the
finest powers of discrimination, and sound judgment must be
exercised during many years. A clearly predetermined object
must be kept steadily in view. Few men are endowed with all
these qualities, especially with that of discriminating very
slight differences; judgment can be acquired only by long experience; but if any of these qualities be wanting, the labour
of a life may be thrown away. I have been astonished when
celebrated breeders, whose skill and judgment have been
proved by their success at exhibitions, have shown me their
animals, which appeared all alike, and have assigned their reasons for matching this and that individual. The importance of
the great principle of selection mainly lies in this power of
selecting scarcely appreciable differences, which nevertheless
are found to be transmissible, and which can be accumulated
until the result is made manifest to the eyes of every beholder.

The principle of selection may be conveniently divided into
three kinds. *Methodical selection* is that which guides a man
who systematically endeavors to modify a breed according to
some predetermined standard. *Unconscious selection* is that
which follows from men naturally preserving the most valued
and destroying the less valued individuals, without any
thought of altering the breed; and undoubtedly this process
slowly works great changes. Unconscious selection graduates
into methodical, and only extreme cases can be distinctly separated; for he who preserves a useful or perfect animal will
generally breed from it with the hope of getting offspring of
the same character; but as long as he has not a predetermined
purpose to improve the breed, he may be said to be selecting
unconsciously. Lastly, we have *Natural selection*, which implies that the individuals which are best fitted for the complex,
and in the course of ages changing, conditions to which they
are exposed, generally survive and procreate their kind. With
domestic productions, with which alone we are here strictly
concerned, natural selection comes to a certain extent into
action, independently of, and even in opposition to, the will of
man. . . .

In attributing so much importance to the selection of animals and plants, it may be objected that methodical selection

would not have been carried on during ancient times. A distinguished naturalist considers it as absurd to suppose that semi-civilized people should have practised selection of any kind. Undoubtedly the principle has been systematically acknowledged and followed to a far greater extent within the last hundred years than at any former period, and a corresponding result has been gained; but it would be a great error to suppose, as we shall immediately see, that its importance was not recognized and acted on during the most ancient times, and by semi-civilized people. I should promise that many facts now to be given only show that care was taken in breeding; but when this is the case, selection is almost sure to be practised to a certain extent. We shall be hereafter enabled better to judge how far selection, when only occasionally carried on, by a few of the inhabitants of a country, will slowly produce a great effect.

In a well-known passage in the thirtieth chapter of Genesis, rules are given for influencing, as was then thought possible, the colour of sheep; and speckled and dark breeds are spoken of as being kept separate. By the time of David the fleece was likened to snow. Youatt, who has discussed all the passages in relation to breeding in the Old Testament, concludes that at this early period "some of the best principles of breeding must have been steadily and long pursued." It was ordered, according to Moses, that "Thou shalt not let thy cattle gender with a diverse kind"; but mules were purchased, so that, at this early period, other nations must have crossed the horse and ass. It is said that Erichthonius, some generations before the Trojan war, had many brood-mares, "which, by his care and judgment in the choice of stallions, produced a breed of horses superior to any in the surrounding countries." Homer (Book V) speaks of Æneas's horses as bred from mares which were put to the steeds of Laomedon. Plato, in his "Republic," says to Glaucus, "I see that you raise at your house a great many dogs for the chase. Do you take care about breeding and pairing them? Among animals of good blood, are there not always some which are superior to the rest?" To which Glaucus answers in the affirmative. Alexander the Great selected the finest Indian cattle to send to Macedonia to improve the breed. . . .

Unconscious selection so blends into methodical that it is scarcely possible to separate them. When a fancier long ago first happened to notice a pigeon with an unusually short beak, or one with the tail-feathers unusually developed, although he bred from these birds with the distinct intention of propagating the variety, yet he could not have intended to make a short-faced tumbler or a fantail, and was far from knowing that he had made the first step towards this end. If he could have seen the final result, he would have been struck with astonishment, but, from what we know of the habits of fanciers, probably not with admiration. Our English carriers, barbs, and short-faced tumblers have been greatly modified in the same manner, as we may infer both from the historical evidence given in the chapters on the pigeon, and from the comparison of birds brought from distant countries.

So it has been with dogs; our present fox-hounds differ from the old English hound; our greyhounds have become lighter; the wolf-dog, which belonged to the greyhound class, has become extinct; the Scotch deerhound has been modified, and is now rare. Our bulldogs differ from those which were formerly used for baiting bulls. Our pointers and Newfoundlands do not closely resemble any native dog now found in the countries whence they were brought. These changes have been effected partly by crosses; but in every case the result has been governed by the strictest selection. Nevertheless there is no reason to suppose that man intentionally and methodically made the breeds exactly what they now are. As our horses became fleeter, and the country more cultivated and smoother, fleeter fox-hounds were desired and produced, but probably without any one distinctly foreseeing what they would become. Our pointers and setters, the latter almost certainly descended from large spaniels, have been greatly modified in accordance with fashion and the desire for increased speed. Wolves have become extinct, deer have become rarer, bulls are no longer baited, and the corresponding breeds of the dog have answered to the change. But we may feel almost sure that when, for instance, bulls were no longer baited, no man said to himself, I will now breed my dogs of smaller size, and thus create the present race. As circumstances changed, men unconsciously and slowly modified their course of selection.

With race-horses, selection for swiftness has been followed methodically, and our horses can now easily beat their progenitors. The increased size and different appearance of the English race-horse led a good observer in India to ask, "Could any one in this year of 1856, looking at our race-horses, conceive that they were the result of the union of the Arab horse and the African mare?" This change has, it is probable, been largely effected through unconscious selection, that is, by the general wish to breed as fine horses as possible in each generation, combined with training and high feeding, but without any intention of giving them their present appearance. . . .

Unconscious selection in the strictest sense of the word, that is, the saving of the more useful animals and the neglect or slaughter of the less useful, without any thought of the future, must have gone on occasionally from the remotest period and amongst the most barbarous nations. Savages often suffer from famines, and are sometimes expelled by war from their own homes. In such cases it can hardly be doubted that they would save their most useful animals. . . .

With plants, from the earliest dawn of civilization, the best variety which at each period was known would generally have been cultivated and its seeds occasionally sown; so that there will have been some selection from an extremely remote period, but without any prefixed standard of excellence or thought of the future. We at the present day profit by a course of selection occasionally and unconsciously carried on during thousands of years. This is proved in an interesting manner by Oswald Heer's researches on the lake-inhabitants of Switzerland, as given in a former chapter; for he shows that the grain and seed of our present varieties of wheat, barley, oats, peas, beans, lentils, and poppy, exceed in size those which were cultivated in Switzerland during the Neolithic and Bronze periods. These ancient people, during the Neolithic period, possessed also a crab considerably larger than that now growing wild on the Jura. The pears described by Pliny were evidently extremely inferior in quality to our present pears. We can realize the effects of long-continued selection and cultivation in another way, for would any one in his senses expect to raise a first-rate apple from the seed of a truly wild crab, or a luscious melting pear from the wild pear? Alphonse De Candolle informs me that he has lately seen on an ancient mosaic at Rome a representative of the melon; and as the Romans, who were such gourmands, are silent on this fruit, he infers that the melon has been greatly ameliorated since the classical period.

Coming to later times, Buffon, on comparing the flowers, fruit, and vegetables which were then cultivated, with some excellent drawings made a hundred and fifty years previously, was struck with surprise at the great improvement which had been effected; and remarks that these ancient flowers and vegetables would now be rejected, not only by a florist but by a village gardener. Since the time of Buffon the work of improvement has steadily and rapidly gone on. Every florist who compares our present flowers with those figured in books published not long since, is astonished at the change. A well-known amateur, in speaking of the varieties of Pelargonium raised by Mr. Garth only twenty-two years before, remarks: "What a rage they excited; surely we had attained perfection, it was said; and now not one of the flowers of those days will be looked at. But none the less is the debt of gratitude which we owe to those who saw what was to be done, and did it." Mr. Paul, the well-known horticulturist, in writing of the same flower, says he remembers when young being delighted with the portraits in Sweet's work; "but what are they in point of beauty compared with the Pelargoniums of this day? Here again nature did not advance by leaps; the improvement was gradual, and, if we had neglected those very gradual advances, we must have foregone the present grand results." How well this practical horticulturist appreciates and illustrates the gradual and accumulative force of selection! The Dahlia has advanced in beauty in a like manner; the line of improvement being guided by fashion, and by the successive modifications which the flower slowly underwent. A steady and gradual change has been noticed in many other flowers; thus an old florist, after describing the leading varieties of the Pink which were grown in 1813, adds: "The pinks of those days would now be scarcely grown as border-flowers." The improvement of so many flowers and the number of the varieties which have been raised is all the more striking when we hear that the earliest known flower-garden in Europe, namely, at Padua, dates only from the year 1545. . . .

On the whole, we may conclude that whatever part or character is most valued—whether the leaves, stems, tubers, bulbs, flowers, fruit, or seed of plants, or the size, strength, fleetness, hairy covering, or intellect of animals—that character will almost invariably be found to present the greatest amount of difference both in kind and degree. And this result may be safely attributed to man having preserved during a long course of generations the variations which were useful to him, and neglected the others.—*Darwin.*

THE DESERT.

The first going-down into the desert is always something of a surprise. The fancy has pictured one thing; the reality shows quite another thing. Where and how did we gain the idea that the desert was merely a sea of sand? Did it come from that geography of our youth with the illustration of the sandstorm, the flying camel, and the over-excited Bedouin? Or have we been reading strange tales told by travellers of perfervid imagination—the Marco Polos of today? There is, to be sure, some modicum of truth even in the statement that misleads. There are "seas" or lakes or ponds of sand on every desert; but they are not so vast, nor so oceanic, that you ever lose sight of the land.

What land? Why, the mountains. The desert is traversed by many mountain ranges, some of them long, some short, some low, and some rising upward ten thousand feet. They are circling you with a ragged horizon, dark-hued, bare-faced, barren—just as truly desert as the sands which were washed down from them. Between the ranges there are wide, expanding plains or valleys. The most arid portions of the desert lie in the basins of these great valleys—flat spaces that were once the beds of lakes, but are now dried out and left perhaps with an alkaline deposit that prevents vegetation. Through these valleys run arroyos, or dry stream beds—shallow channels where gravel and rocks are rolled during cloud-bursts and where sands drift with every wind. At times, the valleys are more diversified, that is, broken by benches of land called mesas, dotted with small groups of hills called lomas, crossed by long stratified faces of rock called escarpments.

With these large features of landscape common to all countries, how does the desert differ from any other land? Only in the matter of water—the lack of it. If Southern France should receive no more than two inches of rain a year for twenty years it would, at the end of that time, look very like the Sahara, and the flashing Rhone would resemble the sluggish, yellow Nile. If the Adirondack region in New York were comparatively rainless for the same length of time, we should have something like the Mojave Desert, with the Hudson changed into the red Colorado. The conformations of the lands are not widely different, but their surface appearances are as unlike as it is possible to imagine.

For the whole face of a land is changed by the rains. With them come meadow-grasses and flowers, hillside vines and bushes, fields of yellow grain, orchards of pink-white blossoms. Along the mountain sides they grow the forests of blue-green pine, on the peaks they put white caps of snow; and in the valleys they gather their waste waters into shining rivers and flashing lakes. This is the very sheen and sparkle —the witchery—of landscape which lend allurement to such countries as New England, France, or Austria, and make them livable and lovable lands.

But the desert has none of these charms. Nor is it a livable place. There is not a thing about it that is "pretty," and not a spot upon it that is "picturesque" in any Berkshire-Valley sense. The shadows of foliage, the drift of clouds, the fall of rain upon leaves, the sound of running waters—all the gentler qualities of nature that minor poets love to juggle with—are missing on the desert. It is stern, harsh, and at first repellent. But what tongue shall tell the majesty of it, the eternal strength of it, the poetry of its wide-spread chaos, the sublimity of its lonely desolation! And who shall paint the splendor of its light; and from the rising up of the sun to the going down of the moon over the iron mountains, the glory of its wondrous coloring! It is a gaunt land of splintered peaks, torn valleys, and hot skies. And at every step there is the suggestion of the fierce, the defiant, the defensive. Everything within its borders seems fighting to maintain itself against destroying forces. There is a war of elements and a struggle for existence going on here that for ferocity is unparalleled elsewhere in nature.

The feeling of fierceness grows upon you as you come to know the desert better. The sun-shafts are falling in a burning shower upon rock and dune, the winds blowing with the breath of far-off fires are withering the bushes and the grasses, the sands drifting higher and higher are burying the trees and reaching up as though they would overwhelm the mountains, the cloudbursts are rushing down the mountain's side and through the torn arroyos as though they would wash the earth into the sea. The life, too, on the desert is peculiarly savage. It is a show of teeth in bush and beast and reptile. At every turn one feels the presence of the barb and thorn, the jaw and paw, the beak and talon, the sting and the poison thereof. Even the harmless gila monster flattens his body on a rock and hisses a "Don't step on me!" There is no living in concord or brotherhood here. Everything is at war with its neighbour, and the conflict is unceasing.

Yet this conflict is not so obvious on the face of things. You hear no clash or crash or snarl. The desert is overwhelmingly silent. There is not a sound to be heard; and not a thing moves save the wind and the sands. But you look up at the worn peaks and the jagged barrancas, you look down at the washouts and the piled bowlders, you look about at the wind-tossed, half starved bushes; and, for all the silence, you know that there is a struggle for life, a war for place, going on day by day.

How is it possible under such conditions for much vegetation to flourish? The grasses are scanty, the grease-wood and cactus grow in patches, the mesquite crops out only along the dry river beds. All told, there is hardly enough covering to hide the anatomy of the earth. And the winds are always blowing it aside. You have noticed how bare and bony the hills of New England are in winter when the trees are leafless and the grasses are dead? You have seen the rocks loom up harsh and sharp, the ledges assume angles, and the backbone and ribs of the open field crop out of the soil? The desert is not unlike that all the year round. To be sure there are snowlike driftings of sand that muffle certain edges. Val-

leys, hills, and even mountains are turned into rounded lines
by it at times. But the drift rolled high in one place was cut
out from some other place; and always there are vertebræ
showing—elbows and shoulders protruding through the yellow byssus of sand.

The shifting sands! Slowly they move, wave upon wave,
drift upon drift; but by day and by night they gather, gather,
gather. They overwhelm, they bury, they destroy, and then
a spirit of restlessness seizes them and they move off elsewhere, swirl upon swirl, line upon line, in serpentine windings
that enfold some new growth or fill in some new valley in the
waste. So it happens that the surface of the desert is far from
being a permanent affair. There is hardly enough vegetation
to hold the sands in place. With little or no restraint upon
them they are transported hither and yon at the mercy of the
winds. . . .

Nature seems a benevolent or malevolent goddess just as
our own inadequate vision happens to see her. If we have
eyes only for her creative beauties we think her all goodness;
if we see only her power of destruction we incline to think she
is all evil. With what infinite care and patience, worthy only
of a good goddess, does she build up the child, the animal, the
bird, the tree, the flower! How wonderfully she fits each for
its purpose, rounding it with strength, energy, and grace; and
beautifying it with a prodigality of colors. For twenty years
she works night and day to bring the child to perfection, for
twenty days she toils upon the burnished wings of some insect
buzzing in the sunlight, for twenty hours she paints the gold
upon the petals of the dandelion. And then what? What of
the next twenty? Does she leave her handiwork to take care
of itself until an unseen dragon called Decay comes along to
destroy it? Not at all. The good goddess has a hand that
builds up. Yes; and she has another hand that takes down.
The marvellous skill of the one has its complement, its counterpart, in the other. Block by block, she takes apart the
mosaic with just as much deftness as she put it together. . . .

The virile and healthy things of the earth are hers; and so,
too, are disease, dissolution, and death. The flower and the
grass spring up; they fade; they wither; and nature neither
rejoices in the life nor sorrows in the death. She is neither

good nor evil; she is only a great law of change that passeth understanding. The gorgeous pageantry of the earth with all its beauty, the life thereon with its hopes and fears and struggles, and we a part of the universal whole, are brought up from the dust to dance on the green in the sunlight for an hour; and then the procession that comes after us turns the sod and we creep back to Mother Earth. All, all to dust again; and no man to this day knoweth the why thereof.

One is continually assailed with queries of this sort whenever and wherever he begins to study nature. He never ceases to wonder why she should take such pains to foil her own plans and bring to naught her own creations. Why did she give the flying fish such a willowy tail and such long fins, why did she labor so industriously to give him power of flight, when at the same time she was giving another fish in the sea greater strength, and a bird in the air greater swiftness wherewith to destroy him? Why should she make the tarantula such a powerful engine of destruction when she was in the same hour making his destroyer, the tarantula wasp? And always here in the desert the question comes up: Why should nature give these shrubs and plants such powers of endurance and resistance, and then surround them by heat, drouth, and the attacks of desert animals? It is existence for a day, but sooner or later the growth goes down and is beaten into dust.

The individual dies. Yes; but not the species. Perhaps now we are coming closer to an understanding of nature's method. It is the species that she designs to last, for a period at least; and the individual is of no great importance, merely a sustaining factor, one among millions requiring continual renewal. It is a small matter whether there are a thousand acres of greasewood, more or less, but it is important that the family be not extinguished. It grows readily in the most barren spots, is very abundant and very hardy, and hence is protected only by an odor and a varnish. On the contrary take the bisnaga—a rather rare cactus. It has only a thin, short tap-root, therefore it has an enormous upper reservoir in which to store water, and a most formidable armor of fishhook shaped spines that no bird or beast can penetrate. Remove the danger which threatens the extinction of the family, and immediately nature removes the defensive armor. On the desert, for instance, the yucca has a thorn like a point of steel. Follow it from the desert into the high, tropical table-lands of Mexico where there is plenty of soil and moisture, plenty of chance for yuccas to thrive, and you will find it turned into a tree, and the thorn merely a dull blade-ending. Follow the sahuaro and the pitahaya into the tropics again, and with their cousin, the organ cactus, you find them growing a soft thorn that would hardly penetrate clothing. Abundance of soil and rain, abundance of other vegetation for browsing animals, and there is no longer need of protection. With it the family would increase too rapidly.

So it seems that nature desires neither increase nor decrease in the species. She wishes to maintain the *status quo*. And for the sake of keeping up the general healthfulness and virility of her species she requires that there shall be change in the component parts. Each must suffer not a "sea change," but a chemical change; and passing into liquids, gases, or dusts, still from the grave help on the universal plan. So it is that though nature dips each one of her desert growths into the Styx to make them invulnerable, yet ever she holds them by the heel and leaves one point open to the destroying arrow.

Yet it is remarkable how nature designs and prepares the contest—the struggle for life—that is continually going on in her world. How wonderfully she arms both offense and defense! What grounds she chooses for the conflict! What stern conditions she lays down! Given a waste of sand and rock, given a heat so intense that under a summer sun the stones will blister a bare foot like hot iron, given perhaps two or three inches of rain in a twelve month; and what vegetation could one expect to find growing there? Obviously, none at all. But, no; nature insists that something shall fight heat and drouth even here, and so she designs strange growths that live a starved life, and bring forth after their kind with much labor. Hardiest of the hardy are these plants and just as fierce in their way as the wild cat. You cannot touch them for the claw. They have no idea of dying without a struggle. You will find every one of them admirably fitted to endure. They are marvelous engines of resistance.

The first thing that all these plants have to fight against is heat, drouth, and the evaporation of what little moisture they may have. And here nature has equipped them with ingenuity and cunning. Not all are designed alike, to be sure, but each after its kind is good. There are the cacti, for example, that will grow where everything else perishes. Why? For one reason because they have geometrical forms that prevent loss from evaporation by contracting a minimum surface for a given bulk of tissue. There is no waste, no unnecessary exposure of surface. Then there are some members of the family like the "old man" cactus, that have thick coatings of spines and long hairy growths that prevent the evaporation of moisture by keeping off the wind. Then again the cacti have no leaves to tempt the sun. Many of the desert growths are so constructed. Even such a tree as the lluvia d'oro has needles rather than leaves, though it does put forth a row of tiny leaves near the end of the needle; and when we come to examine the ordinary trees, such as the mesquite, the depua, the palo breya, the palo verde, and all the acacia family, we find they have very narrow leaves that have a fashion of hanging diagonally to the sun, and thus avoiding the direct rays. Nature is determined that there shall be no unnecessary exhaust of moisture through foliage. The large-leafed bush or tree does not exist. The best shade to be found on the desert is under the mesquite, and unless it is very large, the sun falls through it easily enough. . . .

But nature's most common device for the protection and preservation of her desert brood is to supply them with wonderful facilities for finding and sapping what moisture there is, and conserving it in tanks and reservoirs. The roots of the greasewood and the mesquite are almost as powerful as the arms of an octopus, and they are frequently three times the length of the bush or tree they support. They will bore their way through rotten granite to find a damp ledge almost as easily as a diamond drill; and they will pry rocks from their foundations as readily as the wistaria wrenches the ornamental woodwork from the roof of a porch. They are always thirsty, and they are always running here and there in the search for moisture. A vertical section of their underground structure revealed by the cutting away of a river bank or wash is usually a great surprise. One marvels at the great network of roots required to support such a very little growth above ground.

Yet this network serves a double purpose. It not only finds and gathers what moisture there is but stores it in its roots, feeding the top growth with it economically, not wastefully. It has no notion of sending too much moisture up to the sunlight and the air. Cut a twig and it will often appear very dry; cut a root and you will find it moist.

The storage reservoir below ground is not an unusual method of supplying water to the plant. Many of the desert growths have it. Perhaps the most notable example of it is the wild gourd. This is little more than an enormous tap-root that spreads out turnip shaped and is in size often as large around as a man's body. It holds water in its pulpy tissue for months at a time, and while almost everything above ground is parched and dying the vines and leaves of the gourd, fed from the reservoir below, will go on growing and the flowers continue blooming with the most unruffled serenity. In the Sonora deserts there is a cactus or a bush (its name I have never heard) growing from a root that looks almost like a hornet's nest. This root is half wood, half vegetable, and is again a water reservoir like the root of the gourd. . . .

Is nature's task completed then when she has provided the plants with reservoirs of water and tap-roots to pump for them? By no means. How long would a tank of moisture exist in the desert if unprotected from the desert animals? The mule-deer lives here, and he can go for weeks without water, but he will take it every day if he can get it. And the coyote can run the hills indefinitely with little or no moisture; but he will eat a watermelon, rind and all, and with great relish, when the opportunity offers. The sahuaro, the bisnaga, the cholla, and the pancake lobed prickly-pear would have a short life and not a merry one if they were left to the mercy of the desert prowler. As it is they are sometimes sadly worried about their roots by rabbits and in their lobes by the deer. It seems almost incredible but is not the less a fact, that deer and desert cattle will eat the cholla—fruit, stem, and trunk—though it bristles with spines that will draw blood from the human hand at the slightest touch.

Nature knows very well that the attack will come and so she provides her plants with various different defenses. The most common weapon which she gives them is the spine or

THE TROSSACHS.—SCOTLAND.

thorn. Almost everything that grows has it and its different forms are many. They are all of them sharp as a needle and some of them have saw-edges that rip anything with which they come in contact. The grasses, and those plants akin to them like the yucca and the maguey, are often both saw-edged and spine-pointed. All the cacti have thorns, some straight, some barbed like a harpoon, some curved like a hook. There are chollas that have a sheath covering the thorn—a scabbard to the sword—and when anything pushes against it the sheath is left sticking in the wound. The different forms of bisnaga are little more than vegetable porcupines. They bristle with quills or have hook-shaped thorns that catch and hold the intruder. The sahuaro has not so many spines, but they are so arranged that you can hardly strike the cylinder without striking the thorns.

The cacti are defended better than the other growths because they have more to lose, and are consequently more subject to attack. And yet there is one notable exception. The crucifixion thorn is a bush or tree somewhat like the palo verde, except that it has no leaf. It is a thorn and little else. Each small twig runs out and ends in a sharp spike of which the branch is but the supporting shaft. It bears in August a small, yellow flower, but this grows out of the side of the spike. In fact the whole shrub seems created for no other purpose than the glorification of the thorn as a thorn.

Tree, bush, plant and grass—great and small alike—each has its sting for the intruder. You can hardly stoop to pick a desert flower or pull a bunch of small grass without being aware of a prickle on your hand. Nature seems to have provided a whole arsenal of defensive weapons for these poor starved plants of the desert. Not any of the lovely growths of the earth, like the lilies and the daffodils, are so well defended. And she has given them not only armor but a spirit of tenacity and stubbornness wherewith to carry on the struggle. Cut out the purslain and the ironweed from the garden walk, and it springs up again and again, contending for life. Put heat, drouth, and animal attack against the desert shrubs and they fight back like the higher forms of organic life. How typical they are of everything in and about the desert. . . .

VII—30

Strange growths of a strange land! Heat, drouth, and starvation gnawing at their vitals month in and month out; and yet how determined to live, how determined to fulfill their destiny! They keep fighting off the elements, the animals, the birds. Never by day or by night do they loose the armor or drop the spear point. And yet with all the struggle they serenely blossom in season, perpetuate their kinds, and hand down the struggle to the newer generation with no jot of vigor abated, no tittle of hope dissipated. Strange growths indeed! And yet strange, perhaps, only to us who have never known their untrumpeted history.—*John C. Van Dyke.*

THE SEA.

Who has not heard, amid the heat and din of cities, the voice of the sea striking suddenly into the hush of thought its penetrating note of mystery and longing? Then work and the fever which goes with it vanished on the instant, and in the crowded street or in the narrow room there rose the vision of unbroken stretches of sky, free winds, and the surge of the unresting waves. That invitation never loses its alluring power; no distance wastes its music, and no preoccupation silences its solicitation. It stirs the oldest memories, and awakens the most primitive instincts; the long past speaks through it, and through it the buried generations snatch a momentary immortality. History that has left no record, rich and varied human experiences that have no chronicle, rise out of the forgetfulness in which they are engulfed, and are puissant once more in the intense and irresistible longing with which the heart answers the call of the sea. Once more the blood flows with fuller pulse, the eye flashes with conscious freedom and power, the heart beats to the music of wind and wave, as in the days when the fathers of a long past spread sail and sought home, spoil, or change upon the trackless waste. Into every past the sea has some time sounded its mighty note of joy or anguish, and deep in every memory there remains some vision of tossing waves that once broke on eyes long sealed.

All day the free winds have filled the heavens, and flung here and there a handful of foam upon the surface of the deep. No cloud has dimmed the splendor of a day which has filled the round heavens with soft music and touched the sea with strange and changeful beauty. It has been enough to wait and watch, to forget self, to escape the limitations of personality, and to become part of the movement which, hour by hour, has passed through one marvelous change after another, until now it seems to pause under the sleepless vigilance of the stars. They look down from their immeasurable altitudes on the vast expanse of which only a miniature hemisphere stretches before me. How wide and fathomless seems the ocean, even from a single isolated point! What infinite distances are only half veiled by the distant horizon line! What islands and continents and undiscovered worlds lie beyond that faint and ever receding circle where the sight pauses, while the thought travels unimpeded on its pathless way? There lies the untamed world which brooks no human control, and preserves the primeval solitude of the epochs before men came; there are the elemental forces mingling and commingling in eternal fellowships and rivalries. There the winds sweep, and the storms marshal their shadows as on the first day; there, too, the sunlight sleeps on the summer sea as it slept in those forgotten summers before a sail had ever whitened the blue, or a keel cut evanescent furrows in the trackless waste.

Every hour has brought its change to make this day memorable; hour by hour the lights have transformed the waters and hung over them a sky full of varied and changeful radiance. Across the line of the distant horizon white sails have come and gone in broken and mysterious procession, and the imagination has followed them far in their unknown journeyings. As silently as they passed from sight, all human history enacted in this vast province of nature's empire has vanished, and left no trace of itself save here and there a bit of driftwood. There lies the unconquered and forever inviolate kingdom of forces over which no human skill will ever cast the net of conquest.

The sea speaks to the imagination as no other aspect of the natural world does, because of its vastness, its immeasurable and overwhelming power, its exclusion from human history, its free, buoyant, changeful being. It stands for those strange and unfamiliar revelations with which nature sometimes

breaks in upon our easy relation with her, and brings back
on the instant that sense of remoteness which one feels when
in intimate fellowship a friend suddenly lifts the curtain from
some great experience hitherto unsuspected. In the vast sweep
of 'life through Nature there must always be aspects of awful
strangeness; great realms of mystery will remain unexplored,
and almost inaccessible to human thought; days will dawn at
intervals in which those who love most and are nearest to
Nature will feel an impenetrable cloud over all things, and be
suddenly smitten with a sense of weakness; the greatest of all
her interpreters are but children in knowledge of her mighty
activities and forces. On the sea this sense of remoteness and
strangeness comes oftener than in the presence of any other
natural form; even the mountains make sheltered places for
our thought at their feet, or along their precipitous ledges; but
the sea makes no concessions to our human weakness, and
leaves the message which it intones with the voice of tempest
and the roar of surge without an interpreter. Men have come
to it in all ages, full of a passionate desire to catch its meaning
and enter into its secret, but the thought of the boldest of them
has only skirted its shores, and the vast sweep of untamed
waters remains as on the first day. Ulysses has given us the
song of the land-locked sea, but where has the ocean found a
human voice that is not lost and forgotten when it speaks to
us in its own penetrating tones? The mountains stand revealed in more than one interpretation, touched by their own
sublimity, but the sea remains silent in human speech, because
no voice will ever be strong enough to match its awful
monody.

It is because the sea preserves its secret that it sways our
imagination so royally, and holds us by an influence which
never loosens its grasp. Again and again we return to it,
spent and worn, and it refills the cup of vitality; there is life
enough and to spare in its invisible and inexhaustible chambers to reclothe the continents with verdure, and recreate the
shattered strength of man. Facing its unbroken solitudes the
limitations of habit and thought become less obvious; we escape the monotony of a routine which blurs the senses and
makes the spirit less sensitive to the universe about it. Life
becomes free and plastic once more; a deep consciousness of

its inexhaustibleness comes over us and recreates hope, vigor and imagination. Under the little bridges of habit and theory, which we have made for ourselves, how vast and fathomless the sea of being is! What undiscovered forces are there; what unknown secrets of power; what unsearchable possibilities of development and change! How fresh and new becomes that which we thought outworn with use and touched with decay! How boundless and untraveled that which we thought explored and sounded to its remotest bound!

At night, when the vision of the waters grows indistinct, what voices it has for our solitude! The "eternal note of sadness," to which all ages and races have listened, and the faint echoes of which are heard in every literature, fills us with a longing as vast as the sea and as vague. Infinity and eternity are not too great for the spirit when the spell of the sea is on it, and the voice of the sea fills it with uncreated music.—*Mabie.*

The Sky.

We think little about the sky, can roam for hours beneath it without looking up; and yet it is the most assertive object in the outlook; poets have applied to it more adjectives than to any object beneath. They descant on "the witchery of the soft blue sky," but what of the heartlessness of the steel-blue canopy, when there is not a trace of life within sight or hearing? The cloudless sky of June is not that of January.

Because there were few birds, fewer flowers, and but little green grass where I chanced to wander, I took the hint from Ovid: the skies are open—let us try the skies. So I looked long upon them as they overhung the old meadows, old as the glacial period, and yet how new as compared with the sky that now looked down upon them! Today the sky was blue, fading to violet, with one great white cloud that slowly marched to intercept the sun. It was with keen pleasure that I watched this rolled and rounded mass of drifted snow, for such it seemed, draw near. It did not dissolve nor hurry in torn fragments from the fray, but with bold front shut out the sunbeams. What a marvellous change takes place when the meadows are shifted from sunshine to shade! That short-lived shadow brought in its train a whispering breeze, but so gently did it pass that I fancied it was the shadow itself that whispered.

A word here as to the imagination. If it is kept within too close bounds, your outing is likely to prove so many miles of walking to no purpose. It is not fair to say that inaccuracy is sure to follow the free play of the imagination. Our fancy need not act as a distorting glass, and does not, except with the author's connivance. The greatest blunderers about Nature have been the precise students who occasionally find themselves outside their closets. It is one thing, as Bryant puts it, to

> Go forth under the open sky and list
> To Nature's teachings,

but another to know what to do when you get there. My suggestion is to let your imagination have scope as well as your appreciation of the actual facts you meet with. There need be no conflict in your mind, nor any misleading statement, if you are moved to speak.

To return: quickly again the sky was bright and blue, and the meadows were filled with light—a clear, warm, penetrating light, that was reaching the rootlets and bulbs in the damp soil, quickening them. The grape hyacinth had already responded, and reflected the deepest color the April skies had offered; and the earliest of our larger lilies was above the grass, with the yellow of the noonday glare in its blossoms. These flowers show well together, representing on earth the sun and sky; but how seldom do we turn from them to the high heavens! A few flowers will hold us while the firmament is marked by conditions which may, at least in our lifetime, never again occur.

There is a world of suggestiveness in the words just used, "my summer skies." Therein lies ownership of a wholly satisfactory kind. They are mine without cost, without even the asking, and, better still, without depriving others—mine, yours, the common wealth of all; and yet few, it appears, place any value upon them. To many they are of as little importance as the frame of a picture; yet often they are the real picture and the earth is but the naked platform upon which we stand to view it. It is hard to find a fitting phrase for many a panoramic sky; as the skies of early June, blue of incomparable shade, with white clouds, pink-edged and piled into fantastic shapes—great castles that are unbuilt before you can people them with the merry elves and fays of the month of roses. In June we have those bright skies that deepen when the day is done to blue-black, and, losing their flatness, are lifted to a hollow dome that, star-studded, shows you at last how very far away it really is. The skies that at noon rested on the treetops that hem in the little space about us grow immeasurably grand at midnight; and when from out these starlit skies we hear strange voices, they assume a new importance, and we begin to realize better their significance. The upper region, our sky, is seldom lacking in animal life. Probably hundreds of birds, in the course of a day, pass over us, just out of sight; and when in the silent watches of the night we plainly hear the voices of wanderers, a new chapter of ornithology is opened to us. The clear-toned call of a plover, the hoarse croak of a raven, the chirping of many finches, the fretful scream of an eagle, have all been noted in a single night. We can only follow these birds in fancy, but the fancy will not lead us astray. The direction in which they are going can be determined, the probable elevation of their flight-path estimated, the guiding features of their course made probable. Their purpose can, of course, only be conjectured. It is not strange that birds of many if not all kinds travel in the dark, for this absence of light is but relative. The stars of themselves are nothing to the birds but as they are reflected in the water. When visible in this way, they act as finger-posts along a river valley. Such doubtless is the guide to much of the annual migratorial flight; and the black lines of mountains would be readily recognized as such, while the lights beyond would indicate those of another valley, with its star-reflecting river. So comprehensive is a bird's-eye view that migration has nothing remarkable about it. May it not be, too, that these long journeys are commenced in daylight, and that when great elevation is reached the direction at the outset can be readily maintained? A bird does not fly in a circle, as a man walks when lost in the woods. When fog or excessive cloudiness is encountered, wandering birds drop to the earth, as is shown by water-birds being found upon our upland fields, perhaps miles from their accustomed haunts. . . .

Gossamer and old gold; brown leaves, bleached grasses, and gray twigs; green pines, that now look black in the distance, and frost-defying mosses; such are the salient features of this bright November day. I am in a new country and at every step am met by strangers, but I know their cousins that are dwellers with me on the home hillside. To feel that I am a stranger robs the world of half its beauty. I cannot rid myself of the repressing thought; but, if a stranger today, I am fortunately alone, and that compensates for much; alone today in a wild-wood road, and it is now Indian summer.

It is a long, narrow roadway, with a deep ditch on each side and no special side path for the pedestrian. It is assumed by the traveling community that two vehicles never meet, and the man on foot who meets a wagon must jump into the thicket that hems him in or be run over. So it seemed, at least, until the unexpected wagon did appear, when I found the problem might be solved by climbing over, but I preferred jumping, the ditch, and did so. The teamster, as he passed, hailed me with "What you lost?" and set me down as a liar when I told him "Nothing." No one could be in such a place without an errand, so he thought, and I had no gun to suggest the hunter. But I had an errand, and before the day was done, found I had lost much in not having come to this wildwood road years ago.

Thoreau has said, "Nature gets thumbed like an old spelling-book," but by how many? Carry fringed gentian to town, and by the gaping crowd you will be thought to have plucked it from some garden enclosure or found a hothouse door unlocked. I am surprised the more at Thoreau's remark because my path has so seldom led me among these asserted familiars of the outdoor world. On the contrary, how all-prevalent is ignorance and unusual is earth-knowledge! To be of the earth earthy is beyond question pre-eminently desirable, and yet how generally we study to keep clear of it, lest the black soil may spot our clothing, or, sinking deeper, stain the immaculate whiteness of our ignorance. Nature is like a spelling-book, as Thoreau has suggested, but put our spelling-book into the hands of a Hottentot and what does he find? We are too generally Hottentots in this regard; adepts at misinterpretation, or, fearing a lurking devil in every shadow, huddle in the

glaring light and distort every straight line and rob of beauty
every one with a graceful curve. The pages of nature's spelling-book may be smeared, rumpled, and dog's-eared—too
often they are—but how often are they seriously studied?
We hold it upside down, or study the title-page and turn
away, posing as philosophers. It is well to dig, but all the
bones in a quarry will not make a naturalist of you if they are
merely bones, and the mind's eye cannot see them reclothed in
the flesh. This is thumbing the book and never learning to
spell even a-b, ab. So far Thoreau was right. But this is
Indian summer and no time to preach or grumble, but to meditate. This golden renaissance will teach you a great deal upon
one condition: you must be passive and let the knowledge
come to you. Indian summer is timid. Her efforts to reclothe
the earth with gladness are not free from doubt. Every ray
of reviving sunshine is on the alert lest it be attacked by lurking north winds. Few birds in November sing with a May-
day confidence, but they do sing, and this passing hour I have
seen seventeen different species of birds, and, except in two
cases, several individuals of each species, and not for one second has there been silence. At least the crows were to be
heard, and what a hearty, whole-souled chatter theirs is! The
subject under discussion by them is seldom to be determined,
but now they are scolding at a hawk that has sailed by, and
it heeds them but little. A mere dip of the wing and this
master of flight is above or below its tormentors, or, with a
quick movement of both wings, it rushes far beyond the crows,
and now is heard a wild, triumphant cry that thrills me to the
very finger-tips. But not all the world's life is now in the
upper air. There are birds as much at home in the bushes as
are hawks in the clouds, and I turn to them at their invitation, but as quickly bid them adieu when sounds that smack of
novelty fill the air. The genial sunshine has warmed the quiet
waters by the wood road, and all the chill has left the broad
patches of grey-green sphagnum, and now the chorus of a
hundred frogs recalls the like warm days of early April when
I wander to the meadows. I can scarcely detect these frogs,
however closely I look. They still cling suspiciously close to
mother earth, but from their doubting throats rises a thanks-
giving that floats away like a misty cloud and dies in the si-

lence of the upper air. Again and again I hear it, and then the trembling leafless twigs and rattle of frost-defying leaves gives warning that the sunshine has met its old enemy, the wind, and the frogs sink back to their hidden homes.

Were it not for floating masses of thick, white clouds that shut out the warmth for the moment there would be even more continuous sound these late autumn days. Everything seems to depend upon it. I have often noticed how quickly a bird will cease to sing the moment it is in the shade and how promptly it resumed its song when the bright sun-rays fell upon it. It is really, I think, a matter of warmth rather than the amount of light, but during uniformly cloudy days there is less disposition to sing than when the weather is bright. In short, take the year through, it is a matter of silence in shadows and melody in the sunlit air. While still lingering by the wayside pool and watching a slight ripple on the still surface, a turtle popped its head above the water and gazed about in every direction. I made no motion and so passed for a stick, one of the many hundreds about me. What it thought of the outlook is a matter of doubt in my mind, but following so soon after the chorus of reawakened frogs, it doubtless wondered what all that noise was about, and looked at the world with its own eyes, to determine the truth of the matter. Perhaps it set the frogs down as liars, for the turtle quickly disappeared, and, though I waited long, saw it no more.

It was a short-long journey that I went today—short as the crow flies; long if measured by its wealth of suggestiveness. This swamp, that I would covered thousands of acres, is but a matter of a few hundred, and these will soon be drained, deforested, and despoiled of all its nature-given glory. It is an idle fancy to suppose it foreknows its doom, but so lavish was it of all its beauties it seemed as if hopeful that its brave showing would prove effectual to its preservation. Bright color is not solely a feature of summer or of early autumn leaves; I found it in this solitary swamp, where every leaf had fallen. Bittersweet, fruit laden and so fiery red that the air seemed to glow with heat about it. The summer long this plant had been an unpretending vine, that mingled its green leaves with the common crowd of rank weeds, and gave no hint of its superiority. In the fast and furious struggle for supremacy while the warm days of feverish sunshine lasted, it was content to slowly build for the future, and not then and there exhaust itself in merely overtopping its neighbors, and what of the sequel? Now, in these glorious mid-November days, these bird-full, musical days of misty sunshine and rejuvenating warmth, the vine, that had so long been overlooked, is the chief glory of the roadside. . . .

"If a walk in winter is not simply stumbling over the graves of a dead summer's darlings, what, pray, is it?" In some such way ran the remark of a man who had seen our winters only from car-windows or those of his house on the city street. It is not strange that he held such an opinion. Not even a sleigh-ride affords a fair view of the world in winter. We must be free to move if we would be free to see, and only when on foot and we have the freedom of the fields as well as of the highways can we know what winter really means, and by winter I mean weather that requires us to make war upon the wood-pile. Winter is the crystallization of a summer. A fixedness and quiet now replace the flowing river and music of the many birds that sang throughout its valley. Now are the days of slender shadows that streak the dull gray ground or send narrow lines of darkness over the untrodden snow. The shades of leafy summer are shrunken. There are dimly lighted nooks where cedars cluster and crannies that are well defended by the frozen ferns, but light is all-pervading, in a general sense, and how wide open alike are the fields and forest! The opened door is an invitation to enter, but how slow are we to accept the invitation of winter, when the leafy curtains are withdrawn, and the world more than ever open to inspection! Are we to be forever afraid to look through the bare twigs to the sky above, lest we see the new moon barred by a branch and so tremble for our luck? The naked beam and rafter of Nature's temple are not desolate as the ruin of man's handiwork, for we know that their covering will be renewed in due season. Trees, indeed, in their undress uniform are none the less natural and forever retain their individuality. The wrinkles of the bark are their autographs, and we should learn to read them.

But what is winter to me? The brook, the leafless trees, the frozen grass, and all hungry life, whether bird or beast, protest, but I find no reason to complain. My needs are never many, and I have no sense of want when "fun in feathers," the crested tit, bears me company. We met this morning at the three beeches, and wandered together down the wood road to the edge of the meadow. I have been walking here for so many years there is danger of repetition if I mention today; but no, Nature is never a repetition. The fault lies with ourselves if this is apparently true. Nature cares nothing for us, and we must force her to smile if we would be at all favored. The wind has other errands than to whistle for our amusement; no storm ever passed by on the other side because of our presence. All that we learn comes from our own efforts; we must wrest Nature's secrets from her; she neither invites us nor volunteers any information. Every day has its own history, and the friends of yesterday are often more companionable today. Certainly my jolly, crested tit has gained since first we met, and now is nearer perfection than ever before. I am sure of this, and yet much may be due to a clearer insight as to what a bird really is. Is my companion bird ever convinced I have no weapon about me? Tame as he is, he never destroys the bridges behind him. I cannot quite gain his confidence. I fancy if some of us could see ourselves as birds see us, with what a sense of degradation would we be overwhelmed! Seldom is it that we are not greeted, by every bird we meet, as a red-handed murderer. An exception today, however, for this jolly tit was socially inclined. He peeped over his shoulder as I drew near; called out to me as I was about to pass by, and so we exchanged "good-mornings" as friend to friend. It is difficult to decide whether man or bird was really the leader, we kept so near together as we passed to the end of our woodland journey.

It needs but some such incident as this to give us insight as to winter's real character. There can come no impression of death or desolation when, as we pass, we have birds hailing us from every treetop, and is it not significant that our smallest bird, save one, braves our severest weather? Yet we muffle ourselves in endless wraps and rush frantically from shelter to shelter when the mercury ranges low, as if the frost of a midwinter day was as fatal as some devouring flame.

—*Abbott.*

WONDERS OF POND LIFE.

The microscope is a wonderful instrument. Few purchases will afford so much enjoyment, for after you have learned to use it, it will bring to light thousands of curious minute living animals and plants which, in your oddest dreams, you never thought of.

One who looks through it into a drop of water thickly populated, looks into another world, as it were; for under the objective appear some of the lowest forms of life, from mere masses of gelatine, moving along upon the glass slide, which may belong either to the animal or vegetable kingdom, up to the tiny specimens of *Crustacea,* the water fleas.

Let's go to the pond, down by the willows, this beautiful morning. It is as good a place as any to obtain the tiny wonders, although life is everywhere: in the air, on the earth, flying and crawling; even the mould on this stick, which we pick up on our way, is a collection of living plants that bear fruit; where creatures, perhaps, are crawling among the branches—creatures so small as to be invisible to the naked eye, but which the microscope would reveal.

In place of hooks, lines and baskets we bring two or three wide-mouthed vials and a good dipnet, for we are after smaller curiosities than bream and perch, which seem to be having a kind of dumb carousal in their little world as we approach the shore.

Do you notice this green scum on the surface, around the edge of the pond? Yes, you have seen it a hundred times before. It looks like litter and the commonest filth, does it not? Yet, believe me, this rubbish, as you might call it, is composed of fresh growing plants floating or rolling about in the still or slowly-running water, and getting their nourishment from it, as other plants get their food from the earth. These kinds of plants belong to a family called *Algae,* which really means seaweed, and is so named because so many species grow in the ocean; but those we see in ponds and streams are so very small that the microscope is needed to tell us how curiously they are put together.

Let us now fill our vials with this "green stuff," making sweeps with our nets as we walk around the shores, gathering in not only plants, but green forms of animal life, and hasten home to inspect our booty. To enjoy a few of the interesting things that we see in our walk, each one should be provided with a microscope.

Hold up a vial to the light and look at those little green balls, scarcely a thirtieth of an inch in diameter, rolling round and round in the water, like mimic worlds in space. Let us catch one or two of them with your dipping tube, and place them carefully in a single drop on the glass slide or "live box." Now look down through the instrument, and see how large it has suddenly grown. This is *Volvox globator* (rolling ball). It looks now like a crystal ball, covered over with a delicate network. At the corners of the meshes are seen bright green specks, like small shining emerald beads. We will screw on to the end of the tube another object-glass, which seems to make this revolving globe still larger, and find that these green specks are not specks at all, but little club-shaped bodies, each having two very fine hairs or cilia, as they are called, attached to them, which are continually moving, and which serve as paddles to propel the globe through the water.

These green bodies, of which the *Volvox* is composed, are incorrectly called *Zoospores*, from *Zoon*, an animal, and *Sporos*, a seed, and have the power of moving round so lively from place to place, that at first it seems impossible to believe that they are not animals; but after a great deal of talk among learned persons it has been at last decided that these curious objects are plants, and belong to that great family *(Algae)* of which we have spoken.

How do these plants grow? At certain times each one of those *Zoospores*, or moving seeds, have buds growing from them, or are divided into two parts, and each of these two parts becomes in its turn the parent of other cells which change into moving seeds, and, being very social little bodies, gather themselves in little round balls within the larger globe. There are nine of these small green spheres in the one we see, which, if nothing had happened to them, would finally have burst through the walls of the mother plant, and started off on their rolling excursions to rear in turn other families. Both the parent plant and her children have openings or pores through which the water flows, giving them the food and air they need. These we cannot see because our instrument is not of sufficient power. * * *

The crew of that wonderful submarine ship of Jules Verne's imagination never encountered more surprising creatures than one can collect in a day's search in any pond or stream within a radius of ten miles of the metropolis. The gigantic mollusk seen by Nemo at the bottom of the ocean would be less amazing to me than the larvæ of the May-fly, the common caddis-worm, which have the curious instinct of building for themselves millions of homes for the protection of their dainty bodies against the crafty and greedy fish. There are several species, two of which we will at once put under our glass. They are working amid a thousand perils; here a playful shiner swims up noiselessly to nibble, but the stonemason suddenly quits his labor and goes in. The danger being over, it cautiously shows its head again, and resumes the occupation of clutching with its mandibles and feet small grains of sand, actually turning each grain over and over, as the workman in building a stone wall will turn a rock in his hands to decide its best fitting-place. Then with waterproof cement (saliva) it places grain after grain around the end of the case, until it is completed. In this little round stone house it crawls along on the bottom of the tank, comparatively safe, proving too much for even a fish's curiosity, but at the expense of a very heavy burden, and, when in its native stream, eking out a most precarious existence of two years.

The other species under our observation is quite small and not so clumsy. Its house is made of short, narrow strips of grass, pasted together by the animal, and arranged in regular spirals. From it appear the head and two pairs of legs, by which it propels itself through the water, always maintaining a perpendicular position, and waltzing up to the surface in a most comical manner. We will rob this fellow of his home. The creature offers some resistance, of course, but by careful maneuvering the burglary is committed without taking life. The interior is richly upholstered with fine spun silk, which no doubt secures the animal within the case, and prevents its tender body from rubbing too hard against the coarse material of which it is composed. On each side of the body are six pairs of leaf-like gills, connecting with air-tubes by which this most interesting larva breathes. After viewing its forlorn condition, we thrust it on the cold mercies of the aquarium, wherein it immediately sets about prospecting for another house.

What curious insects are these water-boatmen! Look up through the water at them. A few playful but masterly exhibitions of their skill, and they arrive opposite the judge's stand, lying on their backs. How much their wing-covers resemble a miniature canoe, water-tight, and shining like burnished silver! Evidently they are preparing for the start; see, one of them is cleaning its paddles and brushing its keel, as

———"wet flies twist their thighs
When they wipe their heads and eyes."

Look on deck with the magnifier!

Their hind legs, which they move to propel their boat-like bodies through the water, precisely as a single rower propels a boat, are very long and made broad, like oar-blades, by the thick, long hairs.

What finely constructed row-locks! Old as the world, and never patented! There they go. How nicely they feather their oars—why, Hanlon never dreamed of such a stroke.

Here is a white leech, measuring its slow length along the side of the tank. Has any naturalist noticed this species? What wonderful maternal forbearance and affections! Fourteen little young leeches, all very much attached (literally) to their loving mother.

Twisted around the stem of a water-cress is the *Gordius aquaticus,* or hair-worm. This specimen is one foot long, and no larger than a common hair of a horse's mane or tail. It is continually in motion; now tying itself into a complicated knot, now straightening itself out to its full length. The general belief that they are transformed horse hairs is incorrect. The history of their development from the egg is most interesting. After hatching, the larva escapes into the water and casts about to find some neighboring aquatic fly-maggot, upon which it fastens itself and finally penetrates the body by means of spines on its head. Here it lives as a boarder, inclosed in a tight sack, until some hungry minnow passing by, gulps down the larva, young hair-worm and all. No sooner has the process of digestion set it free from its sack within the body of the maggot than it begins to make another bag for itself within the lining of the fish's intestines, where it lives five or six months. At the end of this period it is cast forth into its world of waters, remaining in a quiet condition until it has grown two inches or more in length, when it turns a rusty color and begins to move as we see it now. . . .

The beetles living in the water are really curious. It is interesting to watch their habits as they go paddling round in the glass tank, as busy as on the first day of their captivity; now swimming here and there as briskly as some of their land relatives run, now diving to the bottom to roll up portions of silt, or to rest on some accommodating snail, which is making its daily tour of inspection along the sides. The gentle vegetable-feeding carp or the smaller dace do not disturb their wanderings, but live with them as a happy family, apparently regarding them as the rightful occupant. How nicely has far-seeing Nature modified the different genera of *Coleoptera* she intended to be aquatic! One pair of legs are altered into oars, or covered with stiff hairs, by which they propel their boat-like bodies through the water, while the wing-covers, and the fine pubescence on the abdomen, and in some species on the thorax, are especially adapted to hold the film or bubble of air for respiration, thus enabling these creatures to remain a long time under water to obtain their food.—*Hunt.*

THE SONG OF THE FLOWERS.

I HID in my garden one night in June
    To listen for fairy and flower lore—
For they danced and sang in this garden of mine
    As they danced and sang in the days of yore.
A troop of daisies, a pink, a rose,
    And jaunty pansies with butterfly wings
Came trooping along with a merry song—
    The song each happy flower sings.
I lurked in the shadows and listened long,
    While whispering breezes gently stirred;
The yellow moonlight spattered around,
    And this at length was what I heard:
A lily spake to a clover bloom—

VII—31

The lily was white and the clover red;
.I could not hear for the busy winds
All of the message that she said,
But she spake of love, and the clover blushed—
Blushed and nodded and hid its face.
Then rose again with a beaming eye,
As one who has said a heartfelt grace.

"God is good, we bloom today,
Others will bloom when we are dead;
Life and death are alike to us,
Though one be white and the other red.
Love and beauty are all of life—
All that the angels have, have we;
For love's flowers shall never cease
Nor love and beauty cease to be.

Back to the earth we give our seeds,
Up from the glad earth spring again:
A merry dance of life and death—
Children we of the sun and rain.
All the dreams that fairies dream,
All the poems that fairies weave,
All the learning of fairy schools,
All the griefs that fairies grieve—
These are in the songs we sing,
Sing in the merry month of June;
Sing to drowsy mortal ears;
Sing to frighten the pallid moon.
We live and we give the best that we have,
Give without grudging heart and life;
He who gives the most is king—
This is the merry flowers' strife.

"God is good, we bloom today;
Others will bloom when we are dead.
Life and death are alike to us,
Though one be white and the other red."

Such was the song the flowers sang
As I hid unseen in the garden there,
And I rose transformed with a glad new thought,
Angel-toned; 'tis nature's prayer:
Living is giving, and love is life;
Beauty is reason enough to be;
Hope is another name for strife,
Death is life in another key.

THOREAU.

HENRY DAVID THOREAU was born in Concord, Massachusetts, July 12, 1817. He died there in 1862. His parents were poor and it was with difficulty that the boy acquired an education, graduating in time from Harvard. He tried teaching but found the school-room too confining, while on the other hand his own eccentric ideas of inculcating knowledge did not generally find favor.

During Thoreau's early manhood many sentiments were written and expressed about a new manner of life. *Simplicity* was the cry of the age—as it has sometimes been since. Various plans for community life were attempted, notably "Brook Farm," in which Emerson, the Alcotts, Margaret Fuller and others were interested. Thoreau had a strong aversion to any form of life which might threaten the *individuality* of man; hence, he turned to solitary life as an existence better suited to himself. While he lived quite a portion of his years in this fashion, he never severed a close relationship with his fellowmen.

Thoreau was a lover of nature rather than a scientist. He made friends with all animate things, communed with trees and found more solace in the fields, the meadows and the forests than in social gatherings and drawing-room conversation. Indeed, he cared little for the conventionalities of society. It is not too much to say that like many another, Thoreau did not object to being thought eccentrical and seems to have cultivated certain individualities for the very purpose of shocking the sensitive. On the other hand, he was himself sensitive, sympathetic and very human, in spite of criticisms to the contrary.

"Walden," "Cape Cod," and "The Week" will perhaps prove his most enduring books.

WHERE I LIVED AND WHAT I LIVED FOR.

At a certain season of our life we are accustomed to consider every spot as the possible site of a house. I have thus surveyed the country on every side within a dozen miles of where I live. In imagination I have bought all the farms in succession, for all were to be bought, and I knew their price.

I walked over each farmer's premises, tasted his wild apples, discoursed on husbandry with him, took his farm at his price, at any price, mortgaging it to him in my mind; even put a higher price on it,—took everything but a deed of it,—took his word for his deed, for I dearly love to talk,—cultivated it, and him to some extent, I trust, and withdrew when I had enjoyed it long enough, leaving him to carry it on. This experience entitled me to be regarded as a sort of real-estate broker by my friends. Wherever I sat, there I might live, and the landscape radiated from me accordingly. What is a house but a *sedes,* a seat?—better if a country seat. I discovered many a site for a house not likely to be soon improved, which some might have thought too far from the village, but to my eyes the village was too far from it. Well, there I might live, I said; and there I did live, for an hour, a summer and a winter life; saw how I could let the years run off, buffet the winter through, and see the spring come in. The future inhabitants of this region, wherever they may place their houses, may be sure that they have been anticipated. An afternoon sufficed to lay out the land into orchard, woodlot, and pasture, and to decide what fine oaks or pines should be left to stand before the door, and whence each blasted tree could be seen to the best advantage; and then I let it lie, fallow perchance, for a man is rich in proportion to the number of things which he can afford to let alone.

My imagination carried me so far that I even had the refusal of several farms,—the refusal was all I wanted,—but I never got my fingers burned by actual possession. The nearest that I came to actual possession was when I bought the Hollowell place, and had begun to sort my seeds, and collected materials with which to make a wheelbarrow to carry it on or off with; but before the owner gave me a deed of it, his wife —every man has such a wife—changed her mind and wished to keep it, and he offered me ten dollars to release him. Now, to speak the truth, I had but ten cents in the world, and it surpassed my arithmetic to tell, if I was that man who had ten cents, or who had a farm, or ten dollars, or all together. However, I let him keep the ten dollars and the farm too, for I had carried it far enough; or rather, to be generous, I sold him the farm for just what I gave for it, and, as he was not a rich man, made him a present of ten dollars, and still had my ten cents, and seeds, and materials for a wheelbarrow left. I found thus that I had been a rich man without any damage to my poverty. But I retained the landscape, and I have since annually carried off what it yielded without a wheelbarrow. With respect to landscapes,—

> "I am monarch of all I *survey,*
> My right there is none to dispute."

I have frequently seen a poet withdraw, having enjoyed the most valuable part of a farm, while the crusty farmer supposed that he had got a few wild apples only. Why, the owner does not know it for many years when a poet has put his farm in rhyme, the most admirable kind of invisible fence, has fairly impounded it, milked it, skimmed it, and got all the cream, and left the farmer only the skimmed milk.

The real attractions of the Hollowell farm, to me, were: its complete retirement, being about two miles from the village, half a mile from the nearest neighbor, and separated from the highway by a broad field; its bounding on the river, which the owner said protected it by its fogs from frosts in the spring, though that was nothing to me; the gray color and ruinous state of the house and barn, and the dilapidated fences, which put such an interval between me and the last occupant; the hollow and lichen-covered apple trees, gnawed by rabbits, showing what kind of neighbors I should have; but above all, the recollection I had of it from my earliest voyages up the river, when the house was concealed behind a dense grove of red maples, through which I heard the house-dog bark. I was in haste to buy it, before the proprietor finished getting out some rocks, cutting down the hollow apple trees, and grubbing up some young birches which had sprung up in the pasture, or, in short, had made any more of his improvements. To enjoy these advantages I was ready to carry it on; like Atlas, to take the world on my shoulders,—I never heard what compensation he received for that,—and do all those things which had no other motive or excuse but that I might pay for it and be unmolested in my possession of it; for I knew all the while that it would yield the most abundant crop of the kind I wanted if I could only afford to let it alone. But it turned out as I have said.

All that I could say, then, with respect to farming on a large scale (I have always cultivated a garden), was, that I had had my seeds ready. Many think that seeds improve with age. I have no doubt that time discriminates between the good and the bad: and when at last I shall plant, I shall be less likely to be disappointed. But I would say to my fellows, once for all, As long as possible live free and uncommitted. It makes but little difference whether you are committed to a farm or the county jail.

Old Cato, whose "De Re Rustica" is my "Cultivator," says, and the only translation I have seen makes sheer nonsense of the passage, "When you think of getting a farm, turn it thus in your mind, not to buy greedily; nor spare your pains to look at it, and do not think it enough to go around it once. The oftener you go there the more it will please you, if it is good." I think I shall not buy greedily, but go round and round it as long as I live, and be buried in it first, that it may please me the more at last.

The present was my next experiment of this kind, which I purpose to describe more at length; for convenience putting the experience of two years into one. As I have said, I do not propose to write an ode to dejection, but to brag as lustily as chanticleer in the morning, standing on his roost, if only to wake my neighbors up.

When first I took up my abode in the woods, that is, began to spend my nights as well as days there, which, by accident, was on Independence day, or the fourth of July, 1845, my house was not finished for winter, but was merely a defence against the rain, without plastering or chimney, the walls being of rough weather-stained boards, with wide chinks, which made it cool at night. The upright white hewn studs and freshly planed door and window casings gave it a clean and airy look, especially in the morning, when its timbers were saturated with dew, so that I fancied that by noon some sweet gum would exude from them. To my imagination it retained throughout the day more or less of this auroral character, reminding me of a certain house on a mountain which I had visited the year before. This was an airy and unplastered cabin, fit to entertain a traveling god, and where a goddess might trail her garments. The winds which passed over my dwelling were such as sweep over the ridges of mountains, bearing the broken strains, or celestial parts only, of terrestrial music. The morning wind forever blows, the poem of creation is uninterrupted; but few are the ears that hear it. Olympus is but the outside of the earth everywhere.

The only house I had been the owner of before, if I except a boat, was a tent, which I used occasionally when making excursions in the summer, and this is still rolled up in my garret; but the boat, after passing from hand to hand, has gone down the stream of time. With this more substantial shelter about me, I had made some progress towards settling in the world. This frame, so slightly clad, was a sort of crystallization around me, and reacted on the builder. It was suggestive somewhat as a picture in outlines. I did not need to go out doors to take the air, for the atmosphere within had lost none of its freshness. It was not so much within doors as behind a door where I sat, even in the rainiest weather. The Harivansa says, "An abode without birds is like a meat without seasoning." Such was not my abode, for I found myself suddenly neighbor to the birds; not by having imprisoned one, but having caged myself near them. I was not only nearer to some of those which commonly frequent the garden and the orchard, but to those wilder and more thrilling songsters of the forest which never, or rarely, serenade a villager,—the woodthrush, the veery, the scarlet tanager, the field-sparrow, the whippoorwill, and many others.

I was seated by the shore of a small pond, about a mile and a half south of the village of Concord and somewhat higher than it, in the midst of an extensive wood between that town and Lincoln, and about two miles south of that our only field known to fame, Concord Battle Ground; but I was so low in the woods that the opposite shore, half a mile off, like the rest, covered with wood, was my most distant horizon. For the first week, whenever I looked out on the pond it impressed me like a tarn high up on the side of a mountain, its bottom far above the surface of other lakes, and, as the sun arose, I saw it throwing off its nightly clothing of mist, and here and there, by degrees, its soft ripples or its smooth reflecting surface was revealed, while the mists, like ghosts, were stealthily withdrawing in every direction into the woods, as at the breaking up of some nocturnal conventicle. The very dew seemed to hang upon the trees later into the day than usual, as on the sides of mountains.

This small lake was of most value as a neighbor in the intervals of a gentle rain storm in August, when, both air and water being perfectly still, but the sky overcast, midafternoon had all the serenity of evening, and the woodthrush sang around, and was heard from shore to shore. A lake like this is never smoother than at such a time; and the clear portion of the air above it being shallow and darkened by clouds, the water, full of light and reflections, becomes a lower heaven itself so much the more important.

Solitude.

This is a delicious evening, when the whole body is one sense, and imbibes delight through every pore. I go and come with a strange liberty in Nature, a part of herself. As I walk along the stony shore to the pond in my shirt-sleeves, though it is cool as well as cloudy and windy, and I see nothing special to attract me, all the elements are unusually congenial to me. The bullfrogs trump to usher in the night, and the note of the whippoorwill is borne on the rippling wind from over the water. Sympathy with the fluttering alder and poplar leaves almost takes away my breath; yet, like the lake, my serenity is rippled but not ruffled. These small waves raised by the evening wind are as remote from storm as the smooth reflecting surface. Though it is now dark, the wind still blows and roars in the wood, the waves still dash, and some creatures lull the rest with their notes. The repose is never complete. The wildest animals do not repose, but seek their prey now; the fox, and skunk, and rabbit, now roam the fields and woods without fear. They are Nature's watchmen,—links which connect the days of animated life.

When I return to my house I find that visitors have been there and left their cards, either a bunch of flowers, or a wreath of evergreen, or a name in pencil on a yellow walnut leaf or a chip. They who come rarely to the woods take some little piece of the forest into their hands to play with by the way, which they leave, either intentionally or accidentally. One has peeled a willow wand, woven it into a ring, and dropped it on my table. I could always tell if visitors had called in my absence, either by the bended twigs or grass, or the print of their shoes, and generally of what sex or age or quality they were by some slight trace left, as a flower dropped, or a bunch of grass plucked and thrown away, even as far off as the railroad, half a mile distant, or by the lingering odor of a cigar or pipe. Nay, I was frequently notified of the passage of a traveller along the highway sixty rods off by the scent of his pipe.

There is commonly sufficient space about us. Our horizon is never quite at our elbows. The thick wood is not just at our door, nor the pond, but somewhat is always clearing, familiar and worn by us, appropriated and fenced in some way, and re-claimed from Nature. For what reason have I this vast range and circuit, some square miles of unfrequented forest, for my privacy, abandoned to me by men? My nearest neighbor is a mile distant, and no house is visible from any place but the hill-tops within half a mile of my own. I have my horizon bounded by woods all to myself; a distant view of the railroad where it touches the pond on the one hand, and of the fence which skirts the woodland road on the other. But for the most part it is as solitary where I live as on the prairies. It is as much Asia or Africa as New England. I have, as it were, my own sun and moon and stars, and a little world all to myself. At night there was never a traveller passed my house, or knocked at my door, more than if I were the first or last man; unless it were in the spring, when at long intervals some came from the village to fish for pouts,—they plainly fished much more in the Walden Pond of their own natures, and baited their books with darkness,—but they soon retreated, usually with light baskets, and left " the world to darkness and to me," and the black kernel of the night was never profaned by any human neighborhood. I believe that men are generally still a little afraid of the dark, though the witches are all hung, and Christianity and candles have been introduced.

Yet I experienced sometimes that the most sweet and tender, the most innocent and encouraging society may be found in any natural object, even for the poor misanthrope and most melancholy man. There can be no very black melancholy to him who lives in the midst of Nature and has his senses still. There was never yet such a storm but it was Æolian music to a healthy and innocent ear. Nothing can rightly compel a simple and brave man to a vulgar sadness. While I enjoy the friendship of the seasons I trust that nothing can make life a burden to me. The gentle rain which waters my beans and keeps me in the house to-day is not drear and melancholy, but good for me too. Though it prevents my hoeing them, it is far more worth than my hoeing. If it should continue so long as to cause the seeds to rot in the ground and destroy the potatoes in the lowlands, it would still be good for the grass, on the uplands, and, being good for the grass it would be good for me. Sometimes, when I compare myself with other men, it seems as if I were more favored by the gods than they, beyond any deserts that I am conscious of; as if I had a warrant and surety at their hands which my fellows have not, and were especially guided and guarded. I do not flatter myself, but if it be possible they flatter me. I have never felt lonesome, or in the least oppressed by a sense of solitude, but once, and that was a few weeks after I came to the woods, when, for an hour, I doubted if the near neighborhood of man was not essential to a serene and healthy life. To be alone was something unpleasant. But I was at the same time conscious of a slight insanity in my mood, and seemed to foresee my recovery. In the midst of a gentle rain while these thoughts prevailed, I was suddenly sensible of such sweet and beneficent society in Nature, in the very pattering of the drops, and in every sound and sight around my house, an infinite and unaccountable friendliness all at once like an atmosphere sustaining me, as made the fancied advantages of human neighborhood insignificant, and I have never thought of them since. Every little pine needle expanded and swelled with sympathy and befriended me. I was so distinctly made aware of the presence of something kindred to me, even in scenes which we are accustomed to call wild and dreary, and also that the nearest of blood to me and humanest was not a person nor a villager, that I thought no place could ever be strange to me again.—

"Mourning untimely consumes the sad;
    Few are their days in the land of the living,
    Beautiful daughter of Toscar."

Some of my pleasantest hours were during the long rain-storms in the spring or fall, which confined me to the house for the afternoon as well as the forenoon, soothed by their ceaseless roar and pelting; when an early twilight ushered in a long evening in which many thoughts had time to take root and unfold themselves. In those driving northeast rains which tried the village houses so, when the maids stood ready with mop and pail in front entries to keep the deluge out, I sat behind my door in my little house, which was all entry, and thoroughly enjoyed its protection. In one heavy thunder-shower the lightning struck a large pitch-pine across the pond, making a very conspicuous and perfectly regular spiral groove from top to bottom, an inch or more deep, and four or five inches wide, as you would groove a walking-stick. I passed it again the other day, and was struck with awe on looking up and beholding that mark, now more distinct than ever, where a terrific and resistless bolt came down out of the harmless sky eight years ago. Men frequently say to me, "I should think you would feel lonesome down there, and want to be nearer to folks, rainy and snowy days and nights especially." I am tempted to reply to such,—This whole earth which we inhabit is but a point in space. How far apart, think you, dwell the two most distant inhabitants of yonder star, the breadth of whose disk cannot be appreciated by our instruments? Why should I feel lonely? is not our planet in the Milky Way? This which you put seems to me not to be the most important question. What sort of space is that which separates a man from his fellows and makes him solitary? I have found that no exertion of the legs can bring two minds much nearer to one another. What do we want most to dwell near to? Not to many men surely, the depot, the post-office, the bar-room, the meetinghouse, the schoolhouse, the grocery, Beacon Hill, or the Five Points, where men most congregate, but to the perennial source of our life, whence in all our experience we have found that to issue, as the willow stands near the water and sends out its roots in that direction. This will vary with different natures, but this is the place where a wise man will dig his cellar.... I one evening overtook one of my townsmen, who has accumulated what is called "a handsome property,"—though I never got a *fair* view of it,—on the Walden

road, driving a pair of cattle to market, who inquired of me
how I could bring my mind to give up so many of the comforts
of life. I answered that I was very sure I liked it passably
well; I was not joking. And so I went home to my bed, and
left him to pick his way through the darkness and the mud to
Brighton,—or Brighttown,—which place he would reach some
time in the morning.

Any prospect of awakening or coming to life to a dead
man makes indifferent all times and places. The place where
that may occur is always the same, and indescribably pleasant
to all our senses. For the most part we allow only outlying
and transient circumstances to make our occasions. They
are, in fact, the cause of our distraction. Nearest to all things
is that power which fashions their being. *Next* to us the
grandest laws are continually being executed. *Next* to us is
not the workman whom we have hired, with whom we love so
well to talk, but the workman whose work we are.

"How vast and profound is the influence of the subtile
powers of Heaven and of Earth!"

"We seek to perceive them, and we do not see them; we
seek to hear them, and we do not hear them; identified with
the substance of things, they cannot be separated from them."

"They cause that in all the universe men purify and sanc-
tify their hearts, and clothe themselves in their holiday garments to offer sacrifices and oblations to their ancestors. It is
an ocean of subtile intelligences. They are everywhere, above
us, on our left, on our right; they environ us on all sides."

We are the subjects of an experiment which is not a little
interesting to me. Can we not do without the society of our
gossips a little while under these circumstances,—have our own
thoughts to cheer us? Confucius says truly, "Virtue does not
remain as an abandoned orphan; it must of necessity have
neighbors."

With thinking we may be beside ourselves in a sane sense.
By a conscious effort of the mind we can stand aloof from
actions and their consequences; and all things, good and bad,
go by us like a torrent. We are not wholly involved in Nature.
I may be either the driftwood in the stream, or Indra in the
sky looking down on it. I *may* be affected by a theatrical
exhibition; on the other hand, I *may not* be affected by an

actual event which appears to concern me much more. I only
know myself as a human entity; the scene, so to speak, of
thoughts and affections; and am sensible of a certain doubleness by which I can stand as remote from myself as from another. However intense my experience, I am conscious of the
presence and criticism of a part of me, which, as it were, is not
a part of me, but spectator, sharing no experience, but taking
note of it; and that is no more I than it is you. When the
play, it may be the tragedy, of life is over, the spectator goes
his way. It was a kind of fiction, a work of the imagination
only, so far as he was concerned. This doubleness may easily
make us poor neighbors and friends sometimes.

I find it wholesome to be alone the greater part of the time.
To be in company, even with the best, is soon wearisome and
dissipating. I love to be alone. I never found the companion
that was so companionable as solitude. We are for the most
part more lonely when we go abroad among men than when
we stay in our chambers. A man thinking or working is always alone, let him be where he will. Solitude is not measured
by the miles of space that intervene between a man and his
fellows. The really diligent student in one of the crowded
hives of Cambridge College is as solitary as a dervish in the
desert. The farmer can work alone in the field or the woods
all day, hoeing or chopping, and not feel lonesome, because he
is employed; but when he comes home at night he cannot sit
down in a room alone, at the mercy of his thoughts, but must
be where he can "see the folks," and recreate, and as he thinks
remunerate, himself for his day's solitude; and hence he wonders how the student can sit alone in the house all night and
most of the day without ennui and "the blues;" but he does not
realize that the student, though in the house, is still at work
in *his* field, and chopping in *his* woods, as the farmer in his,
and in turn seeks the same recreation and society that the latter
does, though it may be a more condensed form of it.

Society is commonly too cheap. We meet at very short intervals, not having had time to acquire any new value for each
other. We meet at meals three times a day, and give each
other a new taste of that old musty cheese that we are. We
have had to agree on a certain set of rules, called etiquette and
politeness, to make this frequent meeting tolerable and that we

need not come to open war. We meet at the post-office, and
at the sociable, and about the fireside every night; we live thick
and are in each other's way, and stumble over one another, and
I think that we thus lose some respect for one another. Certainly less frequency would suffice for all important and hearty
communications. Consider the girls in a factory,—never alone,
hardly in their dreams. It would be better if there were but
one inhabitant to a square mile, as where I live. The value of
a man is not in his skin, that we should touch him.

DESCRIPTION OF ILLUSTRATIONS

IN PART VII

STAGE AND CHORUS—PASSION PLAY.

There are certain comparisons to be made between the old miracle plays given in the Middle Ages and the Passion Play presented every ten years in Oberammergau. To be sure, this last is not given in the streets, as were the old York plays, nor has it the crudities of these. However, in the motive which underlies the perpetuating of an old custom, one may find certain points in common. The audience at Oberammergau is seated under a projecting roof; the chorus and all participating remain under the open sky in sun or rain.

MIDSUMMER NIGHT'S DREAM.

This is a purely fanciful picture of the well-known scene where Titania, queen of the fairies, wakens with the potion on her eyelids, causing her to fall violently in love with the first object she beholds. This chances to be Bottom, who wears the ass's head. One's immediate impression is likely to be that it is not easy to paint fairies. The tiny one on the leaf at the extreme left of the picture alone seems satisfactory.

MRS. SIDDONS—GAINSBOROUGH.

Another celebrated artist has left us a portrait of Mrs. Siddons—one of the first women to adequately interpret Shakespeare's heroines. This time we see her in an afternoon toilette. She wears no jewel and simplicity characterizes her costume. Gainsborough was fond of painting these feathered hats; indeed, they are known by his name on this account. The fine poise of the gifted woman is admirable.

MRS. SIDDONS AS THE TRAGIC MUSE—REYNOLDS.

When Mrs. Siddons was in the height of her popularity, Reynolds was in high favor as a portrait painter. Prolific in his capacity for work, he was eagerly sought by men and women of all classes, for this was before the days of photography and only by this means could one leave his likeness for posterity. Mrs. Siddons conceived this as a fitting pose, while regret and remorse are dimly seen in the background. Reynolds seldom put his name upon his paintings, but in this instance brushed it along the embroidery on her gown. When she noticed it, he paid her the delicate compliment of saying he had chosen thus to go down to posterity on the hem of her garment.

STAIRWAY OF HONOR—PARIS OPERA HOUSE.

The new Opera House of Paris was completed in 1875, having cost approximately $5,600,000. It is still the largest theater in the world, covering about three acres. The Grand Staircase and the Foyer are beautiful indeed. In 1910 the serious floods in Paris threatened this building for many hours.

MONA LISA—LEONARDO.

This great art treasure was stolen from the Louvre in 1912. If only a few of the world's masterpieces in painting could be preserved, we would wish to keep this among them. For an account of the artist and this picture, see Part IX. "He who shall finally understand that smile shall have solved the secret that lies at the heart of nature."

SEA NYMPH—BURNE-JONES.

By some elasticity in the use of the term pre-Raphaelism, Burne-Jones has sometimes been ranked with this school. In the strictest sense of the term, such classification is mistaken. Burne-Jones was a dreamer who never pretended to paint what he saw, but rather what he dreamed. He was a poet-artist if such a term be permissible. In his own words he stated his idea of a picture: "I mean by a picture, a beautiful, romantic dream of something that never was, never will be, in a light better than any light that ever shone, in a land no one can define or remember— only desire."

It was not always possible for the artist to explain what he meant by some of his paintings and surely another can not tell. They must be accepted in the spirit which produced them—dreams and visions—glimpses in a world of fancy; the world of the poet and idealist.

THE SHEPHERD'S CHIEF MOURNER—LANDSEER.

Landseer loved to paint animals—particularly horses and dogs. His dogs are beloved the world over. This touching scene of the dog who refuses to leave his dead master is beautiful indeed. All lovers of fine dogs find Landseer's portrayals most satisfactory.

COLOGNE CATHEDRAL—BRIDGE OF BOATS.

The Cologne Cathedral, like many cathedrals in Europe, was built by devout people in the Middle Ages. Cologne is situated upon the Rhine, a river whose banks are sprinkled over with ruined castles and strongholds. While the trip up or down the Rhine is taken yearly by hundreds of tourists, many declare that aside from the historic associations, the Hudson affords as pleasing and inspiring changes.

THE TROSSACHS—SCOTLAND.

Probably this part of Scotland attracts the traveler more than any other. Here nature has done much to please the eye and he who can escape from the busy cares of life and spend a vacation in this enchanting land, counts himself fortunate indeed.